NOTES ON THE HISTORY AND ANTIQUITIES OF CHAUL AND BASSEIN

NOTES
ON THE
HISTORY AND ANTIQUITIES
OF
CHAUL AND BASSEIN

J. GERSON DA CUNHA

ILLUSTRATED WITH SEVENTEEN PHOTOGRAPHS,
NINE LITHOGRAPHIC PLATES, AND A MAP.

GYAN

Published by

Gyan Publishing House
5, Ansari Road
Daryaganj, New Delhi-110002
Phone: 011-47034999, 9811692060
E-mail: books@gyanbooks.com

Distribution Network
gyanbooks.com
India, USA, Canada, UK, Australia, France

ISBN : 978-81-212-3837-3 (PB)
First Published, 1876

2nd Impression 2020

Printed at: Gyan Press, Delhi.

The book at your disposal is the edition of an old book originally published long back. The Text quality of this book may not be at par as compared to our other books but many readers approached us to reprint this important book so that it could satiate their hunger. We request all the readers of this book to help us to improve its quality by providing the necessary text of those pages which are not properly visible. Your valuable support in this case will be highly appreciated and acknowledged and our future readers will be benefitted immensely.

NOTES

ON THE

HISTORY AND ANTIQUITIES

OF

CHAUL AND BASSEIN.

BY

J. GERSON DA CUNHA,

M.R.C.S. & L.M., Eng.; L.R.C.P., Edin.;

Member of the Committee of Management of the Bombay Branch of the Royal Asiatic Society; Fellow of the Geographical Society of Italy; Corresponding Member of the Adriatic Society of the Natural Sciences of Trieste; Fellow of the University of Bombay; Member of the I. R. Zoological and Botanical Society of Vienna, &c. &c.

ILLUSTRATED WITH SEVENTEEN PHOTOGRAPHS, LITHOGRAPHIC PLATES, AND A MAP.

Bombay:

THACKER, VINING & Co.

1876.

Agents in Europe:—LONDON: Trübner & Co., 57 & 59 Ludgate Hill.

PARIS: M. Ernest Leroux, Rue Bonaparte No. 28.

CHAUL.

THE EXTERIOR GATE OF THE SOUTHERN, OR RIVER GATEWAY AND THE TOWER OF THE CAPTAIN'S PALACE.

PREFACE.

"An important historical work," says a writer, "is its own best introduction." This cannot be the case, however, with unpretending little sketches of two of the earliest European settlements in India, which, having culminated to the eminence of luxury and power, have now dwindled down to the condition of "the City of the Dead," and are almost forgotten, as if overwhelmed, like another Herculaneum or Pompeii, by an inundation of lava, though in reality attesting the influence of that subtle element of gradual deterioration through political vicissitudes which pervades all nations.

The history of such places requires some words of introduction; and the Preface being that part of a work which is by conventional licence set apart to include all explanations relative to its purpose and method, I trust I may be allowed the privilege, and not be considered as laying myself open to a charge of egotism if I enter into personal details to describe the steps by which this work has attained its present form.

Two years have elapsed since I had the honour of reading before the Bombay Branch of the Royal Asiatic Society a communication entitled "Notes on the History and Antiquities of Bassein." The favourable reception accorded to it by the members of that learned body, and the demands, inadequately supplied, that arose for copies among outsiders, —a result that far surpassed the naturally sanguine expectations of a young author in the outset of his literary career,—encouraged me to prepare a second edition with considerable additions. In the interval between the reading of those "Notes" and sending the new edition to the press, a companion paper on "the History and Antiquities of Chaul" was read by me before the said Society, which, being reprinted from the last volume of its Journal, now precedes that of Bassein.

I have thus brought within the narrow compass of a monograph my researches on the history and archæology of an important section of the Northern Koṅkaṇ,—bounded on one side by the sacred Vaitaraṇî and Chaul river, and by the Sahyâdri range and Arabian Sea on the other,—from the earliest mystic times of the Purâṇas to the present.

Though so insignificant in size,—about sixty miles long by twenty broad,—this tract of land has from a very remote period been known as civilized, on account of the numerous architectural and epigraphic monuments existing thereon, and the allusions to its rivers and towns found in the Greek and Arab itineraries of the early Christian and Middle ages. Ethnologically speaking, the region comprised between the above boundaries is the richest for the number and variety of races, ranging from the highly intellectual Brâhmaṇ to the tiger-worshipping Wârlî,—all living, without evincing by any palpable manifestation their ethnic antipathies, among the low-lying plains and detached hills, the fantastic outlines of whose rocky peaks stand out weirdly against the gigantic escarpments of the Western Ghâṭs.

And now—to enhance, doubtless, the historical significance of the place—there has sprung from amidst the two ruined cities, and like the Phœnix of old, as if from their own ashes, the modern city of Bombay, which from a desolate and swampy islet has, by the intelligence and energy of its present rulers, been raised to the rank of the chief port of Western India, and commercial capital of the whole peninsula.

Thus Bombay—like, probably, no capital city in the world—presents to the scholar the contradictory aspect of being at the same time surrounded by seats of very ancient civilization—Buddhist, Śivaite,

Mahomedan, and Portuguese—and wild country inhabited by people as savage as the race living in the deep recesses of the Sâtpûrâs.

It has often been remarked that the European nations who have hitherto held the largest territorial possessions in India have at home little territory themselves. England, which now reigns sovereign on the proud throne of Aurangzebe, was as late as the 15th century known only as a remote island in the German Ocean. Holland, amongst her morasses, dykes, and muddy banks, after successfully resisting the autocratic power of the mightiest monarchs of their time,—Charles V. and Philip II.,—the chivalry of the haughty Spaniard, and the exterminating fury of the Inquisitors, without possessing much land at home, had become rich at the spicy Archipelago at the extremity of Trans-Gangetic India. And Portugal, the smallest of all, the unwieldiness of whose "little body with a mighty soul," as a writer expresses it, and "the narrow bounds of which," as one of her national historians observes, "could no longer contain the greatness of its native hearts," erected a commercial empire in the East, which for extent, opulence, and splendour had until the victory of Plassey no rival in the history of nations.

It is of this vast empire that the now ruined cities of Chaul and Bassein were two important emporia of trade. They were, besides, when in their palmy days, the miniature of the Luso-Indian civilization of the age. Within the compressed area of their walls were contained appliances that imparted grace and dignity to life. Chivalry, religious enthusiasm, scholastic pedantry, and seigneurial arrogance stamped the impress of their character upon every surrounding; and episodes verging on romance, and the passions, misfortunes, reverses and crimes amidst a motley population, made up both the poetry and prose of life, some incidents of which would certainly furnish as rich a pabulum for the novelist as their conquests and triumphs have already lent inspiration to the patriotic mind of Luiz de Camoens in the elaboration of his famous "epic of commerce."

Even at the present day, among the thousand associations which crowd upon the mind when we gaze upon their ruins, none is more moving than the thought that we have before us the relics of a civilization that, whatever its faults, or howsoever anachronistic its institutions may appear to the present dwellers on the globe, there is no doubt that it answered its purpose well, met best all the exigencies of the time, and when it became effete ceased to exist,—a mere question of evolution, and not of revolution. To try to prolong it, however, beyond the period it was intended to serve in the economy of human society, to strive to extend it outside the sphere within which it was designed to move, would naturally amount to involving it in ruin. And that is precisely what took place.

Among the institutions of that civilization which contributed most to the decay of this empire—leaving aside, of course, those causes whose operation appears to be permanent among all nations, such as the rapid accumulation of wealth with corresponding increase of domestic industry, the loss of their most vigorous youth, &c., and those unjustifiable accompaniments of a vicious administration, as peculation, rapine, and corruption of morals—were the Inquisition and the Monastic Corporations.

We know already the harm the *autos da fé* of the Inquisition and the dungeons of the Holy Office did to the Portuguese rule in India; but the monastic bodies did still more. They grew to be an *imperium in imperio*, and at a time when the Portuguese Government was beset on all sides by numerous enemies there were none the Viceroys feared more than the friars and their secular brothers the priests. The Jesuits arrogated to themselves magisterial powers, and, in defiance of the courts of justice, dealt out penalties to members of their congregations before their churches. They also collected the customs duties from vessels sailing in the rivers on the margins of which their convents happened to be situated, such imposition being enforced with the threat that, if they refused to pay, the cannon planted on the towers would shatter them to pieces,*—regardless alike of the extortionate nature or immorality of the black-mail thus levied by these tonsured and cassocked brigands, and the usurpation of the King's rights. The Dominicans, as a tradition has it, ashamed to cross the earth's surface, crawled through underground passages, converting the cowl into a mask, in order to repair to the haunts of dissipation. And the recalcitrant Franciscans, when menaced with the battering of the walls of their monastery by an armed galley unless they showed submission to the Government, replied coolly to the threat by exposing the Sacred Wafer on the window facing the guns, fully aware that only such a proceeding would disarm the enraged mariner.† And the blasphemy of the religious—for such it was—met with but piety, as an ironical commentary on the case states, on the part of the military, who would not fire a single gun as long as the Holy of Holies was liable to be crumbled into dust.

Such were, then, some of the abuses which precipitated the fall of the empire which, having in the beginning of the second half of the sixteenth century given evident signs of brighter times dawning for it in future, had about the end of the first half of the seventeenth century belied such hopes, and the doom of decay was visibly stamped on its forehead.

I have been from the first aware of the great difficulties with which I had to contend, not only in disinterring documents relative to a period that has added romantic pages to Indian history, and to individuals who distinguished themselves either by the brilliancy of their heroism or the magnitude of their vices, and which for the first time see the light of publicity, but also in describing monuments whose decayed state defies the keenest scrutiny, and in portraying an unfamiliar state of society, which requires the hand of a master genius, like a Gibbon, Sismondi, or Michelet, to do it justice.

---

* *Chronista de Tissuary*, vol. ii., pp. 70-71.

† *Ensaio Historico da Lingua Concani, Nova Goa*, 1857, pp. lxxv. *et seqq.*

Conscious, then, of the many imperfections of the work, I have still retained for it the heading of "Notes," first applied to a modest brief paper on the subject, although the latter has now grown into an attempt to give a general description of the two settlements,—written amidst numerous other engagements of both a professional and literary character,—which, with much diffidence, I submit to the judgment of the public, whose indulgence I would crave.

Now a word about the illustrations. These have been a continual source of annoyance to me. No sooner were photographs of the ruins taken than they began to fade away. The ruins that did not admit of the application of the camera had to be submitted to the lithographic art, but in no instance did they come up to the standard of my æsthetics, as they will not, I am afraid, to that of the reader. Wood or copper engraving done in Europe would have certainly pleased me more in all respects, but the distance was the obstacle. I had the alternative of either suppressing the illustrations altogether, or publishing them just as they are. I have preferred to adopt the latter course only in consideration of the fact that the state of the ruins is very precarious, and the villagers, like the mediæval Romans, who built their palaces with the stones of the Flavian Amphitheatre, are removing the materials from the remnants of the convents and churches to build their own houses; so that if deferred, unless there was another man to take my place, of which there is no probability just now, the ruins would run into mounds of earth, and no record of their shape would be left to the present and future generations.

In conclusion, I gladly take this opportunity of recording my obligations to several gentlemen for their kind assistance: to none more so than to Dr. Oliver Codrington, Honorary Secretary, Bombay Branch of the Royal Asiatic Society; Mr. Alexander Kyd Nairne, C.S., author of "The Konkan;" and Mr. James Macnabb Campbell, C.S., on the special duty of compiling the Gazetteer. I am, further, not a little indebted for many valuable suggestions to Commendatore Cristoforo

Negri, of Turin, and Captain Richard F. Burton, British Consul at Trieste, two distinguished names in the department of geographical research. To these and all the other gentlemen who have made me loans of old manuscripts or rare works my hearty acknowledgments are due.

Bombay, 7th August 1876.

TABLE OF CONTENTS.

CHAUL.

BASSEIN.

LIST OF FULL-PAGE ILLUSTRATIONS.

CHAUL.

BASSEIN.

ERRATA.

Page 5, line 3 from bottom, *for* ठाणाजिल्याचें *read* टाणाजिल्ह्याचें.

„ 7 „ 2 „ „ *for* Sir Herbert's *read* Sir T. Herbert's.

„ 7 „ 7, *dele* been.

„ 11 „ 8 from bottom, *for* Sabyâdri *read* Sahyâdri.

„ 13 „ 8, *dele* Tagaras.

„ 13 „ 11, *for* Tagara *read* Tagara râjâs.

„ 17 „ 2, *for* 1385 *read* 1285.

„ 64 „ 5 from bottom, *for* 1625 *read* 1624.

„ 92 „ 5, *for* 1662 *read* 1623.

„ 112 „ 21, *dele* second "now."

„ 155 „ 8 from bottom, *for* 1820 *read* 1780.

„ 189 „ 2, *for* even *read* ever.

„ 203 „ 16 from bottom, the *Pater Christianorum* of Caranjâ belonged to the order of St. Francis, and not to that of St. Dominic.

„ 222 „ last line, *for* Vasca *read* Vasco.

„ 235, „ line 8 from bottom, *for* 1583 *read* 1674.

NOTES

ON THE

HISTORY AND ANTIQUITIES OF CHAUL.

BY

J. GERSON DA CUNHA, M.R.C.S. Eng., &c.

NOTES

ON THE

HISTORY AND ANTIQUITIES OF CHAUL.

THE ancient city of Chaul, now called Revadaṇḍâ, is built on the northern extremity of a narrow strip of territory on the mainland of the North Koṅkaṇ, which with the promontory of the *Mórro*, or Kôrlê, lying about one mile distant off to the south, encloses the well-known harbour of the same name. It is situated in 18° 33′ N. Lat., and 72° 59′ E. Long., and is about 30 miles south-east of Bombay.

Adjoining the above, on the margin of the same creek, is the still more ancient city of Champâvatî, the origin and political existence of which are lost in the dim traditions of the past. It lies as if wedged in between Revadaṇḍâ and the hog-backed hills behind, only two miles further to the north-east, and connected with the former by a long shady street—the dismal remains of what was once a pleasant avenue of trees. It is referred to in old Portuguese chronicles as *Chaul de cima*, or 'Upper Chaul.'

Geologically speaking, the whole tract in and about Chaul is found to consist of horizontal strata of basalt and similar rocks. In the highland of Chaul, comprising an uneven piece of ground broken through by low ridges separated by slightly undulating valleys, the trap is found to be the most conspicuous geological feature of the country. This high land terminates on one side at the foot of the gigantic escarpment which walls in the extensive plateau of the Dakhaṇ from the low plains of the Koṅkaṇ, and rises on the other abruptly in a spur to the northward, which is distinctly seen from the sea. The trap is met with either in tabular masses a few feet below the soil, or projecting through the surface in irregular shapeless boulders varying in size from a few inches to several feet in diameter. Some of these display ferruginous bands of the hydrated peroxide of iron or brown hæmatite, imparting to it a hue not unsimilar in appearance to the lateritic coloration so prominent among the hills of the Southern Koṅkaṇ. The boulders are, moreover, found to be basaltic in structure, and to rest on beds of the fresh-water shales.

Nearer to the seaport, which—notwithstanding accommodation for large vessels has been decreasing for years, owing to silting up and other causes—is a convenient one for the coast craft, being from six to seven fathoms of water in depth, although at the entrance of the bay it is only three fathoms deep, * the shoals are so numerous as to be ranked among the triple lions of Chaul, which, according to the popular notion, consist of 360 temples, 360 tanks, and 360 shoals. There is a tradition current among the maritime population of the place, which is fully borne out by history, that long before Suali, Bassein, and Bombay rose into reputation as harbours, Chaul was a safely navigable river and a very commodious roadstead. It is necessary to remark, however, that this reputation was earned and maintained in the days of the infancy of navigation, when the tonnage of the largest vessel did not, perhaps, exceed that of the ordinary Portuguese caravel. This land-locked inlet, moreover, not unlike several others on the coast, has in course of centuries been gradually filled up, not only by the silt and sand deposited by the stream entering it, but also by other causes. Close to the shore—for instance, where the ruins of the fort stand in picturesque isolation, surrounded by the grey sands of the surf-beaten beach—an agglutinated calcareous mass of shells and gravel is found, bounded on one side by what is neither land nor water, but a muddy compound, which the tropical sun succeeds in a while in rendering fit for a mangrove swamp; and on the other by hillocks of drifted sand periodically bathed by tidal water, in which the *Elymus arenarius*, *Pandanus odoratissimus*, *Scilla communis*, and a few hardy descriptions of reeds and grasses bind together the light covering of the soil, until there is a sufficient consistency for the cocoanut palm to secure a firm hold, or for the rice-fields to make their advances, resulting in the end in that steady though gradual filling up of the river-bed which has rendered it impassable for modern ships.

Thus Chaul has fallen from the proud position of one of the principal commercial centres of Western India into so deplorable an obscurity that even Thornton's *Gazetteer of India* dismisses the whole subject in only two lines.

Though limited in extent, this section of the coast is fully compensated for its scantiness of space by the depth and variety of materials, which afford a wide field for the geologist. There is perhaps no land in

* Horsburgh's *Indian Directory*, Lond. 1817, vol. i., p. 303.

the vicinity of Bombay which will, in all probability, repay the curiosity and careful search of the scientific inquirer as Chaul: for the chemical and lithological peculiarities of its formations, the varieties of minerals contained in them, the fossil shells, though mostly of the littoral or estuary species, found in the intertrappean beds, the mammalian remains of the Miocene and Pliocene conglomerates, which are by no means rare here, and its peculiar flora and fauna, are really worth studying. But archæology, rather than natural history, being the theme of this sketch, I must pause here.

Among the early Hindus the ancient city of Chaul was known by the name of चंपावती (Champâvatî) *, and stated in some of their meagre extant records to have been the capital of an independent kingdom situated in the Paraśurâmakshetra of the Purâṇic geographers. Various accounts of the origin of the name are given, such as 'a place abounding in champa trees' (*Michelia Champaca*)—a supposition that I did not find myself warranted in entertaining, because of the total absence of any mention of that tree in the tolerably exhaustive list of the plants of the district published by Hearn†, until I had the opportunity myself to count them in dozens in a single garden within the fort. The other account, and perhaps the more plausible of the two, is that which ascribes the foundation of the city to a king called Champâ, whose name is, moreover, not unfrequently mentioned in the Purâṇas, and elsewhere. ‡ The city of Champâpura, for instance, is said to have been founded by a king of this name. This is the royal Buddhist city situated on the Ganges near the modern Bhâgalpûr, and formerly inhabited by the descendants of Ikshvâku. This name is traceable again in the designations of several other places, such as Champanîr, Champavat, &c. In the *Bramhottara Khaṇḍa* of the *Skanda Purâṇa*, ch. xvi., a description is given of four Indian cities, which are named Simantinî, Varmanî, Champâvatî, and Mathurâ. Again, mention is made of it in the *Vetâlpanchavinśati* and in the *Kathârṇava;* but unfortunately there is nowhere evidence to connect any of these with Chaul.

The name of Revadaṇḍa appears to be a reversion to one of its ancient Purâṇic designations, 'Reva' being the name of the holy stream of

---

* ठाणाजिल्याचे वर्णन p. 36; *et infra.*

† *Statistical Report of the Colaba Agency*, Bomb. 1854, pp. 26 *et seq.*

‡ H. H. Wilson's *Vishṇu Purâṇa*, Lond. 1820, p. 445.

Narmadâ (Nerbudda), which, like the Gangâ, has given its sacred name to many a rivulet. This is, however, a mere hypothesis. There are other explanations also respecting the etymology of the word Revadaṇḍa, one of which traces it to a tradition current among the Brâhmaṇs of the coast to the effect that when Kṛishṇa was reigning in Gujarât he had assigned the southern part of his kingdom, which embraced a considerable portion of the Northern Koṅkaṇ, for the support of Revatî, the wife of his brother Balarâma, and that the 'Revatîkshetra,' or 'country of Revatî,' which is often mentioned in the Purâṇas, corresponds to the modern Revadaṇḍa.* Others, again, profess to have found its origin from inscriptions. A stone pillar was discovered near Government House, Bombay (Parell?), containing an inscription, dated 1102 A.S. (1181 A.D.), written in the Devanâgarî character, mostly in the Sanskṛit language, but containing a curse in old Marâṭhî, referring to a grant of gardens in the village of Mandauli, in the district of Thaddᴧ (Thulla?), by Śrî-mat-Aparâditya, Prince of the Koṅkaṇ—his ancestors' names being unfortunately omitted, thus leaving us entirely in the dark as to his pedigree or descendants—to the temple of Srî-Vaijanâtha (Mahâdeva), situated in the town of Rabavanti, in which, it is mentioned, there were many merchants living.† This Rabavanti is supposed by the late Professor Wilson ‡ to correspond to Revadaṇḍa, from the circumstance of its having been inhabited by merchants, and from its name being recorded in the monumental stone-pillar—a not uncommon form of memorial—in the neighbourhood of Chaul; while the objection raised against the date 1181 as being that in which the Tagara râjâs of Padma Nâla (Pannalla) ruled the Koṅkaṇ (among whom there is no mention made of such a name as Aparâditya) is easily got over by supposing that this individual must have been simply a chieftain governing the Upper Koṅkaṇ, or Chaul and its immediate vicinity, owing allegiance to the Tagara râjâs, and perhaps from sheer vanity or pretentious exaggeration of his title styling himself "Prince of the Koṅkaṇ."

We tread on comparatively safe ground as we proceed to identify Chaul with its name as given by Western writers. Their itineraries of a coast line which was the best known of any part of India to the

---

* कौकणाख्यान. अ० ४–६, chaps. iv.-vi.

† *Jour. R. As. Soc.*, Lond. 1835, vol. iii., p. 386.

‡ *Ibid.*, p. 387.

Alexandrian merchants, during the first and second centuries of our era, and to the Arabs, the successors in the right line of some of Ptolemy's authorities, in the Middle Ages, although vague on the point of locations of the names with respect to the latitude, afford indications for identification certainly worth recording. Among these writers the foremost are, of course, Ptolemy, Arrian, and the author of the *Periplus Maris Erythræi,* variously estimated to have been written between 80 and 150 A.D. It may be desirable to mention here the approximate dates of the above geographical writers:—*Periplus* 80, Ptolemy 130, Arrian 150. The first calls Chaul Συμύλλα,* the next two Σίμυλλα.† These names are, again, supposed by Reinaud ‡ to correspond to Symola, Chymola, or Malakûta, and by Yule § to Chimolo of the Chinese pilgrim Hwen Thsang. || Another writer, far older than these, tells us that Chaul, if Castaldus' supposition is right, is the *Comané* of Ptolemy. ¶

Among the Arab and Persian writers we have first in the order of chronological precedence Maśûdi, the celebrated Arab historian and geographer, who names Chaul صيمور (Saimûr) and refers to it thus:— "I visited the city of Saimûr, situated on the coast of Lar, and one of the dependencies of Balhârâ, in the year 304 (916 A.D.)." Then he goes on to relate that at that time the reigning prince was named جانج (Janja), which name, Reinaud informs us,** is also found recorded in a copper-plate discovered about eighty years ago in the neighbourhood of Chaul, and which is dated *circa* 1018 A.D., indicating that the prince had reigned there some time previous to the advent of the famous author of the *Meadows of Gold.* This prince is perhaps the Śrî Chhinna Dêva Râjâ, of the Sîlahâra family, descended from the royal line of Tagarâ, and chief of tributary râjâs, who reigned in Ṭhâṇâ over 1,400 villages of the Koṅkaṇ, and whose name is recorded on some copper-plates discovered at the village of

* *Periplus Maris Erythræi,* edit. Blancard, p. 172.

† *Géographie de Ptolémée,* liv. vii., chap. 1.

‡ *Mémoire géographique, historique et scientifique sur l'Inde,* Paris, 1849, pp. 220-221.

§ *Cathay and the way thither,* Lond. 1866., vol. i., p. cxcii.

|| *Foĕ-Kouĕ-Ki,* p. 391, No. 94; and Julien's *Vie de Hiouen Thsang,* p. 420.

¶ *Sir Herbert's Travels,* Lond. 1665, p. 348.

** *Mémoire, loc. cit.,* and *Jour. Asiatique,* Série IV., tome 4, pp. 263-264.

Bhâṇḍûpa.* Maśûdi then tells us that there were about ten thousand Mahomedans in the city of Saimûr from Siraf, Oman, Bassora, Bagdad, &c., exclusive of what he calls بيسر (*baisar*), *i.e.* children of Arabs born in the country. He goes on to relate that the Mahomedans of the place had at their head a man elected from among themselves whose title was هزمة (*Hazama*), who was invested with power by the prince of the country, to whom he owed fealty, and that in our author's time the individual who filled this high post of *Hazama* was called Abû Said.†

The Lar, also called Lardeśa, mentioned by Maśûdi, is evidently the territory of Gujarât and the Northern Koṅkaṇ, embracing Broach, Ṭhâṇâ, and Chaul, and which name is given by Ptolemy as *Larikè*. The connection between Lar and Gujarât is so intimate that Ibn Said speaks, on Abulfeda's authority, of the two names as identical; and it was probably a political rather than a geographical division of the kingdom of Balhârâ. The sea to the west of the coast was also called in the early Mahomedan times, 'the sea of Lar,' and the language spoken on its shores is by Maśûdi named 'Lari.'

As regards Balhârâ, whom Maśûdi mentions as the reigning prince to whom Saimûr was tributary, it has long been identified as the name of the dynasty which reigned at Valabhî (Valabhîpura) in Gujarât, and according to Solimân, a merchant and one of the greatest travellers of his age, was in his time the chief of all the princes in India, the latter acknowledging his preëminence; while the Arabs themselves were shown great favours and enjoyed great privileges in his dominions.‡

Next in order is Ibn Muhalhal, who, it is supposed, visited the city of Chaul, which he also calls Saimûr, in the year 941 A.D., or about twenty-five years after Maśûdi. His whole narrative is unfortunately not extant, and the extracts made from his work by Yâkût, Kazwînî, Kurd de Schloezer, and others have caused doubts to be raised as to the genuineness of his travels, made up, as they are, of so many loose fragments. There are, however, reasons to believe that the traveller was in India about the middle of the tenth century (942 A.D.), when he ac-

* *Jour. R. As. Soc.*, vol. ii., pp. 383-384. The plate was discovered in 1830 at Bhâṇḍûpa, in Salsette. It is dated 948 Śaka (1027 A.D.).

† *Maroudj-al-Dzeheb*, tome 1, fol. 49; and *Les Prairies d'Or*, par MM. Barbier de Meynard and Pavet de Courteille, Paris, 1861-66, p. 66.

‡ Sir H. M. Elliot's *History of India*, &c., Lond. 1867, vol. i., p. 4; and Lassen's *Ind. Alter.*, vol. iii., pp. 533 *et seq.*

companied the Chinese Ambassador from the King of China, Kalin Bin Shakhabar, who had arrived at the court of Nasri Bin Ahmed Bin Ismail, of the Samanidæ at Bokhara, to negotiate a marriage between his King's daughter and Noah the son of Nasri. Ibn Muhalhal speaks of Chaul thus:—"At another foot of the mountain towards the north is the city of *Saimûr*, whose inhabitants are of great beauty, and said to be descended from Turks and Chinese. From this place also *Saimûr* wood is named, though it is only brought thither for sale." * Zakarîya-al-Kazwînî, who compiled his works from the writings of Ibn Muhalhal and others after the middle of the thirteenth century, says of Saimûr:—"A city of Hind near the confines of Sind (an Arabic demarcation). The people are very beautiful and handsome, from being born of Turk and Indian parents. There are Musalmâns, Christians, Jews, and Fire-worshippers there. The merchandize of the Turks is conveyed hither, and the aloes called Saimûrî are named from this place. The temple of Saimûr is an idol-temple, on the summit of a high eminence, under the charge of keepers. There are idols in it of turquoise and *baijâdak* (a stone like a ruby), which are highly venerated. In the city there are mosques, Christian churches, synagogues, and fire-temples. The infidels do not slaughter animals, nor do they eat flesh, fish, or eggs; but there are some who will eat animals that have fallen down precipices, or that have been gored to death, but they do not eat those that have died a natural death. This information has been derived from Misar Bin Muhalhil, author of the *Ajáibu-l-buldân*, who travelled into various countries and recorded their wonders." †

Then follow two contemporary travellers, Shaikh Abû Ishak and Ibn Haukal. They are supposed to have written about the middle of the tenth century (340 A.H., 951 A.D.). The former is a little anterior in point of time to Ibn Haukal, but they both met in the valley of the Indus and compared notes, and exchanged observations The text of Shaikh Abû was first published by Dr. Moeller at Gotha in 1839, under the title of *Liber Clamatum*, and a translation of the same into German appeared in 1845, and of a portion of it into Italian in 1842. He places Saimûr among the "cities of Hind" in contradistinction to the "cities of Sind," and refers to it thus:—"From Kambâya to Saimûr is the land of the Balhârâ, and in it there are several

---

* *Cathay*, *ut supra*, p. cxi.

† Elliot, *ut supra*, p. 97.

kings." Then, again, in reference to distances he says:—"From Sindân to Saimûr five days. Between Saimûr and Sarandib fifteen days."* Ibn Haukal, in his *Ashkálu-l Bilád*, uses the same words as his fellow-traveller in his references to Saimûr.†

Next comes the most accurate of all Arab writers of the time, Abû Rihân Al-Bîrûnî. He wrote about 1030 A.D. He calls Chàul *Jaimúr*, and says: "It is situated to the south of Tâna, in the country of Lârân."‡

Edrisi, who wrote about the year 548 A.H. (1153 A.D.), writes the name of the city thus—صيمور (*Saimúr*), and, as Jaubert has it, fixes its position as follows:—"De là [Barouh, *i.e.* Broach] à Seimur on compte deux journées." Elsewhere he writes:—"Saimûr, five days from Sindân, is a large well-built town. Cocoanut trees grow here in abundance; henna also grows here, and the mountains produce many aromatic plants, which are exported." Then again:—"Kambâya, Sûbâra, Sindân, and Saimûr form part of India. The last named belongs to a country whose king is called Balhârâ; his kingdom is vast, well-peopled, commercial, and fertile. It pays heavy taxes, so that the king is immensely rich. Many aromatics and perfumes are produced in the country."§

Among the later Mahomedan writers we have Sadik Isfahâni, who, in his *Takswin-al Buldán*, written *circa* 1635, gives up the Arabic perversion of Saimûr, and adopts one that is the closest approximation to Chaul, writing چیول (*Chível*), and places it, in accordance with his own system of computation, in Long. 88° and Lat. 36°.‖ The other is the author of the Arabic work on the *History of the Mahomedans in Malabar*, called *Tohfat-al-Majáhidín*, translated by Rowlandson and published by the Oriental Translation Fund in 1833, who writes *Sheiul*, which is not very distantly removed from the modern Chaul.¶

Now putting together all these forms of the name, such as the

* Elliot, *ut supra*, p. 30.

† *Ibid.*, p. 39.

‡ *Jour. Asiatique*, Sept. 1844, p. 263 (p. 121 de Fragments).

§ *Géographie d'Edrisi*, &c., par Amédée Jaubert, Paris, 1826, pp. 175-76; and Elliot, *ut supra*, pp. 85-86.

‖ *The Geographical Works of Sádik Isfaháni*, translated by J. C. Lond. 1832, p. 88.

¶ *Ind. Ant.*, vol. iii., p. 214.

Champâvatî of the ancient Hindus, the Simylla of the Greeks, the Saimûr of the Arabs, the Chîvel of the later Mahomedan writers, and the Cheûval of the Marâṭhâs,* there is no doubt, in the face of the above-noted authorities, and others to be mentioned hereafter, who plead warmly for the identity of these names, that the place they all refer to is but the modern Chaul, a form of spelling I have here adopted, in preference to others, being the one invariably found in almost all the Portuguese records of both olden and modern times.

It was Reinaud, I presume, who first identified *Simylla emporium et promontorium* of Ptolemy and the *Periplus* with the *Saimûr* of the Arab writers,—an identification that has met with the approbation of Yule, who does, besides, identify the above two names with Chaul. Kiepert, in his Map of Ancient India published about twenty-five years ago, under the personal supervision of the veteran Indianist Lassen to illustrate his *Indische Alterthumskunde*, placed Simylla at Bassein, which Yule first removed to Chaul, as evidenced in his recently published Map of Ancient India in Dr. W. Smith's *Historical Atlas of Ancient Geography*, in his *Cathay*, published about ten years before, and other writings,—a removal that has been declared by one of the learned journalists on this side of India to be "much more satisfactory."† Yule, after giving the grounds on which his identifications rest, goes on further to suggest, from the reconstruction of all the loose fragments of the divers spellings of the name, that "it seems likely that the old name was something like Chaimul or Chânwul."‡ Elsewhere he writes:—"Chânwul Châmul or Chânwur would easily run into Semylla or Jaimur on one hand, and into Chaul on the other."§ How difficult it is to settle doubtful points in the ancient geography of India, whether Greek, Chinese, Arab, or Sanskrit, is well known; and some of the above identifications, though not made with rashness, are to be received with caution, being possible but not proveable. They cannot, in fact, be accepted as final, although that they will generally be admitted as satis-

* The Marâṭhâs have a tradition to the effect that this designation is derived from Chyavanarishi, the famous sage mentioned in Râjâvali and Sabyâdri Khaṇḍa of the *Skaṇda Purâṇa*, who had settled himself at Chaul; but this is unsupported by any written authority.

† *Ind. Ant.*, vol. iv., p. 282.

‡ *Cathay*, p. cxcii.

§ *Ind. Ant.*, vol. i., p. 321. Some of the Greek writers, instead of Simylla, write Semylla; just as the Arabs, instead of Saimûr, write Jaimûr or Taimûr. Ptolemy in one place says the natives call the place Timylla, and one of his commentators questions whether it is Tiamylla.

factory in the present state of our knowledge it requires no unnecessary iteration to prove.'

The river of Chaul is no exception to this confused system of nomenclature. Rivers in the Koṅkaṇ have, as a rule, two names,—the one of the uppermost port on the estuary, used by the maritime population; the other of the stream itself, used by dwellers inland: thus the beautiful Kondulîka, the genuine name of the river which debouches into the bay of Chaul, by which name it is known among the people living inland, is called Rohe-Ashṭamîchî-Khâḍî, *khâḍî* meaning literally a brackish part near the mouth of the river. It is fortunate, however, that it has no esoteric name besides,—a practice that is not unfrequent in the Koṇkaṅ, such as Târamatî for the Kâlû or Muslej Ghâṭ river, a name that is chiefly used by the Brâhmaṇs for purposes of worship.*

The history of Chaul during the ancient authentic Hindu period is as much involved in obscurity as the Purâṇic one: Revatîkshetra, for instance, is, as before mentioned, as doubtful in its form and meaning as the inscriptional allusion of Rabavantî, where the temple of Śrî-Vaijanâtha is said to be situated. This uncertainty is, moreover, made palpable by the complete disappearance from the locality of every trace of the elaborate Brahmâṇic Śaivite worship, to which that temple was first dedicated, to make room for the worship of Hingûlzâ, which flourishes at present in all its aboriginal *linga* splendour.

Chaul, there is no doubt, must have been a place of note in the beginning of the Christian era, or else the Greek writers would not have mentioned it. That during the Hindu authentic period the place had attained some degree of civilization cannot also be doubted, for, besides the tradition of its 360 temples and tanks above alluded to, there is the legend that states that the ancient temple of Kâlkâbhavânî, which still exists by the side of a tank having a dome rather like a Musalmân tomb, had in former times an idol of that goddess which, it is believed, sprang—like its cognate of Wâlukeśwara, whose legend was published by me about two years ago †—into the tank beside her temple on the approach of the Musalmâns, and it is not yet known whether that idol has returned to its primitive abode or not.‡

---

* *Ind. Ant.* vol. iv., p. 283.

† *Ibid.*, vol. iii., pp. 47 *et seq.*

‡ *Ind. Ant.*, vol. iv., p. 67.

The peculiar architecture of that temple also would certainly lead one to infer that Châul was a Hindu town that had before the arrival of the Mahomedans reached a marked degree of civilization. Coming down to the undeniably authentic period of copper-plates, inscriptions in stone, and coins, one meets with a number of dynasties disputing among themselves, at various times, the possession of the Koṅkaṇ. Among the struggles for supremacy which ensued at various epochs among the Châlukyas, the Yâdavas, the Tagaras, the Silahâras, and innumerable other petty chieftains, we are at a loss to find out to whom Chaul did really belong. The presumption is that the Silahâra family, a branch of the Tagara, who reigned at Śrí Sthanaka, and whose capital is in the copper-plates called *Purî*, being, as the inscriptions style the sovereign, the "lord of 1,400 villages of the Koṅkaṇ," most probably included Chaul among their dominions, although there is no specification to that effect.* *Puri* seems to be Ṭhâṇâ, *i.e.* the capital *par excellence*, and not Elephaṇṭa Island or Ghârâpurî, notwithstanding that some of the early European writers, such as Garcia d'Orta and Linschoten, call it Pọri and Pory respectively. The same designation must have led Friar Odoric to describe Ṭhâṇâ as *Hæc terra est optimè situata .... et fuit regis Pori, qui cum rege Alexandro prælium magnum commisit,*"† a statement that is, in the face of events, utterly paradoxical. Again, there are no vestiges of any description of an ancient town in the island of Elephanta, while in Ṭhâṇâ there are still some, traceable with difficulty, no doubt; although, when seen by Giovani Botero, these "remains of an immense city" were more plainly visible, and "the town still contained 5,000 velvet-weavers."‡

Of the Buddhists and Jainas we have no record in Chaul, except perhaps an ornamental fragment of a Jaina temple that has been supposed to have existed centuries ago in Chaul, but whose traces are now entirely obliterated. It was discovered by Hearn§ under a banyan-tree, lying along with some other such pieces under a heap of rubbish.

* Besides these, there are other copper-plates found at Ṭhâṇâ in 1787, bearing date Śaka 939 (1018 A.D.), which record a grant by Râjâ Arikeśava Devarâjâ, of the same family, governing the whole Koṅkaṇ, consisting of "1,400 villages with cities and other places acquired by his arm." See *Asiatic Researches*, vol. i., p. 357. For other grants by "a viceroy of the Koṅkaṇ" under a prince of Yâdava descent, see *Jour. R. As. Soc.*, vol. ii., p. 390.

† Hakluyt's *Voyages*, vol. ii., p. 143.

‡ Yule's *Marco Polo, ut supra*, vol. ii., p. 331.

§ *Stat. Rep. of Colaba Agency*, p. 110.

It consists of a marble stone-piece, and its workmanship is, in the opinion of our late deeply lamented Honorary President, Dr. Wilson, of Râjputânâ origin, the most prominent figures being the Tîrthankaras, or saints of the Jaina creed. It is presumable that from the large series of the Kuda caves and cells near Mhar, in the neighbourhood of Chaul, of purely Buddhist construction, Chaul and its vicinity must have undoubtedly been one of the strongholds of Buddhism in Western India. Their position there, however, would not involve any high degree of civilization in the neighbouring town, as it is well known that the Buddhist Śrâmaṇas, not unlike the Christian monks, usually established their monasteries in places remarkable for solitude and beauty of situation.*

It appears that about the end of the 13th century this part of the Koṅkaṇ was conquered by Bhim Râjâ—said by some to be a son of Râmadeva Râjâ of Devagiri, afterwards Daulatâbâd, mentioned by Ibn Batûta as belonging to the Yâdava dynasty—and subverted by the Mahomedans in 1317 A.D., and by others to the Chelia or military Banian caste. But, whatever be his origin, the conqueror did not long preserve the integrity of his dominions, which were soon divided into fifteen Mahâls, the principal portion being inherited by his son Pratâpa Shâh, who was at last defeated and dispossessed of his kingdom by the invaders from Chaul, under the leadership of his brother-in-law named Nâgar Shâh, until the latter was in his turn defeated by the Mahomedans.†

Coming down to the Mahomedan period, it strikes us as probable that when the Mahomedans had established themselves in the Dakhaṇ, they lost no time in securing to themselves, for both strategical and commercial reasons, the seaports of the Koṅkaṇ, and that they did so there is historical evidence to prove.

As early as 1347 A.D., when Sultan A-la-u-din Hussain Kangoh Bâhmany became king of the Dakhaṇ and fixed his residence at Kulburga or Affnâbâd, all the country lying between the river Bhima and the vicinity of the fortress of Rudrâ, and from the port of Chaul to the city of Bidar, was soon brought within the circle of his possessions.‡

In 1356, when the dominions of Ala-ud-din became divided into sepa-

---

* See my *Memoir on the Tooth-Relic of Ceylon*, p. 18.

† *Trans. Bom. Geog. Soc.*, vol. vi., p. 132; Tod's *Western India*, p. 150.

‡ Scott's *Ferishta*, vol. i., pp. 9-10.

rate governments, Chaul and three other cities, with some territory around, were committed to Mahómed, son of his brother Ali Shâh. This prince, who is said to have been a man of sweet disposition, humane and just, established schools for orphans, with ample funds for their maintenance, in 1378 A. D., in both the cities of Dâbul and Chaul. The Bâhmani and the Shâhî dynasty of Ahmednagar promoted by all means in their power the prosperity of Chaul. It was from this city, as well as from Goa, that Sultân Féroz Shâh used to despatch vessels every year to procure him the manufactures and curious products from all quarters of the then known globe, and to bring to his court persons celebrated for talent.*

But both Féroz Shâh and his successors were not entirely engaged in the pacific course of trade; a little campaigning with the neighbouring Hindu chieftains, and occasional skirmishes with the rebels in their own dominions in the Koṅkaṇ, were by no means rare. In 1469 Mallik-al-Tûjâr Khajeh Jehan Gawan had to march with a powerful army against the Rai of Kellna and refractory rajas in the Koṅkaṇ; and, as on other occasions, the troops were ordered from Chaul to join him in this service.†

Of the fourteenth century we have no traveller recording his impressions of the city of Chaul, except, perhaps, he whom Yule not inaptly calls "the lying Mandevill." The compass of his travels, which, if true, would certainly equal, if not surpass, that of "the Moor," includes Chaul among his other numerous peregrinations. He refers to Chaul thus: "Est et non longè ab ista insula regio seu insula Cava vel Chava (here Hakluyt adds a marginal note—"Insula Chava vel Chaul forte)" quæ a primo statu multùm est minorata per mare. Hi sunt infidelissimi Paganorum. Nam quidam adorant Solem, alii Lunam, ignem, aquam, et terram, arborem vel serpentem, vel cui de manè primò obviant. Ibi magni mures, quos nos dicimus rattas, sunt in quantitate parvorum canum. Et quoniam per cattos capi non possunt, capiantur per canes maiores."‡

Now this is, *mutatis mutandis,* what Friar Odoric about the same

---

* Briggs's *History of the Rise of the Mahomedan Power in India*, Lond. 1829, vol. ii., p. 368.

† *Ibid.*, p. 483.

‡ Hakluyt's *Collection of Voyages*, vol. ii., p. 104.

time* wrote on Thâṇâ, which he had visited about the beginning of the second quarter of the 14th century. Sir John Mandevill here openly plagiarizes not only facts, but even the mongrel Latin of the Friuli monk. It appears strange that Jordanus, having been at Thâṇâ only a few years before Odoric, should, like Odoric himself, have omitted to mention so close and flourishing a place as Chaul; but most probably they confined themselves to their missionary track, and did not care for describing places they did not visit. It is still stranger that Marco Polo and Ibn Batûta, who traversed the peninsula on its western side about the middle of the 14th century, should have remained absolutely reticent about a city which, according to the testimony of the Arab writers who preceded them, was a flourishing emporium of trade with the West. Rennell, the Father of Indian Geography, remarks that "little can be gleaned from Marco Polo," and that "the travels of Cosmas in the 6th century, and of the two Mahomedan travellers in the 9th, afford few materials for history."† It was so, I dare say, in the days of Rennell; since then it has been ascertained that the omission of the name of the Koṅkaṇ by Marco Polo is more apparent than real, for his Thâṇâ stands for the Koṅkaṇ,— Thâṇâ being, as it was in the time of Al-Bîrûnî, the capital of the Northern Koṅkaṇ.

Rashîd-ud-din, in 1310 A.D., and Ibn Batûta, about 1350 A.D., call that city Konkan-Tâna and Kukin-Tâna respectively, while an Italian writer of the same century names it Cucintana,‡ and Barbosa Tana mayambu, which latter designation Yule considers to be the first indication of the name of Bombay.§ Ibn Batûta, owing perhaps to the political aspect of India being in a state of transition, from the form assumed in consequence of the Afghan conquests of the preceding century, to the general disorganization which paved the way for the establishment of the new empire of Timûr, could not visit all renowned places as Thâṇâ, nor be precise about the government and other particulars of the maritime cities like Chaul, although he maintains no reserve regarding the condition of different other places he visited on the southern coast. His spelling of the Hindu names

* Odoric's travels refer to the year 1330 A.D., while the spurious peregrinations of Mandevill extend between the years 1322 and 1356 A.D. For Odoric's travels see Hakluyt, *ut supra*, p. 143.

† J. Rennell's *Memoir of a Map of Hindustan*, Lond. 1788, p. xli.

‡ *R. A. S. Journal*, New Series, vol. iv., p. 340.

§ Yule's *Marco Polo, ut supra*, vol. ii., p. 331.

is, however, highly problematical. Marco Polo was at Thâṇâ about 1385 A.D., and describes the manners of the people of that neighbourhood, and the trade in horses and other traffic, much as travellers in the next two centuries describe Chaul, which we shall see further on, as we follow the sequence of events.*

Cosmas Indicopleustes, who flourished in the reign of Justinian, describing the city and population of Kalliâna—which is according to some the Kalyânapura near Uḍupi, while others, with more plausible reasons, assert it to be the old city of the Koṅkaṇ to the north of Ṭhâṇâ—refers to *Sibôr*, which, in accordance with the order of his names, indicates it rather as the *Saimûr* of the mediæval Arabs, or the modern Chaul, than Supâra near Bassein, as it has been supposed by some of his commentators.

"The two Mahomedan travellers" mentioned by Rennell were for a time an enigma for me, until the work of Eusebius Renaudot, who first edited and translated the manuscripts of these two travellers of the 9th century, in the year 1718, solved it. An English version of them appeared in 1733, and was reprinted in Pinkerton's *Collection of Voyages* in 1811.† A new edition reprinted in French, by Reinaud and Alfred Maury, has also been lately published. Now all these writers seem to agree that the reason why "the two Mahomedans" are silent on the Koṅkaṇ is because a portion of their manuscripts, which refer to the voyage between the Indus and Goa, is missing. But of the two the genuine traveller seems to be only the one known by the before-mentioned name of Solimân, who is supposed to have travelled in India about 898 A.D. ; while the other, named Abu Saíd Hussain of Siraf, never once left the latter place for India, although, like Mandevill, he had the knack of fabricating a Ulysses-like travelling episode, in which he fixes his start in the year 237 A.H. (851 A.D.)

During part of the 13th and the 14th centuries, the city of Chaul had, like Diu, in the opinion of Baldæus,‡ sunk into a state of comparative obscurity.. The Arabs, as mentioned by their own historians, made during that time several descents upon the west coast, and, though they made no fixed stay in it, a number of individual merchants established themselves there and carried on a brisk business.

* Yule's *Marco Polo, ut supra*, vol. ii., p. 230.

† Pinkerton's *Collection of Voyages*, Lond. 1811, vol. ii., p. 179.

‡ Churchill's *Collection of Voyages*, vol. iv., p. 150.

It again rose by degrees to become a place of considerable note in the 15th century, during the prosperity of the Bâhmani dynasty and its Ahmadnagar branch.

It was during these times that the Russian traveller Athanasius Nikitin first visited the city of Chaul. He writes in 1470 A.D. thus:—"We sailed six weeks in the tava (a vessel) till we reached Chivil, and left Chivil on the seventh week after the great day (Easter Sunday). This is an Indian country. People go about naked, with their heads uncovered and bare breasts; the hair tressed into one tail, and thick bellies. They bring forth children every year, and the children are many; and men and women are black. When I go out many people follow me, and stare at the white man.

"Their kniaz (Russian word for prince or chief) wears a *fata* (a large silken garment still worn by the women of the lower classes of Russia round the head or over the upper part of the body) on the head; and another on the loins; the boyars (noblemen) wear it on the shoulders and the loins; the *kniaginies* (princesses) wear it also round the shoulders and the loins.* The servants of the kniaz and of the boyars attach the *fata* round the loins, carrying in the hand a shield and a sword or a scimitar, or knives, or a sabre or a bow and arrow—but all naked and barefooted. Women walk about with their heads uncovered and their breasts bare. Boys and girls go naked till seven years, and do not hide their shame."†

As the accounts of travellers, in the absence of better materials, are the only natural and easy method of attaining a tolerably accurate knowledge of the place, each illustrating the other and serving as a commentary too on the brief text of its precursors, showing at the same time the advance or decline the place has undergone during the course of ages, I quote here from the travels of a Roman who followed the Russian about thirty years after. He describes the place and manners of the inhabitants in much the same style as the Russian does.

Ludovico di Varthema, who travelled in India from the year 1503 to 1508, and was an eye-witness to the first commercial enterprise of the Portuguese on the western coast, writes:—"Departing from the said city of Combeia (Cambay), I travelled on until

---

* Varthema's *Alla Apostolicha*.

† *India in the Fifteenth Century*, edited by R. H. Major, Lond. 1857, part iii., pp. 8 and 9.

I arrived at another city named Cevul, which is distant from the above-mentioned city twelve days' journey, and the country between the one and the other of these cities is called Guzerati. The King of this Cevul is a pagan. The people are of a dark tawny colour. As to their dress, with the exception of some Moorish merchants, some wear a shirt, and some go naked with a cloth round their middle, with nothing on their feet or head. The people are warlike : their arms are swords, bucklers, bows and spears made of reeds and wood, and they possess artillery. This city is extremely well walled, and is distant from the sea two miles. It possesses an extremely beautiful river, by which a very great number of foreign vessels go and return, because the country abounds in everything excepting grapes, nuts, and chestnuts. They collect here an immense quantity of grain, of barley, and of vegetables of every description ; and cotton stuffs are manufactured here in great abundance. I do not describe their faith here, because their creed is the same as that of the King of Calicut, of which I will give you an account when the proper time shall come.* There are in this city a very great number of Moorish merchants. The atmosphere begins here to be more warm than cold. Justice is extremely well administered here. This king has not many fighting men. The inhabitants here have horses, oxen, and cows in great abundance.†

We shall now pass on to describe the most interesting of all the periods of the history of Chaul—the Portuguese period. But before doing so it is necessary, for the better elucidation of the subject, to go back to a previous period, and survey briefly the condition of the Portuguese on their first arrival on the coast.

During their ascendancy in the Indian seas the Portuguese never aspired, in spite of splendid opportunities both in Gujarât and the Dakhan, to acquire political and territorial influence, but confined themselves merely to the acquisition of maritime and trading power by the establishment of factories on the coast and small garrisons for their defence.

---

* On the religion of the king of Calicut he says that the king of Calicut is a pagan, and worships a God whom the people call the Creator ; while they also believe in one spirit, *deumo* (*deva ?*) besides God, whom they call Tamerani (Malabar *Tambaran*, meaning lord or master), and the king keeps his *deumo* in, a chapel in his palace, &c. : *see* pp. 136-137.

† *The Travels of Ludovico di Varthema,* edited by G. P. Badger, Lond. 1863 pp. 113-114.

Although their real dominion was on the ocean, where their ships, armed and manned in a manner superior to that of the Eastern potentates, were victorious in almost every encounter, still their seaports, with a chain of forts, were in a very short time extended along the coast line from Mozambique and Sofala in Eastern Africa, Ormuz in the Persian Gulf, Diu and Damaun in Gujarât, Bassein, Chaul, Goa, Angediva, Cannanore, and Cochin on the Malabar Coast, Ceylon, the Coromandel Coast, Malacca, and the Moluccas, to China and Japan. This sudden rise of a small nation in the west of Europe originated in a handful of enterprising men and bold adventurers.

When Vasco da Gama arrived, on the 20th May 1498, at Calicut,* which was then the principal emporium of trade in that part of India, sending out every year above five hundred ships to the Red Sea, he endeavoured to open communication with the Zamorin (Samondry Râjâ) in order to obtain such privileges and facilities as would enable the Portuguese to carry on an advantageous commerce with this rich country. He landed, and with great pomp made his appearance before that prince, who, actuated by motives of the soundest policy, showed a decided disposition to favour the admiral and his crew. Soon after, however, the intrigues and malicious reports of the Mahomedans from Egypt and Arabia, who commanded then the whole commerce of the Indian seas, carrying away not only rich cargoes, but shiploads of pilgrims, and who were jealous of the foreigners' interference with their own prerogatives, wrought a sudden change in the mind of the sovereign, who consented to make Vasco da Gama a prisoner. The prudence and firmness of the latter, however, availed him much at this juncture, for, observing ominous signs in the behaviour of the people on the release of two of his officers who had been detained by the Zamorin, Vasco da Gama weighed anchor and set sail; and although pursued by the enemy's fleet, a breeze springing up, he got clear off and reached home in safety on the 29th August 1499.

A new expedition was now fitted out, under Pedro Alvares Cabral, with a fleet comprising 13 vessels and 1,200 men. On their arrival at Calicut the Zamorin received them with imposing ceremonies, although the Mahomedans, whose resources in intrigue were otherwise inexhaustible, were not less demonstrative. Permission being neverthe-

* A pretty good representation of the city of Calicut as it was in 1574 is given by Brun and Hosenburg, and copied by Beveridge in his *History of India*, vol. i., p. 156.

less obtained to establish a factory, under the charge of Ayres Correa, in one of the Zamorin's palaces, a fair start was then made by the Portuguese to trade on a systematic plan with India.

It was, notwithstanding, highly impolitic under the circumstances to overlook the fact that the Mahomedans, thus brought into close competition with the foreigner, would beneath this seeming friendship nourish hostile intentions, moved as they were, beyond the feelings of political ambition and mercantile cupidity, by their natural hatred towards the Christians. But Cabral, it appears, in spite of all his excellent qualities, allowed himself, through Ayres Correa, to fall too easily into the snare thus laid for him.

The consequence was that the king and his myrmidons who never ceased for a moment to plot against them, and watch for an opportunity to attack them, profited by the uncircumspect conduct of the Portuguese, who had been treacherously induced to capture a merchant vessel with seven elephants on board. This affording them a pretext for the outrage, they stormed the building and overpowered the inmates. Their number amounted to seventy, and being unable to resist the thousands of Moors, Nairs, and others who in a body assailed the factory, fifty of them, the factor Ayres Correa included, were slaughtered on the spot, the rest escaping into the sea to swim over and seek shelter on board their vessels. The factory was first plundered and then reduced to ashes. This may be appropriately described as the inauspicious beginning of the hostilities which raged almost uninterruptedly for two centuries between the Portuguese on the one side and the Moslems and Hindus on the other, with a short interval of peace, until the whole fabric of the former tottered to its very foundation, and fell a rich prize to the energetic and moral endeavours of a great nation, which now happily sways the destinies of this important country.

Cabral's retaliation was severe. The Zamorin, perceiving that the matter was taking a grave turn, manifested an anxiety to cultivate the friendship of such powerful strangers. This is in accordance with the singular character of the Orientals, who from the days of Taxiles, Porus, and others of the time of Alexander of Macedon downwards have been always playing a similar *rôle*. But Cabral, determined to avenge their brutality, on a sudden made a furious onset, captured ten Moorish ships, transferred their cargoes to his own vessels, made their crews prisoners, and then ranging the captured vessels in a line before the city set them on fire, exhibiting them in full blaze before the citizens of Calicut. He then drew his ships up in line of battle and opened a furious cannonade upon the city, which was destroyed in several places, hundreds of its inhabitants being killed. The Zamorin himself had a narrow escape, as one of his favourite Nairs was struck down beside him by a cannon-ball; and he hastily fled into the interior of his country. Cabral then set sail for Cochin, and after an encounter or two with the Calicut fleet started on his homeward voyage, arriving in Lisbon on the 31st July 1501.

Before Cabral's arrival at Lisbon, a third armament, under Joaõ da Nova, was on its way to India; it consisted of three ships and one caravel with 400 men. He was followed by Vasco da Gama, in his second voyage, with a fleet of twenty ships and the title of Admiral of the Eastern Seas. The details of the conflicts which ensued, although highly entertaining, possess little interest for my subject. Vasco, however, succeeded in forming a triple alliance with the kings of Cochin and Cannanore, and sailed for Europe on the 20th December 1503, reaching Lisbon in the following September.

Some time after, the Viceroy, Dom Francisco d'Almeida, arrived in India. He sailed on the 25th March 1505 from Lisbon in command of a magnificent fleet of twenty-two ships,* carrying, in addition to the crew, 1,500 trained soldiers, and arrived at Angediva on the 8th September of the same year.† Cabral, though his resentment was sufficiently gratified, had thought of applying to the Zamorin for further redress; but learning that he had countenanced the outrage, he left the reprisals to Vasco da Gama in his second voyage and to Almeida. A powerful fleet was then equipped by the latter to demand satisfaction for the injuries that had been sustained by his countrymen. All this, to cut the story short, was at last obtained.

There was thus a respite; but the calm was not unlike that which forebodes greater disasters. While most of the Portuguese officers were engaged in the conquest of Sofala, the Zamorin of Calicut, always instigated by his Mahomedan subjects, was secretly making exertions to raise up enemies against the Portuguese, and entering into an offensive and defensive alliance with the king of Gujarât, Mahomed Shâh, was through him invoking the assistance of the

* Of these ships eleven were to return with merchandize to Portugal, and the rest to remain in India.

† See my *Historical and Archæological Sketch of the Island of Angediva*, *Jour. Bo. Br. R. As. Soc.* 1876, vol. xi., pp. 288 *et seq.*

Mameluke Sultân of Egypt to drive away the dreaded *Farangîs* from the Indian seas. Almeida, being made aware of these machinations, sent his son Dom Lourenço d'Almeida with eleven vessels to cruise about the coast and counteract the designs of the Zamorin by destroying the fleet he had equipped. Dom Lourenço fell in with them at the port of Cannanore while on his way, and after a severe engagement put them to flight. A great booty, consisting of ships laden with spice, was taken; and after sinking some, and running others aground, Dom Lourenço returned to relieve the garrison of the Angediva island, which was being besieged by the Mahomedans under the command of a renegade, who, on the approach of Dom Lourenço, made, with his barbarous host, a precipitate retreat, and in their hasty flight they lost several of their vessels.

These two signal victories, one following the other, achieved by the valour of the younger Almeida, seemed to have inspired the enemy with terror, and made them (so it was imagined) more cautious than ever in any new attempt against their rivals. But this was a mistake. The irrepressible Zamorin, relying on the predictions of his wizards and soothsayers, was arming afresh a fleet against the Portuguese, who this time were somewhat distracted by a petty strife with the Socotrines. No sooner was the news heard than the Viceroy sent his son, Dom Lourenço, with a squadron of ten ships to cruise about the sea. On his way in search of the Calicut fleet, which had sailed northwards, Dom Lourenço for the first time cast anchor at the entrance of the port of Chaul, into which seven vessels of the enemy entered without saluting his standard. Dom Lourenço upon this followed them in his boats, and the Moors, having no other resource left, leaped overboard and attempted to escape to the shore; but while in the water many of them were barbarously slain. This almost unprovoked cruelty was soon followed by another still more execrable, in which Gonçalo Vas was the chief actor. While on his way from Cannanore to join Dom Lourenço, Vas fell in with a Mahomedan ship having a Portuguese pass, but in spite of this he sunk the vessel with her crew sewed up in sails, that they might never be seen again. Scarcely even for a day did this inhuman action remain secret, as the perpetrator had perhaps thought it would, for the body of one of the Moors who had been thus basely destroyed was washed ashore, the victim being recognized as the nephew of Mamale, a rich merchant of Malabar. From that moment the latter swore vengeance against the

Portuguese, which terrible oath was the harbinger of all the calamities that subsequently befell the Portuguese at Chaul and elsewhere, as the sequel will show.

Dom Lourenço, on returning from Chaul with vessels laden with horses and other goods captured there, fell in with the Calicut fleet near Dàbul. He anchored off the mouth of the river, eager to destroy it; but on calling a council of his officers to consult with them as to what measures were best for an attack, they gave their opinion unanimously against any offensive action, the fleet having entered the river, which was too narrow for a successful combat. On his arrival at Cochin, flushed with victory and bearing rich spoil from Chaul, Dom Lourenço expected to be received with honour by his father; but he was, on the contrary, much to his disappointment and mortification, threatened by the Viceroy with punishment for not having engaged the enemy at Dâbul and destroyed their fleet, notwithstanding that he had the excuse to urge of having been overruled by the votes of his officers. This severe treatment preyed on the young man's mind, and, finding that all efforts to conciliate his father and regain his favour were of no avail, he sacrificed his valuable life in an action at Chaul. In the river of Chaul have his bones lain for the last three centuries and a half, and of the millions who have frequented the port since then none have known the spot which was the last resting-place of the brave Dom Lourenço d'Almeida.

But I am afraid I anticipate. Some time after the first victory of Dom Lourenço at the Chaul river, while Albuquerque was engaged before Ormuz, the Sultan of Egypt—to whom a deputy, reputed to be a man of sanctity, was despatched from Calicut by instigations of Mamale, the uncle of Vas's victim—fitted out a fleet of twelve sail with 15,000 Mamelukes, which he sent, under the command of Amir Hussain, to oppose the Portuguese in India. At this time the Viceroy, who was on the Malabar coast, had ordered his son Dom Lourenço with eight ships to scour the coast as far as Chaul, and wait there to join another fleet from Cochin, which was being prepared,—orders that were well received by his son. His fleet having arrived off Chaul put into the bay to take in provisions and refreshments. On his arrival there Dom Lourenço received intelligence of the fleet of the Sultan of Egypt being on its way to India, but, believing it to be an unfounded rumour, went ashore with most of his officers. Chaul was then a place of considerable trade, rising from its former decadence through the exer-

Plate 1.

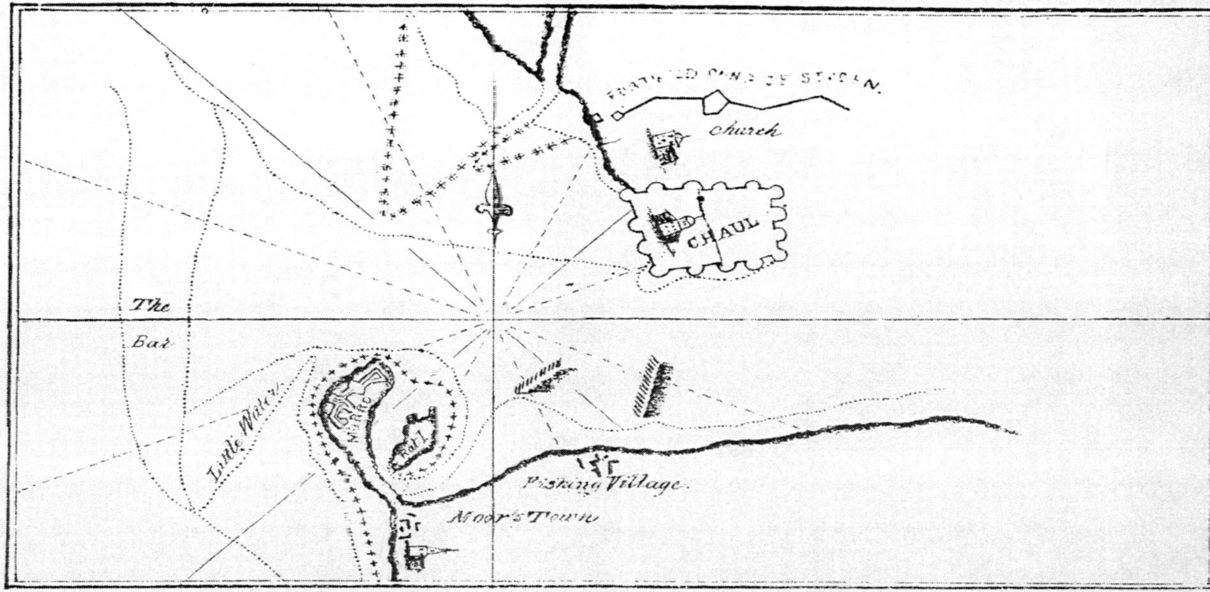

REDUCED & DRAWN BY. ARDASEER, BOMBAY.

CHAUL.

THE CHAUL PORT, WITH DRAKES' TRACK.

FROM A DRAWING DATED THE 19TH JULY 1764. IN THE LIBRARY BY. GEOG. SOC.

tions of the Ahmadnagar kings, who had but one maritime city for their extensive territory. This renovation was, moreover, facilitated by its convenient situation as an entrepôt between Gujarât and Malabar, and an outlet to the exports of the Dakhan.

To resume, however, the thread of our narrative. The news of the arrival of the Egyptian fleet having been confirmed by the Governor of Cannanore, who was informed of the fact by the well-known pirate Timoja, the Viceroy despatched Pedro Cam to Chaul to direct Dom Lourenço to proceed and engage the fleet. This has been regarded as a wrong step on the part of the Viceroy. It is by some opined that he should himself have started for Chaul to reinforce his son's fleet. Others, again, say that Dom Lourenço himself on the approach of the enemy's fleet should have steered out of the river and engaged the enemy on the sea. But we are all apt to be wise after the event.

Hussein, a Persian by birth and admiral of the Egyptian navy, had once before, on his way from Egypt to India, experienced in a formal engagement very harsh treatment from the two Almeidas, and was thirsting for vengeance. Malik Eyâz, a native of Sarmatia, who had renounced Christianity for Mahomedanism, and through his singular dexterity as an archer had not only regained his liberty—he had been a slave of the king of Cambay—but through his skill got himself nominated Governor of Diu, was also a sworn foe of the Portuguese. The hatred that both these men bore towards their common enemy was a bond of unity between them, and they combined to plan the destruction of their rivals.

Hussein and Malik Eyâz met amid great rejoicings at the point of Diu, and while consulting how to lay the ambuscade, or discussing other more or less well-devised schemes to annoy the Portuguese with their joint fleets, news was brought to them that Dom Lourenço d'Almeida had anchored his vessels before Chaul, and had landed his men, being ignorant of the arrival of the Egyptian fleet in the Indian seas. Dom Lourenço, on being made aware of this, did not at first take much heed, depending upon the friendship of Nizâm-ul Mulk, and believing that this sovereign would not permit any surprise in his dominions; although it was for his own interest that this pseudo-friend of theirs had advised his subjects to keep on good terms with the Portuguese trafficking in his ports.

Dom Lourenço, believing in this outward show of friendship, thought he might safely remain a little longer on land with some of his officers, entertaining himself in shooting and athletic sports, until he had the opportunity of joining the fleet from Cochin. It was indeed rumoured abroad that the combined fleets had been seen on the coast sailing southwards; but Dom Lourenço made no account of this, imagining them to be the ships from Mecca which were here daily expected, or, as others state, to be the fleet of Albuquerque, who was sent out to succeed the Viceroy.

One of the ship's crew at last espied an extensive fleet from the top of the mainmast, but he could not discern their strength. They began now to suspect the truth. Hussein was really advancing that way with his red and white ensigns adorned with the black crescent, and a display of ornamental bunting as if on a gala day; while the astute Eyâz was following in the rear to concert an attack against the Portuguese.

Dom Lourenço had no sooner given the necessary orders to his men than he saw the Egyptian ships advancing against them. The Mamelukes had buoyed themselves up with the hope that they would surprise the Portuguese, and they gave undignified expression to their feelings by shouting and gesticulating and making divers other demonstrations of joy at having so opportunely found the enemy whom they were in search of, at their mercy. The Portuguese, having just had time enough to place themselves in a good position of defence, gave the enemy a warm reception. Hussein, believing himself secure of victory as he had surprised the Portuguese ships, determined to board in person the flag-ship commanded by Dom Lourenço. For this purpose he opened the attack with a volley of shells, arrows, hand-grenades, and other war-engines, enveloping the fleet in clouds of flame and smoke, but his attack was returned with such determination and skill that he at last desisted from attempting to board the vessel. Other Egyptian vessels attacked the Portuguese squadron throughout the day, though from a distance, but as night approached and separated the combatants, Hussein retreated with his vessels to the opposite bank of the river, among the sands, for his greater safety, to prepare for the renewal of the fight the next morning.

This brief respite for the night was spent by the Portuguese in preparations for the combat the next day. Dom Lourenço, being still ignorant of the confederacy between Amir Hussein and Malik Eyâz gave, at daybreak, the signal to renew the fight. The attack was made with great energy and ardour, and Dom Lourenço was sanguine of boarding Hussein's ship, which hope was shared by Pedro Barreto and the other captains; but, not being able to approach close enough, on account of the sandbanks, he was obliged to rest satisfied with cannonading them, and this he did the whole day, and succeeded, notwithstanding the greater numerical strength of the enemy in ships and men, in capturing two galleys, all the men on board being put to the sword. The combat was carried on with much ardour and intrepidity on both sides, and the Portuguese seemed fast gaining ground, when Almeida, favoured by the wind and tide, made the attempt to board the Egyptian flag-ship. The victory was almost achieved, and the Moors were leaping overboard to escape to the shore, when the inconsiderate valour of Francisco de Nhaya, who began to pursue with a lance the enemy in the water, turned the scales against the Portuguese. The Moors returned to the combat with the heroism of despair, and Dom Lourenço was unsuccessful in his attempt, on account of the contrary current, to board the vessel. Malik Eyâz, the Governor of Diu, in the meanwhile put in his appearance in the harbour with a well-manned fleet, consisting of forty vessels, coming at the most decisive moment to the relief of his *confrère* Hussein, the Egyptian admiral. Not daring at once to engage the Portuguese, he came to anchor at the entrance of the creek, near enough to Hussein to join him the next day, the Portuguese slackening their efforts a little, being somewhat alarmed at this formidable and unexpected circumstance.

On observing this state of things, Dom Lourenço, although twice wounded by arrows, retained his presence of mind. He despatched two galleys and three caravels to hinder the union of the two fleets of the enemy, and this they did so effectually that Eyâz was obliged to change his position and retreat for shelter to another site. Dom Lourenço was then advised by his captains to set fire to the enemy's vessels, but he said he wanted to spare them to take them over as trophies to his old father. This little vanity had blinded him to the danger of the moment.

The battle, however, still continued between Dom Lourenço and Hussein until night again parted them, both sides endeavouring to conceal their losses. In the evening, after the cessation of the fight, the Portuguese captains met in council on board the flagship to deliberate on what was next to be done, and they were unanimously of opinion that as it was unsafe to defend themselves in the narrow river of Chaul, which was being rapidly blockaded by the enemy's fleet, it was well to exercise prudence, and endeavour to bring their ships out of the river into the open sea during the night, to effect a decent retreat, before Malik Eyâz, who was a much more formidable antagonist than they had been accustomed to deal with, had joined the reinforcing fleet. But Dom Lourenço, remembering the displeasure of his father at his having declined to force the Calicut fleet to action in the river of Dâbul, and being besides of a temper more valiant than discreet, resolved not to steal away by night, fearing that his retreat to the open sea might be construed as a flight. He determined to make the best of his way by broad daylight, resolutely awaiting in the meanwhile the events of the next morning.

The morning arrived, and Malik Eyâz, perceiving that the Portuguese ships were ready to set sail with the first tide after daybreak, interpreted the alteration in the arrangements as a preparation for a retreat, and advancing, therefore, from the place where he had taken shelter, boldly attacked them, and, undismayed by the havoc wrought among his own crew by the constant cannonade of the Portuguese, pressed close in front in order to intercept their passage. Unfortunately at this time the ship of Dom Lourenço ran foul of some fishing-stakes in the bed of the river, and then was cast upon the rocks. Pelagio de Souza, who commanded the nearest galley, fastened a rope to the stranded vessel, and plying all his oars was making ineffectual efforts to tow her off, when, a ball happening to strike her hull near the rudder, she took in much water and was in danger of sinking. Then Pelagio cut the rope off, and his own ship was irresistibly borne out by the current to the sea. The officers seeing the impossibility of extricating the Admiral's vessel from so perilous a position, a boat was sent to Dom Lourenço entreating him to save his person and preserve himself for another combat. The gallant and high-spirited youth replied, however, that "he would never be guilty of such a piece of treachery as to leave in the lurch those who had hitherto been his companions in danger." Accordingly, he exerted himself to the utmost extremity in this precarious situation, animating his thirty men (out of a hundred, seventy being *hors de combat*) both with words and by his example to defend themselves. They fought like lions, and, rejecting all proposals of honourable surrender, armistice, &c., offered them by the enemy, resolved either to save the ship or die in the attempt. In the midst of this engagement a ball broke the Admiral's thigh. Ordering his men to place him upon a chair resting against the mainmast, or directing them, as others write, to lash him to the mast, he continued to encourage them with his orders as occasion required, when another bullet pierced him through the chest and he was killed. His body was thrown below deck, that the sight of it might not give the enemy cause to rejoice. Here it was followed by his faithful page Gato, who, threw himself upon his master's corpse, lamenting his fate with literally bloody tears, one of his eyes having been pierced with an arrow. When at last, after a vigorous resistance, the Moors boarded the ship, and found Gato upon his master's body which he defended, he rose and slew as many of the Moors as approached the body of Dom Lourenço, until he himself fell dead among them. At length the ship sank, and out of the hundred men who belonged to her only nineteen escaped. At the close of the action it was found that, in all, the Portuguese had lost one hundred and forty men, besides one hundred and twenty-four wounded, while the enemy's loss is estimated at upwards of six hundred. The accounts given by the Portuguese chroniclers and the Mahomedan historians differ widely as to the loss in men, Ferishta adding that although 400 Turks were honoured with the crown of martyrdom, no fewer than 4,000 Portuguese infidels were sent to the infernal regions. But they all agree that the Portuguese on this occasion experienced a severe check, losing both the flag-ship and their Captain.* Among those who distinguished themselves most in this engagement was a sailor by name Andrea van Portua—others call him André Fernandes—a native of Oporto, who, standing on the top of the mainmast, although having previously lost the use of his right arm by a musket-ball, defended himself with only his left for a long time against the enemy, till at length they promised to spare his life. Upon this he surrendered himself, and was afterwards restored to the Portuguese. He returned at last safely to his country, and was well rewarded for his rare bravery by the King. The rest of the squadron continued their flight to Cannanore.

Such was the end of poor Dom Lourenço. Still young, he was one of the most distinguished sons Portugal ever gave birth to. He was much loved by his men, not only because of the constant exhibition of his bravery and prodigies of valour in the battle-field, but also on account of his other qualifications and his general good conduct. In the taking of Mombaza ; in obtaining satisfaction from the regent of Quilon, who had

* Barros, *Decadas*, edition of Lisbon, 1777, tome ii., pt. i., pp. 186-199.

once offered an insult to his countrymen; in the naval combat with the fleet of the Zamorin which was being secretly prepared against them, and whose preparation was made known to him by the afore-mentioned traveller Ludovico di Varthema; in a successful combat at Panane; in establishing negotiations with the Maldives and Ceylon, the principal king of which island he compelled to submit to the King of Portugal; and in several other actions both on sea and on land,—in all these he played a most distinguished part, displaying an undaunted courage, and a noble and considerate interest for the welfare of his companions in the field. He had been about four years in India, and it may truly be said of him what a British essayist has said of Blaise Pascal, only in a different line of thought and action:—"When we think," says Rogers, "of the achievements which he crowded into that brief space, and which have made his name famous to all generations, we may well exclaim with Corneille, 'À peine a-t-il vécu, quel nom il a laissé!'"*

The combat being now ended, the policy of the victors was to pursue the vanquished by going down to Calicut to join the fleet of the Zamorin prepared there in order to make a general attack against the Portuguese. Hussein was of this opinion, in which, however, Malik Eyâz did not agree, for he took altogether an opposite view of the matter, and persuaded his fellow-admiral to sail with his fleet back to Diu. Malik Eyâz had, besides a clear mind, tact, politeness of manners, and an air of gallantry, qualities which are held in such high repute among the Orientals, and which made him take special care of his prisoners and render their captivity as light as possible. He also tried to get possession of the corpse of Dom Lourenço in order to consign it to a decent grave, but it could not be found, or, if found, could not be recognized. Eyâz at last wrote a letter to the Viceroy on the death of his son, to console him on his loss, saying, among other platitudes, that it was a subject for consolation to a father who loved glory to learn that the son he had lost in the midst of such a high and hopeful career was worthy of him, dying as he did on the bed of honour.

The Viceroy, long before receiving this condoling letter, was made aware of the unfortunate event by the fugitive remnants of the fleet which had, in the meanwhile, arrived at Cannanore and given him all the details of the action, concealing from him, however, the death

---

* Rogers' *Essays Critical and Biographical*, Lond., 1874, vol. i., p. 212.

of his son, or rather disguising the fact by stating that they were not quite sure whether their leader was dead or taken captive. In the midst of this perplexity the Viceroy sent a *yogi* to Cambay with a ball of wax containing a letter to the captives there, asking for particulars regarding Dom Lourenço. The *yogi* returned in due time with the news of his death. The elder Almeida sustained with all fortitude this severe shock to his paternal feelings, and although he spoke in public of the death of his son as the death of a Christian hero, and worthy of one who had maintained hitherto by his conduct the traditions of his noble ancestors, he subsequently withdrew to his apartment, from which he did not come out for three days, neither did he speak of his heavy misfortune to any one.

The victors were in the meanwhile overwhelmed with joy, and the whole of India rang with the cry of victory from the lips of the blatant Mahomedans. They then spoke but of Amir Hussein and Malik Eyâz as the most celebrated men of the day; all the kings of the country sent them ambassadors with congratulatory addresses, and the people celebrated the triumphs of their generals with fêtes and pageants of rare splendour. The victors were their tutelary deities, and the people believed that the moment had arrived for their deliverance from the oppressive yoke of the foreigner. These demonstrations of joy added to the affliction of the bereaved father, and tended also to inflame his wrath. Taking advantage of the two fleets which had arrived from Portugal, the venerable general set out to wreak his vengeance upon the Mahomedans, or revenge the death of his brave son. It would have been indeed difficult for him to hold the sea, but for the opportune arrival of the fleets of Tristaõ da Cunha and Affonço d'Albuquerque. The Viceroy had thus under him the combined armaments of nineteen vessels commanded by able officers, with 1,300 Portuguese soldiers and mariners and 400 Malabarese on board, with which force he set sail on the 12th November 1508, and, having first sunk and burnt some Calicut ships on his route, anchored off the city of Dâbul, which he destroyed, making a descent upon it. The resistance was, however, vigorous. Piles of the dead formed a barrier more formidable even than the palisades erected round the city, but the assailants striving among themselves who should be the foremost, the artillery of the besieged being happily of high range and passing over their heads, they pressed on to the ramparts, which were scaled, and the city devastated and razed to the ground. It was then given to plunder,* and ultimately reduced to ashes. Their cruelty was on this occasion of so glaring a nature that it gave rise to the proverbial curse: "Let the wrath of the Farangî fall on you as it did on Dâbul." Having accomplished this unpleasant task, he set out for Diu on the 3rd February 1509, where he achieved a splendid victory. Of this engagement there is no mention made in the Mahomedan history of Gujarât, but the Portuguese annalists' accounts are too circumstantial to be doubted. Having at last concluded a treaty of peace with Malik Eyâz, who now hastened to court the friendship of the Portuguese, the Viceroy returned to Cochin, and on his way made the sovereign of Chaul, Nizâm-ul-Mulk, who was intimidated by the accounts of the late victory, a tributary to the King of Portugal.† This took place in April 1509.

One year subsequent to this event the Viceroy was, through the imprudence of his officers, involved in a scuffle with a band of Hottentots at Saldanha Bay, where he had stopped on his way home, and died, being wounded by a javelin in the neck. Besides his prudence and valour which had contributed so much to extend the conquests of his nation, Dom Francisco d'Almeida, the seventh son of the Conde d'Abrantes, had also other accomplishments. It was he who first discovered the island of Madagascar and gave it the name of St. Lawrence, which name, according to Mandelslo,‡ was meant either to honour his son, or the saint of the day on which the discovery was made. His disinterestedness was equal to his valour, for, unlike some of his successors, he returned home poorer than when he left Lisbon for India. His death has been a never-ending theme for philosophical discourses, and, among others, there is a contemporary writer who moralizes on the sad event thus:—"That the man who had trampled upon countless thousands of Asiatics, who had humbled their sovereign powers, and annihilated in the seas the powers of the Egyptian Soldan, should perish on an obscure strand

* Faria y Sousa adds that, the Viceroy not having laid in any considerable store of provisions when his expedition was organized, it was thought fit to seek for food in Dâbul when it was given to plunder. In the search they found locusts preserved in pots, which the Portuguese tasted and found palatable, and not "unlike shrimps."

† Some of the chroniclers state that the amount of 2,000 *pardaos* in gold, which Nizâm-ul-Mulk used voluntarily to pay to Dom Lourenço for the defence of his port, was now made compulsory.

‡ *Voyages du Sieur Albert de Mandelslo*, Amsterdam, 1727, p. 654. But others say it was the fleet of Tristaõ da Cunha; Camoens is of this opinion—see *Lusiadas*, canto x., stanza xxxix.

by the hands of a few savages, should be a salutary lesson for human ambition.* Soon after this event a factor was placed at Chaul, where he is mentioned in 1514 by Duarte Barbosa, who, under the name of Cheul, describes the place thus :—

"Leaving the kingdom of Cambay, along the coast towards the south, at eight leagues' distance, there is a fine large river, and on it is a place called Cheul†,—not very large, of handsome houses, which are all covered with thatch. This place is one of great commerce in merchandize, and in the months of December, January, February, and March there are many ships from the Malabar country and all other parts, which arrive with cargoes. That is to say, those of Malabar laden with cocoanuts, arecas, spices, drugs, palm sugar, emery, and there they make their sales for the continent and for the kingdom of Cambay; and the ships of Cambay come there to meet them laden with cotton stuffs, and many other goods which are available in Malabar, and these are bartered for the goods which have come from the Malabar country. And on the return voyage they fill their ships with wheat, vegetables, millet, rice, sesame, oil of sesame, of which there is much in the country; and these Malabars also buy many pieces of fine muslin‡ for women's head-dress, and many beyranies, of which there are plenty in this kingdom. A large quantity of copper is sold in this port of Cheul, and at a high price, for it is worth twenty ducats the hundredweight, or more, because in the interior money is made of it, and it is also used throughout the country for cooking-pots. There is also a great consumption in this place of quicksilver and vermilion for the interior, and for the kingdom of Guzarat, which copper, quicksilver, and vermilion is brought to this place by the Malabar merchants, who get it from the factories of the King of Portugal; and they get more of it by way of the Mekkah, which comes there from Diu. These people wear the beyranies put on for a few days nearly in the raw state, and afterwards they bleach them and make them very white, and gum them to sell them abroad, and thus some are met with amongst them which are torn. In this port of Cheul there are few inhabitants, except during three or four months of the year, the time for putting in cargo, when

* Knight's *Universal Biography*.

† *Chaul, Ortelius*, 1570.

‡ *Beatilla, bétille* in French.

there arrive merchants from all the neighbourhood, and they make their bargains during this period, and despatch their goods, and after that return to their homes until the next season, so that this place is like a fair in those months. There is a Moorish gentleman as governor of this place, who is a vassal of the King of Decani, and collects his revenues, and accounts to him for them. He is called Xech, and does great service to the King of Portugal, and is a great friend of the Portuguese, and treats very well all those that go there, and keeps the country very secure. In this place there is always a Portuguese factor appointed by the captain and factor of Goa, in order to send from this place provisions and other necessaries to the city of Goa, and to the Portuguese fleets; and at a distance of about a league inland from Cheul is a place where the Moors and Gentiles of the cities and towns throughout the country come to set up their shops of goods and cloths at Cheul during the before-mentioned months; they bring these in great caravans of domestic oxen, with packs like donkeys, and on the top of these long white sacks placed crosswise, in which they bring goods; and one man drives thirty or forty beasts before him."*

During the Governorship of Lopo Soares d'Albergaria, in the year 1516, permission was obtained from Nizâm-ul-Mulk to establish on a larger scale a factory at Chaul, and to have freer access than the Portuguese had hitherto had to this important harbour. It is on this occasion that the Portuguese chroniclers make the first mention of Mahim and Bandora, although it has no great historical importance attached to it. It was but a skirmish by Dom Joaõ de Monroy, who, while the Governor was engaged in the Red Sea, having orders to cruise along the coast, entered the Mahim river and met a native merchant vessel, the crew of which on the approach of the Portuguese dragged her on shore, and, taking as much of the cargo as they could carry, ran off in haste. Monroy then took the ship and steered towards Chaul. Passing near the Mahim fort he ordered a discharge of artillery against it, and went on his way; the native captain of the fort, by name Haguji, extremely vexed for this outrageous provocation, equipped in haste ten vessels, and followed in pursuit of Monroy. They met at the entrance of the Chaul river, where Haguji was defeated.

---

* Barbosa's *Description of the Coasts of East Africa and Malabar*, translated by the Hon. Henry E. J. Stanley, Lond. 1866, pp. 69 *et seqq.*

Plate 8.

DRAWN BY ARDESHEER, BOMBAY.

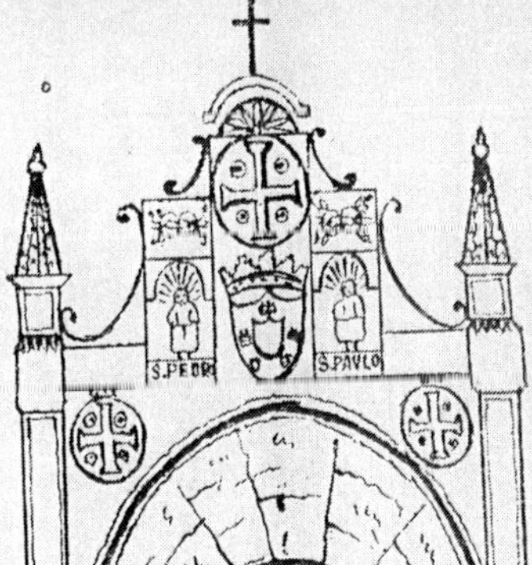

DRAWN BY ARDESHEER.

CHAUL.

RUINS OF THE CAPTAIN'S PALACE OR THE CASTLE.

In the year 1521 the Governor, Diogo Lopes de Siqueira, who, like his predecessor, Soares d'Albergaria, was more a merchant than a soldier, on his return from Cambay, where everything had gone amiss with him, put into Chaul. His principal misfortunes were the firing of the powder-room of the ship commanded by Antonio Correa, by the Mahomedan crew of a vessel captured by him on his voyage from Ormuz to Diu, on board of which they were made prisoners, and by which they blew up the poop into the air along with the brave conqueror of Bahrayn and all his rich booty. This was followed by the defeat of the little fleet that was sent under Beja to make the old demand in regard to a site to construct a fort at Diu, which not only met with a stern refusal, but in the scuffle which ensued on that occasion one of their galleys was sunk. Diogo Lopes at last, owing to these disasters, abandoned the project and retired precipitately, harassed as he was by Malik Eyâz and his compeers in the rear, until he arrived at Chaul.

At Chaul, Diogo Lopes met Fernaõ Camello, who had come with permission from Nizâm-ul-Mulk to erect a fort on the site of Revadaṇḍa, where the Portuguese had already built, in 1516, a miserable-looking little house called a factory.[1] They were, however, practically masters of the place to such an extent as to enrage the Mahomedans, who through sheer jealousy had murdered the first factor, Joaõ Fernandes, whose place was then filled by Fernaõ Camello.*

Some of the chroniclers state that the permission for the erection of the fortress was not only willingly granted by Nizâm-ul-Mulk, but almost pressed on them to be executed expeditiously, in order to spite the Gujarât king, with whom the Nizâm was then at war. For this purpose the king of Ahmadnagar, who had, a short time before, had his city burnt by the Dâbul fleet of Adil Khân, despatched to the Portuguese factory a person whom Barros calls Letefican (Latîf Khân) to concert measures and draw up an agreement or treaty between the two parties. The governorship of the Mahomedan city of Chaul had then fallen vacant, and was in dispute between two rival brothers named Sheikh Ahmad and Sheikh Mahomed, the highest bidder for the prize succeeding to the place.

Diogo Lopes was not slow to profit by so advantageous an offer. The treaty being ratified and signed, the building of the fort was

---

* Barros, *Decadas*, tome i., pt. 2, p. 295: also tome ii., pt. 1, p. 182.

begun without delay on the northern margin of the creek, about half a league to the south of the other, as the most convenient site for warlike purposes.*

The walls being once erected, the workmen, to whose toils a great impetus was imparted by the receipt of letters from the King of Portugal desiring them to build a fort at Chaul as well as at Diu, applied themselves *à couvert* to perfect the inner apartments of the building. Within this time the charge of the factory had passed over from Camello to Diogo Paes. Being aware that the erection of the fortress of Chaul was begun, which would eventually prove prejudicial to his interests, Malik Eyâz lost no time in making his appearance before Chaul with more than fifty vessels, and sunk a large Portuguese ship of Pedro da Silva de Menezes sailing with a rich cargo from Ormuz. He then continued to blockade the fort of Chaul for three weeks, doing considerable damage to the squadron which was opposed to him, and altogether harassing them greatly. Notwithstanding this, the construction of the fort was perseveringly carried on. About this time Diogo Lopes, learning that his successor had arrived at Cochin and his presence was necessary at that place, and being chagrined, moreover, at the inglorious result of the naval encounters above alluded to, forced his way through the enemy's fleet, leaving his nephew Henrique de Menezes to command the fort, and Fernaõ Beja in charge of the ships, consisting of two galleys, three caravels, one foist, and one brigantine, to oppose the aggressions of Malik Eyâz.

While thus forcing his way, escorted by his vessels, Diogo Lopes was, besides some untoward accidents of tide and head winds, met with a vigorous attack by Âgâ Mahomed, who was then commanding the Cambay fleet, and, being indefatigable in seconding every intention of his master, had himself done all in his power to hinder the establishment of the Portuguese at Chaul. He was, however, defeated, although the victory cost the Portuguese the death of Fernaõ Beja, who is crowned by the annalists with the pompous title of "General of the Sea." This memorable engagement was seen with

* Among the stipulations of that treaty was one concerning the importation of horses for the use of Nizâm-ul-Mulk. Barros says that on the subject of horses the Indian Mahomedans had the following adage:—"Se naõ houvesse soffrimento, naõ houvera já mundo; se naõ houvesse cavallos, naõ houvera guerra:" "Without sufferings there would be no world, nor without horses any war."

exciting interest from the shore by multitudes of people, who seemed to enjoy the affray and carnage so long as their own lives were not at stake. Beja was much regretted, and his place was temporarily occupied by Antonio Correa (not the one blown up near Ormuz),* pending the arrival of Dom Luis de Menezes, brother of the new Governor, who had been appointed in his place "General of the Sea."

To secure the entrance to the river, the Portuguese had constructed a redoubt or bulwark on the side opposite to the fort, and placed it under the command of Pedro Vaz Permeo, an old officer who had seen service in Italy, with a garrison of thirty men. Âgâ Mahomed landed 300 of his men by night to surprise this bulwark; but the small garrison, though the captain and several men were slain, valiantly opposed them, and maintained their ground till relieved by Ruy Vaz Pereira with a reinforcement of two armed boats containing sixty men, who put the enemy to flight, after having lost two of their chief officers and a hundred men. By this signal success of the Portuguese the enemy were much daunted, particularly a certain Sheikh Mahomed, a great man in the city, who pretended to be a friend of the Portuguese, but yet did everything in his power secretly to molest them. On the occasion of the defeat of Âgâ Mahomed, this Sheikh, believing him ignorant of his perfidy, sent to congratulate Antonio Correa; but the latter, well knowing his treachery, sent him in return the heads of his messengers, and hung up their bodies, for his edification, along the shore. The Sheikh was taken aback at this act, and in revenge proceeded to open hostilities, encouraging Âgâ Mahomed to persevere in the blockade, giving him at the same time intelligence that the Portuguese were in want of ammunition; but Dom Luis de Menezes arrived in the nick of time with reinforcements and a supply of ammunition and provisions, beside the new captain of Chaul, Simaõ d'Andrade; to them Correa resigned the command, and the blockade was raised. Some of the chroniclers relate wonders of this siege. They tell us of a soldier's shield on which a crucifix was represented being spiked with sixty darts, none of which touched the crucifix; and of others having twenty or more darts on them, which were likewise uninjured.

* This, though apparently preposterous, is a necessary parenthesis. Some of the translators of Faria y Souza have expressed doubts on the subject.

The next historical event in connection with Chaul is the arrival of Vasco da Gama in its port on his third and last voyage to India as the second Viceroy of the Portuguese dominions in the East. On his way to Goa, off Dâbul, he met with a fierce tempest which was about to engulf his fleet, and which Vasco da Gama, with his usual *sang froid*, used to explain away as a symptom of the ocean's fright at his presence; he was driven safely to Chaul, where he cast anchor on the 8th September 1524, and took, according to Barros, his title of Viceroy, following the example of Dom Francisco d'Almeida, who had taken the same title on his arrival at Cannanore. He did not land at all, but on his arrival Simaõ d'Andrade, Captain of Chaul, went at once to pay his respects to the Admiral on board his vessel, where, says Gaspar Correa, "the Viceroy did him great honour, and gave him and all the Captains of the fleet large presents of refreshments, because he was very grand and liberal in his expenditure."* Then the Viceroy appointed Christovaõ de Souza captain of the fortress, and having made, in conformity with his instructions from the King, several other minor appointments, he sailed, after a stay of three days, to Goa, carrying with him all the officers who did not belong to the local garrison and were unmarried, or had no pretext whatever for staying at Chaul, promising to each a share of the rich spoil of a Mahomedan ship which he had captured at sea on his way from the Red Sea to India. The goods on board that ship, when valued, were found to contain one hundred thousand ducats in gold, and two hundred thousand more in merchandize and slaves.

Dom Duarte de Menezes, on entering upon the government of India on the 22nd of January 1522, had sent his brother Dom Luis de Menezes, the General of the Sea in Chaul, to Ormuz to quell a rebellion of the Mahomedans, and afterwards followed himself. The Mahomedans showed opposition to the obnoxious measure adopted by Dom Duarte's predecessor of appointing Portuguese officers to the custom-house of Ormuz, to prevent certain frauds that had been practised by the native officers of the customs. On Dom Luis going to Ormuz, Chaul was left entirely to the care of Simaõ d'Andrade, who had begun his career here by capturing two Turkish galleys and gaining a victory over the people of Dàbul. By this success that city was reduced, and made to pay tribute, and also to cede to him two of the enemy's

* Stanley's *Three Voyages of Vasco da Gama*, Lond. 1869, p. 384.

ships. In the meanwhile the fort of Chaul, which had begun to be built in 1521, had been completed about 1524, and commanded even the entrance of the harbour of Bombay, in which from this date the Portuguese fleets were moving freely.

On Dom Duarte putting in at Chaul, where he met Christovaõ de Souza as Captain, he was informed that the Viceroy, Vasco da Gama, had left orders not to allow him to land. Malik Eyâz in the meanwhile appears to have been terrified by the repeated successes of the Portuguese, for he at once withdrew his fleet from before Chaul, to return again in 1528, when a great number of the ships of the fleet, which comprised 83 barques, were destroyed by the allied forces of the Portuguese and the King of Ahmadnagar. A valiant Moor named Alexiath (Ali Shâh) was in command. He had done much injury to the subjects of Nizâm-ul-Mulk and to the Portuguese trade at Chaul during the captaincy of Christovaõ de Souza. In consequence of this, the present Captain, Francisco Pereira de Berredo, demanded aid from the Governor, Lopo Vaz de Sampayo, who accordingly set sail with 40 vessels of different sizes, in which were 1,000 Portuguese soldiers, besides a considerable force of armed natives. In this expedition Heitor de Sylveira commanded the small vessels that were rowed—they all being Malabar vessels, which by the early writers are called *parâos, tonys, caturs*, &c., and are in fact rowing-boats—while Sampayo took charge of the sailing vessels. On arriving at Chaul, Sampayo sent 80 Portuguese, under the command of Joaõ de Avelar, to the assistance of Nizâm-ul-Mulk, and then sailed towards Diu. It was on this occasion that Bombay was for the second time visited by the Portuguese. Off Bombay the Cambay fleet, of which he was in search, was descried; some of the ships were detached and sent round to secure the entrance to the Bandora creek, to prevent the enemy from escaping; while Sylveira with his brigantines and rowing-boats bore down upon them. During the night, which was spent in the Bombay harbour, the crews of both fleets observed in the sky a comet of extraordinary size, sword-like in shape, which, says Barros, the Greeks used to call *Xiphia*. This appearance was held by the Mahomedans as an ominous sign, foreboding their proximate defeat. Notwithstanding, the engagement took place. A little before this, however, Sampayo got into one of his swift little boats and ordering all the ships of his fleet in a line made a short speech to each of them, encouraging them to action, and then gave the order for fighting. After a furious cannonade about or in front of the Bombay harbour the Portuguese gallantly boarded the enemy, who attempted to flee round the harbour through the Bandora creek, but found it blockaded, and Ali Shâh escaped with only ten of his barques, all the rest being taken. Of the 73 vessels captured, with a vast number of prisoners and much artillery and abundance of ammunition, 33 were retained as serviceable, the rest being burnt. It was on this occasion that Thâṇâ, Salsette, and Bombay were made tributary. All this took place in February 1528.

In this naval engagement Francisco de Barrio de Paiva was the first to board the enemy's vessels, and obtained the prize of 100 ducats which had been previously offered by Sampayo for such an act. The Portuguese historians state that, although the enemy lost so many ships and lives, the Portuguese lost not a single man. On this Lafitau remarks:—"Peut on les croire sans leur faire tort et sans diminuir beaucoup l'éclat de leur victoire en concevant trop de mépris pour les ennemis, à qui ils avaient affaire?"*

The detachment sent to Nizâm-ul-Mulk, assisted by 1,000 native soldiers of that king, acquired great honour by their gallantry, their commander, Joaõ de Avelar, being the first to scale, with their assistance, a fort belonging to the Gujarât king till then thought impregnable. Having slain the defenders, he delivered it up to Nizâm-ul-Mulk, who had for this purpose first implored the aid of the Portuguese.

In 1530 the Portuguese had a squabble with Nizâm-ul-Mulk, who had at length come to the determination, in spite of all his amicable overtures, to show the Portuguese his undisguised displeasure at having been compelled to cede them a few roods of the ground at the Chaul creek. This misunderstanding appears to have originated from the then captain of Chaul, Francisco Pereira Berredo, having, at the request of Nizâm-ul-Mulk, proceeded with a detachment of 200 men under his personal command to overthrow his enemy the king of Cambay, who was at the head of an army of 12,000, but only to return after suffering a severe repulse. Hence the determination of Nizâm-ul-Mulk to show his displeasure, which indicates to what extent the friendship he bore to the Portuguese was induced by self-interest. However, differences were soon made up, but the good understanding, superficial in its nature, lasted only for a decade, during which period Chaul was the only powerful Portuguese naval station on this part

* *Hist. des Descouvertes*, etc. Paris, 1736, vol. iii., p. 196.

of the coast, as well as the chief place of their army prior to the establishment of Bassein, honoured often by the visits of men so remarkable as statesmen and warriors as Nuno da Cunha, Martim Affonso de Souza, and others.

The success of the Portuguese under Sampayo had terrified all the princes of India who had been hitherto their enemies. Nizâm-ul-Mulk and Adil Khân sent in consequence their ambassadors to the Viceroy, Dom Garcia de Noronha, to renew their former treaties of peace, and the Zamorin was to obtain more honourable treatment from his employing the mediation of a commandant of the fort of Chalé, near Calicut.*

The next important event in connection with the history of Chaul is a grand naval review held in the harbour of Bombay. The largest fleet that ever crossed the Bombay waters, comprising four hundred vessels of all descriptions, principally from Chaul, were assembled under the command of Nuno da Cunha, Góvernor-General in India, conveying 22,000 men, of whom no less than 3,600 soldiers and 1,450 sailors were Europeans. There were, besides, 2,000 Canara and Malabar soldiers, 8,000 slaves, and about 5,000 native seamen. All of them were paraded on the site of the present Esplanade, and it was a splendid spectacle, say the chroniclers, to see these soldiers, in the quaint gaudy costumes of the time, moving on the then almost desolate island of Bombay, having for a background the array of vessels lying at anchor in the harbour, and all preparing to sail for the conquest of Diu. This took place in January 1531. They sailed towards Diu on the 7th February, and carried by assault a strongly fortified position in the island of Beyt, in the Gulf of Cutch.

Some time after, Chaul was visited by one of the greatest Portuguese travellers, the yet little known Fernaõ Mendes Pinto. He came down on board the same fleet which brought a new Captain of Chaul, appointed by the King, by name Jorge de Lima. On arrival at Chaul, in 1538 or the beginning of 1539, he met here Simaó Guedes, who was then the Captain of Chaul, and to whom he mentioned all the untoward accidents that befell him on the way.†

---

* The renewal of the treaty with Nizâm-ul-Mulk in the Governorship of Dom Garcia de Noronha is published in the *Subsidios para a Historia da India Portugueza*, by Rodrigo J. de L. Felner, Lisbon, 1868, pp. 115-117.

† *Peregrinaçaõ de Fernaõ Mendes Pinto*, Lisbon, 1762, pp. 3 and 8.

In the year 1540 Nizâm-ul-Mulk being determined to gain possession of the fortresses of Sangaça and Carnala (Sanksî and Karnâla), held by two subjects of the king of Gujarât, on the frontiers of that kingdom, and which were formidable from their strength and situation, took them by assault in the absence of their commanders. Dom Francisco de Menezes, the captain of Bassein, having been applied to for help, went to their assistance with 300 Europeans and a party of native troops, and the fortresses were stormed, retaken, and restored to their former owners, and Portuguese garrisons left with both for their protection. After a short time Nizâm-ul-Mulk, with an army of 5,000, having ruined and pillaged the two districts, the commanders in despair abandoned the places, and, resigning their titles to the Portuguese, withdrew to Bassein, whence Menezes sent supplies and relief, intending to defend them. On hearing of this, Nizâm-ul-Mulk sent an additional force of 6,000 men, of whom 1,000 were musketeers, and 800 well-equipped horsemen. This great force having besieged the fortress, which they twice assaulted in one day, they were repulsed with great slaughter. They again assaulted the trenches, and were opposed with determination, until, being much fatigued, and suffering from hunger and excessive heat, both parties were under the necessity of declaring by mutual consent a truce. In this interval Menezes having arrived with 160 Europeans, twenty of whom were cavalry, several naiks and 2,000 native soldiers, the attack was renewed, and after a sharp encounter the enemy fled, leaving the ground about the fortresses strewed with arms and ammunition.

In this engagement a Portuguese soldier of gigantic stature and prodigious strength, named Trancoso, in the heat of the battle seized by the waist a Mahomedan wrapped up in a large veil, and carried him as if he were a buckler to shelter his breast, receiving upon him all the strokes from the enemy's weapons. He continued to use this strange shield with marvellous effect, and did not once drop it on the ground till the close of the action. This soldier was the brother of Dom Antonio Trancoso, a magistrate, and having settled at Thâṇâ died there at a very advanced age, having two of his grand-daughters married to Dom Francisco de Souza and Dom Diniz d'Almeida, officers of the Diu garrison. The house and family of this distinguished warrior are now extinct.*

* Diogo do Couto's *Decadas*, vol. ii., pt. 2, p. 193.

When the battle was over, the Governor, Dom Estevaõ da Gama, happened to arrive at Chaul, and considering that these fortresses cost more than they produced, and Nizâm-ul-Mulk was their ally, restored them to that prince for an additional tribute of 5,000 *pardaos* in gold, to the great regret of Captain Menezes of Bassein, who showed to the last his reluctance to deliver them up to him.*

A curious episode, connected with the history of Chaul, as illustrated in the "*Vida de Dom Joaõ de Castro,*" by one of the most elegant and popular, though by no means trustworthy, of the Portuguese chroniclers, Jacinto Freire d'Andrade, is the patriotic zeal of the matrons and maidens of Chaul, who, having heard that the Viceroy of India, Dom Joaõ de Castro, had requested the municipality of Goa to lend him 20,000 *pardaos,* for the use of his army of defence at Diu, which was being besieged by Khoja Sofar, sending at the same time a lock of his moustaches as a pledge for the sure and punctual repayment of the money, sent him their earrings, necklaces, bracelets, and other jewellery, to be applied to the public service. The Governor, however, restored them all in the same condition in which they were sent, having been in the meantime amply supplied with funds by the capture of a rich ship of Cambay. This took place in 1546.

The above statement has been written and reproduced several times for more than three centuries, and, remaining uncontradicted, is universally believed. It was only lately that the discovery of documents that lay buried for years in the Government archives at Lisbon led some writers to cast a doubt on the veracity of that story. The truth is that when Dom Joaõ de Castro wrote a letter, dated the 3rd May 1516, addressed to the municipality, magistrates and inhabitants of Chaul, requesting their aid in the preparation of a fleet to resist the king of Gujarât, a reply, dated the 22nd of the same month, was sent, saying, "We are ready to aid you not only with persons, arms, horses, ships and states for all the time you wish; but if our states be not sufficient for that purpose, our wives will gladly offer us their jewels." The enthusiasm of the reply is so palpable that, caught by it, and faithful to the tradition of being the Spartans of the time, a lady from Chaul, who was then at Goa, sent to the Viceroy by her daughter a case of jewels, stating that

* This second treaty is found in Felner's *Subsidios, ut supra,* pt. ii., pp. 117-120.

having heard that the ladies of Chaul had offered their jewels to him, she was desirous to have the honour of sending hers. Another part of this curious letter worth noting is her allusion to the wealth of Chaul at that time. She writes :—" Do not think, Sir, that because my jewels are so few, there are not more at Chaul. I assure you that I have the least portion, having distributed them among my daughters. There are jewels in Chaul which alone are sufficient to carry on the war for ten years."*

During the entire period from 1540 until the Governorship of Francisco Barreto, in 1555, Chaul enjoyed the blessing of peace, which circumstance accounts partly for the amount of wealth above referred to. It was only in 1557 that the Governor having been informed of the death of Nizâm-ul-Mulk in the preceding year, and not being quite sure of meeting the same friendly treatment at the hands of his successor, expressed his desire to secure the promontory of Kôrlê (*Môrro*), and fortify it into an outwork of defence for the city of Chaul, when a scuffle ensued, as we shall see hereafter.

The Portuguese chroniclers of the time pass a glowing encomium on the memory of the deceased Nizâm-ul-Mulk, who, it is stated, was endowed with great natural and political sagacity, his court being an hospitable resort of the best men of the time. He had among his courtiers a Portuguese renegade, by name Simaõ Peres, who had embraced Mahomedanism, and was held in such high estimation by the king that he appointed him his minister and general of his army. Notwithstanding his apostacy, Peres was always friendly towards his countrymen, and entertained no respect for those who imitated his perfidy. The king, on his death-bed, recommended his successor to the good offices of this faithful servant, and Peres executed with fidelity all his charges.

Soon after the death of the king, the young prince had an unpleasant affray with Adil Khân, in which the old minister lost his life, and the new Nizâm-ul-Mulk was left to his whims, unguided alike by the advice of his sober minister and the example of his wise father. In reference to the latter, Diogo do Couto is the only chronicler who points out a trait

* *Instituto Vasco da Gama*, vol. iv., pp. 29 and 57. Dom Joaõ de Castro was often at Chaul, and a fourth treaty of alliance, confirmatory of all the three previous ones, was signed by him with Nizâm-ul-Mulk. *Subsidios, ibid.*, pp. 120-123.

Plate **7.**

CHAUL.

THE "MORRO DE CHAUL" OR THE FORTIFIED HILL OF KORLE.

in the character of the deceased king which really mars the effect of his otherwise eminently eulogistic memoir. He informs us, in his *Decada* V., liv. VIII., cap. vi., that this prince being affected by what he calls St. Lazarus' malady, *i.e.* leprosy, and all medical efforts to cure him having failed, was recommended by one of his court physicians to try as a last resource the effect of bathing in children's blood. Large tanks were filled, says the historian, with that liquid, but with no better result. This wanton immolation of innocent little lives on the altar of this prince's tyranny differs perhaps only in degree from the murder of the innocents by Herod. However, Nizâm-ul-Mulk, in spite of his leprosy, lived to the advanced age of ninety, having reigned for the unusually long period of fifty-eight years. The disposition of this prince was perhaps not dissimilar to that of Sultân Mahomed, king of Gujarât, who, like Mithridates, had accustomed himself to the use of poison, to guard himself against being poisoned. When any of his women, Faria y Souza tells us, happened to be nigh delivery, he opened their wombs to take out the fœtus. And being out hunting one day accompanied by some of his women, he fell from his horse and was dragged by the stirrup, when one of his female companions bravely made up to his horse and cut the girth with a scimitar; in requital for this service he killed her, saying that "a woman of such courage had also enough to kill him." He was at length murdered by a page in whom he had great confidence. "For tyrants," adds the historian, "always die by the hands of those in whom they repose most trust."*

When Barreto arrived at Chaul he had neither the friendly assistance of the old king nor the coöperation of the patriotic minister to back him in his project to secure and fortify the rocky promontory of Kôrlê, called by the Portuguese, as already stated "o Môrro de Chaul." It was really this friendship that had hitherto prevented the Portuguese from attacking Chaul, while the neighbouring city of Dâbûl had been between 1503 and 1557 four times burnt and plundered. The possession of the promontory of Kôrlê commanding the entrance of the harbour, would, he thought, compensate for all the drawbacks and imperfections of the fortress of Chaul, especially at a time when all the Mahomedan powers of India were,

* *Asia Portuguesa*, Spanish edition of 1674, vol. ii., p. 278.

conjointly with the Rûms,* striving to enlist the support of the natives of the country in their efforts to make the Portuguese abandon their conquests in India.

The project of fortifying the promontory had, however, according to the stipulations of the treaty, before being carried into effect, to be submitted to, and approved of by, the King of Chaul, Nizâm-ul-Mulk II. For this purpose an ambassador with rich presents was sent. The young prince regarded the proposal as an insult to his dignity, and as displaying an occult desire on the part of the Portuguese to undermine his independence. Then apprehending that such a project was a mere pretext to levy duties on merchandize leaving or entering his port, and thus deprive him of this important item of state revenue, he not only refused permission, but made the ambassador a prisoner, and despatched his General, Farate Khân, with 30,000 men, and instructions to build as speedily as possible an impregnable fortress there on his own account. He ordered his General at the same time not to show any hostility towards the Portuguese in the fort, nor to those who were settled in their city. Garcia Rodrigues de Tavora, the Governor of the fortress of Chaul, alarmed at this state of things, made representations to the Viceroy, and obtained a fleet, under the command of Alvaro Peres Souto Maior, to stop the progress of the work begun.

Soon after the Viceroy himself went in person to their relief with a numerous and well-manned fleet conveying 4,000 Portuguese troops, besides natives, who kept on pouring shells and bullets on the workmen, preventing progress being made with the fortifications. Whereupon Nizâm-ul-Mulk, unwilling to continue the conflict, sent a *parlementaire* with the following message :—"that he was a friend to the King of Portugal, having inherited that feeling from his predecessor, who had given them a place where they had already built a citadel, a gift which he certainly never thought of revoking, but that he had reasons to apprehend that by allowing them to build a new fort it would eventually lead them to place him under their yoke, and deprive him of the customs duties, which belonged, as hitherto, to him alone, as the sovereign of the place." The arguments being found convincing, the

* The European Turks were called Rûms by the Portuguese, from their occupying the seat of the Lower Roman Empire, just as the Asiatics used to call Franks all nations of the Latin race, from their first acquaintance with them in the time of the Crusades.

conflict ended in a pacific arrangement being made by both parties that Kôrlê should remain as it was.

During the above affray, the chroniclers add, a miracle was wrought at the promontory of Kôrlê, where the Moors, utterly unable to cut down with swords a small wooden cross fixed upon a stone, tried to remove it by the force of elephants, but without success. Faria y Souza adds to this miracle the following :—" Likewise about this time a Portuguese soldier bought for a trifle from a jogue (*yogî*) in Ceylon a brown pebble about the size of an egg, on which the heavens were represented in several colours, and in the midst of them the image of the holy Virgin with the Saviour in her arms; this precious jewel fell into the hands of Francisco Barreto, who presented it to Queen Catherine, and through its virtues God wrought many miracles both in India and Portugal."*

This was also an occasion on which the Portuguese of Chaul, not yet intoxicated with the spirit of luxury or insolence of wealth, which rendered them in subsequent encounters as difficult to control within the bounds of prudence as to bring them under a moderate discipline, evinced such a zeal for the public welfare as to feed at their expense all the soldiers of the garrison. One of the inhabitants, by name Lopes Carrasco, a man of considerable wealth, placed daily at his door tables with every sort of eatables for the use of the garrison during the time the conflict with Nizâm-ul-Mulk continued, and his excellent example was followed by others with alacrity and praiseworthy emulation.

In 1570, five years after the famous battle of Talicota, in which the memory of the old empire of Narsinga was destroyed by the Mahomedan sword, a serious combination was formed against the Portuguese by the kings of Bijapûr and Ahmadnagar, assisted by the Zamorin, to drive them out of India—not unlike the one that in 1857 was concocted against the British. This confederacy, which had been under negotiation for five long years with remarkable secrecy, flattered itself so much with the certainty of extirpating the Portuguese from this country that they agreed beforehand on the distribution of their expected conquests.

Princes are, however, more than ordinary individuals, apt, as M. de la Clède rightly observes, to mistrust each other, even when profess-

* *Asia Portuguesa, loc. cit.*, p. 314.

ing apparently entire confidence.† In spite of the alliance being sealed with the most solemn oaths, each of the princes was disinclined to strike the first blow, suspecting his ally would not follow suit. Nizâm Shâh or Nizâm-ul-Mulk, anxious as he was to get rid of the Portuguese from Chaul at all hazards, and share their dominions as a part of his spoil, was on various pretences putting off besieging Chaul until Adil Khân had first invaded Goa.

The secret at last got out: Farate Khân being appointed the commander of Nizâm-ul-Mulk's army, advanced with it about the end of December, in fulfilment of the stipulations of his master. His army consisted of 26 elephants, 8,000 horse, and 20,000 infantry, men of courage and willing to fight, but wanting in one thing—discipline—to make them fine soldiers.

Their march into the environs of the old city was made amidst the deafening sound of cymbals, beating of drums, and a variety of martial music. Four thousand of the Ahmadnagar cavalry then marched along the north of Chaul to cut off the reinforcements and supplies from Bassein, and the small fort of Caranja with its garrison of 40 men under Duarte Perestrello. All this amazing ostentation did not, however, in the least alarm the Portuguese citizens, who, being fully awake as to what was to happen, displayed the same serene determination, intrepidity, and willingness to fight as their countrymen at Goa. The chroniclers attribute this disposition of mind to the Viceroy, Dom Luis d'Athaide, the Lord Canning of those days, whose good example had, more than anything else, inspired them with confidence. He was recommended by many, especially the Archbishop, to abandon Chaul for the greater security of Goa; but he undauntedly resolved to defend both.

This was a time pregnant with grave events. Goa was then in the throes of a formidable invasion. However, those were the days in which the capital of Portuguese India had not entirely declined from its former proud eminence of luxury and power, and romantic incidents and deeds of valour were not uncommon.

Luis Freire d'Andrade, a man of acknowledged merit, was then the Captain of Chaul, which he hastily fortified, taking in all necessary provisions to last during a siege, which, it was feared, would be a long one. The fortifications were then in so contemptible a

* *Histoire Général de Portugal*, Paris, 1735, tome vi., p. 52.

condition that they well merited the hard epithet of "*un misérable bicoque*" applied to them by Lafitau. They gave, moreover, origin to that curious dialogue reported by chroniclers between Nizâm-ul-Mulk and his general Farate Khân, in which the former made use of the not very complimentary phrase "a stable of beasts" in reference to the Chaul fort, the general excellently retorting that "the beasts were lions." Some of the citizens of Chaul, however, enervated by luxury and abuse of the blessings of twelve years' peace, were every way thwarting the general Dom Francisco Mascarenhas' plans. They seemed to care more for their houses and gardens than the honour of the nation. The houses were, however, pulled down, some of the gardens outside the town fortified, and every nook and corner put in the best state of defence.

The Viceroy was in the meanwhile preparing to send him reinforcements after the 600 men, five foists and four galleys already despatched under the command of Mascarenhas, a gallant officer of his time, who had also brought with him some shiploads of ammunition and other supplies. These reinforcements were followed by others under the command of Ruy Gonsalves, who brought 200 men, and Dom Luis de Menezes Baroche, who eventually became captain of Chaul in succession to Freire d'Andrade.

Farate Khân, immediately on his arrival at Chaul, about the end of December 1570, marshalled his artillery and elephants in battle array, and having made sure that in pursuance of the league Adil Khân had taken the field before Goa, without awaiting further orders from the king Nizâm Shâh, who was himself expected to join the campaign, gave orders to carry the place by a *coup de main*. His attempt, however, proving unsuccessful, he retreated into the chapel of Madre de Deus and waited there until the king arrived, about the 16th January 1571, with the rest of his army, which, with that under General Farate Khân, amounted now to 34,000 horse, 100,000 foot, 30,000 pioneers, and 4,000 men consisting of smiths, masons, and other artizans, of different nationalities, such as Turks, Persians, Abyssinians, and a few European renegades. He had also 300 elephants with 40 pieces of artillery of enormous size with such names as 'the cruel,' 'the devourer,' 'the butcher,' 'the honour,' &c., and every kind of ammunition. This prodigious force was encamped in the environs of Chaul, which place, though but poorly fortified and with only a handful of men to carry on its defence, had a few officers of such extraordinary courage, as Dom Luis de Menezes, who had earned through his exploits the appellation of *solus mundi*, and others, that one of them was surely worth a hundred of the enemy. The Nizâm-ul-Mulk had, besides, an auxiliary naval force to assist him from the Zamorin, which mustered twenty-two *paraus*, carrying 1,500 fusiliers; this fleet he ordered to engage the Portuguese in the port, and ascended the top of one of his own mosques to observe the progress of the action. He had, however, the mortification to behold from this place the crushing defeat of the Malabarese allies, in whom he had placed more dependence than in his own army.

"Thus," says Faria y Souza, "an army of 150,000 men sat down to besiege a town that was defended merely by a single wall, a fort not much larger than a house, and a handful of men. Farate Khân took up his quarters near the church of Madre de Deus with 7,000 horse and 20 elephants; Agalas Khân in the house of Joaõ Lopes with 6,000 horse; Nimiri Khân between that and Upper Chaul with 2,000 horse: so that the city was beset from sea to sea. The Nizâm encamped with the main body of the army at the further end of the town, where the ground was covered with tents for the space of two leagues; and 5,000 horse were detached to ravage the district of Bassein."*

Although at the commencement of the siege the Portuguese garrison was, as above stated, a mere handful of men, and the works being very slight no particular posts were assigned, all acting wherever their services were most wanted, yet soon afterwards, the news of the siege having spread abroad, many officers and gentlemen flocked thither with reinforcements, so that in a short time the garrison was augmented to 2,000 men. It was then resolved to maintain particular points, besides the general circuit of the walls. The monastery of the Franciscans was committed to the charge of Alexandre de Souza; Nuno Alvares Pereira was entrusted with the defence of some houses near the shore; those between the Misericordia and the church of the Dominicans were confided to Gonsalo de Menezes; others in that neighbourhood to Nuno Vello Pereira, and so on in other places. In the meanwhile the priestly party continued more than ever to recommend that Chaul should be sacrificed for the safety of Goa; but the Viceroy thought otherwise, in which opinion he was seconded only by Ferdinando de Castellobranco, and he immediately despatched succours under Ferdinando Telles and Duarte de Lima. Before their arrival, Nimiri Khân, who had pro-

* *Asia Portuguesa, ut supra.*

Plate 10.

CHAUL.

RUINS OF THE CHURCH TOWER, AND FORTIFIED MONASTERY OF THE FRANCISCANS.

mised the Nizâm that he would be the first person to enter Chaul, vigorously assaulted the posts of Henrique de Betancourt and Ferdinando de Miranda, who resisted him with the slaughter of 300 of his men, losing seven on their own side.

At last the reinforcements arrived, in spite of all the efforts of the enemy to intercept them. The enemy had erected a battery against the monastery of the Franciscans, where the Portuguese had some cannon ; and as the gunners on both sides used their utmost endeavours to burst or dismount the opposite guns, the cannon-balls were sometimes seen to meet by the way. On the eve of St. Sebastian the Portuguese made a sally upon some houses which were occupied by the Moors, and slew a great number of them without the loss of even one man. Enraged at this affront and the late repulse, the enemy made that same night an assault on the fortified monastery of the Franciscans with 5,000 men, expecting to surprise the Portuguese, but were soon undeceived by losing many of their men. This assault lasted with great fury for five hours ; and as the Portuguese suspected the enemy were undermining the wall, and could not see by reason of the darkness, one Christovaõ Corvo thrust himself several times out from a window, with a torch in one hand and a buckler in the other, to discover, if possible, what they were doing. During this assault those in the town sent out assistance to the garrison in the monastery, though with much hazard. When morning broke and the assailants had retired, the monastery was found all stuck full of arrows, and the dead bodies of 300 Moors were seen around its walls, while the defenders had not lost a single man.

The enemy renewed the assault on this post for five successive days, and were every time repulsed by the Portuguese with vast slaughter, the garrison often sallying out and strewing the field with slain enemies. It was at length judged expedient to withdraw the men from this place into the town, lest its loss should occasion greater injury than its defence could do service. Seventeen of the Portuguese were here slain. One of these used to stand on a high place to notice when the enemy fired their cannon, and on one occasion said to the men below, " if these fellows should now fire *Raspadillo* (a cannon 18 feet long to which that name was given), it will send me to sup with Christ, to whom I commend my soul, for it points directly at me." He had hardly spoken these words when he was torn to pieces by a ball from that very gun. On getting possession of the monastery of the Franciscans the Moors fired a whole street in the town of Chaul, but on attempting to take post in some houses they were driven out with the loss of 900 men. At this time Gonçalo da Camara went to Goa for more reinforcements, as the garrison was much pressed, and brought a relief in two galleys.

About this period the 500 men that had been detached by the Nizâm to ravage the district of Bassein attempted to get possession of some of the Portuguese garrisons. Being beaten off at Assarin and Damaun, they invested Caranja, at this time commanded by Estevaõ Perestrello with a garrison of only 40 men, but was reinforced, on the reappearance of the enemy, by Manuel de Mello with 30 more from Salsette. With this small band of only 70 soldiers Perestrello sallied out against the enemy, and with such success that after covering the little island with dead bodies, the rest fled, leaving their cannon and a considerable quantity of ammunition and provisions.

In the meantime the Moors continued to batter Chaul without intermission for a whole month with 70 pieces of large cannon, every day expending against its weak defences at least 160 balls. This tremendous cannonade did much damage to the houses of the town, in which many of the brave defenders were slain. On one occasion six persons who were eating together were destroyed by a single ball. This furious battery was commenced against the bastion of the Holy Cross, and was carried on for a considerable way along the defences of that front of the town, levelling everything with the ground. The besieged used every precaution to shelter themselves by digging trenches; but the hostile gunners were so expert that they elevated their guns and made their balls plunge among those who considered themselves in safety. On observing that one of the enemies' batteries beyond the church of the Dominicans never ceased its destructive fire, Perestrello detached 120 men under Alexandre de Souza and Augustinho Nunes, who drove the enemy, after a vigorous resistance, from the battery with great slaughter, set their works on fire, and levelled them with the ground, without sustaining any loss. Among the arms taken in this successful sortie was a scimitar inscribed 'Jesus salva me.'

Having ruined the defences of the town, the enemy attacked several large houses in which they endeavoured to establish themselves, but were repulsed from some of these with considerable loss, while the defenders lost but one man. On attacking the house of Heitor de Sampayo, which was undermined by the Portuguese with the intention of blowing it up when occupied by the enemy, some fire was accidentally communicated to the mine during the conflict, and it blew up while still occupied by the Portuguese, by which 42 of their soldiers were destroyed, without the least injury to the Moors, who then planted their colours on the ruins. Nimiri Khân made an assault by night with 600 men upon the bastion of the Holy Cross, in which Ferdinando Pereira was posted with 30 men, reinforced by Henrique de Betancourt with a few more. The assailants were beaten off, and five of their colours taken which they had planted on the works. In this action Betancourt fought with his left hand, having previously lost the right; and Dominico del Alama being lame caused himself to be brought out in a chair. April 1571 was now begun, and the enemy were employed in constructing new works, as if determined to continue the siege. Alexandre de Souza and Gonçalo de Menezes were appointed to head a sally upon these new works, but their men to the number of 200 ran out without orders and made a furious assault upon the enemy, whom they drove from the works after killing fifty of them, and losing a few of their own number. The two commanders hastened to join their men, and then directed them to destroy the works they had so gallantly won. Perplexed with so many losses, the Nizâm made a general assault at night with his whole army, attacking all the posts at one time. Every one almost they penetrated; but the garrison exerted themselves with so much vigour that they drove the Moors from every point of attack, and in the morning above 500 of the enemy were found slain in and about the ruined defences, while the Portuguese had only lost four or five men. About this time the defenders received a reinforcement of above 200 men from Goa, Diu, and Bassein, with a large supply of ammunition and provisions; but at the same time they were much afflicted by a troublesome though not mortal disease, by which they became swelled all over so as to lose the use of their limbs.

Having ineffectually endeavoured to stir up enemies against the Portuguese in Cambay on purpose to prevent relief being sent to the brave defenders of Chaul, the Nizâm made every effort to bring his arduous enterprise to a favourable conclusion. The house of Nuno Alvares Pereira, being used as a stronghold by the Portuguese, was battered during forty-two days by the enemy, who then assaulted it with 5,000 men. At first the defenders of this post were only forty in number, but twenty more came to their assistance immediately, and several others afterwards. The Moors were repulsed with the loss of 50 men, while the Portuguese only lost one. The house of Nuno Velho was battered for thirty days and assaulted with the same success, only that the Portuguese lost ten men in its defence. Judging it no longer expedient to defend this house, it was undermined and evacuated, on which the enemy hastened to take possession and it was blown up, doing considerable damage among them, but not so much as was expected. The summer was now almost spent; above 6,000 cannon-balls had been thrown into the town, some of which were of prodigious size,* and the Nizâm seemed determined to continue the siege during the winter. About 200 Portuguese, appalled by the dangers of the siege, had already deserted; but instead of them 300 men had come from Goa, so that the garrison was even stronger than before. On the 11th of April, Gonçalo da Camara made a sortie upon 500 Moors in an orchard, only fifty of whom escaped.

Fortune could not be always favourable to the besieged. By a chance ball from the enemy, one of the galleys which brought relief was sunk with 40 men and goods to the value of 40,000 ducats. But next day Ferdinando Telles made a sally with 400 men, and gained a victory equal to that of Gonçalo da Camara, and brought away one piece of cannon with some ammunition, arms, and other booty. This action was seen by the Nizâm himself, who mounted his horse to join in it in person, for which purpose he seized a lance, which he soon changed for a whip, with which he threatened to chastise his men, upbraiding them as cowards. The Portuguese were now so inured to danger that nothing could terrify them, and they seemed to court death, instead of shunning it, on all occasions. Some of them being employed to level those works from which the enemy had been driven near the monastery of the Franciscans, and being more handy with the sword than the spade, drew upon themselves a large party of the enemy, of whom they slew above 200, yet not without some loss on their own side. About this time Farate Khân, one of the Nizâm's generals, made some overtures towards peace, but without any apparent authority from his sovereign, who caused him to be arrested on suspicion of being corrupted by the Portuguese, though assuredly he had secret orders for what he had

* Such balls, if they are the real relics of the siege, are still found scattered all over the area in the city of Chaul.

done. Indeed, it was not wonderful that the Nizâm should be desirous of peace, as he had now lain seven months before Chaul to no purpose, and had lost many thousand men; neither was it strange in the Portuguese to have the same wish, as they had lost 400 men, besides Indians.

When the siege had continued to the beginning of June, the attacks and batteries were carried on by both sides with as much obstinacy and vigour as if then only begun. The house of Nuno Alvares was at this time taken by the enemy, through the carelessness of the defenders, and in an attempt to recover it 20 of the Portuguese lost their lives, without doing much injury to the enemy. The Moors, in the next place, got possession of the monastery of the Dominicans, but not without heavy loss, and then gained the house of Gonçalo de Menezes, in which the Portuguese suffered severely. The hostile batteries kept up a constant fire from the end of May to the end of June, as the Nizâm had resolved to make a breach large enough for the whole army to try its fortune in a general assault. On the 28th of June, everything being in readiness, the Nizâm's whole army was drawn up for the assault, all his elephants appearing in the front with castles on their backs full of armed men. While the whole army stood in expectation of the signal for the assault, an officer of note belonging to the enemy was slain by a random shot from one of the Portuguese cannon, which the Nizâm considering as an evil omen ordered the attack to be deferred till next day. On this occasion six of the garrison ventured beyond the works and drew a multitude of the enemy within the reach of the Portuguese fire, which was so well bestowed that 118 of the assailants were slain and 500 wounded, without any loss on the side of the defenders.

About noon on the 29th of June 1571 the Nizâm gave the signal for assault, when the whole of his men and elephants moved forward with horrible cries and a prodigious noise of warlike instruments. The Portuguese were drawn up in their several posts to defend the ruined works, and Dom Francisco de Mascarenhas, the Commander-in-Chief, placed himself opposite the Nizâm with a body of reserve to relieve the posts whenever he might see necessary. The day was alternately darkened with smoke and lighted up with flames. The slaughter and confusion were great on both sides; some of the colours of the enemy were planted on the works, but were soon taken or thrown down, along with those who had set them up. The elephants were made drunk by the naiks who conducted them, that they might be the fiercer; but, being burnt and wounded, many of them ran madly about the field. One that was much valued by the Nizâm, having his housings all in flames, plunged into the sea and swam over the bar, where he was killed by a cannon-ball from one of the Portuguese vessels. The Moors continued the assault till night, unable to gain possession of any of the works, and then drew off, after losing above 3,000 men, among whom were many officers of note. On the side of the Portuguese eight gentlemen were slain and a small number of private soldiers.

Next day the Moors asked leave to bury their dead, and a truce was granted for that purpose. "While employed in removing their dead, some of the Moors," adds Faria y Souza, "asked the Portuguese what woman it was that went before them in the fight, and if she were alive. One of the Portuguese answered, 'certainly she was alive, for she was immortal.' On this the Moors observed that it must have been the Lady Mariam, for so they call the Blessed Virgin. Many of them declared that they saw her at the house of Lourenço de Brito, and that she was so bright that she blinded them. Some of them even went to see her image in the church of Chaul, where they were converted, and remained in the town."*

The Nizâm was now seriously disposed for peace, and the Portuguese commander equally so, yet neither wished to make the first overture. At length, however, advances were made, and a treaty set on foot. Farate Khân and Azaf Khân were commissioners from the Nizâm, while Pedro da Silva and Antonio de Teive were deputed by the Portuguese commander-in-chief, and Francisco Mascarenhas by the captain of the city. Accordingly a league offensive and defensive was concluded in the name of the Nizâm and the King of Portugal, which was celebrated by great rejoicings on both sides and the interchange of rich presents. This, however, might easily have been accomplished without the effusion of so much blood. The Nizâm now raised his camp and returned to his own dominions. Thus the simultaneous attacks or sieges of Nizâm-ul-Mulk and Adil Khân had failed to capture Goa and Chaul. The Zamorin scarcely kept his engagement, and the old jealousies between Bijapûr and Ahmadnagar soon began to revive. The most memorable of all the combinations among the native princes was now triumphantly defeated, a new lustre being added to the Por-

* *Asia Portuguesa, ut supra.*

tuguese arms. Their power, it was thought, had never before been established on a firmer basis than now, and would assume larger proportions. But such predictions are apt to fail or mislead.

Chaul had now entered again into a period of peace and prosperity. Its trade was active, and the city improving in splendour and architectural beauty. Cesar Frederic, a merchant of Venice who visited the city in 1563, seven years before the siege, describes it from a merchant's point of view, thus:—

"Beyond this (Thâṇâ) is Chaul on the continent, where there are two cities, one belonging to the Portuguese, and the other to the Moors; that which belongs to the Portuguese is lower than the other, commands the mouth of the harbour, and is very strongly fortified. About a mile and a half from this city is that of the Moors, belonging to their king, *Zamaluco*, or Nizam-ul-Mulk. In time of war no large ships can go to the city of the Moors, as they must necessarily pass under the guns of the Portuguese castles, which would sink them. Both cities of Chaul are seaports, and have great trade in all kinds of spices, drugs, raw silk, manufactures of silk, sandalwood, *Marsine Versine*,* porcelain of China, velvets and scarlets, cloth from Portugal and Mecca,† with many other valuable commodities. Every year there arrive ten or fifteen large ships, laden with great nuts called *Giagra*,‡ which are cured or dried, and with sugar made from these nuts. The tree on which these nuts grow is called the *Palmer* tree, and is to be found in great abundance over all India, especially between this place and Goa. This tree very much resembles that which produces dates, and no tree in the world is more profitable or more useful to man; no part of it but serves for some useful purpose, neither is any part of it so worthless as to be burnt. Of its timber they build ships, and with the leaves they make sails. Its fruits, or nuts, produce wine, and from the wine they make sugar and *placetto*.§ This wine is gathered in the spring of the year from the middle of the tree, where there is then a continual stream of clear liquor like water, which they gather in vessels placed on purpose under each tree, and take them away full every morning and evening. This liquor, being distilled by means of

---

* A species of velvet; but the words marsine and versine were inexplicable in the days of Hakluyt.

† The velvets and scarlet cloths from Mecca were probably Italian manufactures brought through Egypt and the Red Sea.

‡ These must necessarily be cocoanuts.

§ Possibly molasses is here meant.

fire, is converted into a very strong liquor, which is then put into butts with a quantity of white or black *Zibibs*, and in a short time it becomes a perfect wine. Of the nuts they make great quantities of oil. The tree is made into boards and timbers for building houses. Of the bark cables and other ropes are made for ships, which are said to be better than those made of hemp. The branches are made into bedsteads after the Indian fashion, and into *Sanasches* (?) for merchandize. The leaves being cut into thin slips are woven into sails for all kinds of ships, or into thin mats. The outer rind of the nut stamped serves as oakum for caulking ships, and the hard inner shell serves for spoons and other utensils for holding food or drink. Thus no portion whatever of this *Palmer* tree is so worthless as to be thrown away or cast into the fire. When the nuts are green, they are full of a sweet water, excellent to drink, and the liquor contained in one nut is sufficient to satisfy a thirsty person. As the nut ripens, this liquor turns all into kernel.

"From Chaul, an infinite quantity of goods are exported for other parts of India, Macao, Portugal, the coast of Melinda, Ormuz, and other parts; such as cloth of *bumbast* or cotton, white, painted, and printed, indigo, opium, silk of all kinds, borax in paste, asafœtida, iron, corn, and other things. Nizam-ul-Mulk, the Moorish king, has great power, being able to take the field with 200,000 men and a great store of artillery, some of which are made in pieces,* and are so large that they are with difficulty removed, yet are they very commodiously used, and discharge enormous stone bullets, some of which have been sent to the King of Portugal as rarities. The city of *Abnezer* (Ahmadnagar) in which Nizam-ul-Mulk resides, is seven or eight days' journey inland from Chaul." Elsewhere he writes :—"The Portuguese trade all the way from Chaul along the coast of India, and to Melinda in Ethiopia, in the land of Cafraria, on which coast are many good ports belonging to the Moors. To these the Portuguese carry a very low-priced cotton cloth, and many *paternosters*, or beads made of paltry glass, which are manufactured at Chaul, and from thence they carry back to India many elephants' teeth, slaves, called Kafrs or Caffers, with some *amber* and gold."†

* Probably meaning that they were formed of bars hooped or welded together, in the way in which the famous *Mons Meg*, long in Edinburgh Castle, and now in the Tower of London, was certainly made.

† Robt. Kerr's *Collection of Voyages*, Edin. 1824, vol. vii., pp. 153 and 206.

About twenty years after the Venetian Cesar Frederic, the city of Chaul was visited by a party of English merchants, the first, so far as is known, who ever crossed overland to India. The party consisted of Ralph Fitch, John Newbery, William Leeds, the jeweller, and James Story, the painter. They visited Chaul in 1584. Their letters to their friends in London, though they relate chiefly to commercial subjects, are full of interest. Of Chaul Fitch writes :—" The 10th November we arrived at *Chaul* on the firm land, at which place there are two towns, one belonging to the Portuguese, aud the other to the Moors. That of the Portuguese is nearest the sea, commanding the bay, and is walled round ; and a little above it is the Moors town, subject to a king called *Xa-Maluco.* At this place is a great trade for all kinds of spices, drugs, silk, raw and manufactured, sandal-wood, elephants' teeth, much China work, and a great deal of sugar made from the nut called *gâgara* (cocoanut ?)."* He then goes on describing the customs of the natives of the country, and a variety of the articles of trade, in much the same style as Cesar Frederic. There is one part of it, however, which evidently strikes as a repetition of what Marco Polo wrote on Ṭhâṇâ two hundred years before. He says elsewhere :—" They worship the cow, and plaster the walls of their houses with its dung. They will kill nothing, not so much as a louse. They will eat no flesh, but live on roots, rice, and milk. When the husband dies, his wife is burnt with him ; if she refuses, her head is shaved and she is held in no account. They will not bury their dead, because the body would generate worms, and when it is consumed the worms would starve." Then Fitch with his companions went to Goa, and returned to Chaul alone on the 2nd November 1590. Having remained twenty-three days there, he sailed homeward at last, arriving in London on the 29th April 1591.

Now we come to a curious incident in the history of Chaul, one that has often been described by historians and travellers. It occurred in 1594. This was a time signalized by events of no little historical interest. The seeds of European policy and Christian religion sown broadcast during the century which was coming to a close, by the Portuguese in India, were bearing fruit; and, although the national power was on the decline, incidents of bravery and deeds of heroism among those who had adopted the creed of the Portuguese were not uncommon. The old city of Goa, the capital of the Portu-

* Hakluyt's *Collection*, vol. ii., pp. 382 *et seqq.*

guese establishments in the East, was now in the full zenith of fame and power.

"Opposite to our city of Chaul," says Diogo do Couto, "and running half across the mouth of the river, is a high and precipitous hill called the Rock (Môrro), which the forces of Melique (the Ahmadnagar king) had converted into a great fortress, as strong as any in the world. This Rock was surrounded on three sides by the sea, and on the fourth was a ditch which extended from the sea to the river, and which was crossed by a wooden drawbridge. On the inner side of the ditch was a high and strong wall, also extending from the sea to the river, and relieved by two great bastions. Between the bastions, and looking down from the wall, stood a bronze lion with this inscription—'None passes me but fights.'

"Crossing the Rock about the middle was another wall with bastions, and on the top of it a great and strong tower which commanded the summit, and was called the 'Tower of Resistance.' From the highest point of it looked down a bronze eagle with extended wings and with this inscription—'None passes me but flies.' At the point of the rock stretching further into the river was another great and strong bastion. There were thus seven in all, armed with more than 70 pieces of heavy artillery. Inside the walls the Moors had a deep cistern or tank, well built of costly cut stone, several magazines full of warlike stores of all sorts, and some good houses. The garrison consisted of about 8,000 troops, horse and foot, among whom were many rich and noble Moors, who were quartered outside the walls in costly tents of gay colours. Adjoining this camp was a bazar of nearly 7,000 souls, all engaged in trade, which contained everything necessary for the wants of such a population, and here also was great store of rich stuffs, money, and merchandize."*

It was from this place that the Mahomedans, notwithstanding the alliance that existed between Ahmadnagar and the Portuguese, began to molest the latter by cannonading occasionally the Portuguese fort from so commanding a position as the Rock. The Portuguese had several encounters with them, and, though fortune was not always propitious, they seemed to have fought with some success, particularly on the occasion of the arrival of a party of Moguls who had come to witness the defeat of the Portuguese, which they considered a certainty.

* Couto, *Decadas*, II., cap. 30, vol. xiii., pp. 165 *et seqq.*

Plate 2.

CHAUL.

REDUCED & DRAWN BY ARDA-EER.

VIEW OF THE CHAUL FORT FROM THE SEA.

FROM DALRYMPLE'S DRAWINGS IN THE LIBRARY BY. GEOG. SOC.

These hostilities were of course countenanced by Burhân Nizâm Shâh, though contrary to the peace which had been established when Francisco Barreto was Governor. They were said now to be justified by the conduct of Mathias d'Albuquerque, the present Viceroy. But this was a mere pretext. In addition to the troops ordered out to lay siege to Chaul, several military parties belonging to Nizâm Shâh were sent to infest the districts around the Portuguese forts of Bassein and Chaul, where they did their work spreading havoc and desolation in their train. As the Moors considered the capture of Chaul to be near at hand, seeing that their cannon had made considerable impression on its walls, fourteen Mogul chiefs, as above stated, came to be present at its reduction; but in a sortie made by the Portuguese nine of these were slain and two made captives, the remainder saving themselves by ignominious flight. The eunuch Thanadar, commander of the besiegers, was mortally wounded, and died soon afterwards, as did a Turk who was next in command. On this Farhad Khân succeeded in the conduct of the siege, and gave the Portuguese no respite by day or by night, continually battering their works with his powerful artillery. The garrison in Chaul consisted of 1,000 men, to whom Alvaro de Abranches brought an additional force of 300 from Bassein and 200 from Salsette; and being now at the head of 1,500 Portuguese troops and an equal number of natives, mercenaries so brave and faithful, however, that, says Faria y Souza, "they often voluntarily interposed their own bodies to protect their masters," Abranches appointed a day for making an attack upon the enemy. All the soldiers having on 2nd September attended mass and confessed before starting, and all the churches and convents being kept open for prayers, the Portuguese embarked in a number of small vessels and crossed the river, after which they forced their way to the Môrro, where the battle was renewed, Abranches having the vanguard, and Dom Cosme de Lafeitar the rear. Ten elephants were turned loose by the Moors, in expectation that they would force the Portuguese troops into disorder; but one of these being severely wounded by a Portuguese soldier turned back and trampled down the enemy, till falling into the ditch he made a way like a bridge for passing over. Another of the elephants forcing his way in at a wicket in the works of the enemy enabled the Portuguese to enter likewise, and they slaughtered the enemy almost without opposition up to the "Tower of Resistance," where they made their last stand. Some accounts say that 10,000 men were slain on this occasion, while others estimate the loss at no less than 60,000; but this is a childish exaggeration. The Mahomedan historian, however, acknowledges the loss of 12,000 men. Farhad Khân with his wife and daughter were made prisoners, and only 21 Portuguese were slain. The principal booty consisted of 75 pieces of cannon of extraordinary size, a vast quantity of ammunition, many horses and five elephants. Farhad Khân became a Christian before he died; so did his daughter, who was sent to Portugal, but his wife was ransomed. This action, which was at first a pitched battle, eventually degenerated into an irregular fight of hand-to-hand conflicts, when the power of a little handful of disciplined men fighting against overwhelming odds was made patent in the crushing of the barbarous legions of the enemy. The result once more flattered the pride of the Portuguese of Chaul, and obtained for them privileges which up to that time the citizens of Goa only had enjoyed.*

We now enter upon a stage in the history of Chaul which, for want of a better designation, may be named the stage of decrepitude. Having spent the bloom of her youth, so to speak, in settling herself firm in the boggy marshes of Revadaṇḍa, surrounded by a host of treacherous enemies, and the vigour of her middle age in resisting the repeated incursions and sieges of her neighbours, the noble city of Chaul now falls gradually into a stage of dotage which forebodes proximate dissolution. The decade from 1590 to 1600 is spent in useless scuffles among the civil population and some parochial *brouillerie*, in which the inevitable priestly element occupies the foremost place. Surfeited with the rich endowments from the Portuguese fidalgos, and the not less welcome fees from the poor native Christians, whose numbers were rapidly increasing, the priests turned their energies from the field of evangelization and education of the people to the less congenial arena of athletes. Some of the friars at last, in opposing the establishment of a custom-house at Chaul, acted in a way so disloyal and disorderly as to provoke a rebellion, and compel the most priest-ridden of Spanish monarchs, Philip II., who was then also the King of Portugal, to write to the then Viceroy, Conde da Vidigueira, giving vent to his unfeigned regret and indignation at their conduct.†

Then followed a long interval during which Chaul enjoyed a state of comparative security, less from the terror inspired by the Portuguese

* *Archivo Portuguez Oriental*, fasc. iii., pt. 2, pp. 593, 675, and 848.

† *Ibid.*, pp. 700-701.

power, or the good condition of its defences, than from the internecine feud between the Ahmadnagar sovereign and his subjects, and also from the menacing attitude assumed by the Mogul towards the Dakhanese kings. This much-desired calm was, however, destined to last but for a very short time.

During this period Chaul was visited by the French traveller François Pyrard, who was in India between 1601 and 1608. He writes:—"The city and fortress of Chaul differs from others (Damaun and Bassein), in being extremely rich and abounding in valuable goods, which merchants from all parts of India and the East come here to seek for. But the principal article is silks, of which there is so large a quantity as to supply both the markets of Goa and India, and are far nicer than those of China. In Goa it is highly appreciated and they make fine clothing of it, besides of the cotton stuff which is also woven here."

Then our author goes on describing the two cities of Chaul in much the same way as other travellers before quoted have described them. He alludes especially to the state of peace in the country, and to the manufacture of lacquered articles in Upper Chaul. He states that the reigning Prince of Chaul is called *Melique* (Malik), and is a vassal of the Great Mogul. The Malik, he adds, has a large number of elephants. When he dines he sends for many handsome women, who sing and dance during the meal. Then some of them cut a piece of cloth called taffety into bits so minute that they have no other use than that of being carried away by the spectators, who stick them on to their breasts as if they were so many medals. When the spectacle is over, the king remains alone in his palace, his mind absorbed in the contemplation of the vanity and uncertainty of life, until he goes to sleep at last.*

In 1609 the Mahomedan Governor of Chaul sent out a fleet of 30 *padáos* to cruise against the Portuguese, whose power being on the wane no redress could be got from the Ahmadnagar government, notwithstanding the act being in contravention to the articles of the treaty. In 1611, again, the natives of Chaul introduced into the Portuguese city some Mahomedan outlaws from the neighbouring island of Caranja, who murdered the Portuguese captain of the fortress, Baltazar Rebello d'Almeida. His vacant place was, however, soon filled up by Fernando Sampaio da Cunha. In the meanwhile Nizâm-ul-Mulk, al-

* *Viagem de Francisco Pyrard, Nova Goa*, 1862, vol. ii., pp. 227-228.

though much troubled at home, did not think it desirable at this juncture to leave the Portuguese and their subjects unmolested, and, taking advantage of the rebellion, sent an army to take possession of Salsette and Bassein. His object was, however, defeated.

The year 1612 saw the Mogul before Chaul, as well as before Damaun and Bassein, with the intent to set fire to it, in revenge for the injury done by the Portuguese to his fleet near Surat. He besieged the town, desolated the surrounding country, and when peace was purchased by concessions and presents the arrangements for the defence gave once more to Chaul the best governor it ever had, one whose name has already been mentioned as a valorous and genial officer—one of those who are, says Lafitau, destined to do honour to the nation in which they are born,—Ruy Freire d'Andrade.

On taking possession of the governorship of Chaul vacated by Manuel d'Azevedo, who was appointed to a similar post at Diu, his active spirit being unable to remain idle, Ruy devoted his time and attention, in the absence of military enterprise, in which he was as skilful as intrepid, to the study of the native courts of Chaul and the adjoining countries, their manners and customs, and made the native princes, by his behaviour towards them, so attached to the Portuguese, that it is said that during his governorship more solid conquests were made by his suavity of manners and thorough understanding of the peculiarities and interests of the native population, together with a display of fine diplomatic tact in his intercourse with them, than by the force of arms. Two treaties of peace were, during this interval, made with the Mogul and Nizâm Shâh. The former was signed by two commissioners from their respective governments, and the latter brought to a favourable conclusion by the intervention of Adil Khân.*

Such a state of things was productive of tranquillity and peace, and of this we have evidence in the writings of travellers who during the first quarter of the 17th century visited Chaul, and have left us a record of their impressions.

Of these travellers Pietro della Valle comes first in the order of priority. He visited Chaul twice, in 1623 and 1625. His accounts of the two cities of Chaul are, however, too long to enter here. But we shall have to refer to him hereafter again.

Now we come to a period in which Chaul is in a state of rapid de-

---

* See *Chronista de Tissuary*, tome iii., p. 269, and tome iv., p. 6.

cline. Still, instead of being despondent at the gradual decline so obvious to every one's eyes, the Chaulese continue raising buildings, which serve perhaps the purpose of disguising all appearance of imminent ruin.* They seem, indeed, to be supremely indifferent to the inevitable decay and dissolution which awaits misgoverned settlements, and which overtakes them almost unawares. This is partly accounted for by the fact that while the military spirit of the Portuguese at Chaul declined, the ecclesiastical power went on ever increasing, and the native converts they made gave to the government a support scarcely to be surpassed by any of their political transactions.

The middle and end of the seventeenth century, which were marked in Western India, as in some kingdoms of Europe, by revolutionary events of vast and lasting importance, could not pass over without drawing Chaul into their turmoil. During this period a new empire was founded by the genius of one man, who has not unaptly been compared to Gustavus Adolphus and Julius Cæsar, although his rival Aurangzebe nicknamed him "the mountain rat." The conquests which in the 14th century the King of Delhi had made in the Deccan, subsequently divided among his lieutenants, who established themselves as independent rulers, were in the course of this century absorbed into the dominions of Śivaji. Welding together into a powerful nation the people, who seemed to have lost, if they ever had it before, all sense of nationality, and who, although sturdy and enthusiastic under a fit leader, had never had any systematic training, Śivaji, himself rising to the position of a powerful Eastern monarch, raised his native subjects to so high a condition as even the Portuguese converts, in spite of their various privileges, never dreamt of. His dominions grew eventually to such a height as to create an empire that forty years after its founder's death was extorting at the gates of Delhi, from the Great Mogul himself, grants of revenue and privileges, which, to use Sir Henry Lawrence's words, "not only confirmed them in their own possession, but authorized their inquisitorial interference in every province of the Deccan," and "where," adds Captain West, "the Marâṭhâ had the right of interference, he soon gained the sovereignty."† They had, in fact, by the year 1758 fulfilled the prophecy of Śivaji "that they should water their horses in the Indus and in the Hooghly." This state of things, however efficient

* See Inscriptions further on.

† *Diary of the late Raja of Kolhápur*, by Capt. E. West, Lond. 1872.

at the time, could not last long. Their acquisitions proved only delusive A soldiery, naturally of a predatory type, brought under discipline by the influence of a great man, was soon broken up into a mob on the death of their leader and of a few of his wise successors. Both in the rise and fall of their power Chaul's destiny was intimately involved.

If I were to enumerate their series of attacks or plundering expeditions in and about Chaul, it would carry me far beyond the limits assigned to this sketch, but I shall allude to a few salient points on the way as we proceed on tracing the sequence of events.

In 1664, while Śivaji was meditating a blow against Surat, whither he went, it is said, in disguise, and remained three days gathering information and marking the opulent houses in that city, Chaul was startled by the formation of his camp in its vicinity, as if his designs were against it. But this was a stratagem, for a similar camp was also formed before Bassein, both made with the object of concealing his intentions against Surat.*

About this time the Portuguese had to deal with, besides the Marâthâs, two rival European nations, who were by degrees trying to deprive them of their former conquests. The English, after capturing Ormuz in 1622, which place was one of the principal ports from which Chaul imported horses, whereby at least a show of trade was kept up there, had the island of Bombay ceded to them, whose rising prosperity was soon destined to eclipse Chaul for ever. It is not really in the nature of things that two cities of any great pretensions, even if under two powerful rival nations, should at the same time flourish in such proximity as Bombay and Chaul. The Dutch had on their side captured Cochin in 1663 and deprived Chaul of one of her best fellow-seaports; and when in the following year peace was concluded, the Portuguese abandoned their claim to the monopoly of the Eastern trade, which had for about a century and a half been achieved "by the enterprising valour, military skill, and political sagacity of the officers who had supreme command in India, and who have a title to be ranked with persons most eminent for virtues or abilities in any age or nation."† Mr. Nairne writes: "A comparison between their (Portuguese) exploits and settlements in a hundred years and those of

---

* Orme's *Historical Frag.*, Lond. 1805, p. 12.

† J. Robertson's *Historical Disquisition*, Lond. 1809, p. 150.

the English in the first hundred years after their coming to India is as much in favour of the Portuguese as any one could wish."*

In 1667 Sivaji was in possession of the whole sea-coast from the river of Râjâpur to the river Penn, which flows into the harbour of Bombay, excepting Chaul.† During this time the Nizâm Shâhí dynasty had ceased to affect the course of history at Chaul. Even in its declining days, when the Abyssinian minister Malik Ambar was patching up that kingdom, the jurisdiction of the King of Ahmadnagar is said by Ferishta to have extended to within eight *kos* of Chaul.‡ This statement leads one to suppose that the ancient Mahomedan city and creek had by this time glided away into the hands of a separate governor. Malik Ambar died in 1626, and in 1636, or ten years after, the whole of the Koṅkaṇa dominions of the Ahmadnagar kingdom were ceded to the king of Bijâpur, and then taken by the Mogul. About thirty years after they were in the possession of Śivaji.

On the 18th October 1679 a petty naval fight took place off Chaul between Daulat Khân's fleet and the English grabs under Keigwin, the commander of the Bombay garrison. The English lost the grab called Dove, but the enemy's gallivats, amounting to fifty, were pursued into shoal water to the bar of Nagôṭna, until several of them were captured, some sunk, and others put to flight.§

About this time three famous travellers—an Englishman and two Frenchmen—refer to both the cities of Chaul. The first in chronological order is M. de Thevenot, who was at Chaul in January 1666. He refers to the Portuguese city thus :—" Le Port de Chaoul est de difficile entrée mais très seur, et à l'abri de toute sorte de gros tems. La ville est bonne et défendue par une forte citadelle qui est sur la cime d'une montagne, appellée par les Européens *il Morro di Ciaul.*"¶ Fryer speaks of the Mahomedan city in 1672 as a city utterly ruined by the troops of Śivaji ; while of the Portuguese city mention will be made further on. Carré visited Chaul in the same year, from whence he went to Upper Chaul, where he says he was treated with much civility by Śivaji's officers, and having received his pass, which

* The *Konkan*, Bombay, 1875, p. 43.

† Orme's *Historical Fragments*, Lond. 1809, p. 22.

‡ Briggs, *ut supra*, pp. 117, 315.

§ Orme, *ut supra*, pp. 80-81.

¶ *Les Voyages aux Indes Orientales*, Amsterdam, 1727, vol. v., pp. 248-249.

carried him without hindrance to the city of Bijâpur, he arrived there in January 1673.* About the same time Ogilby, in his *English Atlas*, a work of some merit, although his pictures of the cities of the coast, like those of Faria and Lafitau, could never have been the least like them, describes at length the fortifications of Chaul, and gives the following description of the temperature and natural products of the place:—"The air at Chaul is more hot than cold: the soil thereabouts produces all things except raisins, nuts, and chestnuts. Oxen, cows, and horses are here in great numbers." This vagueness about the agricultural products of the country strikes one as something similar to that of Varthema, who refers to them in almost identical terms. Ogilby's work in five volumes was published about 1670.

In 1676 Moro Pant was the Subedâr of Śivaji in Upper Chaul, from which place he despatched a letter in the beginning of December, through an agent named Nârâyan Shenvi, to the Bombay Government to settle payment of what remained due from Śivaji on Oxenden's agreement.

Besides the Marâṭhâs, the Portuguese of Chaul had another enemy in the neighbourhood, who continuously harassed and worried them. This was the well-known Sidî.† This individual, about the middle of December 1681, without the least provocation, sent a large number of his gallivats down to Chaul, and, passing the Portuguese fort without showing any offensive sign there, ravaged unceremoniously the adjacent country, and proceeded to assault the town of Upper Chaul, which belonged then to Sambhâji, but was unable to do so. On this sudden appearance of the Sidî in the Chaul waters, Sambhâji, anxious for the security of his town, sent forthwith messages to the Bombay Government and the Portuguese of Chaul threatening the former with invasion of the English territory of Bombay if they continued to admit the Sidî's fleet into their harbour, and to fortify the island of Elephanta, which would then have divided the command of the harbour. To the Portuguese at Chaul he wrote upbraiding them for suffering the descent of the Sidî in his territory within sight of their walls, and demanded ground under their fort to build a fortification

* La Haye's and J. C. Carré's Travels, quoted by Orme, *ut supra*, p. 173.

† Yet only a few years before, the Sidî had entered into an alliance with the Portuguese. See *Boletim do Governo do Estado da India*, 1873, pp. 358 and 363. About the same year—1670—another treaty was signed between the Portuguese and Śivaji.—*Ibid.*

which should prevent the landing of the enemy in future. In case his demand was not complied with, he threatened to take possession of the island of Angediva, and thus enthral the trade at Goa.*

The Portuguese, thus forewarned of the intention of Sambhâji to take possession of Angediva, put that fortress into a good position of defence. In the meanwhile Sambhâji, regardless, like his father, of the unsuitableness of the season, came down the Ghâṭs in June with 30,000 men, and from his own town of Upper Chaul invested the neighbouring citadel of Chaul, but could make no progress, owing to the discipline and fortifications of the Portuguese. The Portuguese Viceroy, in the meanwhile, as if to divert Sambhâji's attention, laid siege to his castle of Ponda; but Sambhâji, although he set off from Chaul with the reinforcement of 8,000 horse and 14,000 foot in order to raise the siege, did not discontinue his own against Chaul.† This siege was again assisted by a fleet of Sambhâji, which kept cruising about Nagôṭnâ, Kenery, and Chaul, but could not prevent a Portuguese frigate from landing a supply of military stores and provisions.‡ This siege was at last raised, and the troops of Sambhâji then marched off and took possession of the island of Caranja on the 24th December 1683. In September of the following year the latter island, as well as the hills of Santa Cruz and Assari, was surprised and retaken by the Bassein fleet, and although Sambhâji came down the Ghâṭs soon after with 15,000 horse to Callian to ravage the Portuguese territory around, from Chaul northwards to Damaun, he did not succeed in capturing either Caranja or Chaul.§ Thus the Portuguese of Revadaṇḍa, although submissively waiting their doom from the host of Marâṭhâs in the neighbouring city of Chaul, showed still a bold front, either from that innate feeling of superiority which did not desert them in the last extremity, or from the peevishness of decrepit old age, of which we have abundant illustrations at the end of the seventeenth and beginning of the eighteenth century in repeated quarrels with the Marâṭhâs, the Angria, the Sidî, and last, though not least, the English, as opportunities were afforded them, supremely regardless alike of the imminent decay undermining their whole fabric, which at last tumbled down in the tremendous catastrophe of 1739, and the growing power of their European rivals in the East.

---

* Orme, *ut supra*, pp. 109-111.

† *Chronista de Tissuary*, vol. i., pp. 124, 175.

‡ Orme, *ut supra*, pp. 122-123.

§ *Ibid.*, p. 141.

Add to all these neighbouring enemies the powerful Mogul; and the Portuguese, between the Marâṭhâs, the Angria, and the Sidî on the one side, and the Mogul on the other, must have really had a hard time of it.

In 1694 Aurangzebe declared war against the Portuguese, and during this and the following year treated their subjects with such cruelty that numbers were obliged to take refuge in the forts of Damaun, Bassein, and Chaul. Peace was at last concluded, with a view to obtain cannon from the Portuguese for the reduction of the Marâṭhâ forts.* At the same time the Portuguese burnt three of the Marâṭhâ ships in the Râjâpur river, the largest of which is said to have carried 32 guns and more than 300 men.†

About this time Chaul was visited by a very trustworthy traveller, Dr. John Francis Gemelli Careri. He was in Chaul in February 1695, and refers to it as follows:—

"Tuesday the 22nd, after sailing nine miles further, we anchored opposite to the city and fortress of Chaul. It is seated on a plain, six miles from the sea,‡ on the bank of a river, which at flood will carry any ships up to the city. It is enclosed with good walls, and other works, and furnished with excellent cannon. A fort, called *El Morro*, secures the entrance of the harbour, being built by the Portuguese in the year 1520,§ on the hill, by their General *Sequeira*, with leave of the tyrant *Nizzamaluc*; ‖ who granted it upon condition they should bring him over three hundred horses of Persia or Arabia, at reasonable rates, because of the scarcity of them there was in India, to serve him in his war against *Hidalcon*."¶

Then our author goes on relating how Malik Eyâz tried to obstruct the building of the Portuguese fortress of Chaul, and how the building was raised, their attack repulsed, and the fleets of the enemy disabled. He concludes thus:—"Afterwards the Portuguese made themselves masters of the city with ease. Its territory does not extend above six miles in length. On the south it borders on *Savagi*, and on the

---

* Grant Duff's *History of the Marathas*, Bombay, 1873, p. 168.

† *O Chronista de Tissuary*, vol. ii., p. 201.

‡ This calculation is rather exaggerated.

§ This error has been corrected elsewhere.

‖ Nizamaluco, the Portuguese equivalent for Nízâm-ul-Mulk.

¶ Hidalcaõ, another Portuguese designation for Adil Khân.

north with another fort belonging to the *Sydi*."* He stayed only one day at Chaul, sailing on the 23rd to the north.

The next writer—the last as far as is known—who refers to Chaul before its fall, is Hamilton, who writes: "And two leagues to the south of *Culabee* (Colâba) is *Caul*, a town belonging to the Portuguese, whose river affords an harbour for small vessels. The town is fortified, and so is an island on the south side of the harbour, called *Chaul Moar*, which may be known five or six leagues off at sea, by a white church built on it. *Chaul* in former times was a noted place for trade, particularly for fine embroidered quilts; but now it is miserably poor."†

On the fall of Bassein in 1739, Chaul was still in the hands of the Portuguese, but when the Marâṭhâs threatened to besiege Goa it was surrendered to them as a sort of compromise.‡ The Marâṭhâs gladly took it and ceased to trouble the Goa people, but the unfortunate remains of the Portuguese armies, which were marching from Bassein and Chaul to Goa after the rains, were attacked by Khem Sanvat on the way, and numbers of them miserably perished. A writer in the *Bombay Quarterly Review* asserts that Chaul was delivered to the English for surrender to the Marâṭhâs. As his description of the events that followed the fall of Bassein is circumstantial and interesting, I quote the following extract from him:—

"The Marâṭhâs, on being invited to propose their terms, showed none of that moderation which had astonished even their enemies at the capitulation of Bassein, but assumed the haughty tone of Oriental conquerors, and treated the prostrate Portuguese with indescribable contempt. At first they not only demanded the cession of Chaul, but also of Damaun, and insisted upon having assigned to them a portion of the customs at Goa, which they were to collect by stationing a guard at the port,—thus hoping to insert the thin end of the wedge by which they would eventually obtain the whole of the small, but most fertile, territory. Captain Inchbird, however, having been deputed by the Portuguese, with the consent of the English Government, to treat for them, obtained for them more favourable terms, and induced their scornful enemies to show some forbearance. On

---

* *Churchill's Collection of Vayages*, Lond. 1732, vol. iv., pp. 200-201.

† A. Hamilton's *New Account of the East Indies*, Lond. 1744, vol. ii., p. 243.

‡ *Bosquejo Historico de Goa*, Nova Gôa, 1858, p. 51.

the 14th of October 1740, articles of peace were signed on behalf of Bâji Râo, the Peshwâ, on the one side, and the Viceroy of Goa on the other. The Portuguese engaged to deliver up to the Marâṭhâs the forts of Chaul and Mahim, which were to be temporarily occupied by the English until the Marâṭhâs should have fulfilled their part of the conditions by withdrawing their forces from Salsette in the Goanese province and Bardez. A brief delay occurred, in consequence of the repugnance which the Portuguese priests of Chaul felt for any measure by which the possessions of Christians would be delivered to heathens, and they seditiously excited their people to resist the transfer. Their own envoy, perplexed by their obstinacy, admitted that he had discovered in them 'a malignant spirit,' and Inchbird, throwing aside all restraint, exclaimed in disgust, 'Surely such unheard-of villains and inconsiderate men are hardly to be met with!' However, this clerical opposition was hopeless from the first; in November Chaul was delivered by the English to the Marâṭhâs, and all parties expressed themselves satisfied with the honourable manner in which the conditions of the treaty were fulfilled."*

The treaty of the capitulation of Chaul was drawn at Puṇâ between Bâlâji Bâji Râo and the Portuguese Commissary, Dom Francisco Baron de Galenfles. Two copies of the treaty, one in Marâṭhî and the other in Portuguese, were sent for his sanction to the Viceroy, Dom Pedro Mascarenhas, Conde de Sandomil, who was residing at the time in the territory of Goa. The former copy was despatched to its destination by the English General, Stephen Law, of the Bombay garrison. His letter accompanying it is dated the 25th April 1741. The treaty consists of 14 chapters. The 11th chapter of the Portuguese copy states:—"The city and *Môrro* of Chaul shall be delivered over to the Marâṭhâ, with all the cannon and ammunition belonging to it. The gates of the city shall be garrisoned by English troops until the Marâṭhâ has evacuated the provinces of Salsette and Bardez (Goa). In the meanwhile the Marâṭhâ troops shall remain encamped at St. Joaõ (St. John's Fields), one of the quarters of the city of Chaul. On receiving intelligence that the Marâṭhâ has withdrawn from the provinces of Salsette and Bardez, the English garrison will deliver over to the Marâṭhâ the city and Môrro of Chaul, after making a list, with the assistance of a Marâṭhâ clerk, of all the cannon, powder and balls, on their delivery to them."

* *Bombay Quarterly Review*, vol. iv., p. 89.

The 3rd chapter of the Marâṭhî copy is as follows:—"The Portuguese shall cease their hostilities against the jurisdiction of Bassein, Salsette, Damaun, Belâpur, Uran (Caranja), Revadaṇḍa (Chaul), and Corlâ (Môrro). The same will be observed by us (Marâṭhâs) in the provinces of Salsette and Bardez, as well as in the Pragaṇâ Nahor, which shall be delivered over to Damaun, which latter place we will allow the Portuguese to possess as heretofore, without our ever molesting, disturbing, or showing any hostility towards them."

One chapter refers to the liberty allowed to the residents of the city of Chaul to remain in or quit the place with all the objects belonging to them, and the other to the assistance that will be afforded to the Portuguese in their contests with the Angria. Another clause binds the Marâṭhâs to defend the Portuguese when provoked to a fight by Bounsulo (Bhonslê), and *vice versâ*.

This treaty was at last, after obtaining the approval of the Goa Government, signed at Puṇâ by Dom Francisco Baraõ Galenfles on the part of the Portuguese Viceroy, Pedro Mascarenhas, Conde de Sandomil, and Captain Inchbird on that of the English General, Stephen Law.*

The inhabitants of Chaul who professed the Catholic religion, and had means to do so, emigrated in successive bands to Goa, and those who had no means still remain (their descendants, of course) in the neighbourhood of the fort, living in the miserable hovels nestled in deep and beautiful palm-groves round Kôrlê and Revadaṇḍa.

Chaul fallen into the hands of the Marâṭhâs did not remain long in their possession. Amidst constant quarrels among themselves, an attempt was made in 1775, by an adventurous Frenchman named Chevalier Paillebot de Saint-Lubin, who landed at Chaul from a French ship and went to Puṇâ pretending to be an envoy from the Court of France, to negotiate for the surrender of Chaul and Revadaṇḍa or Lower Chaul, but he was discovered to be an impostor and his object defeated.† But even after the detection of St. Lubin the question of the cession of these ports to France was again under discussion in 1786, as was, some time in the 18th century, that of the cession of Bassein to the Dutch,

* *Boletim do Governo do Estado da India*, 1874, pp. 172 and 176.

† Grant Duff's *History of the Mahrattas, ut supra*, p. 399; and Wilks' *Historical Sketch of the South of India*, vol. ii., pp. 228-229. On the French side see Langlés' *Monuments Anciens et Modernes de l'Hindoustan*, Paris, 1821, vol. i., p. 255, and Dubois de Jaucigny's *Inde*, Paris, 1845, pp. 442-443.

who greatly wished to establish a factory there. These facts point to both these rival nations after the fall of the Portuguese trying to settle themselves near Bombay,—as desirous to share, perhaps, in the prosperous trade the English were carrying on in their settlement.

In December 1802 the Peshwâ Bâji Râo, on the army of Holkar pursuing him, put into Chaul, where he stayed some days and then embarked for Bassein. On his overthrow at last in 1818, Chaul and the districts around passed over to the British, in whose possession we find them at the present time.

The present condition of Chaul is that of an obscure little village, included in the tâlukâ Alibâg of the Colâba collectorate. The population consists principally of Bhaṇḍârîs, Parabûs, Beṇe-Israels, Musalmâns, and native Christians. The Bhaṇḍârîs often had their services recorded, in the official documents of the Portuguese of Chaul as very praiseworthy in their contests with the Marâṭhâs and others. Some of the testimonials given them by the Captains of the Fort are still in the possession of their descendants. The Parabûs appear to have settled in the locality from a very remote time, and had some share in its government. They must have been characterized by some local peculiarity, for a colony of theirs having settled in Bombay in a lane parallel to the main road of Kâlbâdevî has been a sufficient *raison d'être* to designate that locality "*Chaul Vâḍi,*" and their whole tribe with the patronymic of *Chaulkar*.* The Bene-Israels have settled in Chaul and its vicinity from time immemorial, while the Koṅkaṇî Musalmâns, from their distinctly Arab physiognomy, seem to be descended from Mahomedan settlers in Saimûr, referred to by Maśûdi and other travellers of the Middle Ages.

The class of the native Christians is in all respects the poorest of all. I had occasion to meet only two of them. They had nothing striking about them ethnologically, except what I have already written on the native Christians of Bassein elsewhere; but pathologically they were excellent specimens.

Thus far the historical portion of my Notes. The facts relating to the Portuguese period from the day the factory of Chaul was erected —about the beginning of the sixteenth century—to its cession to the Marâṭhâs in the middle of the eighteenth, are drawn up from so large

* See जातिभेद विवेकसार, p. 49.

a number of chronicles and documents, both printed and manuscript, that it would but encumber the text with references and be a work of supererogation to cite them after each event recorded. I have, therefore, beyond the chief authorities mentioned in the body of the work and in occasional footnotes, reserved for the end to refer in brief to the various sources from which I have culled my historical information, in accordance with the division of time during which my authorities flourished, so as to obtain all the important and accurate details from a contemporaneous writing.

From the year 1448 to 1550 my authorities have been Barros' *Decadas*, Gaspar Correa's *Lendas da India*, Felner's *Subsidios para a Historia*, &c. These have been supplemented by the works of Fernaõ Lopes de Castanheda, whose narrative ends at the first siege of Diu in 1538, and of Maffei, who stops his work at the death of Dom Joaõ III. in 1557.

From 1550 to 1640 I have followed Diogo do Couto's *Decadas*, the hitherto published *Decadas* of Antonio Bocarro, and Faria y Souza's *Asia Portugueza*—the latter written in Castilian, from which edition of 1674 I have translated select extracts and compared them with the translation of Captain Stevens reprinted in Kerr's *Collection of Voyages*.

These authorities have again been supported by consulting the excellent compilations of Lafitau and *Os Portuguezes*, as well as Chronicas, Vidas, Historias, and Archivos; such as *Historia das Inquisições*, *Chronica Serafica*, *Vida de D. Joaõ de Castro*, *Archivo Portuguez Oriental*, &c. All these authorities, however, have, with few exceptions, a style so replete with redundancies and exaggerations, that to prune here and retrench there has been not the least difficult part of my work.

In some places where more elucidation was desirable, amplification has been substituted for curtailing.

From 1640 downwards my chief authorities are Transactions and Journals of learned Societies of Portugal and other countries, too numerous to mention here. I must, however, particularize the *Chronista de Tissuary*, *Instituto Vasco da Gama*, and *Boletim do Governo do Estado da India*.

The accounts of Chaul by travellers at various times, which are laid under contribution, have been referred to the original sources at their respective places.

One word more. As the chroniclers generally differ much in narrating events, some recording facts which others entirely omit, I have dovetailed them together, and formed them into as continued and complete a narrative as possible, without allowing a single event of the least historical importance to Chaul to escape.

Passing on now to describe the Antiquities of Chaul, we will begin with its fortifications. The Fort, whose circuit occupies about one mile and a half, is a fifteen-sided figure, its angles being formed by eleven bastions abutting in a semicircular outline from the walls, and four redoubts, which contain rooms large enough to hold a guard of twenty-five soldiers. Each of the bastions is, with the exception of one named Santa Cruz, or Holy Cross, dedicated to a saint, and is named after him—Sam Pedro, Sam Paulo, Sam Thiago, Sam Jacintho, Sam Luis, Sam Diniz, Sam Francisco, Sam Domingos, Sam José, and Sam Jeronimo. The walls are of varying height, being from twenty-five to thirty feet on the land, and from twenty to twenty-five on th sea side; the disparity is owing to the land side being more exposed to the enemy's attacks than the other. The walls have generally little appearance of strength, although possessing in some places the support of ramparts and terraces on the inner side, which seem to be well devised for the purposes of both attack and defence. The grim old crenellated battlements and embrasures of bulwarks, on which were mounted as late as 1728 fifty-eight pieces of cannon ranging from three-pounders to forty-pounders, or from the diminutive swivels to huge mortars and basilisks, are now in a dilapidated state, the only relics of their former greatness being a few rusty old pieces of ordnance lying about in utter neglect on the ramparts; while the walls themselves bear to the present day, besides signs of the ravages of time, the marks of having withstood the effects of a raking fire from outside. Several of the guns, which were once in considerable number, were carried away by Dom Martim Affonso to Malacca, and although Antonio Bocarro in 1634 recommended to have them replaced, it appears that this advice was not heeded at all. In 1728, about a century afterwards, the factor of Bassein, André Ribeiro Coutinho, was sent by the Government to inspect and report on the condition of the fort, and his recommendations to remedy innumerable defects about it seem also to have met with a similar fate.* The remaining guns were mostly taken

† *Chronista de Tissuary*, Nova Gôa, 1866, vol. i., pp. 35 and 59; and also vol. iv., pp. 17 *et seqq.*

COPIED BY ARDESEER, BOMBAY.

CHAUL.

THE EXTER OR GATE OF THE EASTERN OR LAND GATEWAY.

possession of by the Marâṭhâs on their occupation of Chaul, who carried them away for better use elsewhere, leaving behind only those that were found unserviceable.

The same factor, who otherwise eulogizes the fort as "the most ancient, most celebrated, and most estimable fort of Chaul, which having been rebuilt by modern rules, and all the military usages punctually observed by the garrison, is now become the most important of all the other forts," finds fault with several parts of the fortifications, and recommends especially to have the bastions Sam Jacinto and Sam Luis, with the intervening wall, repaired; the adjoining moat, which was being rapidly filled with sand, dug up; and a stockade planted on the sea side to oppose the tidal wave, which was undermining their foundations. The changes which Nature has since wrought are really remarkable. Places where the sea surf was then but slowly advancing have since been completely encroached upon; the wall breached at five to seven different points along the beach; and the tidal current placidly enters into the fort and washes away the foot of the ruins of the monasteries within, which are in imminent risk of falling. A few of the bastions and a large portion of the wall have within the last twenty years tumbled down, and in a few years more the remaining portion facing the sea will perhaps be hardly visible. The sands that were once filling up the ditch have now formed a hillock of their own, so that the enemy, if there be one, would require no scaling at all. Stepping up the sands would easily place him at the top of the wall. On its inner side this part of the wall is surrounded by a small bamboo thicket, which probably dates its origin from the Portuguese period, and was devised, it would appear, as an outwork, to have a counteracting influence against the enemy using the encroaching sands as ladders for scaling.

The fort of Chaul has, like several others on the coast, two gateways, viz. a 'Porta do Mar' and a 'Porta da Terra,' or the sea and the land gateway; the former having, besides, a thin wall a few paces in front to screen it from the river-side, and the latter, which bears also the name of 'Porta de Casados,' or 'married men's gate,' having the remains of a drawbridge over the ditch, which is now completely filled up with sand, although formerly it was broad and deep, encompassing the whole wall towards the land, and could be flooded at pleasure. Each of these gateways consists of two gates, viz. interior and exterior.

The southern gateway is situated on the northern margin of the Chaul creek, where is also the *bandàr*. The first object that strikes a tourist on landing here is an enormous Indian fig tree (*Ficus indica*), which has nothing unusual about it except its roots displacing and hiding some stepping-stones which have the appearance of having belonged to a pier which once led the way from the landing-place to the gateway of the fort. It appears that a jetty formerly stretched as far as the water's edge, on which, according to the testimony of Della Valle, Careri, and others, people used to disembark by means of a wooden plank thrown as a bridge from their galleys. The tree appears also to be an ancient one; for Lafitau, in his fantastic picture of the fort of Chaul, has not, apparently, forgotten to stick up just in the foreground a big tree, which is probably meant to represent the present Indian fig tree.

The southern gateway has now the thin wall to its right-hand side, which once screened it completely from the river view, partly knocked down. A slab 4 feet 3¼ inches long by 2 feet 3¼ inches broad, containing the figure of a warrior in high relief in military uniform, with the insignia of the Order of Christ and with a helmet, is let into the remaining outer part of the wall, and was intended, it is believed, to represent one of the kings of Portugal, with the scarcely discernible legend of six letters in two lines O I O A and T O at the foot—the remains, perhaps, of the name of King Dom Joaõ or Dom Sebastiaõ, during whose unhappy reign this wall was built. The figure is now converted by the devout villager into the idol of Khaṇḍobâ, his face besmeared with oil, and the head daubed over with a thick coating of red paint. An altar to the *tulsí* is raised just in front of it, which receives the daily offerings of flowers and rice, and shares them with the warrior's figure. That the figure of one of the Kings of Portugal, who in days gone by made every exertion in their power and spent millions from their treasury to abolish idolatry in India, should now minister to the superstitious propensities of the descendants of their former subjects, is a very humiliating reflection indeed. There is one consoling trait in this whole transaction, however, Vandalism though it may appear to the sober imagination of an antiquarian: some conscientious iconoclast has clearly knocked off the hands, ears, and nose of the saintly warrior, and made the facial surface as smooth as a slab of marble. So strong was the stigma attached to representations of living objects by the professors of Islâm, that the most disreputable prince among the Mahomedans felt a scruple of conscience in showing even a tacit acquiescence in the naturally ignorant display of the religious zeal of the Hindus. Though politically commendable, their indifference towards such an object would be represented by their sanctimony as the mortal sin of encouraging idolatry; hence this state of intolerance of these otherwise uncontrite individuals against innocuous images, resulting in the end in such irrational practices as the hideous disfigurement of the warrior-sculpture at Chaul.

The greater part of this outer wall is now demolished, only a small portion with a little oblong window above a well of water, and an open passage towards the west with the doorposts and lintel rapidly crumbling away, remaining.

The exterior southern gateway is built of black basalt, and is surmounted by a crown and armorial bearings carved in the same stone, but now almost entirely overgrown with rank vegetation. It is still in a fair state of preservation, although devoid of the massive teak gates cased with iron bars and spikes which once existed there.

On entering the gate the visitor finds himself in a little square area walled in on all sides except at the two gates. To the right is a stone 2 feet 3¼ inches long by 2 feet and 2 inches broad, let into a hole, from which it is half-loose. The inscription on it, with an artistic attempt at heraldic ornamentation consisting of three stars and a mace—possibly a coat-of-arms of the Captain of the fort at the time this wall was built—and the motto of *Ave Maria, gratiā plena,* slovenly carved around, shows plainly enough that there is not only no excellence of epigraphic art to be expected in this, as in other inscriptions of Chaul, but that they even fall far short in complying with the ordinary rules of caligraphy, especially in their absolute want of regard for the sense of the clause or sentence.

It may perhaps be necessary to mention that this, as every other of the inscriptions of Chaul, is written in Portuguese.

Here is a faithful copy of the inscription, which, like several others, was made by Mr. Hearn (see plate A).

Surmounting the interior gateway is observed the well-known D. Manuel's terrestrial globe to the left, three arrows in a sheaf to the right, and the Portuguese royal coat-of-arms in the middle, the whole placed under a Maltese cross of the Order of Christ. Each of these emblems is about 2 feet long by 2½ broad, and the circles about 2 feet in diameter. The stones are mouldering to pieces, and being covered by vegetation are not so distinguishable now as when seen and described by Mr. Hearn, in 1854. The globe denotes power, the broad belt which encircles it being intended to represent the conquests and discoveries of the Portuguese throughout the world, and the three arrows tied together peace, which the Portuguese of Chaul had, before the building of this part of the fortifications, uninterruptedly enjoyed for thirty long years, which was an unusual occurrence in those troublous times. To the left are the remains of a staircase which once led, it appears, to the story above, which is now without both floor and roof.

On the opposite side of this gate are two other slabs 1 foot 6 inches by 1 foot 4½ inches broad, with inscriptions. One is towards the east (see plate B), and the other towards the west (see plate C). On the latter side a rampart leads to a terrace, where are found some old rusty cannon sheltering many a venomous reptile.

Having crossed the gates, the tourist has before him a scene which may be equalled, but not surpassed, by any of the ruined cities of the Portuguese on the coast, except the old city of Goa. A pretty large town surrounded on all sides, save where the sea has made some ugly breaches, by a high wall, regular though narrow unpaved streets, and huts of bamboo plastered with mud or cowdung and clay, and covered with a roof of palm-leaves and straw, ensconced in deep groves of trees, where many a carved stone and painted wood that once belonged to the Portuguese churches and monasteries is seen in grotesque patch-work. The natives of Chaul, like the modern Goanese and the mediæval Greeks and Romans, have found it cheaper to dig and carry away cut stones than to quarry them; but, unlike the inhabitants of the Eternal City of the day, they will never learn to have a grand object in preserving them.

At Chaul the material interests seem to have prevailed over the scientific, or the utilitarian to have got the upper hand of the artistic; for on no other ground could the presence there of the broken fragments of dispersed masonry be accounted for, as well as the heads of the little wooden cherubim with squint eyes, flushed cheeks, and elaborately curled wigs, which were once to be found in profusion in almost every village and hamlet, as they are still in some. All these things can suggest to the passing traveller no just estimate of the general strength and symmetry of the edifices wherein these fragments once

Plate 4.

CHAUL.

THE INTERIOR GATE OF THE SOUTHERN GATEWAY.

occupied not only a definite though subordinate place, but some of which must have doubtless had assigned them a distinguished place in the Roman Catholic altars of Chaul. The villagers' utilitarianism is displayed, moreover, in some places in so debasing a form as to make the wall of a church or monastery serve the same purpose for his own snug little square hovel, where three walls are built of mud, and the fourth is part of a convent.

One does not meet at Chaul the indications of that power and influence which is conferred on a city by years of prestige and tradition; for Lower Chaul is, not unlike Bombay, a modern creation. It was first a low swampy ground reclaimed and converted into a town, and as such it soon took a high rank among the other numerous settlements on the coast. Its ruins, as the earliest Christian ruins, however, deserve special mention. They consist mostly of roofless churches and convents, and stately mansions of noblemen and merchants, embowered amidst pleasant gardens, now encumbered with the *débris* of fallen edifices, and overgrown with wild vegetation; lofty steeples soaring high in the sky, with arched belfries which once contained bells that sounded many a merry peal, now mute for ever—nay, the abode of the ominous owl, whose discordant screech simply adds to the desolation of the place. All these things have a melancholy interest of their own, which will make, I hope, the ruins of Chaul, for many a year to come, before they are quite swept off the earth's surface, a place worthy of a visit from Bombay excursionists, a class daily increasing in number.

A little active imagination will not fail to bring life back again into this ruined scene of the former power and glory of the Portuguese, where are still to be found the relics of their past heroism and memorials of their dominion—now, alas, irrevocably passed away!—and of their enterprises of piety and laudable zeal for the spread of Christianity, which they prosecuted with all mediæval enthusiasm. It would be easy, perhaps, to trace the footsteps of those who have, it seems, but lately deserted it; to recall for a moment the ancient aspect of the city; to reclothe the altars and walls of churches with their usual lively drapery, as they stood before the devastations caused as much by the sacrilegious Marâṭhâs as by the leaden hand of Time; to fill again the desolate naves and aisles with the sound of the grand Gregorian chant; and to impart to it that historical interest which, more than architecture itself, strikes the mind of the beholder with admiration and awe. I have often, while gazing on these ruins, felt the necessity and fancied that the application of the words of Mr. Dyer on Pompeii to Chaul—to compare for a moment great things with small—would not be entirely inappropriate. "If the romantic fictions of the Middle Ages," says that writer, "could be realized, which tell of mirrors framed with magic art to represent what had formerly passed or was passing in distant parts of the earth, the happy discoverer might soon make his fortune in this age of exhibition." *

Chaul, long before Bassein rose to be "the capital of the North," was the principal entrepôt of trade of the Portuguese in this part of India, as well as their chief naval station and arsenal. It was also a place from whence numerous missionary expeditions started almost every year, and was visited by many celebrated generals and saints, notably Affonço d'Albuquerque on his way to Aden, and St. Francis Xavier *en route* to Bassein, and whose presence more than once hallowed its soil. I have already said enough of the prolonged sieges, naval encounters, and other actions, in which, though engaged with hordes of the enemy who tried their best to crush it, the civic honour and the military reputation of Chaul until its ultimate downfall remained unsullied. A settlement so famous in the Portuguese annals could not easily escape the patriotic mind of the author of the great national epic, who in several stanzas refers to it as connected with only those events or thrilling episodes which display the heroic side of his countrymen's nature and happened during his lifetime. He has thus immortalized the sad occurrence of the death of Dom Lourenço d'Almeida at Chaul, and the exploits of Heitor da Sylveira in the great naval engagement which took place in its neighbourhood during the governorship of Lopo Vaz de Sampayo, in the two following stanzas :—

† XXIX.

Mas de Deos a escondida providencia,
(Que elle só sabe o bem de que se serve)
O porá onde esfôrço nem prudencia
Poderá haver, que a vida lhe reserve.

---

* T. H. Dyer's *Pompeii*, Lond. 1867, p. 2.

† XXIX.

But God's hidden prudence known alone
To Himself for His wise purposes intended,
Shall place him where no strength or prudence of his own
Shall avail, his life to save, doomed to be ended.

* Em Chaul, onde em sangue e resistencia
O mar todo com fogo e ferro ferve,
Lhe faraõ que com vida se naõ saia
As armadas d'Egypto e de Cambaia.

LX.

E naõ menor de Dio a fera frota,
Que Chaul temerá de grande e ousada,
Fará co' a vista só perdida e rota
Por Heitor da Sylveira, e destroçada:
Por Heitor Portuguez, de quem se nota,
Que na costa Cambaia sempre armada
Será aos Guzerates tanto dano,
Quanto já foi aos Gregos o Troiano.

Luiz de Camoens' *Lusiadas*, Canto X.

Now groping among the ruins, where there is still enough, in spite of what the Vandalism and cupidity of the natives could do to remove them, to repay for the trouble of the search, it is impossible, notwithstanding, to resist the first impulse of indignation at the culpable neglect with which the ruins appear to have been formerly treated, and at the havoc wrought by the natives, more so than by the destructive action of the weather or the prolific *pípal* tree. The display of bad taste, moreover, in daubing with red ochre and oil every striking piece of sculpture or masonry that pervades the whole desolate city, is really painful to behold.

Going now along a circuitous street flanked by low fence-walls of cocoanut gardens, and encumbered here and there with *débris* of ruined

---

* In Chaul, where under fire and blood shall Ocean groan,
And boil beneath two powerful armadas blended,
Of Egypt and Cambaya, in desperate strife;
Fighting while able, shall the hero lose his life.

LX.

And not the less to Dio shall the fierce fleet,
Which Chaul shall also fear as bold and grand,
Do by its sole appearance, when these are beat
By Hector da Sylveira, vanquished out of hand:
The Portuguese Hector who must yet prove so great
Along the Cambayan coast, where he shall plan
As much mischief to the Guzerats he shall seek,
As the Trojan formerly wrought unto the Greek.

—*The Lusiad*,
Translated by Lieut.-Col. Livingstone Mitchell, Kt., D.C.L., Lond. 1854.

buildings, a street that in its outline much resembles the tortuous course of the Chaul creek as it meanders through the extensive valley fringed with cocoanut trees and other palms, one is led at last to the eastern or land gate. Half-way between the two gates, where the street approaches the wall, a breach in an arched door about ten feet wide has been effected, through which the traffic from the *bandar* passes in a curved line to the north-eastern part of the district.

The land gateway, like its sea counterpart, has two doors, interior and exterior. The latter is half buried in sand, leaving the lintel still visible, where a crown and a few other royal emblems carved in *alto-relievo*, with an oblong vacant space for the insertion of an inscriptional stone, is observed. The inscription has disappeared; but it may be identical with the one discovered by Mr. Hearn in 1854 in the Agent's bungalow at Colâba, whither it had been carried from Revadanda some eight years before, and which is 2 feet 2½ inches long by 2 feet 6 inches broad, broken horizontally into two unequal parts. The stone eventually found its way to the Museum of the Bombay Branch of the Royal Asiatic Society, where it is now lying. (See plate D.)

In the month of May 1868 a translation of this inscription by the Rev. Joseph Poli, S.J., was read at the monthly meeting of the Society. It runs thus:—

"This work was made during (in the lapse of) the year 1636 (5?)... and at the beginning of 1636, being Captain of this fortress of *Chaul*" (here the Father adds a footnote stating that *Chaul* is at Mahim close to the bridge) "Joaõ de Thobar de Velasco, and was taken as Patron of this city the glorious Father St. Francis Xavier, of the Society of Jesus."*

This translation, as was to be expected, was found fault with by Mr. J. H. da Cunha Rivara, Chief Secretary to the Goa Government, who sent his own translation as follows:—"This work was made at the end of the year 1635......... and at the beginning of 1636, being Captain of this fortress of Chaul, Joaõ de Thobar de Velasco, and was taken as Patron of this city the glorious Father St. Francis Xavier, of the Society of Jesus."

The above translation was accompanied with a note correcting the misstatement made by the Jesuit Father Poli, thus:—"*Chaul* is not a place at Mahim close to the bridge, but is situated on the coast 23

* *Jour. Bom. Br. R. As. Soc.*, vol. ix., p. xlvii.

Plate 6.

CHAUL.

THE INTERIOR GATE OF THE EASTERN OR LAND GATEWAY.

A

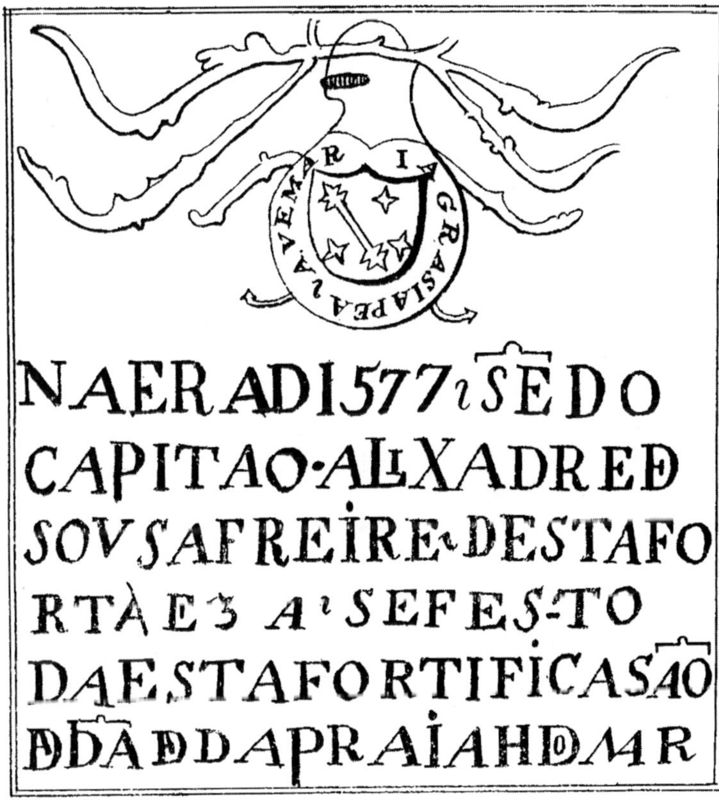

Translation.

In the year 1577 Alexandre de Souza Freire being Captain of this Fort, the whole of this fortification along the beach was built.

B

ESTAPORTA
COARDANS
DOR·OVEHF
SVA

Translation

This gate is under the protection of our Lady of Dolours
N.B. It admits of no other translation, mutilated as it is.

C

NAERADE
1638 SERE
DEFICOV
ESTAPORTA

Translation

In the year 1638 this gate was rebuilt

D

ESTAOBRASEFESNOREMA
TEDOANNODE635 EPRI
NCIPODE·636·SENDOCAPITA
ODESTAFORTALEZADCH
AVLIOÃODETHOBARDEVE
LASCOESETOMOVRORPAD
ROEIRODESTACID.OGLO
RIOZOP·S FRANCISCOXA
VIER·DACOMP·DEIESVS

Translation.

This work was done at the end of the year 1635 and the beginning of 1636, João de Thobar de Velasco being Captain of this Fortress of Chaul, and was taken as Patron of this city the glorious Father St. Francis Xavier, of the Society of Jesus.

E

SENDOVRDAINDIA
FRco DETAVOR·CON
DE·DEAIVOR:Mdo Iom
DEIEMO:DEBRITO
FZeo ESTÃ·ATALAIA
ASVACVSTASENDO
CAPam MOR·DESTA
CANPO·NAERADI688

Translation.

*Being Viceroy of India Francisco de Tavora, Conde d'Alvor, Joaõ de Mølo de Brito commanded this tower to be built at his expense, while Chief Captain of this Camp in the year 1688.**

* *Here there is a chronological error, Conde d'Alvor ceased to be Viceroy in 1686, being succeeded by D. Rodrigo da Costa.*

F

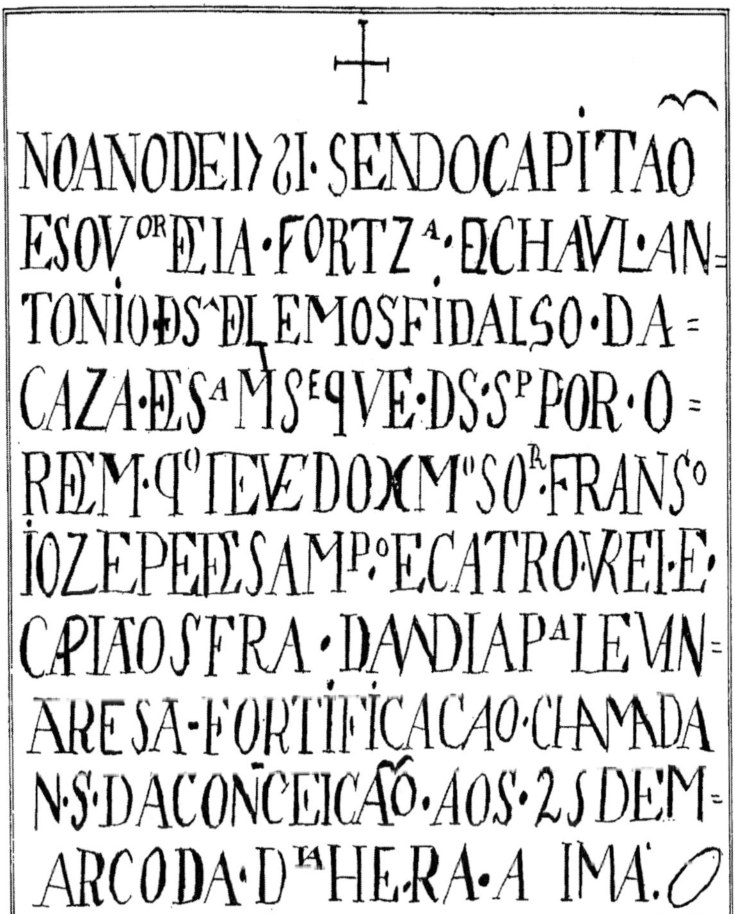

Translation

In the year 1721, being Captain and Governor of this Fortress of Chaul Antonio de Souza de Lemos, Nobleman of the Household of His Majesty, whom God may always protect, by the order sent by His Excellency Senhor Francisco José de Sampaio e Castro, Viceroy and Captain General of the Portuguese India, this fortification, named N S. da Conceição, was commanded to be built on the 25th March of the abovementioned year

G

ESTECASTELOMANDOV·FAZER
OVIZORI·DAINDIADFELIPHE
MZ SEDNOVBROE1646ANOS Q
SENDCAPITAOECHAVL·FE
RNAOEMIRADA·E RI·QEAS·EA
CABOVSEMMAIOE1680SENDO
CAPITAÕDESAPRACACRISTVAO
DABREVDAZEVEDO

Translation.

This Castle was commanded to be built by the Viceroy of India D. Felippe Mascarenhas in November of the year 1646, being Captain of Chaul Fernaõ Miranda Henriques(?), and was finished in May 1680, being Captain of this Fort Christovaõ d'Abreu d'Azevedo.

H

CONSAGRADA AETERNIDADE IOAM IV REI DE PORTU
GAL: EM AS CORTES Q CELEBROV NO ANNO DE 1646
FES TRIBVTARIO A SI E A SEVS REINOS O ANNVA
PENCAM A IMMACVLADA CONCEICAM DA VIRGEM
SENHORA E COM PVBLICO IVRAMENTO PROMETEO
DEFENDER Q A MESMA SENHORA ELEITA PADROEIRA D
E SEV IMPERIO FOI PRESERVADA DE TODA A MACVLA D
E PECCADO ORIGINAL. E PERA Q A PIEDADE PORTVGE
ZA VIVESSE MANDOV ABRIR NESTA PEDRA ESTA PERPETVA L
EMBRANCA NO IS ANNO DE SEV IMPERIO E NO DE CHRISTO
1655 FESE ESTA OBRA NA EB DE 1586 ~

Translation.

Consecrated to Eternity. D. Joaõ IV, King of Portugal, in the Cortes which he assembled in the year 1646, made tributary himself and his kingdom, with an annual pension, to the Immaculate Conception of the Virgin Lady, and under a public oath promised to defend that the same Lady, the elect Patroness of his empire, has been preserved from the stain of original sin. In order that Portuguese piety should last, he commanded to carve this perpetual memento on this stone in the 15th year of his reign and the year of Christ 1655. This work was done in the year 1656.

PORHAVERMORADONESTELVGAR
SFRCO XAVIERO CO PASSOVAONOR
TELHEFESESTAERMIDADO
CILIANESDEN RA SENDOCAPIT
ÃODESTAFORTALEZA.PA
MEMORIAELOVVCRDOSANC
TOOANODE1640

Translation.

St. Francisco Xavier having resided in this place on his way towards the north, this Chapel was built by Dom Gilianes Noronha, Captain of this Fort, to the memory and praise of the Saint, in the year 1640.

miles south of Bombay, and has been a remarkable town and port in the time of the Portuguese."*

A round tower in the neighbourhood of the eastern gateway also bears an inscription, surmounted, as usual, by a coat-of-arms. It is cut out in the most confused manner, which makes the translation of it, in part at least, mere guess-work. (See plate E.)

This tower has four embrasures, and rooms for a guard of about twenty-five soldiers. From the top of this fortification the Portuguese cannon could sweep the whole plain outside the walls.

Another inscription, 2 feet long by 1 foot 9 inches broad, bearing a cross at the top, on the same side of the fort, refers to that part of the wall which was known by the name of N. S. da Conceiçaõ. It is the most recent of all, and withal the worst engraved. The decline of the power of the Portuguese in India seems now to be reflected even in their lamentable decay in epigraphy, which had otherwise never risen to any high degree of perfection. This stone was some years ago removed to the house of the medical officer of Alibâg, and faithfully copied by Mr. Hearn. (See plate F.)

Besides these, all the towers and bastions of the fort have the names of the saints, to whom they are dedicated, inscribed on them, although they have now become almost illegible. Outside the wall landwards there was a fortified camp, remains of which are still visible. It was named *O Campo de Sam Joaõ*, or "the Camp of St. John." It was occupied by the Marâṭhâ troops before they got possession of the forts of Chaul and the *Mórro*, and was garrisoned and equipped with 30 cannon of from 2 to 40 pounders when inspected in 1728 by the above-mentioned factor of Bassein.† To the garrison of Chaul I shall have to refer hereafter, but in the meanwhile we will describe the adjacent fort of the *Mórro*, or the Kôrlê hill.

The fort of Kôrlê, both in its plan and works, is entirely different from that of any other fort on the coast. It has no traces of Marâṭhâ work in it, nor is it built quite after the Portuguese model. I have already referred to its general outline, and the battle that was fought for its conquest.‡ It appears to have been rebuilt on the

* *Jour. Bom. Br. R. As. Soc.*, pp. lv.-lvi., and *Chronista ds Tissuary*, vol. iii., p. 165.

† *Chronista de Tissuary*, vol. i., *ut supra.*

‡ See Diogo do Couto's *Decadas*, vol. xiii., pp. 165 *et seqq.* See also *Ind. Ant.*, vol. iii., p. 181, and Mr. Nairne's *Konkan*, p. 61.

Musalmân plan after the Portuguese had destroyed the first fortress. It is, though strong, of no great size or height compared with many hill-forts, and derives certainly its whole importance from its position. Nor could it possibly have held the garrison described by some of the chroniclers at any time, although a considerable auxiliary force could have lain outside it, as stated by Diogo do Couto and others. It is nevertheless a very striking monument of the Portuguese, and unlike anything else in the district.

The fort stands on a narrow ridge of the rock which stretches across the mouth of the river opposite to the fort of Chaul, and is completely surrounded by a strong wall. The Water Battery, named Santa Cruz, lies lowest of all the works, and vessels of over fifty tons must enter the river almost within pistol-shot of it. Inside the wall there are two other walls crossing the ridge at the top, each being protected by towers and bastions, and dividing the whole virtually into three different fortresses. The bastions are seven in number, and, like those of Chaul, were dedicated to saints, whose names engraved on them are still faintly visible. The names of Sam Thiago, Sam Francisco Xavier, Sam Pedro, and Sam Felippe, over both the bastions as well as gateways, are still legible, others being entirely worn out. There is, besides, a bastion about the centre, with a parapet all round; this, being the highest, was named by the Portuguese *baluarte cavalleiro*. On the north side the hill slopes gently down to the water's edge, and this slope, being enclosed, like the rest of the rock, by the fortified wall, forms a broadway, which is also crossed by walls and bastions, and ends at the bottom in a wide level space. Here were the quarters of the garrison of the Cuirass, or Water Battery, above noticed. On the most prominent point of the hill stood a large cross, and there are still existing in the highest part of the fort, close to the ruins of a magazine, the remains of a chapel, which in 1634 had only the chancel of stone and mortar, the nave being built of bamboo mats and palm-leaves, and the roof thatched with straw, while that of the chancel was tiled. It appears that, later on, the whole of the chapel was built of stone, the walls of which are still standing, although now entirely roofless, and the sacred precincts converted into a cattle-pen. There are, besides, the ruins of a large rain-water cistern, which, according to Diogo do Couto, dates from the Mahomedan period.

The following was the garrison of the fort of the *Môrro*, with their corresponding military pay :—

One captain..............................	60,000 reis a year.*
One constable	50,000 do.
Fifty soldiers, who were altogether paid...	2,772 xerafins.†
Ten do. who had only provisions, amounting to	288 „

A chaplain, or a priest, who used to be supplied by the neighbouring city of Chaul, to perform mass in the chapel of the *Mórro* every Sunday and holyday, had five *larins*‡ for each mass. The garrison had besides at their service a passage rowing-boat equipped with seven rowers, including the *muccadam*, each rower being paid at the rate of five *larins* and a maund of rice a month, the *muccadam* having double the amount of both money and rice. The hire of the passage-boat was three xerafins a month. Then the cost of maintenance of the *Mórro* fort, excluding the expense of ammunition and provisions, repairs and improvements, and masses said in its chapel for the souls of those who had died in the fort, amounted to 3,426 xerafins, 3 tangas, and 20 reis a year.

Of inscriptions in the fort of the *Mòrro* there are only three remaining. One is placed over a doorway in the centre and highest part of the fort, about 400 feet above the sea-level. (See plate G.)

The armorial bearings at the top of the above inscription consist of the Portuguese *quinas* in the centre and seven castles around, the whole being surmounted by an ordinary cross upon a disproportionately long pedestal.

There are two other inscriptions in this fort: one is situated over the principal entrance, and the other is over an altar in the chapel before described; but both are worn away and illegible, and even the process of *estampage* or rubbing would not, I believe, be as successful as the eye has been.

The fort of Kôrlê is still in a perfect state of preservation, with the exception of an outer wall on the eastern slope, which has almost disappeared. Its situation on a hill is, however, so favourable to its preservation that the fort, it is presumed, will probably be standing quite perfect when not a vestige of Chaul or Revadaṇḍa is remaining, owing to the encroachments of the sea, and other causes before adverted to.

* One thousand reis are equivalent to rupees two, annas two, and pies four.
† A *xerafim* is equal to about half a rupee; so is a pardao.
‡ Each *larim* was worth ninety reis.

There is another remarkable change in this fort which remains to be noticed, although in no way affecting its integrity and preservation. The names of Christian saints, after whom the bastions were named, have all been changed into Marâṭhâ names. The last Marâṭhâ commandant of the fort, a Wanjâri by caste, who died a few years ago, must, like his predecessor, have wrought this nationalization of Portuguese names. A very large gun belonging to this fort is said to have been given as a present by the English Government to the Habshi of Jinjîrâ, from the Pusanti Burj, or South-East Bastion. The Pâṭîl family of Kôrlê still worship the remaining guns once a year, as they worship every material and mortal thing there, from the red-ochred idol to the bat-haunted cavern.

Returning once more to the ruins of Chaul, the first object to attract one's attention is the gateway which leads to the stately enclosure, half palace half fortress, which was the house of the captain of the fort, one of its apartments being set aside for the *tronco*, or jail. This was the first building constructed in Chaul, and is often named 'the Chaul Castle.' It was first erected as a factory in 1516, and when fortified in 1521 was set apart for the captain's residence, the factor being lodged in a private house rented by the Government specially for that purpose. The gateway has the figures of St. Peter and St. Paul in two conspicuous niches on either side over the entrance, and the royal arms of Portugal and the Maltese cross in the middle, carved in alto-relievo, the whole being surmounted by an ordinary cross. The whole façade is ornamented with designs of more or less artistic merit, and is flanked by two little obelisks on the sides. The figures of the saints have been sadly injured either by rough weather or by still rougher natives, and in a few years more there will, perhaps, remain no traces of them.

The garrison at the fort of Chaul varied constantly, in accordance with the exigencies of war and peace. In 1728 it consisted of three companies of 62 men each. The fortified camp of St. John, outside the wall, was also garrisoned by companies of the same strength, and equipped with nineteen cannon. It had, besides, an auxiliary force of 234 Bhaṇḍârîs, who were paid four xerafins, or nearly two rupees, a month. Although poorly paid, the Battalion of the Bhaṇḍârîs, as it was called, proved a valuable aid to the Portuguese in many a pitched battle, and especially in their contests with the Angria and other recalcitrant neighbours. The service rendered to the State by this class of mercenaries was duly appreciated by Viceroys and Captains of Chaul, whose testimonials on rags of mouldering paper are still preserved as inestimable heirlooms in many a Bhaṇḍàrî family of the district. Two of these, with *facsimiles* of the signatures of Dom Rodrigo da Costa dated the 13th July 1711, and of Caetano de Souza Pereira dated the 21st January 1737, are published by Mr. Hearn.*

The fort of the Môrro was garrisoned in 1634 by 50 soldiers, increased to 130 in 1728, besides a detachment which was daily sent from the opposite fort of Chaul. The Captain or Governor of Chaul, usually a nobleman of the King's household and appointed by him to that important post, was the head of the settlement, and as such had a large establishment under him paid by the State. Some of the appointments are now obsolete and deserve to be recorded. Their salaries were paltry sums, and every officer, from the highest to the lowest, was paid in Portuguese reis, one thousand of which, in round numbers, are equivalent to a little more than two rupees. There are only two printed documents besides some manuscripts existing, from which we glean the following information. One of these works was written in 1554, and is entitled *Tombo da Estado da India,*† by Simaõ Botelho, and the other was written in 1634 by Antonio Bocarro, and styled *Livro das Plantas das Fortalezas da India.*‡ Although there are some discrepancies—occasioned, doubtless, by the long interval of almost a century which elapsed between the two writers,—they agree tolerably on the main subject of appointments in each of the military, civil, judicial, and ecclesiastical departments, and their respective salaries. Here is the salary list:—

The Captain..............................	400,000	reis	a year.
His Naik	600	,,	a month.
His two Naffars and fifteen peons § .	300	,,	each ,,
His Oriental translator..................	600	,,	,,
Three torch-bearers, usually African negroes ‖	one pardao each a month.		

* *Colaba Report, ut supra*, pp. 66 *et seqq.*

† *Subsidios, ut supra*, pp. 126 *et seqq.*

‡ *Chronista de Tissuary*, vol. iv., pp. 19 *et seqq.*

§ This number was by the celebrated financier Martim Affonso de Souza reduced to nine, and in 1634 there were only eight.

‖ The number of torches and the maunds of oil were eventually reduced to two.

Three maunds of cocoanut oil for the torches	3 tangas a maund, or about 6 annas.
Six bombardiers	1,200 reis each a month.
The gatekeeper of the fort, whose pay, at first 7,200 reis per year, besides his military pay and allowances, was eventually raised to	15,600 ,, a year.

Next to the Captain, the Factor was the *grand seigneur* of Chaul. His establishment was as follows:—

The Factor, who was also an *Alcaide mór*, or police magistrate	100,000 reis a year.
His two clerks, at 30,000 reis each......	60,000 ,, ,,
(This number was eventually reduced to one).	
His Oriental translator	7,200 ,, ,,
Nine peons (this number was in 1634 reduced to four)	300 ,, each a month.
Two torch-bearers, also negroes	1 pardao each ,,
Two maunds of oil. (The maunds, as well as the torches, were reduced to one.)...	3 tangas a maund.
The 'Almoxarife dos Almazens,' or receiver of customs. (This appointment was eventually absorbed into that of the Factor, without any further increase of pay)	20,000 reis a year.
His clerk (eventually abolished)	15,000 ,,
Constable of the Fort had at first 24,000 reis, raised to..............................	30,000 ,,
'Sobre-rolda,' or chief of the night-watch department	18,000 ,,
'Alcaide do mar,' or sea magistrate (also abolished)	12,000 ,,
Tinoeyro, besides his military pay and provisions	21,000 ,,

It is not clear what the duties of this last high functionary were, but that he was found to be more ornamental than useful, and that at last the sinecure was suppressed, there is every evidence in the documents above quoted from to prove.

The Administration of Justice had the following staff:—

One 'Ouvidor' or judge....................	100,000 reis a year.
One 'Meirinho'—a sort of bailiff, or an officer to apprehend criminals and serve summonses, &c.	15,000 ,,
His six peons..................................	300 reis each a month
The 'Alcaide da cidade,' or police magistrate	15,000 ,, ,, a year.
His six peons..................................	300 ,, ,, a month.
The 'Tronqueiro,' or jailor, raised from 7,200 to	15,600 ,, ,, a year.
One maund of oil for do.	3 tangas a maund.
The Government also contributed for the monthly rent of a house for the Factor eight patacoons of 360 reis each, the total being	34,560 reis a year.

But to go back once more to the description of the ruins. Half-way between the southern gateway and the newly-made breach in the wall towards the land side, the visitor finds himself confronted by the magnificent ruins of two churches. The highly ornamented façade of Corinthian columns to the left are the ruins of the Church of the Jesuits, while the thin wall with the friezed and columnar porch to the right are the only remains of the 'Matriz' or Cathedral standing. This stately building has almost entirely disappeared, every square yard of the available space being now occupied by cocoanut and other trees.

The 'Matriz' was one of the earliest ecclesiastical institutions of Chaul. It was built soon after the conquest of Bassein in 1334, by that indefatigable Franciscan friar Antonio do Porto, of whom we shall hear more hereafter. He built it on the eastern margin of the river, and named it 'Igreja de Nossa Senhora do Mar,' or 'Church of our Lady of the Sea.' It was then a small church, but became by degrees the centre of a considerable parish, and was affiliated to the Church and Convent of the Franciscans, which was dedicated to St. Barbara. Some time after, the connection between the two ceased, and the 'Church of our Lady of the Sea' was increased in dimensions, assuming at last the proportions of a Cathedral, and was then raised to the dignity of 'Matriz' or 'Sé' of Chaul, as it was styled.

Some of the travellers have mistaken this Sé for an extramural church, when the Sé ought to be always placed, from the nature of its foundation, as in all fortified cities of the Portuguese in India and elsewhere, within the walls. Pietro della Valle, who visited this church in 1662, says of it:—"Scesi, che fummo in terra, poco lontano dalla casa della Dogana, che stà fuor delle mura, la prima cosa ch' io vidi, fù la Chiesa maggiore, ò Cathedrale, che pur fuori delle mura stà sù la riva del mare," &c.* John Ogilby, who wrote in 1670, refers to Chaul in his *English Atlas*, and as his short description of the harbour and fort of Chaul appears to have been principally drawn from the accounts of Varthema and Della Valle, he falls into the same error as Della Valle in saying that the cathedral was situated on the margin of the river, outside the walls. This misstatement may perhaps have arisen from there being, besides the two principal gateways, a postern on the river-side, through which the population outside the fort could easily communicate with the cathedral within the wall. This postern was a little behind the Custom-house, or Toll-house as Ogilby calls it, the latter being always placed outside the wall, about the very spot where the modern dingy little Custom-house is situated. Ogilby, however, does not rest contented with copying this erroneous statement of Della Valle, who in other respects is admirably accurate. He must add something new of his own. So he informs his readers that the "Morro di Ciul" means in the Portuguese tongue "A member of Ciul"; but Môrro simply means a hillock.†

The following list of salaries and other disbursements and charges paid by the State in connection with the Cathedral is extracted from the before-mentioned documents. There being no bishop at Chaul, the vicar of the cathedral, with the exception of the episcopal functions, which were naturally denied him, was to all intents and purposes the head of the ecclesiastical establishment of Chaul.

The vicar	20,000	reis a year.
Four "beneficiados" or canons	12,000	,, each.
One treasurer	6,000	,, a year.
Two 'meninos do coro' or choir-boys	400	,, each a month.

* "The moment we landed at a short distance from the Custom-house, which is outside the walls, the first thing I saw was the Great Church or Cathedral, which is also outside the wall, on the sea-shore."—*Viaggi, ut supra*, vol. ii., p. iii., p. 134.

† Ogilby's *English Atlas*, vol. i., pp. 243-244.

Two maunds of wax for candles........	14,400 reis a year.
" " of oil for lamps	4,320 " " "
One cândie of wheat for wafers	1,860 " " "
Wine for masses	4,320 " " "
Palm-leaves, &c., for the ornaments of the church on festive occasions	2,100 " " "
It appears that in later years the above five items were brought under the heading of "serviço da sachristia," or the vestry service, and reduced to...	37,400 " " "
Eight surplices to the above-mentioned eight members of the cathedral were usually presented to them on Easter Sunday, at the outlay of ...	300 " " "

A few yards behind the space once occupied by the building of the Cathedral are the ruins of the "Misericordia." This was an old Portuguese charitable establishment under the management of a religious brotherhood named "a Irmandade da Misericordia." The documents relating to its first introduction into India are now no longer extant, the oldest being a provision of the Governor, Nuno da Cunha, dated the 18th June 1532*; although tradition ascribes its foundation to the great Affonso d'Albuquerque in the year 1514, with all the rights and privileges belonging to a similar institution in Lisbon after the pattern of which it was instituted in Goa. From the latter place it soon spread over every important settlement of the Portuguese in India. That of Chaul is one of the oldest of the kind, and had an hospital and a chapel, as is usually the case, attached to it. The State contributed annually the following sums of money and articles of food, &c. for its support:—

Thirteen candies of rice—in pardaos 566, tanga 1, and reis 20.

To the hospital, including the pay of one physician, one surgeon, and one barber— pardaos 666, tangas 3, and reis 20.

In time of war the allowance was increased to 2,000 pardaos, on account of the larger number of admissions into the hospital, as in the year 1546, when the second siege of Diu brought crowds of the wounded and sick to the hospital of Chaul.† The Chapel of "the

---

* *Bosquejo Historico de Goa*, by M. V. d'Abreu, Nova Goa, 1858, pp. 175-176.
† *Subsidios, ut supra*, p. 129.

Misericordia," which was first in the charge of the Franciscans, eventually passed over to the Jesuit Fathers on their landing at Chaul, where they won the reputation of good nurses to the sick and excellent comforters to one's troubled soul, and thus gained a number of contributions to build their own church, as we shall see hereafter.

The ruins of the "Misericordia" consist now of a few mouldering walls mercilessly invaded by the rank vegetation, which makes its approach repulsive, and of an underground apartment which was probably the store-room of the hospital in connection with it, but now the abode of a great many offensive creatures. The visitor who would find out the place has simply to ask the natives where the '*Misri*' or '*Misri Kot*,' is; for such is the phonetic degeneration to which the sublime name of 'Misericordia' has now been reduced.

Opposite the ruins of the 'Matriz,' on the other side of the main street, are the ruins of the church and convent of the Jesuits. Its front resembles, mutilated as it is, the façade of the church "de Santo Nome" (Holy Name) at Bassein, or the church "de Santa Fé" (Holy Faith) and that of "Bom Jesus" (Good Jesus) at Goa, all of which were built after the model of the mother-church of the Jesuits in Rome. The Jesuits' church at Chaul was dedicated to SS. Peter and Paul, and was built in 1580. We are told by the Jesuits' chief chronicler in India* that as early as 1552 St. Francis Xavier was requested by the pious inhabitants of Chaul, who already had the Franciscans and Dominicans among them, to found a Jesuits' College there; but as only thirty Jesuits were then in India, and the saint was desirous of multiplying, as he was wont to say, 'missions rather than colleges,' the request could not be complied with. The saint sent them in his reply the following characteristic bit of advice:—"It is not so good to have many persons engaged in one fortress, as to have many fortresses given to the missionary work of one man."† However, the efforts of the Chaulese to have the Jesuits among themselves did not cease until they actually had them, although not without some opposition from both lay and religious bodies. The Jesuit chronicler thus narrates circumstantially all that happened at the time the Jesuit missionaries were first introduced into Chaul. He tells us that in 1580 two Jesuit Fathers

---

* *Oriente Conquistado*, by Pe. Francisco de Souza, Lisbon, 1708, vol. ii., p. 156 *et seqq*.

† *Resumo Historica da Vida de S. Francisco Xavier*, by F. N. Xavier, Nova Goa, 1861, p. 179.

and two Brothers were sent as missionaries to Chaul. The names of the Fathers were Pe. Christovaõ de Castro and Pe. Miguel Leitaõ. The names of the Brothers are not known, for which the author expresses his great regret, it being "desirable," he says, "to have the names of such able coadjutors in that mission duly recorded ;" and the omission, I dare say, is really to be regretted. On their arrival at Chaul these missionaries were soon placed in charge of 'the Royal Hospital of Misericordia'— as it was styled, the one above mentioned, to minister both spiritual and bodily solace to the sick and wounded there. This their truly pious work soon attracted to them the sympathy of the inhabitants of the city of Chaul. The Fathers were besides in the habit of preaching, every Sunday and holyday, in the chapel of the 'Misericordia.' Their sermons were so highly appreciated that crowds of people flocked to listen to them.

In the 'Matriz' or Cathedral they were not allowed to preach by the jealous members of other religious orders, who had long settled themselves in Chaul, and considered this to be a privilege appertaining to priority. But this, like every other short-sighted policy, was suicidal. The right of exclusivism was defeated in its purpose by the people crowding to the chapel of the 'Misericordia' to hear the Jesuit preachers, either for piety or novelty's sake, the other churches—and especially the Cathedral—being left empty. The consequence was that the Jesuits were at last allowed to preach also in the Cathedral. The fruit of their preaching was so profitable that they resolved to remain at Chaul. This was bad news for those who did not like their presence in the city, and unfair means, such as the stoppage of provisions that had been given them daily at the hospital, were soon had recourse to in order to compel them to abandon the place. In this object, however, their enemies did not succeed, for the moment their provisions were stopped D. Jeronimo de Menezes and his wife, Dona Maria de Castro, came forward to supply them with their own provisions, which were, the chronicler says, a great luxury to them, and in this comfortable state they continued to carry on their ministrations until in the month of July, on the day of St. Mary Magdalen, the Jesuits were invited by the Prior of the Dominicans to preach in their church. The invitation being accepted, the Father Christovaõ de Castro preached an excellent sermon, explaining to the immense auditory assembled there the institution of the Society of Jesus, and entreated them to contribute their mite towards the erection of a residence for the Jesuits. The effect of the preaching was magical. No sooner was the sermon over than contributions began to pour in from all sides, and the Captain of Chaul, Dom Fernando de Castro, son of Dom Garcia de Castro, alone, contributed a large sum, and promised to bequeath to them his valuable library in Evora, which eventually on his death was divided between the Jesuits' college in that town and their residence at Chaul. In a very short time the church was built, which was then followed by the building of a college, which was attended by above three hundred alumni. The number of the Jesuits was increased from two to seven, and their collegiate institution divided into two sections—the upper, which taught Latin, logic, theology, &c., having 40 boys on its roll; and the lower one 300, in which the rudiments of Portuguese grammar, music, and Christian doctrine were taught.

The Kings of Portugal made to the Chaul Jesuits many valuable donations and conferred on them high privileges. One of these was to receive every year five hundred ducats from the customs, but as these duties were not collected, for several reasons, until the year 1633, as we shall see hereafter, the grant was exchanged for a daily pension of one *larim*, a silver coin worth ninety reis, to each of the Fathers. The decree of this exchange of allowance is dated 11th May 1607, before which year they were paid, it appears, five hundred ducats from the Royal Treasury. They were, besides, the builders of a great portion of the Chaul fortifications, and this was not quite a profitless work.

Among the subscribers to the fund for building the church and school of the Jesuits, which latter was some time after raised to the dignity of a college, are found the names of the Viceroy, Dom Luis d'Athaide; Dom Jeronimo de Menezes, brother-in-law to Padre Christovaõ de Castro; Jorge Neto, and several others. Dom Francisco Mascarenhas, the Commander-in-Chief in the siege of 1571, made a donation to the church of two thousand *pardaos*, the interest of which was destined to be applied to the repair and maintenance of the church, a fund which was known by the Portuguese under the name of "Fabrica da Egreja." But the principal contributor was Sebastiaõ Pinto, Knight of the Order of Christ, whose portrait is still to be seen in the convent of 'Bom Jesus' at Goa.*

Several other facts in connection with the church and convent of the Jesuits at Chaul are mentioned in detail by their chronicler,

* *Vida de S. Francisco Xavier, ut supra*, p. 180.

Pe. Francisco de Souza, but the limits I have assigned to these "Notes" prevent me from drawing further from so rich a fountain of historical facts. There is one fact, however, which deserves special mention, and that is the church and college of the Jesuits of Chaul were under the immediate superintendence of the Jesuit church and college at Bassein.* In later years, about three-quarters of a century before their expulsion from the Portuguese dominions in 1759, the Jesuits at Chaul suffered great losses. The English Government seized their lands on account of their being active in promoting the views of the Sidî during the invasion of 1688.

Of the ruins of the church and convent of the Jesuits at Chaul there are at present only the handsome façade already referred to, and a few low walls surrounding a garden where wild plants now grow thickly, but signs are not wanting of its having once contained some choice fruit and flower trees, for which the Portuguese Jesuits had earned once a really enviable reputation. Among the remnants of those trees I observed the guava (*Psidium pyriferum*), the rose-apple (*Jambosa vulgaris*), the custard-apple (*Anona squamosa*), the jack-fruit (*Artocarpus integrifolia*), and several others.

The natives of Chaul point out to the visitor the ruins of the church and convent of the Jesuits as 'St. Paul the Small' and 'St. Paul the Great,' the former being the church, and the latter the convent and the college ruins.

Leaving now the remains of the buildings of the Jesuits, and proceeding on northward along the main road as far as the recently made arched breach in the wall, about ten feet wide, and then turning to the right, the visitor is shown by the village *cicerone* into a little, dark, square room overgrown with rank vegetation. In one of the corners of this room a door leads to an intramural gallery which is almost blocked up by *débris*, and is disagreeably tenanted by that species of bat (*Rhinolopus tridens*) which seems to take special delight in living in desolate places, such as the tombs and the recesses and chambers of the pyramids of Egypt, and also find a congenial retreat in the caverns of Chaul. The villager does not know the use of this little labyrinth ; but there is no doubt it had some military purpose of attack and defence for its object.

* I must here acknowledge with grateful thanks the assistance I have derived from the notes and extracts, some of which were expressly made for me, by the Rev. Theodore Hauser, S.J., whose zeal in studying the chronicles of the religious order of which he is an ornament is really commendable.

Then going along the road that runs parallel to the wall, and turning to the first street to the right, the visitor is confronted by the ruins of a church and convent, of which the façade and the belfry are still preserved, but the walls lowered to form a fence to the cocoa-nut trees which now occupy the former nave and aisles of the church. This was the Church of the Augustins. The chancel is still traceable, but the little oval niche over the altar, the sacrarium, is now broken into a round hole for an irrigation pipe to fit in ; and, to make this sacrilegious operation still more shocking, the pedestal, which once evidently served to hold a cross close by, is now converted to the use of an altar to the *tulsî*. But in this the Portuguese have merely met with a tardy retribution for what they did in their own days with the Hindu temples.

By the side of this church is now a new Hindu temple, with its indispensable *dipamâhars* or light pillars, having an old *pîpal* tree on one side, and a well of water, to the bottom of which leads a still well-preserved flight of stone steps, on the other.

But to return to the Church of the Augustins. This order was the fourth that came to Goa. They came first in 1572, under the guidance of their Provincial, Fr. Antonio da Paixaõ, and it was not until 1587 that they had a branch of their church and convent at Chaul. This church was erected in the latter year by Fr. Luis de Paraiso, under the invocation of *Nossa Senhora da Graça*, or 'Our Lady of Grace,' and their convent contained from twelve to sixteen monks, including their superior, which number in the last century dwindled down to only two. In 1841, when Chaul was taken possession of by the Marâṭhâs, this was one of the best-preserved buildings, and they were not slow to take advantage of the circumstance, occupying it the moment they entered the Virgin Fort, the Metz of the Portuguese in India. The State used to contribute an annual pension of 500 xerafins to the Augustinian convent at Chaul, besides several other donations, and the monks were apparently leading a very easy life on them.

A little in front of these ruins are the remains of the Court-house of Chaul. It must have been a large building, and its *Ouvidor*, or Judge, was elected by the people of Chaul,—a privilege which was conceded to them, after the fashion of that enjoyed by the inhabitants of Goa, in 1697.

The duties and rights of this obsolete order of judicial functionary are graphically described by my learned friend Senhor Abranches

CHAUL.

RUINS OF THE CHURCH AND CONVENT OF THE AUGUSTINIANS
AND THE HINDU TEMPLE.

Garcia, one of the Judges of the High Court of Goa, in the *Instituto Vasco da Gama*, vol. iii., p. 162.

Then going to the end of the street are observed, close to the sea-beach and almost parallel to the promontory of the Môrro, the ruins of the Church and Convent of the Franciscans, which played always so conspicuous a part in the numerous sieges that the city of Chaul underwent. This was a fortified convent, and some of its cloisters still remaining are remarkable for their castelline appearance. This was after the Matriz, the earliest church and convent of Chaul, built by that remarkably active Franciscan, Fr. Antonio do Porto, under the invocation of St. Barbara. It was the next in chronological precedence to their church and convent in Goa, which was built soon after the conquest of that place in 1510. That of Chaul was built in 1534, and the church of N. Sra. do Mar, which was eventually raised to be the Matriz, was, when a mere parish church, subject to it.

The Franciscans were the second religious order that came to India after the discovery of the Cape route. On the first expedition of Vasco da Gama two monks of the order of 'the Blessed Trinity,' by name Rodrigo Annes and Pedro Covilham, were, at their own request, brought over to India. The former died at Melinde, and the latter while preaching on the shore of Calicut was murdered by the natives. Then Pedro Alvares Cabral brought with him in 1500 nine secular priests and eight Franciscans, whose names were Henrique Alvares, the Superior, F. Gaspar, Francisco de Cruz, Simaõ de Guimaraes, Luis de Salvador, F. Massen, Pedro Neto, and the Brother Joaõ de Victoria. They had with them as interpreter the Jew Gaspar de Gama, of whom I have spoken more at length in my *Historical and Archæological Sketch of the Island of Angediva, ut supra*.

These Franciscans preached at every place they touched at on their way to Calicut. At Quiloa, on the African coast, they had a narrow escape from being murdered by the savages, several of them being badly wounded. In the island of Angediva, where Cabral first landed on Indian soil, they are said to have made twenty-two converts. At Calicut three of the Franciscans were killed, and F. Henrique severely wounded. The latter after his recovery returned home to inform the King of the state of religious affairs in India. He was made Bishop of Ceuta, and then of Evora, where he died on the 24th September 1532. From that time, year after year, every fleet that came to India brought from Portugal a certain number of these Fran ciscan missionaries. The fleet under the command of Joaõ da Nova, and that under Vasco da Gama on his second expedition, had a pretty large number of them. On their arrival in India these Franciscans met their four fellow-missionaries who had been left by Cabral, two at each of the stations of Cochin and Cannanore, on his way to Europe.

But to write the Franciscan Chronicles, very interesting though they are, is not within the scope of these "Notes."

Now the only striking object amidst a vast mass of ruins of the Franciscan church and convent at Chaul that exists at the present day is the tower, which, it appears, served for the double purpose of a church steeple, and of a beacon for ships entering the harbour. It is about 96 feet high, and the natives, to express their admiration of its height, name it *Sâtkhanî*, or the 'seven-storied.' The staircase of the steeple has been removed, and there is now no means of access to the belfry, from which a most delightful view might be obtained of all the ruins around and the beautiful scenery in the background. The tower threatens to fall down, and its top is now a little forest of the prickly pear (*Opuntia vulgaris*), and other parasitic plants, which seem simply to hasten its decay. In spite, however, of the invasion of all these enemies of its security and duration, the 'Sâtkhanî' has been for more than three centuries there on the sea-beach; the waters have encroached upon the walls surrounding it; but notwithstanding the periodical wave at the spring-tide enters there and almost washes its foot, it still bids fair to weather the storms of many years to come.

The arched roof of the church has now fallen in, and the heap of *dèbris*, which is many feet high, would perhaps, if removed, disclose many a grave-stone of no little local interest to the history of Chaul. I had, however, no time nor inclination to excavate. This church when visited by Mr. Hearn in 1847 "was perfect, and there were many little figures standing out in relief from the roof—for instance, those of the Crucifixion, the Ascension, and Incarnation;" but in 1854, when his Report was written, it was "completely choked up with ruins." Mr. Hearn then thought, and rightly, that "before long they (the ruins) will all disappear, and cocoanut plantations and Bhaṇḍâris' houses will rise in their stead. Even now," he adds, "it is becoming a famous nursery for cocoanut plants, owing to the place being so well protected by walls from the strong south-westerly winds during the monsoon."* Mr. Hearn's prediction has been fulfilled, and the things

* *Colaba Report*, p. 113.

that he saw are now no longer there. The principal arched door, for instance, "with an aperture in the wall agreeing in size with the stone" which "was lying in the Agent's bungalow," and is now in the Museum of the Bombay Branch of the Royal Asiatic Society, does not exist. The inscription had, like the other stone above referred to, the deciphering abilities of Father Poli bestowed upon it, and his decipherment then, not unlike the other, was found faulty and corrected in the same way as the other by Mr. J. H. da Cunha Rivara.* The stone, which is 5 feet 11 inches long by 2 feet 2¼ inches broad, is broken longitudinally into three unequal parts (see plate H).

This inscription testifies to the vow made by King Dom Joaõ IV. of Portugal in the Cortes in the year 1646 to defend by all means in his power the Immaculate Conception of the Virgin Mary, for which purpose a decree was passed with an order to carve such inscriptions in every city and fort of the Portuguese in India. That of Diu is in Latin.†

The Franciscans of Chaul had from the royal treasury 371 xerafins and 3 tangas for the purchase of the following articles:— A candie of wheat, 6 candies of rice, 2 packs of sugar, 50 dimities, a certain amount of linen, 6 maunds of butter, 12 do. of cocoanut oil, 7 do. of wax, 2 do. of raisins, 1 maund of almonds, ½ do. of dry plums, and 6,000 reis for medicines.‡

Now turning from the west, where the ruins of the Church of the Franciscan friars are situated, towards the south, one meets the ruins of the Church and Convent of the Dominicans. The area occupied by the ruins of this church and the adjoining monastery is immense, but of the ruins the only part recognizable is the chancel and a portion of the steeple, all the rest being a hideous mound of rubbish.

The Church and Monastery of the Dominican friars were built in the year 1549 by Fr. Diogo Bermudes, under the invocation of 'Our Lady of Guadalupe.' The Dominicans, who came first to India in 1513 and landed at Goa, did not build their church and convent there until the year 1548. Fifty Dominicans were once brought by Affonço d'Albuquerque's fleet, and placed in charge of the first wooden church built by Albuquerque in St. Thiago's fort at *Cochin* and dedi-

---

* *Jour. Bo. Br. R. As. Soc.*, and *Chronista de Tissuary, ut supra.*

† See *Inscripçoẽs de Diu*, by J. H. de Cunha Rivara, Nova Goa, 1865, p. 28.

‡ *Chronista de Tissuary*, vol. iv., pp. 20-21.

cated to St. Bartholomew. However, although built one year later than that of Goa, theirs was the richest and most extensive priory at Chaul, containing between thirty and forty monks. It had also a noviciate attached to it, the novices being elected under the careful scrutiny and searching inspection of the Prior, and after obtaining special permission from their Vicar-General at Goa. The Government used to grant them yearly the sum of 904 xerafins for buying the following commodities:—23 candies of wheat, 8 do. of rice, two barrels of wine, and 7 *cantaros* (a kind of pot) of olive oil. They had also 60,000 reis in cash.

Governor Duarte Menezes gave to this order the privilege of electing from among themselves the *Pay de Christaõs* or *Pater Christianorum* at Chaul, whose business it was, besides many other things, to take care of the neophytes. Juvencius explains all these functions in short thus:—"Præest rei Christianæ promovendæ, Christianos jam factos fovet, et omnem dat operam ut ad Christum alii aggregentur."*

The office of the *Pater Christianorum* was, like the Misericordia, to be found in almost every one of the numerous settlements of the Portuguese in India. But it was not confined to one religious order. It was given to several of them at different places: thus the Jesuits had the field of Goa and Cochin exclusively for themselves; Salsette and the island of Caranja were given to the Franciscans; Negapatam to the Augustins; and, lastly, Chaul, Diu, and Macao to the Dominicans. This was a dangerous appointment, and the indiscreet zeal of many of the *Patres Christianorum* often led them into unseemly affrays. The State used to contribute 20,000 reis a year towards the maintenance of this dignitary at Chaul.

But to return once more to the ruins. The next object to attract one's attention is a little chapel, scarcely larger than a vestry-room; but it is now well known as a site consecrated by many a Roman Catholic pilgrimage. This place has been rendered famous as the residence of the great missionary St. Francis Xavier during his stay at Chaul. His numerous biographies are silent on the dates on which he visited Chaul; but it appears that during the three visits which he paid to Bassein he must have halted at Chaul. The fact of his having resided there is, however, plainly recorded by an interesting little tablet of white marble, emblazoned with a coat-of-arms, about 4 feet

* See Juvencius' *Epitome Historiæ Soc. Jesu*, tome II, ad annum 1560.

Plate 11.

CHAUL.

RUINS OF THE CHURCH AND CONVENT OF THE DOMINICANS.

1 inch long by 2 feet 9½ inches broad, with an inscription. It would be far better to have this slab removed to one of our Museums, if not carefully looked after, as the natives are allowed to do whatever they like with the ruins; and this was also the opinion of Mr. Hearn. (See plate I.)

The author of the *Oriente Conquistado* informs us that this chapel was built by contributions of the inhabitants of Chaul, that every Friday a Jesuit Father used to say mass in it, and that on the octave of the feast of the saint a solemn mass, with the accompaniment of music and a sermon, was performed, all the expense being defrayed by the senate or municipality of Chaul.*

Close to this was another small chapel dedicated to St. Ignatius, but it has now entirely disappeared.

The space of ground in front of the chapel of St. Francis Xavier and the southern gates on one side, and the gate of the Captain's palace to the eastward on the other, was once occupied by *almazens*, or store-rooms; it is now but a vast cocoanut garden intermingled with some fruit trees and much rank vegetation.

Thus far the intramural public buildings, or their ruins; besides which are the remains of numerous private mansions and houses, whose outlines are barely traceable, their sites being now almost entirely occupied by cocoanut gardens. Among the extramural buildings the first place deserves to be assigned to the Custom-house, the establishment of which began to be talked about in the year 1585, but it was not constructed until 1633. It was situated in just about the same place as the present little Custom-house, to the right of the southern gateway. That building was however, much more imposing in appearance than the modern one, which is no better than an ordinary police *chauki*.

Although the average revenue yielded by the customs at Chaul hardly exceeded the expense first incurred in maintaining it, the custom-house having been established too late to be of any great use, when the trade at Chaul was declining, still it yielded a pretty good sum. But there were other sources of revenue from which a constant supply to the coffers of the King was derived. Deducting all expenses, the budget showed annually, until the year 1634, a balance of about 27,000 xerafins, which was sent to the royal treasury at Goa.- To enter into details would be contrary to the design of my "Notes;" but the reader will find

---

* *Conquista*, I., *Decada* I., p. 95.

them in the *Subsidios para a Historia da India Portuguesa*, pt. ii., p. 123 *et seqq.*, and in the *Chronista de Tissuary*, vol. iv., pp. 33-35. I give, however, only a *résumé* of it in the footnote below.*

The other ecclesiastical buildings *extra muros* were the churches of St. Sebastian, St. John, and *A Madre de Deus*, or 'the Mother of God.'

---

* Before the Custom-house of Chaul was established several articles of trade were taxed, as well as a certain class of professions from which almost all the revenue was derived, besides the tribute of 7,000 xerafins paid by the Nizâm. Chaul being, unlike Bassein and Damaun, a settlement that depended more on the sea trade than landed property, it was entirely supported by the yield of those taxes.

The traders from Ormuz and Cambay at Chaul used to pay annually	700	patacoons.	Each patacoon of the value of 360 reis.
" revenue from opium, &c., as well as *bangue* and soap, amounted to	560	"	
" " " the bazâr (this tax was by D. Joaõ de Castro, during the Captainship of Vasco da Cunha, ceded to the Chaul Municipality as a remuneration for their help to the State during the siege of Diu, subject to the approval of the King	335	"	
" " " from brokerage and weight of merchandize	3,330	"	
" " " tobacco, which was until lately a royal monopoly.................	9,714	"	
" " " *urracas*, or spirit distilled from palm juice, which was once given, at an insignificant quit-rent, as a reward for her relatives' service to the State, by the Viceroy Francisco Mascarenhas, to Dona Catherina de Castro, daughter of Dom Garcia de Castro, but the King would not sanction such an arrangement. This tax yielded in 1593 more than 2,250 pardaos of 4 larins each, and in 1634 1,900 patacoons. (See *Archivo Portuguez Oriental*, fasc. 3, pt. ii., pp. 393 and 476-477..............			
The revenue derived from shroffs at Chaul amounted to	450	"	
There was, besides, a tax called *Guanguaõ*, which was paid by a gambling-house for the African slaves, but D. Joaõ de Castro suppressed it as immoral.			

The King had also some revenue derived from ground-rent, such as the *ribeira* (dockyard), *cordoaria* (rope-yard); but, as no ships were built here, these places were eventually given over for a mere nominal rent, during the Captainship of Francisco da Cunha, to officers to build houses on, subject to certain rules. See *Archivo, ut supra*, p. 563.

The Church of St. Sebastian was built about the middle of the seventeenth century. It was situated somewhere between Upper and Lower Chaul, but there is no trace of it now. The vicar of this church had from the royal treasury 30,000 reis a year, besides the sum of 12,000 reis for vestry expenses. It was neither a rich nor extensive parish. Fryer informs us that when in 1675 an English embassy was sent to Śivaji, the ambassador, together with two English factors, embarked on a 'Bombaim Shebar,' and, "about nine o'clock at night arrived at *Choul*, a *Portugal* city on the main, into which he could not enter, the gates being shut up, and watch set; so that they passed this night in the suburbs, in a small church called *St. Sebastians*, and the next day about three in the afternoon receiving advice that Śivaji was returned to *Rairee* from *Chiblone*, departed thence to Upper *Choul*, a town belonging to the *Rajah*, about two miles distant from the *Portugal* city," &c.*

The Church of St. John belonged to an important parish. Its vicar had the same pay and emoluments as that of the Church of St. Sebastian. Its ruins are still visible.

The church of "A Madre de Deus" was the centre of a rich and large parish. It was in charge of the Capuchin friars, who had, besides emoluments and revenue derived from parishioners, 7,300 reis under the heading of *mesinhas da botica*, or medicinal drugs. This church is now in ruins. The only church that forms a nucleus of a small community of native Christians at the foot of the Kôrlê promontory is dedicated to "Our Lady of Carmel," and appears to be a recent building. There is also one small chapel, outside the fort, dedicated to 'A Madre de Deus,' which is at the same time a cemetery. It is a very poor little chapel, of the size of an ordinary vestry-room.

The other remains of the Portuguese in Chaul are three inscriptions, which require yet to be noticed, although they are insignificant. One is that of a gravestone, on which are the following nine words:—"Sepultura de Luis Alvares Camello e de seus herdeiros," *i.e.* "The grave of Luis Alvares Camello and his heirs." It is found in the house of a Bhaṇḍâri, who uses it to sharpen his knives on.

* John Fryer's *A New Account of East India and Persia*, Lond. 1698, p. 77. Elsewhere this traveller writes:—"In whose opening arm, that is, from *Choul Point* to *Baçein* [two famous cities belonging to the *Portugals*) some 30 leagues distance, lie those spots of ground, still disputable to which side to incline," &c. And again—"Bombaim is the first that faces *Choul*," which indicates that even in Fryer's time Chaul was an important place: p. 62.

The other inscriptions are on two bells. The one runs thus :—

"AO PR' DEIANR DE 1720." Translation :—"The 1st of January 1720."

This bell is now in the Mâmlatdâr's Kacheri at Revadaṇḍâ.

The other bell has the date of 1739 A.D. engraven on it, and the following inscription in Latin, surmounted by the monogram I.H.S. :— "Ave Maria, gratia plena, Dominus tecum." It is now in the temple of Ambâbaî or Mahâlakshmî at Kolâpur.* There are reasons for supposing that this bell was carried away by the Marâṭhâs from one of the churches of Chaul to Kolâpur.

The antiquities of Upper Chaul, or Chaul Proper, are of quite a different nature. There is not a single Christian inscription there, all the ruins belonging either to the Hindus or the Mahomedans.

The Hindu antiquities consist mostly of temples and tanks. There are no inscriptions or copper-plates to trace their origin or foundation, but there are legends in hundreds about gods which are recorded in their *purâṇas*, and piously believed by their votaries. Two or three traditions about the foundation of the defunct city, and some of the buildings of temples there, are really worth translating from amongst a large mass of manuscripts in Sanskrit and Marâṭhî† which I have been able to collect.

One of the traditions is to the effect that in the *Dvâpara Yuga* the name of this place was Champâvatî,‡ when the king was called Nagara. His successor, Pithora Râja, had a minister by name Chava, who, having murdered the king, established his own rule, and changed the designation of Champâvatî into Chaul. This name, again, on the

* Major D. C. Graham's *Statistical Report of the Principality of Kolhapoor*, Bombay, 1854, p. 319.

† I am indebted for the collection of these MSS. to the diligent care of Messrs. Eshvant F. Danaite and Keshavrao Mâdhavrao, the latter a native of the place.

‡ I have already given different conjectural meanings of this word; there is one more, which, although not so plausible as the others, it may be worth while to give as well. In Kâṭhiâvâḍ "the people along the shores use a peculiar sort of net for catching fish, called *champa*. It is made of six sticks 3 feet 6 inches in length, all secured at the upper end; the net is fastened to the lower end of the sticks, and it is spread like an umbrella when ready for use, and covers a circle of six feet in diameter."—*Jour. Bo. Br. R. As. Soc.*, vol. v., p. 114. May not the manufacture of this *champa* at Chaul have given it the name of Champâvatî? One cannot tell whether in olden times there was any fishing in Chaul, but at present, since the city once so famous has shrivelled up to a small village it has become a fishing village.

conquest of the place by the Emperor of Delhi, was changed into Mâmalê Mortezâbâd, a name that is said to be still found recorded in various ancient manuscripts and records in possession of the natives of the district.

The ancient city of Chaul was divided into sixteen equal parts, called *pâkhâḍyas*, or rows of buildings separated by paved alleys, and were named thus :—

1	Pâkhâḍya or	Pâkhâḍî	Prathama.
2	,,	,,	Mokhava.
3	,,	,,	Veshvî.
4	,,	,,	Dakhavâḍa.
5	,,	,,	Bolâvê.
6	,,	,,	Tuḍâl.
7	,,	,,	Usavê.
8	,,	,,	Muraḍa.
9	,,	,,	Ambepurî.
10	,,	,,	Vejârî.
11	,,	,,	Koparî.
12	,,	,,	Peta.
13	,,	,,	Bhovasî.
14	,,	,,	Zivaḍî.
15	,,	,,	Doḍ.
16	,,	,,	Kasabê.

Out of these the three pâkhâḍyas of Dakhavâḍa, Muraḍa, and Doḍ were ceded to the Portuguese. At the present day the Fort of Chaul has for several purposes been marked out into forty different gardens, and named in Marâṭhî. There are, however, some traces of the Portuguese language among them, though sorely mangled. Such names as Sam Pâl Diul (Igreja de Sam Paulo), Misri or Misri-Kot (Misericordia), Padri Vigar (Padre Vigario or Matriz), Manel Coterel (Manuel Cortereal), Ales Perer (Aleixo Pereira), Mâm Gonsâl (Simaõ Gonsalves), and several others, are derived from the names of the Portuguese, who were probably in former times owners of those places.

The tradition continues that when the Portuguese applied for a piece of ground to build their factory, the sovereign of Chaul granted their application, provided the space ceded did not exceed that covered by a certain number of cow-hides, a system of mensuration that really admits of equivocal interpretation. The consequence was that the Portuguese were not slow to profit by so vague a formulation of the grant; they got the desired number of cow-hides, cut them into thin strips and then measured the ground, thus occupying an amount of land that far exceeded what was originally intended by the donor. The sovereign of Chaul got alarmed at this usurpation, but the Portuguese stuck firmly to the letter of the gift, which could not be revoked. This is the way they invent history in India, and that is, moreover, the credulous silliness with which it is recorded in the papers in my possession. We know better; the cession of Revadaṇḍa to the Portuguese had nothing to do with cow-hides.

The ground thus acquired by the Portuguese occupied, we are told, the following *pâkhâḍyas*, viz., Doḍ, Dakhavâḍa, and Muraḍa. The tradition does not stop here; it goes on to assert that these facts are recorded on the foundation-stone of the fort of Chaul, a name that was then given to it by the Portuguese, and changed into Revadaṇḍa on its occupation by the Marâṭhâs.

The old city of Chaul, the *bakars* or Hindu chronicles tell us, had, besides 360 tanks and 360 temples, 1,600,000 public buildings and private mansions. This is another instance of the fondness of the Hindus for multiplying objects, as they have done their gods, whose number now exceeds the whole population of the globe. But how to account for the disappearance of this immense number of buildings? They inform us that in the year 1313 of the Śâlivâhana era a fisherman by name Parasubhagela, a native of Kolvân Salsette, conquered Chaul, and the war that he waged with that object, and which lasted for a long time, caused the destruction of all these buildings by fire, &c.

The temples of Chaul were really numerous, and of these twelve are dedicated to Śiva, nine to Vishṇu, seven to Durgâ, eight to Gaṇapatî, eight to Bhairava, an incarnation of Vishnu, and four to different *Rishis*.

Those dedicated to Śiva are named thus:—

1. Śac'iramana.
2. Someśvara.
3. Revaneśvara.
4. Amṛiteśvara.
5. Vaijanâtha.
6. C'ivaleśvara.
7. Nâmeśvara.
8. Muraḍeśvara.
9. Hareśvara.
10. Sidheśvara.
11. Maleśvara.
12. Kâśiviśveśvara.

Those dedicated to Vishṇu are the following:—

1. Keśava Nârâyaṇa.
2. Lakshmî Nârâyaṇa.
3. Mâdhava Nârâyaṇa.
4. Sundara Nârâyaṇa.
5. Narasiñha Nârâyaṇa.
6. Trivikrama Nârâyaṇa.
7. Udâra Nârâyaṇa.
8. Sûrya Nârâyaṇa.
9. Adhya Nârâyaṇa.

Those dedicated to Durgâ are:—

1. Champâvatî.
2. Śitalâdevi.
3. Bhagavatî Yekavirâ.
4. Padamâvatî.
5. Kaḷâlagî.
6. Hingulzâ.
7. Chatursitî.

The temples dedicated to Gaṇapatî are as follows:—

1. Sidhivinâyaka.
2. Dhuṇḍivinâyaka.
3. Mukhyavinâyaka.
4. Bodhyavinâyaka.
5. Tri Gaṇeśa.
6. Chiṇtâmaṇivinâyaka.
7. Hari Gaṇeśa.
8. Samayaharavinâyaka.

The following are dedicated to Bhairava, an *avatâr* of Śiva:—

1. Kâlabhairava.
2. Âdyabhairava.
3. Samayasidhabhairava.
4. Budhabhairava.
5. Hatabhairava.
6. Śivabhairava.
7. Dinabhairava.
8. Kolâṭabhairava.

Places, or rather hermitages, dedicated to *Rishis* are:—

1. Kapilamunî.
2. Śakunî.
3. Datâtrayamunî.
4. Yâdnyavalkyamunî.

Several of these temples and hermitages are no longer traceable; but the following are not only existing, but are renowned places of pilgrimage among the Hindus:—

1. Râmeśvara.
2. Maleśvara.
3. Sidheśvara.
4. Kudeśvara.
5. Hingulzâ.

The temple of Râmeśvara is mentioned in the *Mangesha Mâhâtmya,** a section of the *Sahyâdri Khaṇḍa* of the *Skanda Purâṇa*. It is

* इति संचिंत्य मनसा सर्वसंगविवर्जितः। तदाहं पार्वतीं त्यक्त्वा जगाम तपसे वनं ॥ १॥ तस्मात्स्थानाद्विनिर्गत्य कृष्णावेण्याश्च संगमे। तपश्चकार भगवान्संगमेश्वरनामतः ॥ २ ॥ सूत उवाच। इति प्रचोदिता ताभ्यां सखीभ्यां पार्वती तदा। गमनाय मतिं चक्रे ताभ्यां सह द्विजोत्तम ॥ ३ ॥ भगवानपि विश्वेशश्चंपावत्यां समाययौ। तत्र किंचित्स्थितः कालं तपस्तप्तुं महेश्वरः ॥४॥

therein recorded that Śiva having been laughed at by Pârvatî for having lost a game of *saripâta* in Kailâsa, his paradise, in the presence of several of her maid-servants, the god became so annoyed that he left her company and went to a place where the river Kṛishṇâ meets the Veṇâ. He lived for a considerable time there, and to commemorate 'his stay his liṅga was established,' which in after-years became famous as Saṅgameśvara, or 'lord of the junction of the two rivers,' a place that is considered to be holy, and is resorted to by a great many pilgrims.*

The legend then adds that Śiva left Saṅgameśvara for the Bhargava Kshetra, or the Koṅkaṇ Proper. Pârvatî, who was all the while anxious to meet her husband, followed him to this place; but Śiva had in the meanwhile left for Champâvatî. Now there is no doubt that the connection of places so close to each other as Saṅgameśvara, Bhargava Kshetra, and Champâvatî points out the last as the modern Chaul. Śiva lived for a very long period at Champâvatî, and during his residence caused a *liṅga* of his, by name Râmeśvara, to be placed in it, whence arose the temple which still exists there. This is, then, one of the three Râmeśvaras, which are celebrated places of worship in India, viz., one between Ceylon and Cape Comorin, mentioned in the *Râmâyaṇa* and several Purâṇas; the second near the frontier of Goa, between the latter territory and the British district of Carwar; and the last that of Chaul. It is said that around this temple there are three *kuṇḍas* dedicated to the three Vedic elements, *vayu*, *agni*, and *parjyanya*, or air, fire, and water.

Pietro della Valle has left us a description of this temple of Râmeśvara at Chaul as it was in his time, and given a plan of the building with its tanks and other works around. It is a faithful representation of

---

तपस्तत्वाथ विपुलं लिंगं कृत्वा स्वनामकं । रामेश्वरेति नाम्ना वै प्रथितो न्यवसन्मुने ॥५॥ मं० म० स० स्कं० अ० २–३.

Another Mâhâtmya, by name *Manjuleśvara Mâhâtmya*, chap. 2—म० म० अ० १—२—also refers to the temple of Râmeśvara at Chaul in the following ślokas, the purport being that Râghava, *i.e.* Râma himself, was the god who first established the liṅga or phallus called Râmeśvara, that this *shetra* as a place of pilgrimage is soul-saving, and that to all the best and greatest *tirthas* in the world the Râmatîrtha excels.

Here follows the text :—

रामेश्वरं महालिंगं स्थापयामास राघवः । सिंधुलिंगांतरालं यत्सा तत्र मणिकर्णिका ॥
तारकं तन्महाक्षेत्रं सर्वप्राणिविमुक्तिदं । रामतीर्थमिति ख्यातं सर्वतीर्थोत्तमं महत् ॥ १ ॥

* A notice of some inscriptions of this place by the Hon'ble Ráo Sâheb V. N. Maṇḍlik is found in the *Jour. Bo. Br. R. As. Soc.*, vol. xi., pp. 101 *et seqq.*

what it is at the present day. This is at least the one advantage of the Hindu conservatism. While the changes and innovations going on in European society have upset the Portuguese government of Chaul, and reduced to ruin its numerous and excellent buildings, the Hindu temples of Upper Chaul are still left in a good state of preservation, and, what is more to the purpose, are preserved in just the same state as they were found centuries ago.

But to return to our Roman traveller: he informs us that having started on the 2nd December 1624 for what he calls *Ciaùl de riba*, or Upper Chaul, he visited on his way to it the *Bazar*, Mahomedan mosques, Portuguese gardens, and Hindu temples. Close to the *Bazar* of Upper Chaul he saw a large tank which he names *Tanlè Nave Naghèr*, probably the Tank Nagersî, which is still extant. Then he relates that he visited several of the Hindu idols in Chaul, among which he mentions that of *Zagadanbâ*, another name for Durgâ, which he takes care to inform his readers is the same as *Leksemi* (Lakshmî), wife of Vishṇu; then the idol of *Amrùt Suêr* (Amṛiteśvara), which, he tells us again, is identical with that of Mahâdeva, the round stone phallus. He then refers to the different temples of Nârâyaṇa, and at last to that of, Râmeśvara, which he says is "the largest, and the principal among all others." He describes its tank very minutely, and the figure of an animal which is called, he says, in Canara *Bassuanà* (Basvâ), and *Nandì* in Chaul, *i.e.* the bull of Siva.*

The celebrated tanks of Upper Chaul, which are still in a good state of preservation, are the following:—

1. Bhavalê Talê or Tank.
2. Giryachî.
3. Sarai.
4. Kâjî.
5. Nârâyaṇa.
6. Shahachî.
7. Jânnavî.
8. Bhivalê.
9. Shâraḷî.
10. Majid.
11. Khabâlê.
12. Tragaris.
13. Nagersî.

Some of these tanks have their own curious legends; for instance, the tank of Jânnavî, which is said to be very deep and to possess the magic power of dissolving the bones of cows, which disappear the moment they are thrown into it.

---

* *Viaggi di Pietro della Valle*, Venetia, 1667, vol. ii., pp. 410 *et seqq.*

Another curious thing about these tanks is that there is one which is supposed to contain milk, and is hence called 'Dudhâlî' 'or milky tank.'

Other objects of antiquarian curiosity about the place are the *yâtras* or fairs held in honour of the Hindu gods. These are as follows :—

1. Śhripanta, a place where a *yâtra* or *jatra* is held every year on the 14th of the month Margaśirsha Śudha, which corresponds to a date between September and October.

2. Śrîbhagavatî, a place where a feast for nine days, called *Nahuratra-utsâha*, is held in honour of the goddess after which the place is named, once a year, in the month of Aśvina Śudha, corresponding to a date between July and August.

3. Śrî Râmeśwara, where also yearly, on the 15th of the month of Kârttika, about the phase of the new moon, an illumination is made in honour of Kṛishṇa.

Where the temple of Hingulzâ is situated on the slope of a hill is a *kuṇḍa*, or small square well, built under that goddess's *âsana* or seat. The belief is that when fruits or flowers are thrown into this well they go direct to Kâśî or Benares. There was an old *pîpal* tree (*Ficus religiosa*) near this place, which was supposed to have always had leaves of a golden colour. It is now quite dried up. This is now the great place of worship of the Khole tribe.*

The remaining object of worship is a *Sona Champaka* tree (*Michelia Champacą*), each of whose flowers is said to weigh exactly one tolâ, or three drachms. In connection with this flower there is a legend current among the people to the effect that the Kalâlagî Devî, whose temple is at Chaul, was so fond of this flower that a wealthy man, whose name is not given, made a vow to indulge this caprice of the goddess by throwing every day around her neck garlands of this flower of the value of one thousand rupees, without redeeming which promise he would not eat his food. But one day it so happened that there were no *champa* flowers to be got in any bazâr or market, when the opulent devotee of Kalâlagî, instead of throwing the garland of flowers round her neck, got only one, for which he paid the same price,

* A tradition is current among the people at Chaul to the effect that about fifteen years ago a Sanskṛit inscription being discovered on the wall of the *kuṇḍa*, or as some people say, under the *âsana* of Hingulzâ, it was reported to some of the *savants*, who wished much to see it; but a Bhangasali, indignant at the outsiders' inquisitiveness, to prevent their ever coming to the temple, removed the inscription, and nobody knows what became of it

which acted as if a string of a thousand rupees had been placed round her neck, and from that date her neck became bent downwards as if by the weight of the silver. The effect was most unpleasant: the goddess grew vexed with her devotee, and from that fatal moment the rich man became poor.

Of the Mahomedan antiquities of Chaul, there are the remains of a mosque, which appears to have been of good size and design, on the banks of the creek. It was once a massive structure; but " the Portuguese cannon, " Hearn tells us, " made sad havoc of the whole of the western side and the minarets," by which means a whole line of arches was swept away, and were it not that peace was soon made, the remaining portion would have been levelled with the ground. There is also, not unlike the Hindu system, a legendary tale connected with the erection of this masjid, but the Mahomedans themselves seem to disbelieve it. The dimensions of this building, which was built of black basalt, were 88 feet long and 45 broad. Its height is not known.

At a little distance from this place are the remains of an apparently strong Mahomedan fort, partly invaded by a mangrove swamp, which cuts off the village from the creek. The walls that remain now are not more than three or four feet high.

The other prominent architectural remains of the Mahomedans in Chaul are those of a striking building called Hamâmkhânâ, which is still in a fair state of preservation. It was a bath-house; the interior is divided into three circular chambers, the central being the largest, and each lighted by a circular opening in the cupola above. The walls, it is said, have been nearly undermined by people, who are digging for treasure, under the impression that the Mahomedans deposited here large sums of money on their evacuation of the fort. The pavement, which was almost all of marble flags, has thus been removed, and the impression that money is hidden there has found confirmation in the fact of some persons having got some large sums in it from time to time.

The other Mahomedan antiquities of Chaul are tombs of the ordinary and domed variety. One of these, called Dadi-Pamâlî Pîr, belonging to a saint, is held in high veneration, and an *urus* or annual feast is celebrated in his honour on some variable date between the months of Ramzân and Shawal, corresponding to our September and October.

Besides these there are the remains of large houses and buildings, of which, however, only the foundations, and in some cases the plinths, are now observed. It was thus thoroughly destroyed by Śivaji and his successors. From the large area over which these ruins are scattered, it appears that this city must really have been a very large and remarkable one, as described by mediæval and other writers.

BASSEIN.

THE RUINED GATEWAY OF THE CITADEL.

NOTES

ON THE

HISTORY AND ANTIQUITIES OF BASSEIN.

BY

J. GERSON DA CUNHA, M.R.C.S. Eng., &c.

NOTES

ON THE

HISTORY AND ANTIQUITIES OF BASSEIN.

"*A good description of Bassein, with an account of the inscriptions to be there found, is still a desideratum.*"—E. B. Eastwick, *Handbook for India*, Lond. 1859, pt. ii., p. 311.

THE island of Bassein lies between 19° 24′ and 19° 28′ N. Lat., and 72° 48′ and 72° 54′ E. Long. It is bounded on the north by the Vaitaraṇî or Dantura river, on the south by the Strait of Bassein, on the east by a narrow channel separating it from the mainland, and on the west by the Arabian Sea. It is about 11 miles long, about 5 broad, and has an area of nearly 35 square miles. It is distant 29 miles from Bombay.

Its original name, *Vasai*, has been the object of innumerable surmises, the most plausible, perhaps, being what connects it with the Sanskṛit root वस् (*vas*) to dwell, whence a dwelling or residence,* and by which it is still designated by the natives. It was by the Mahomedans first changed into *Basai*, which the Portuguese made *Baçaim*, and the English *Bassein*.†

Bassein is one of a multitude of islands situated on the north-western shore of India which, varying from a few yards to a hundred square miles, fringe that coast from 9° to 20° N. Lat. It belongs to that picturesque group between 19° and 20° which once consisted of about twenty-five islands, known as the Bombay group, and probably the Heptanesia of the Greeks, viz.—Bassein; Dharavi; Versova, just off the shores of Salsette; Salsette itself, the largest of them all; Trombay; Mazagon; Mahim; Varli; Bombay or Mumbai; Old Woman's Island; Colaba; Elephanta; Butcher's Island; Gibbet or Cross Island; Caranja; Heneri; Keneri; and other detached and small rocky islets of lesser note, some of which are scarcely capable of containing a fisherman's hamlet, complete the group. Several of them

---

* Confer वनवसई (*Vanavasai*), conjectured to mean 'forest residence.'

† It would perhaps be more correct to writê Basaiṅ, which should differentiate it from the Burmese Bassein; but the old spelling is so well known that it is thought better to retain it.

are now connected either by causeways, breakwaters, and embankments to shut out the sea, or by the deposition of silt and sand; while others are on the way to being rapidly united, though still separated by merely tidal creeks easily forded at low water.

The island of Bassein is, like Bombay, trapezoidal in form, having its long axis nearly north by east and south by west. Its short parallel side, which is about four miles in length, lying northwards, is separated by the Vaitaraṇî river from the mainland; while its opposite, which is longer by one mile, embraces with the adjacent islands the Bassein Strait, so as to form a pretty spacious, though shallow, harbour, with a width of about two miles at its broadest part. This harbour is used only in fair weather by vessels of small tonnage engaged in the coasting trade, being rock-bound and not sufficiently land-locked to protect shipping during the prevalence of the south-west monsoon.

It is on the south-western extremity of this line, on a low flat ground about fifteen feet above the level of the sea at low water, that the famous Portuguese fort and city named after the island is situated.

The outer or seaward side of the island, about eleven miles long, is bounded by ridges of hills scarped towards the west and gently sloping towards the east. The inner, about ten miles in length, is separated from the undulating plains of the neighbouring continent by a narrow channel of water, which, beginning at Panjao close to the Bassein railway bridge and passing by Mânikpûra and Baling, ends at Dongray, where it joins the Dantura creek, and has about its middle the ancient famous port of Suparâ, of which we shall have to speak more at length hereafter.

At the two short sides of the figure there are sandy beaches lined by cliffs of blown sand, * which, as natural barriers, prevent, except at two or three places, the sea from overflowing. Between these lines of

* Blown sand is a conspicuous feature of a considerable space along the coast from Bassein to Bombay. Their cliffs are supposed to have begun to be formed at a somewhat remote period. Dr. Carter mentions the discovery of a grave-yard on a sandy bank near the Mahim Fort, which was exposed in the monsoon of 1854 and was covered with six and a half feet of sand and soil above its top, and "on the ground was a cocoanut plantation with trees whose stems were some forty, and some fifty feet high." This fact, then, plainly indicates the antiquity of those islands as inhabited localities.—*Geological Papers of Western India*, 1857, p. 161, and Dr. Leith's *Report on the Sanitary State of the Island of Bombay*; 1864, p. 34.

demarcation the mountainous ravines and the rugged and swampy grounds of the villages of Agaśî, Sayavâna, Nirmâla, Pâparî, and others are situated.

Geologically considered, and in accordance with the division of insular regions proposed by L. von Buch into round and longitudinal, Bassein would belong to the latter category; while following the system adopted by Hoffman, of distinguishing islands into continental and pelagic or oceanic, it would appertain to the former.

It is not necessary to enter here into geological details of Bassein, a subject that has been freely treated of in numerous excellent geodesic memoirs that have been published within the last half-century.* Their authors seem all to agree that there have been in ancient times not only long intervals between the successive outpourings of which its strata are composed, but that it is a broken fragment from the mainland

---

* As a bibliographical note on these memoirs may be of some interest to the reader, I append it below :—

A *Sketch of the Geology of the Bombay Island*, by Robert D. Thomson, M.D.; Madras Journal of Literature and Science, 1836, vol. v., pp. 154 *et seqq.* This paper is somewhat discursive, and has only the interest of being the first on the subject.

Geological Notes of the Northern Conkan, by Dr. C. Lush ; Journal of the Asiatic Society of Bengal, 1836, vol. v., pp. 761 *et seqq.* This writer was the first to describe the horizontal strata of sandstone containing shells as overlying the trap rocks.

A paper in the Quarterly Journal of the Geological Society by G. F. Clark, Lond. 1847, vol. iii., pp. 221 *et seqq.* The chief portion of this paper refers to the Koṅkaṇ and Dakhaṇ, with occasional allusions to the islands, a short but clear and correct outline of whose fresh-water formations is given.

Geology of the Island of Bombay, by Dr. G. Buist, F.R.G.S., April 1851, Trans. Bo. Geog. Soc., vol. x., pp. 167 *et seqq.* In this valuable paper Bassein's basaltic ridges and their composition are often referred to. It treats of the economic geology of the island.

Geology of the Island of Bombay, with a geological map and plates, by Dr. Henry Carter; Jour. Bo. Br. R. As. Soc., July 1862, vol. iv., pp. 161 *et seqq.* This is another valuable essay that deals with scientific and speculative inquiries.

Both the above papers were published in a collection entitled *Geological Papers on Western India*, 1857.

On the Geology of Bombay, by A. B. Wynne, *Memoirs of the Geological Survey*, Calcutta, 1866, vol. v., pp. 173 *et seqq.* An elaborate and exhaustive treatise on the subject, evidently benefitted by previous publications.

Besides these there are several other publications of great merit from the pens of Col. Sykes, Malcolmson, Newbold, and others, most of which are embodied in the *Geological Papers on Western India*, above referred to. Other papers on the subject by modern geologists, such as Mr. Blanford and others, will be found in the volumes of *Records of the Geological Survey of India*, a valuable periodical publication that is still alive.

during the many upheavals and depressions to which it has been subjected.

Though closely allied in structure to adjoining islands and the neighbouring coast, Bassein presents local differences of considerable interest. The rocks, which with the exception of the freshwater strata are all of volcanic origin, belong to the trappean system. The basaltic tract runs in a ridge, maintaining for some distance the elevation of about 200 feet above the sea, and rising often into somewhat bolder cliffs of beautiful groups of black and compact columns, from amidst which the stones that compose the fronts of the Portuguese churches at Goa and elsewhere were quarried. This basalt ridge runs as a great sea-wall from Bassein to Chaul, a distance of about 60 miles, only broken through by creeks, especially the one that opens into the Bombay harbour.

In two places the resemblance to a ridge ceases, and it assumes the shape of hills of considerable elevation, their crests attaining the altitude of about 400 feet. One flat-topped or table-form hill rises to a greater eminence than the other, which when viewed from the sea presents a round conical peak of a strange outline, backed as it is by the mural ranges and other peculiarly pinnacled summits of the great Sahyâdri range or Western Ghâṭs. Its seaward slope is abrupt and precipitous, while the landward one is, on the contrary, gently falling away in terraces. The level plain of Bassein, broken and rugged, is covered over mostly with recent marine deposits of the alluvial and littoral species, overlying generally the dark grey trap, and in some places by drift sandbanks. Thus it will become evident that, though comparatively small in size, what the island lacks in extent of area is fully compensated for by an infinite variety of woodland, surrounded by creeks, which, assuming capriciously the aspect of lakes, rivers, or estuaries, presents a wild landscape. Its banks are, moreover, covered with underwood down to the water's edge, bordered by mangrove bushes and fine belts of lofty palms, which for picturesqueness and beauty can scarcely be surpassed by any other island in the neighbourhood. Add to this the considerable historical importance which from time immemorial Bassein had attained in connection with the sacred places of Vaitaraṇî and Tuṅgâri, or the political and commercial reputation from its relation to the ancient celebrated places of Kalyâṇa and Śrîsthânaka, or from its becoming at a later period famous as the principal Portuguese settlement of the

Northern Koṅkaṇ, and the subject will commend itself to the study of all.

Ancient Hindu geographers included Bassein in the Varâlâṭâ (Varâr), one of the seven divisions of the Paraśurâma Kshetra.*

Among the Greeks the island of Bassein was, according to Mercator,† known as *Borace;* but the *Borace* of the *Periplus* and *Baris* of Ptolemy, the name applied to the mouth of a river, is supposed by D'Anville‡ to be the channel that separates the province of Bardez from the island of Goa. Again, Lassen § affirms Bassein to be *Simylla*, which is placed by Gosselin ‖ at Suali, and is now finally identified with Chaul.¶ The truth, however, appears to be that Bassein, like Surat, was a place of little or no importance in the time of the Greeks, and that, as says D'Anville of the latter place, "*l'état florissant* qui la distingue aujourd'hui ne paroit pas d'un temps bien reculé."**

The Chinese pilgrim Hwen-Thsang refers to a place which he calls *Kong-kien-na-pu-lo*, or Koṅkaṇapura.†† This place is identified by General Cunningham ‡‡ with *Annagundi*, on the northern bank of the Tuṅgabhadrâ river, and formerly the capital of the Yâdava dynasty; but Vivien de Saint-Martin has suggested that Banavâsî, which is mentioned by Ptolemy as *Banauasei*, the ancient seat of the Kadamba dynasty, may be the place referred to. Then the Chinese traveller describes from hearsay a place called *Malayakuta* or *Malakuta*, which has been identified by General Cunningham with Madura. We have already seen that this name in its Chinese form is also transliterated by Julien

---

* The seven divisions of the Paraśurâma Kshetra are "केरलाश्चतुलंगाश्च तथा गोराष्ट्रवासिनः कौंकणाः करहाटाश्च वरालाटाश्च बर्बराः :" *i.e.*, Kerala, Tulaṅga, Gaurâshtra, Koṅkaṇa, Karahâṭa, Varâlâṭa, and Barbara. These seven divisions of land correspond to seven different tribes of the Brâhmaṇs inhabiting it and speaking different dialects. In ancient Hindu works this region is often described as Sapta-Koṅkaṇas.—*Sahy. Kh.*, bk. ii., ch. viii., and *Maṅgesh Mâhât.*, ch. ii.

† Gérard Mercator, quoted by John Ogilby in his *English Atlas*, Lond. 1670, vol. i., p. 214.

‡ *Eclaircissemens Géographiques sur la Carte de l'Inde*, par M. D'Anville, Paris, 1753, p. 91.

§ Map to *Indische Alterthumskunde, ut suprà.*

‖ *Recherches sur la Géographie Systématique et Positive des Anciens,* tome iii., p. 307.

¶ *Antè*, p. 5.

** *Ut suprà*, p. 73.

†† S. Julien's *Hiouen-Thsang*, vol. iii., p. 146.

‡‡ *The Ancient Geography of India*, by Alexander Cunningham, Lond. 1871, pp. 552 *et seqq.*

into *Chimolo*, which being read by Cunningham as *Jhimura* is merely a variant form of the Arabic *Saimûr*, or modern Chaul. Now the Chinese traveller repairs first to *Kanchipura*, which is said to be Conjeveram on the Palâr river, and at last to *Koṅkaṇapura*. From the latter place he proceeds to *Mahârâshṭra*, Broach, &c. But having once found out that *Malakuta* or *Jhimura* is Chaul, may not the next place of *Koṅkaṇapura* (*Kong-kien-na-pulo*) be Bassein, or some place in its neighbourhood, and *Mo-ho-la-cha* or *Mahârâshṭra*, Kalyâṇ, which place, according to the distance of *lis*, says General Cunningham, accords better with the position assigned to Broach? All this is, however, highly problematical, and the *lis* of the Chinese pilgrim make the different distances indicated between the places visited very difficult of solution indeed.

Among the Purâṇic accounts relating to the island of Bassein and the district around are the *mâhâtmyas* or legendary chronicles extolling the sacredness of the places or glorifying the shrines they describe. These are three, viz. the *Vaitaraṇî, Tuṅgârî*, and *Nirmâla mâhâtmyas*. They are mostly found incorporated with the Purâṇas, the chief of which are the *Padma* and the *Skanda Purâṇa*.

The Vaitaraṇî (*vulgò* Dantura), also written Vaithârnâ, river is held in high estimation by the Hindus as a sacred stream, its waters cleansing from all sin. This was the oldest river known to the Greeks. Lassen has identified it with the *Binda* of Ptolemy, while others regard the latter as the Kâmevâdi or Bhivaṇḍî (*vulgò* Bhimḍî), which falls into the so-called Ṭhâṇâ creek, which is not, however, properly a creek at all, but a "depression or backwater reaching from the head of the Bombay harbour to Bassein."* Other writers suppose the *Binda* of Ptolemy to be the estuary of the Ulâs, which is said to be a noble river from the point of junction with the Kâlu, eight miles above Kalyâṇa, to its entrance into the Ṭhâṇâ depression.† Col. Yule ‡ identifies *Binda* with the river Bhîmâ; and from the characteristic tendency of the ancient Eastern nations to connect rivers running in different ways, it is believed that it is but the *Goaris* of Ptolemy that stands for the conjunct of the Godâvarî and Vaitaraṇî, as the *Bindâ* for that of the Bhimâ and Ulâs.§

The Vaitaraṇî river takes its rise from Nâsik, and running through the Mahim Tâlukâ debouches into the creek bearing its name. Its

---

* *Ind. Ant.*, vol. iv., p. 283.

† *Ibid.*

‡ *Map of Ancient India, ut suprà.*

§ *Ind. Ant., ut suprà.*

head-waters are close to an affluent of the Gangâ at the Thal Ghâṭ, and within two days' march of the highest salt-water there is the town of Gore, situate on its margin, which, although not a large place, keeps up still some trade in rice and timber with the ports at the mouth of the river, and is supposed to have had more in former times.

In the *Mahâbhârata Bhîshmaparva*, ch. 9, in the description of Jambudvîpa, the Vaitaraṇî is enumerated among the four sacred streams:—Mandâkinî, Vaitaraṇî, Kosha, and Mahânadî.*

Again, the *Harihareśvara Mâhâtmya* of the *Skanda Purâṇa* refers to it thus:—"Among the *tîrthas*, Vimala or Nirmala is the best, emancipating the world from all trammels of sin. Those who resort to it are in the position of the Supreme Spirit. The river Vaitaraṇî is joined to the Western Ocean. He who bathes in it and gives alms will always be free from torments inflicted by Yama."†

In the *Vanaparva* of the *Mahâbhârata Tîrthayâtrâparva*, ch. 83, the river Vaitaraṇî is described thus:— "Let men go to Tripishṭâpa, which is famous in the three worlds, where is the meritorious Vaitaraṇî river, which destroys sins. Let them bathe there and worship the god Śiva, who has a trident in his hand and a bull for his emblem; whereby their souls defiled by sins will be purified, and then they will go to a final beatitude."‡

In the *Matsya Purâṇa*, ch. 113, the famous Vaitaraṇî and the Veṇî are mentioned as sacred rivers.§

The *Vaitaraṇî Mâhâtmya*,‖ a part of the *Padma Purâṇa*, mentions that the Vaitaraṇî, which means 'truly saving'—from वै (*vai*) truly, and तरणि (*taraṇî*) saving—was brought to the earth by Paraśurâma, the well-known sixth *avatâr* of Vishṇû, and son of Jamadagni, from the Pâtâla

* मंदाकिनीं वैतरणीं कोषां चापि महानदीम्। म० भी ज० अ० ५.

† ततस्तीर्थेषु विमलं निर्मलं नाम सुंदरं। संसारमलनिर्मुक्तं यत्र यान्ति परं पदं ॥ ततो नदी वैतरणी युक्ता पश्चिमसिंधुना। यत्र स्नानेन दानेन नश्यंति यमयातनाः। ह० ह० मा० अ० २ श्लो० ४४, ५०.

‡ ततस्त्रिपिष्टपं गच्छेत्त्रिषु लोकेषु विश्रुतं। तत्र वैतरणी पुण्या नदी पापप्रणाशिनी ॥ तत्र स्नात्वार्चयित्वा च शूलपाणिं वृषध्वजं। सर्वपापविशुद्धात्मा गच्छेत्तु परमां गतिम् ॥ म० व० ती अ० ८३.

§ वेणीवैतरणी चैव–म० पु० अ० ११३.

‖ The *Vaitaraṇî*, *Tungârî*, and *Nirmala Mâhâtmyas* are supposed to be pretty old compositions, originally in Sanskṛit, but they have now been translated into Marâṭhî in *ovi* metre with the *placet* of the representative of Śaṅkarâchârya. The editions from which the text is translated are dated Śaka 1785 (1863 A.D.).

after his having killed the demon Pâlapañjara. Paraśurâma repaired to Kailâsa, and having performed religious austerities Śiva was so pleased with his devotions that he promised Paraśurâma to grant him any boon he should ask. Paraśurâma rejoined: "O great Śiva, after the expiration of *Dvâpâra*, the *Kali Yuga* will set in, when people will commit great sins. For their remission grant, O God, that the river Vaitaraṇî be carried from the Pâtâla to the earth's surface." The request being granted, the Vaitaraṇî was brought to the place where it is now found—to the north of Bassein, and separating the latter on that side from the continent. It was then the resort of numerous Ṛishis and others, such as Nârada, Vaśishṭa, Indra, Yakshas, Gandharvas, Kinnâras, who used to go there both for bathing and sacrificial purposes.

The river is now held in such high veneration as a place of sanctity by the Hindus that it is piously believed that one who bathes in its waters on the 11th day of Kṛishṇapaksha in the month of Kârtika has secured his eternal happiness in the next world, for which purpose pilgrimages are annually held on that day.

The *Tuṅgârî Mâhâtmya*, or "the greatness of Tuṅgâr," a part of the *Padma Purâṇa*, gives an interesting account of the establishment of *Tuṅgâreśvara* and its *tîrtha* in the Tuṅgâr hill. It is therein stated that Paraśurâma had a fight with the *asuras* or evil spirits under the championship of Vimala, who was in the habit of harassing the people in the Varâlâṭa in revenge for affronts given to the Brâhmaṇs. Paraśurâma being invincible, the demons were compelled to make a hasty retreat westward, but being pursued, had to run into the sea. Here Vimala brought a mountain on his head, named Tuṅgâ, which in Sanskṛit means a hill, placed it in the sea, and fixed there his residence. His defeat, however, having counselled him repentance and religious austerities, he pleased Śiva so much that he obtained from the deity immunity from death, and the privilege of a *tîrtha*, along with a *divyaliṅga* or divine phallus. This he was told to establish on the Tuṅgâr hill, and provided he desisted from being aggressive towards the Brâhmaṇs in future he need fear nobody in the three worlds. The condition being acceded to, the *liṅga* was settled on the Tuṅgâr hill, and named *Tuṅgâreśvara*, or "the Lord of the Mountain."*

This event is said to have taken place in the *Tretâ Yuga*, or Silver

* This is the modern Tungâr Hill, about 2,300 feet above the sea level, on the east side of the railway, which promises to become a rival to Matheran Hill as a sanitarium; but of this more hereafter. See Appendix.

Age of the Hindus, before Paraśurâma had reclaimed the Koṅkaṇa from the sea.

It is recorded in the *Skanda* and other Purâṇas that Paraśurâma, after reclaiming and colonizing the Koṅkaṇa* with the Brâhmaṇs, established a certain number of *tîrthas*† in it, one of which was Nirmala or Vimala in Bassein.

The *Nirmala Mâhâtmya*, also a part of the same Purâṇa, states that while some Ṛishis were praising the name of Paraśurâma, Vimala, angry at hearing the praises of his deadly enemy, came down from the Tuṅgâ hill, and commenced to annoy the Ṛishis by placing a big stone on their *homakuṇḍa*, or hole in the ground for receiving the consecrated fire for an oblation. The Ṛishis made a complaint to Śiva, who sent Paraśurâma to chastise the *râkshasa* or demon, forgetful of his promise. This hero arrived just in time to afford protection to a young daughter of Lomaharshaṇa Ṛishi, who, while engaged in performing her devotions on the banks of the Vaitaraṇî, was being carried off by Vimala. Paraśurâma had a fight with Vimala, but every time he cut off his hands and feet they were renewed more vigorously than ever by the blessing of Śiva, whereupon Paraśurâma had recourse to Śiva himself, and, duly backed by the latter, succeeded at last in defeating Vimala with his classical *paraśu* or axe.

Vimala, now fallen, began to invoke Parasurâma's clemency and praise his name. Paraśurâma pardoned him and established then on the spot where Vimala fell a *liṅga*, which he called *Vimaleśvara*, or

---

* The *Sahyâdri Khaṇḍa* of the *Skanda Purâṇa* mentions that Paraśurâma having vanquished the emperor Kârtavîrya Sahasrârjuna and annihilated the race of the Kshatriyas, gave over their lands to the Brâhmaṇs, but having no place for himself, asked Varuṇa, the Indian Neptune, to grant him a part of his dominions, which having been refused, Paraśurâma repaired to the top of the Sahyâdri and, in spite of the opposition offered by Varuna, discharged fourteen arrows. From the points where they fell the sea receded, and the land thus extorted from the ocean was then divided into seven parts. This is said to have taken place between the *Tretâ* and *Dvâpâra Yugas*. The legend typifies both the contests among the Âryas themselves and the geological changes in the Dakhaṇ.

† The *Tîrthas* are "विमलं निर्मलं चैव खदिरं तीर्थमुत्तमं। हरिहरेश्वरं तीर्थं मुक्तेश्वरं तथैव च ॥ वालुकेशो महाश्रेष्ठो बाणगंगा सरस्वती। तस्यास्तु दक्षिणे भागे कुशस्थलीसमुद्रिणी ॥ मठग्रामं तथा चान्ये गोमांताख्ये च पर्वते। तत्रैव स्थापितं तीर्थं गोरक्षं च कुमारिजं ॥ रामकुंडं कुड्मलं च प्राचिसिद्धं गुणोपमं" ॥ *i.e.* the Vimala, or Nirmala, Khadira the best, Harihareśvara, Mukteśvara, Vâlukeśa the great, Bâṇagaṅgâ, and Sarasvati; to the south of these the Kushastalî river and Maṭagrâma: and on the Gomânta mountain the Goraksha Kumârija, Râmakuṇḍa, Prâchîsiddha, Guṇopama, and several others.—*Sahy. Kh.*, bk. ii., ch. i.

"the lord of Vimala," and erected a temple to commemorate the event.

Vimala is now called Nirmala, or *stainless,* since it was purified by Paraśurâma—from निर् (nir) *without,* and मल (mala) *stain.*

This mythic fight of Paraśurâma with the *asuras* in the Tretâ Yuga may possibly typify the contests of the Âryas with the aborigines; while the shelter Vimala found in the Tuṅga hill, to which Paraśurâma could get no access, seems to point to some geological change in and about Bassein previous to the reclamation of the Koṅkaṇa from the ocean.

The Nirmala Tîrtha is so celebrated a place among the Hindus that numerous *mâhâtmyas* of Western India allude to it. To name only a few:—first the *Trimbakeśvara Mâhâtmya,* ch. 10, refers to it thus:—"Nirmala Tîrtha not only destroys sins committed in the present life, but even those of the former lives."*

Again, the *Skanda Purâṇa* states: "The Nirmala Tîrtha, which is the best of all the *tîrthas,* is the seat of perfection, yielding fruit seven *karor* times. He who repeats a *mantra* thereat and abstains from sin acquires perfection seven *karor* times. He who lives there in sanctity is sure of obtaining supreme happiness."†

In the *Badari Mâhâtmya* also a dialogue between Skanda and Śiva is given on the subject of the Somakuṇḍa and Nirmala tîrtha, wherein Śiva is made to say that Nirmala is the best for all purposes of acquiring heavenly bliss.‡

Besides these, there are numerous small *kuṇḍas,* or consecrated pools and *tîrthas* in Bassein of great sanctity, but of little historical interest.

But to return to Vimaleśvara. The Portuguese, or rather the Inquisition, pulled down the temple, desecrated the *tîrtha,* and made the *liṅga* of Śiva disappear. On the Marâṭhâs taking possession of Bassein, Nirmala was again purified, Pâdukas of Śrî Dattâtreya substituted for

---

* विमलं निर्मलं तीर्थं सद्यो मानसदोषहृत्। यत्र स्नात्वा न लिप्यन्ते मलैर्जन्मांतरार्जितैः॥ अ० १०.

† सिद्धिपीठं तथा ख्यातं निर्मलं तीर्थमुत्तमं। सकृत्सप्तकोटिगुणं तदक्षयफलप्रदं॥ अथोपकारकं मंत्रं पाठयेद्वात्र कीर्तयेत्। न पापं चिन्तयेत्तत्र ततः कोटिगुणं भवेत्। न तत्र वासं कुर्वीत पापभीरुः कदाचन॥ पुण्यनिश्चयवान्स्थित्वा महासिद्धिंलभेन्नरः। स्कं०

‡ नमो निर्मलतीर्थाय सोमकुंडाभिधाय च। कथं वा लभ्यते स्वर्गः सर्वेषामुत्तमोत्तमः। अत्रिरुवाच। दुर्लभं रुपसाधूनामिह लोके परत्र च। ततस्तु नारदाच्छ्रुत्वा क्षेत्रं परमनिर्मलम्। ब० म०

the *liṅga*, and a tank constructed in the neighbourhood for religious ablutions in lieu of the *tîrtha* destroyed.

The legendary lore of Bassein, full of extravagant and wild chaff, such as the abduction of the daughter of Lomaharshaṇa Ṛishi on the banks of the Vaitaraṇî by the terrible *asuras*, and other fictional matter—hopeless mazes of tradition and mythology, without even the redeeming feature of probability—contains, however, some obscure hints from which grains of truth may be extracted. Besides, the ***Mâhâtmyas***, if they have no historical value, have at least some philological importance, and as they are fast disappearing, I have thought it advisable to save those of Bassein, in defiance of those who deem them but nonsensical.

The present temple, endowed at the public expense, is under the management of Gurû Śaṅkarâchârya Swâmi, who occasionally pays a pastoral visit to Nirmala, as well as to the other divisions of the Koṅkaṇa, and is regarded in the same light by the Śaivas as Madhavâchârya by the Vaishṇavas. Attached to the shrine there is an *annachhatra* or inn, where the Brâhmaṇs are fed gratuitously. A *jatrâ* is annually held on the 11th day of the month of Kârtika, which is attended by numerous pilgrims.*

Very little is known concerning the ancient authentic history of Bassein, a few incidental allusions to it only being found in the writings of some old Hindus and Greeks. The latter, since the expedition of Alexander, found their way into the country both by sea and land, and entered into commercial intercourse with the natives. Ptolemy Philadelphus was the first to send one Dionysius to the southern part of India to inquire into the produce and manufactures of the Dakhaṇ. At that time,† it appears, there were three famous kingdoms in Central and Southern India, viz. *Plithana* which is supposed to be Paithaṇa or Pratishṭhâṇa on the Godâvari; *Tagara*,‡ modern Devagaḍa or Daulatâbâd, the capital of a kingdom then called *Ariake* (Sansk. *Âryakshetra*) or Âryan-speaking country), which comprehended a great part of Aurangâbâd and the Southern Koṅkaṇa; while *Larikè* is said, as above noted,

* There is also said to be here the tomb of the first Śaṅkarâchârya Swâmi, who healed the schism between the Jainas and the orthodox Brâhmaṇs, but the great Śaṅkarâchârya is known to have died in Kashmîr, and as there were many of his spiritual descendants who assumed his name, one of them may have been buried at Bassein.

† The campaign of Alexander, B.C. 330, and Ptolemy's *Geography*, A.D. 130, or 460 years later.

‡ Mr. Bhagvânlâl Paṇdit informs me that the *Tagara* of the Greeks corresponds better to modern Junâr or Junâgaḍa.

to correspond to the modern Gujarât, and Kalyâṇa, Ṭhâṇa, Bassein, Chaul, &c.*

The author of the *Periplus* records that long before his time the Greeks traded with Kalyâṇa,† but that since the conquest of Egypt by the Romans, who had monopolized the Indian trade and would not allow foreigners to enter the Red Sea, the trade of the Dakhaṇ was wholly carried on by land. The king of the country about Kalyâṇa, Bassein, and Bombay was in the second century of our era called Sâraganos‡ (Sâraṅga or Sâraṅgesha), who was friendly towards the Greeks, but Sândanes having conquered that king, not only strictly prohibited those foreigners from trading at Kalyâṇa and its neighbourhood, but even sent some of them under a strong guard to Barygaza (Broach). The writer does not give any reason for such a proceeding, but others are of opinion that the Greeks had attempted to effect a settlement on the island of Salsette with a view to its acquisition, and to facilitate their meditated conquest in the Dakhaṇ. The king of Tagara had several harbours south of Kalyâṇa in his possession, but they were all infested by the pirates,—a fact testified to by Arrian, Ptolemy, Pliny, and others.

One of the few incidental allusions to Bassein is found in an inscription of the Kânheri caves. It runs thus:—

बस्यायि आमात्यस्य शतेरकस्य पानीय भाजन्य देयधम्म:

This has been translated by the Rev. Dr. Stevenson as follows:—"The charitable establishment of a place for the distribution of water by Śateraka, the minister in the Bassein province of the Satrap..." To this the author adds the following note:—"This inscription is over a water-tank, but it appears that visitors had water served out to them."

---

* D'Anville's *E'claircissemens Géographiques sur la Carte de l'Inde*, p. 69; Vivien de St.-Martin's *E'tude sur la Géographie Grecq. et Lat. de l'Inde*, p. 204.

† A few of the early Greek writers are minute in describing the kinds of articles of commerce for which they had made Kalyâṇa a port of considerable resort and enterprise. The names of some of those articles have been transmitted to us in Greek, and of others in Latin, nomenclature, viz. *ξύλα σησαμινὰ* or *sesamin* (*śîśu ?*), logs; *Φαλάγγων ἐβενινων*, or spars of ebony, *othonium vulgare*, dangarî or lighter sail-cloth; *sindones omnis generis*, muslins of all kinds; *molochyna*, a kind of cotton stuff dyed of a purplish colour, &c. Cosmas also mentions *χαλκος*, which is said to be intended for steel. Heeren (*Hist. Researches*, Oxford, 1833, vol. ii., p. 442) mentions among other products native brass.

‡ *Καλλίενα πολίς, ἡ ἐπὶ τῶν Σαραγάνου τοῦ πρεσβυτέρου Χρὸνων ἐρπόριον ἔνθεσμον γενόμενον.*—Hudson, *Geog. Vet.* I. 30.

The date of this inscription cannot be ascertained with precision, for the construction of the caves itself has been surmised by Dr. Stevenson* to date from shortly before to the 5th century of the Christian era, while Mr. Fergusson allows it a range from the 4th to the 10th century.† General Cunningham, however, places it in the first or second century of the Christian era.‡

In the reign of Justinian the trade of Kalyâṇa was as active as ever. Cosmas, the aforementioned Egyptian merchant, who had made some voyages to India, for which he received the surname of Indicopleustes, informs us that Kalyâṇa was a place abounding with Christians, who were subject to a Persian Bishop of the Nestorian sect.§

About one century after Cosmas, we have the account of Hwen Thsang, a Chinese traveller, who was, it is believed, in the neighbourhood of Bassein in June or July A.D. 640. He mentions a place called Mo-ho-la-cha or Mahârâshṭra, close to the western coast, which is said to correspond to Kalyâṇa;‖ but *Kong-kien-na-pu-lo* appears, as before stated, to accord more precisely with the position indicated, where it is supposed he embarked on his return. About two centuries and a half before the latter Chinese pilgrim, another of his compatriots and a Buddhist priest by profession, by name Fah-Hian, had, it is supposed, visited the caves of Kânheri, and possibly his *Ta-thsin* (Sansk. *Dakshiṇa*), the Dakhaṇ, refers to the country in the neighbourhood of Bassein as his *Po-lo-yu* (Sansk. *parvata*) mountain, to the hill where the Kânheri caves are situated. The subject is, however, controversial, and both Sykes and Beal think it refers to Ellora.¶ Of Kalyâṇa, however, as an emporium of trade, Bassein seems to have been the chief entrepôt of foreign commerce, from its being at the head of inland navigation.

It appears that during the whole of this period the country in and about Bassein was subject to the Châlukya kingdom of the Dakhaṇ, of which Kalyâṇa was then the capital.

---

* *Jour. Bom. Br. As. Soc.*, vol. v., p. 15.

† J. Fergusson's *Rock-cut Temples of India*, Lond. 1864, pp. 35 *et seqq.*

‡ *Ancient Geography of India, ut suprà*, p. 554.

§ *Jour. R. As. Soc.*, vol. vi., p. 329.

‖ Stanislas Julien's *Hist. de la Vie de Hiouen-Thsang*, p. 202; and Alex. Cunningham's *Ancient Geography of India*, p. 554.

¶ *Travels of Fah-Hian and Sung-yun*, by Samuel Beal, Lond. 1869, pp. 139 *et seqq.*

The long interval between the travels of the Byzantine monk Cosmas* and the eleventh century of our era is filled up by several Arabian geographers before mentioned, but there is no reference made to Bassein, although several places in the neighbourhood, such as Ṭhâṇâ, Supâra, &c., are mentioned.

We learn from some inscriptions and copperplates† that in 1017 A.D. Śrîsthânaka (Thâṇâ) was the seat of a reigning family called Silâra, or Silâhâra, who date their ascent to the throne from the time of Kapardi, which may be computed to be about 900 A.D. He traces his lineage to Jimutavâhana, 'the cloud-borne,' of the race of Rajputs and Râja of Tagara, exhibiting a long series of about nine princes who claimed to be the masters of 1,400 villages in the Koṅkaṇa, the principal of which was termed *Puri*, which, being a generic term for city, appears to stand for Ṭhâṇâ, the city *par excellence*.

These princes had frequent contests with the Kâdamba and Châlukya kings; of the latter Śrî Kambhadeva is said to have made a grant of land to Vimaleśvara in 1261 A.D. The royal grant is that of a place called Jâtakeśvara, while another piece of land in its vicinity is given to Mahâdeva of the Bharadvâja lineage, for serving in the above temple, which plainly shows that Vimaleśvara was revered as early as the thirteenth century. The grant is rather interesting, and deserves to be reproduced here in a very concise form. It begins thus:—"Svasti Śrî. In the year of Śaka 1282, the cycle being called Raudra, on the seventh of the dark half-moon of Pausha, Saturday...... residing in the city of Kalyâṇa, Kambhadeva Râja of the Châlukya race being sovereign, and Śrî Keśava Mahâjana minister, a place called Jâtaka Sivara was given to Vimaleśvara, and land lying near, to Mâdhavadeva, of the Bha-

---

* Cosmas was in Kalyâṇa about 530 A.D. On returning home (A.D. 535) he betook himself to a monastery and wrote various works, among which his *Topographia Christiana* contains particulars about the trade and people of Kalyâṇa. Don Bernard de Montfaucon, one of the Cosmas translators, suspects him to be a Nestorian, for which he gives what La Croze calls historic and dogmatic proofs. (*Hist. du Christianisme des Indes*, by V. La Croze, vol. i., pp. 40-50.) Some writers contend that the Kalyâṇa of Cosmas is modern Kalyâṇapura, near Uḍupi, about 32 miles north of Mangalore; but Col. Yule is of opinion that it is identical with the one here referred to: *Ind. Ant.*, vol. i., p. 321; vol. ii., p. 273. See also *antè*, p. 15, and Priaulx's *The Indian Travels of Apollonius of Tyana*, Lond. 1873, p. 214; the latter writer doubts that Cosmas ever visited India, although his narrative is, he says, "sober as facts and commonplace as reality:" p. 226.

† *As. Res.*, vol. i., pp. 363-4.

radvâja race for sacrifice, service, and offerings. The copper vessel and house near the temple were given to Brâhmaṇs for holy purposes, and four orchards called Râjâṭaka to Jelâva Raula's son Jvê Raula."* One of the princes of the house of Kâdamba, named Jayakeśi Deva I., king of Goa, is said to have slain the king of Kapardikadvîpa, or the island of Kaparda; it has not yet been ascertained whether this is Salsette or Bassein.

Bassein eventually passed from the Silâra family into the hands of the Yâdavas, whose inscriptions, dated 1272 and 1290 A.D., have been discovered near it.†

Until the submission of the Yâdavas to the Mahomedans, this part of the Koṅkaṇa was subject to constant political changes, being divided and subdivided between Bhimrâja of Mahim and Râmadeva of Devagaḍa, as well as between other petty chieftains of the Nâyaks, Baṅgolîs, and Bhaṇḍârîs.‡

It was in 1311 A.D. that the fury of the Mahomedan invaders was first felt in this part of Aurangâbad, which was ravaged by Malik Kafur, the general of Allâ-u-din, under whose sovereignty it continued for about forty years, and was subsequently subject to other Mahomedan rulers until its conquest by the Portuguese.§ About 1285 A.D. Marco Polo, the celebrated Venetian traveller, was at Ṭhâṇâ, and describes it as the capital of a great kingdom in the West, its inhabitants as idolaters, speaking a language of their own, and under a sovereign subject to no other. He speaks of its great trade in leather finely dressed, and cotton goods, and also of imports of gold and silver. He likewise alludes to the pirates issuing from the Ṭhâṇâ river and infesting the coast.

The defeat of Râmadeva by All-â-u-din, the emperor of Delhi, in the year 1294, placed the Dakhaṇ and, some years subsequently, the

---

* स्वस्तिश्रीशक ११८२ वर्षे रौद्रसंवत्सरे॥ पौषवदिसप्तमी शनिदिने॥ .... कल्याणपुरवराधीश्वर॥ ...... चालुक्यकुलकमलकलिकाविकासभास्कर॥ .... श्रीकांबदेवराय .... तद्राज्यभारचालनसमर्थ॥ .... श्रीकेशवमहाजनिना॥ झाटसीवारसंबंधिनीशूद्रभोजोप॥ जीविनीसमग्रभूमिर्विमलेश्वरद्देवस्य॥ तथा देवस्यसन्निधौ या भूमिः॥ सा॥ भारद्वाजगोत्रस्य॥ माधवदेवस्य॥ गंधधूपनैवेद्यार्थं॥ .... देवसन्निधौ॥ ताम्रभाजनपूर्वक॥ शाश्वतमठं॥ धर्मकार्यार्थकं झाटकवाटिकाचत्वारि अंक संख्याजाल्हण राउलसुतगोइराउलस्य दातव्यं .... श्रीगोविंदेन विलिखितं॥ ......॥

† *Jour. R. As. Soc.*, vol. ii., p. 380.

‡ *Trans. Bomb. Geog. Soc.*, p. 129.

§ Briggs' *Ferishta*, vol. i., p. 304.

greater part of the Koṅkaṇa under the sway of the Mahomedans. It was while under the Mahomedan rule that the neighbourhood of Bassein acquired the notoriety of being the scene of the martyrdom of five Franciscan missionaries, and their burial-place, which happened about forty years after Marco Polo. But of this I shall have to speak more at length hereafter.

The coast of Bassein, according to Faria y Souza, was first visited by the Portuguese in the year 1509, when Dom Francisco d'Almeida on his way to Diu captured a Mahomedan ship in the harbour of Bombay with twenty-four Moors, belonging to Gujarât, by which means he procured a supply of sheep and rice, whilst some cattle were got in other places, and a further supply at the fort of Mahim, all the people flying to the mountains from terror of the Portuguese, having heard of what had happened at Dâbul,* but it was not till about seventeen years later that they established a factory there. Duarte Barbosa says of it, about this period, under the Mahomedan name of Baxay, that "Having passed this town of Deudi, twenty leagues further on to the south is another town of Moors and gentiles, a good seaport, which also belongs to the King of Gujarât, in which much goods are exchanged; and there is a great movement of the shipping which comes there from all parts, and many Zambucs† from the Malabar country laden with areca, cocoas, and spices, which they delight in, and they take thence others which are used in Malabar."‡

In 1528 Lopo Vas de Sampaio fought, as above stated, the great naval battle in its neighbourhood, when Heitor de Sylveira was sent round to assault the Mahomedan fort of Bassein ; and it was in 1530 that the Portuguese made the first descent upon the coast from Chikli Târâpur to Bassein, and levied contributions on Ṭhâṇâ and Kalyâṇa, compelling both places to promise to pay annual tributes of 4,000 pardaos to the crown of Portugal,§ Bombay being held in the meanwhile as a security for the tribute due. The geographical position of Bassein inspired them with a desire to possess it permanently, and as a quarrel soon arose with Bahâdur Shâh, King of Gujarât, whom the Portuguese historians

---

* Faria y Souza, *ut supra*, tome I., pt. VI., ch i., p. 117. This must have taken place in January 1509, for we are told that on the 2nd of February the Viceroy had arrived at Diu.

† *Sambucs* are Arab undecked boats.

‡ *Description of the Coast of East Africa and Malabar*, p. 68.

§ Faria y Souza, *ibid.*

call *Sultao de Cambaia*, or *Melique*,* recourse to arms could no longer be avoided. The result was a treaty by which they obtained formal cession of Bassein, and the confirmation of the former cession of Ṯhâṇâ, Salsette, Bombay, and Mahim, permission to erect forts, and the right of levying duty on the Red Sea trade; engaging themselves in return to afford him assistance against the emperor Humâyun of Delhi.† In virtue of these concessions the fort of Bassein was in 1536 founded by Nuno da Cunha, on the southern extremity of the island of that name, facing the narrow inlet of the sea which divides it from Salsette, and was placed under the command of his brother-in-law, Garcia de Sá, who is known as the first Captain of Bassein, and was subsequently appointed Governor of India on the death of the last of the Portuguese heroes, Dom Joaõ de Castro, in 1548.

But to enter into details. It was in 1530 that Antonio de Sylveira made the first descent upon the coast of Bassein, and burnt and pillaged it to an enormous extent. His march of depredation was, however, arrested at the island of Bombay, where the King of Ṯhâṇâ, panic-stricken at the news of the ravages made by the Portuguese, came down to offer, as a check to further waste, the islands of Bombay and Mahim, now united into one, which being duly accepted, an annual tribute was also imposed on him.

In 1531 Antonio de Saldanha, on his way to Goa from Cambay,‡ partly to retrieve his misfortunes in the court of the King of Gujarât, and partly to punish the recalcitrant Sultân Bahâdur, who had refused to cede Diu to the King of Portugal, made a second descent upon the coast from Chikli Târâpur to Bassein, setting fire to it again.§ Saldanha was followed in 1533 by Diogo de Sylveira, who, having already gained elsewhere the unenviable reputation of an incendiary,‖ was

* *Melique*, from the Persian ملک a king. Some writers also call him "Rei de Cambaia," or King of Cambay, his principal port.

† *Tuhfat-ul-Mujahidin*, pp. 136-7.

‡ J. P. Maffei, *Hist Ind.*, p. 428.

§ J. T. Lafitau, *Hist. des Descouv. et Conq. de Port.*, vol. ii., p. 215.

‖ Diogo de Sylveira, though so fierce in temper, had also his better side of nature. It is written that once while cruising in the Red Sea, Sylveira came across a vessel under a Mahomedan captain, who saluted him, and, having obtained an audience, brought him a letter from a Portuguese, which the Mahomedan believed to be a recommendatory letter. Its contents, however, disclosed the fact that the ship was laden with valuables, and the writer wished Sylveira to seize it as a very good prize, and make a prisoner of the captain, whom he described as a wicked man. Sylveira did not know which to admire most, the impudence of the one or the rashness of the other. He treated the captain with extreme kindness, gave him a passport in better form, and told him that he rather preferred that the world should learn that a man of his nation would willingly lose an opportunity of enriching himself than show bad faith.

chiefly instrumental in burning and plundering the whole sea-coast from Bandora along Ṭhâṇâ and Bassein up to Surat, which scarcely had had time to recover from the devastating effects of the two previous invasions of his comrades Saldanha and Antonio de Sylveira. Having accomplished this, Sylveira returned to Goa rich with the spoils of his pillaging, among which there were four thousand slaves, who were afterwards employed in the building of convents and churches of Goa.

While this summary castigation of their deadly foes was going on under the immediate supervision of Captains Saldanha, Sylveira, Martim Affonso de Souza, and others, the General Nuno da Cunha was all the while devising means to take possession of Diu. His whole mind appears at this time to have been engrossed in this object, while Bassein seems scarcely to have been thought of. Having, however, of a sudden been made acquainted with the fact that Malik Tokan, son of Malik Eyâz, Governor of Diu, was fortifying Bassein, which would certainly prove a useful addition to the Mahomedan citadels on the coast, especially as this place and the country around yielded timber of the best quality for the building of fleets, he set out to put a stop to it. In the meanwhile Malik Tokan had built his citadel of Bassein, fortified both margins of the river with trenches and ramparts surrounded with a ditch that admitted the water from the sea, and garrisoned the fortress with cavalry and infantry amounting to about 15,000. He had, besides, improved its condition by facilitating means for the increase of the general population, attracted there by the commercial importance of the place, which, however, dated from very remote times, and by the building of edifices, both public and private, the vestiges of which are now with difficulty traced, especially among the ruins of the circular castle in the centre of the fort, to be described hereafter.

The General Nuno da Cunha, solely intent on putting down any fortified place that might prove troublesome to his ambitious views, prepared a fleet of 150 ships manned by 4,000 men, half of whom were Portuguese, and the rest Canarese and Malabarese.

Malik Tokan, on seeing this formidable array of the naval power of the terrible *Farangí*, lost no time in making overtures of peace, which being entertained by Cunha only under extremely hard stipulations, Tokan had no resource left but to try his fortune on the battle-field. Thereupon the Portuguese landed a little to the North of the citadel, and, led by Diogo de Sylveira and Manuel de Macedo, glided on to the moat of the fortress, scaled its ramparts, mounted its parapets, and gained a position from which Malik Tokan, with his whole host, could not dislodge them. Once within the citadel, the Portuguese, not at all daunted by their numerical insignificance—for only the vanguard of the Portuguese army was engaged in the combat—threw themselves amidst the ranks of the enemy with such impetuosity and rancour that Malik Tokan's troops were entirely dispersed. The terrible havoc wrought among the Mahomedans caused them to retreat precipitately, leaving behind a prodigious quantity of stores and munitions of war. This mere handful of valorous Portuguese, whose daring deeds in this action often extorted the admiration of their foes, fought with success so decisive that the whole island of Bassein fell into their hands. Only two persons of mark and a few soldiers, says Lafitau, were killed, while the whole field seemed to be strewn with the corpses of the enemy. This action took place on the 20th January, on the day of St. Sebastian as the chroniclers call it.

Nuno da Cunha, naturally elated by so signal a victory, intended to celebrate this action by bestowing the honour of knighthood—in imitation of which, perhaps, Estavaõ da Gama, son of the great admiral Vasco da Gama, knighted his young companions at the shrine of St. Catherine on the mount Sinai—on a few of his officers, distributing among his brave troops the spoils of war; but the council of war having determined, like the Roman senate's decree *de delenda Carthagine*, that the ramparts should be demolished and the whole citadel razed to the ground—more on account of its proximity to the fort of Chaul, and its consequent uselessness, than, like the Romans, from hatred—the Portuguese General retired without further ceremony with four hundred pieces of artillery to Goa, where he was received with rejoicings.

After his defeat, Malik Tokan endeavoured to console himself with a systematic series of intrigues, underhand machinations, and organized hypocrisy with Bahâdur Shâh on the one side, whom he hated from the very bottom of his heart, and with the Portuguese on the other, also his detested enemies, and it would be simply tedious, if not unpleasant, to write about it. The General Nuno da Cunha, at the request of each party, sent an emissary to treat of peace, Vasco da Cunha going to Malik Tokan, and Tristaõ de Ga to the court of Bahâdur Shâh; their missions, however, having proved fruitless, the General himself sailed with a fleet of eighty ships, and began that brilliant course of diplomacy which eventually secured for him not only the possession of Bassein, but even the realization of the *songe doré* of his life, the building of the fort of Diu, which the Portuguese had hitherto failed to accomplish, from the King Dom Manuel, who had in 1519 sent Diogo Lopes de Siqueira with a fleet of eighty ships to conquer it, which utterly failed; Henrique de Menezes, who followed Siqueira, but whose premature death put a stop to his otherwise well-conceived tactics; down to Lopo Vaz de Sampayo, who, having spent an incredibly large sum of money, had prepared one of the most formidable armadas that India ever saw, but with the same result. The King, Dom Joaõ III., frequently wrote to the Governor, Nuno da Cunha, not to slacken his efforts to gain possession of a place that commanded the whole trade of India, Persia, and Arabia, and whose possession subsequently gave rise to those two memorable sieges which have been sung by poets, and have few rivals in deeds of valour and gallantry in the annals of warfare.

Bahâdur Shâh, who had succeeded in winning the confidence of Ibrâhim II., and obtaining the governorship of Gujarât, succeeded on the death of his sovereign in making himself an independent king. The Mogul, however, would not forgive the treachery of his former servant; and Bahâdur Shâh, being left without a single friend to help him against the threats of Humâyun of Delhi, had recourse to the Portuguese, who having, under the eminent general Martim Affonso de Souza, reduced Damaun—the loss of which citadel Bahâdur Shâh had felt most poignantly—and knowing the great value of such an alliance, accepted the offer of a treaty of peace, which was concluded and sworn to under the following conditions:—"That Sultân Bahâdur Shâh should cede to the King of Portugal the sovereign right to Bassein, with all dependencies: that the Portuguese should have the right to levy duties on the Red Sea trade; that all his vessels should sail with a passport from the Portuguese Crown; that his harbours should no longer have any armed boat; and that the Rumîs should have no protection from the Sultân." This took place in 1533.*

Again, being about the following year invited by the Mogul to an alliance offensive and defensive, which request was highly flattering to his feelings as being sought after at the same time by two of the most powerful of the kings of India, Nuno, though rather vacillating at first, came to the conclusion to reject the Emperor of Delhi's proposal, and remain content with that of his former ally, Bahâdur Shâh, who then entered into another league, the conditions of which gratified to the full the ambition of the Portuguese general. They were:—That the Sultân Bahâdur Shâh should cede to the King of

* *Subsidios, ut supra*, pt. ii., pp. 134 *et seqq.*

Portugal a site for the búilding of a fortress in Diu; that the Ṣultán should in particular give the King the ramparts that were on the seaside close to the port, and at the same time confirm the cession he had made the preceding year of Bassein and the territory around. Another clause was to the effect that the Portuguese should engage in return to afford him assistance against the Emperor Humâyun, which assistance was eventually given, and proved highly valuable to Bahâdur Shâh, though it has not been acknowledged by the Mahomedan historian Ferishta.

This treaty, containing conditions so hard for Bahâdur Shâh, although signed on the 23rd December 1533, did not urge the Portuguese general to found the city of Bassein until 1535, when, the Mogul having threatened to take possession of it, he was obliged to appoint his brother-in-law Garcia de Sá to conduct its defence; but Garcia, as it had but a factory established there by the Portuguese several years before, and some slight fortifications hastily constructed, thought it better to abandon the place. Thereupon Antonio Galvaõ, whom the chroniclers call the great Christian hero,—who in after-time as a governor of the Moluccas not only distinguished himself by repairing the ruins caused by his predecessor, the inconsiderate Tristaõ de Ataide, but made himself beloved by the whole native population,—opposed a resolution so unworthy of the Portuguese, and determined on fighting. Galvaõ is better known to scholars by his work *Tratado de diversos e desvairados caminhos*, &c., translated under the heading of *Discoveries of the World* for the Hakluyt Society by Vice-Admiral Bethune, C.B., Lond. 1862. The Mogul's hope of becoming master of Bassein being thereby frustrated, he, in view of the warlike attitude assumed by the dauntless Galvaõ with his gallant company, thought it prudent not to risk an attack, and retreated without even firing a shot. Nuno, who had arrived soon after the Mogul had withdrawn from the field, commenced to lay the foundation of his citadel of Bassein, and was so pleased with the valorous action of Galvaõ that, in order to do him honour, he asked him to lay the corner-stone of the fort.

Having once built Bassein, Garcia de Sá was made its first Captain or Governor, who continued to improve, by all means within his power—in spite of the siege which was laid to it in April 1540 by the King of Gujarât, and which turned to the honour and glory of Bassein—the condition of the place until the year 1548, when, on the death of Dom Joaõ de Castro, the *cartas de successaõ*, or royal letters of succession, being opened with the usual formalities, the following names in succession were read out:—Dom Joaõ Mascarenhas, Dom Jorge Telles e Menezes, and Garcia de Sá. The two former being absent in Portugal, Garcia de Sá was proclaimed Governor of India, while his place of Captain of Bassein was given to Jorge Cabral, who eventually, on the death of Garcia de Sá, which took place in 1549 at Goa, where his remains lie buried in the church of Nossa Senhora do Rosario, was also called from this place to Goa to occupy the position of acting Governor until the year 1551, when the Viceroy Affonso de Noronha came down to hold the reins of the Portuguese empire in Asia. Jorge Cabral, being of a retired disposition, historians tell us, was at first averse to leaving the humble post of Captain of the fort of Bassein, for the more splendid but burdensome position of acting Governor; but induced by his wife, who was young, handsome, and ambitious, he accepted the situation and returned to Goa, where he was received with all the honours due to his high post, which, however, he endured rather than enjoyed.

The founder of Bassein belongs to that brilliant galaxy of intrepid soldiers of old Lusitania who for about half a century dazzled the world with their splendid achievements.* (See Plate 12.) He was not less known as an accomplished general and statesman than as a man of culture and attainments. Musgrave writes of him: "His conquests were numerous, and his measures so skilfully and nicely framed and concerted, that he stands preëminent amongst the Viceroys who acquired the most

* A Sampaio feroz succederá
Cunha, que longo tempo tem o leme;
De Chalé as torres altas erguerá,
Em quanto Dio illustre delle treme:
O forte Baçaim se l'he dará,
Nao sem sangue porém; que nelle geme
Melique, porque á força so de espada
A tranqueira soberba vê tomada.

Camoẽs, *Lusiadas*,
Canto X., lxi.

Then the fierce Sampaio shall be succeeded by
Cunha, who the helm long time shall wisely guide,
The lofty towers of Chalé he shall raise on high,
While famous Dio shall tremble when by him tried.
Strong Baçaim shall not its artillery deny,
But not without bloodshed; Melic with humbled pride
Shall see her superb palisades downtorn,
And not less because the work of the sword shall mourn.

Mitchell, *ut supra*, p. 257.

Plate 12.

BASSEIN.

GOVERNOR NUNO DA CUNHA, FOUNDER OF BASSEIN,—(1529—1538.)

COPIED FROM AN ANCIENT OIL PAINTING IN GOA.

brilliant reputation."* His sayings are characteristic of his ready wit. It is stated that at the siege of Diu a soldier by his side being struck with a bullet on the head, Nuno da Cunha coolly exclaimed, in the words of the Holy Scriptures, "*Humiliate capita vestra Deo,*" "Humble your heads to God." His case affords one of the many illustrations of the proverbial ingratitude of princes. He was, notwithstanding his great services to his king, recalled at the instigation of his enemies, but died near the Cape of Good Hope on his way home, in February 1539, uttering with the indignant Roman the words "*Ingrata patria, ossa mea non possidebis,*" "Ungrateful country, thou shalt not possess my bones." His will, when opened, disclosed his dying wish that his king should be paid for the iron chain with which he would be buried in the sea, for he had incurred no other debt. The irony, as it was, met with another stern mind to carry it into effect, for his old father, the distinguished navigator Tristaõ da Cunha, presented himself to the King, Dom Joaõ III., and offered to pay the amount. What followed the chroniclers have not transmitted to us. We are simply told that the King regretted the way he had treated his subject, as great and as unfortunate as Affonso d'Albuquerque.

The Portuguese were in possession of Bassein for about two hundred and ten years, during which period it gradually rose to a state of grandeur and opulence that obtained for it the noble appellation of "a Côrte do Norte," or "the chief city of the North,"† in relation to the capital of Goa; for it had become the resort of the most prosperous *fidalgos* and the richest merchants of Portuguese India, so much so that it became proverbial in those times to call a great man "Fidalgo, ou Cavalheiro, de Baçaim." It abounded with sumptuous edifices, both public and private, civil and religious, which latter, besides the *Matriz* or Cathedral, consisted of five convents, thirteen churches, and one *Misericordia* or asylum for orphans and maidens; and the ruins of which even at the present day serve as a silent epitaph of departed greatness.

The writings of several travellers, both foreign and Portuguese, afford us an insight into the state of Bassein during its palmy days, and as some of them have never been published before in English, I shall make no apology for quoting passages from them. Diogo do Couto writes:—"The city of Bassein is the largest, and comprehends

* Musgrave's *Lusiad*, p. 565.

† *Dic. Hist. Exp.*, Art. *Baçaim*, Nova Goa, 1848, p. 10.

more territory than all the others of India, because towards the east it extends to the forts of Assari and Manorá, which are about eight leagues, and contain rich villages yielding great revenue. Towards the north it extends to the river of Agaçaim, and towards the south to the river of Bombay, or even a little further—to another arm which is called Carania, as it makes between the one and the other a small island in which we have a castle of that name. The river which surrounds the island of Salsette has two branches; that to the north is the river which runs along the city of Bassein, and continues its course to the south in several windings; and about halfway, in a place distant about three leagues, the Portuguese established a colony called Taná, which is the residence of about sixty Portuguese, who possess in that island their villages, which are very productive. Here the river has two very narrow passages, and a person can ford it at low water from the country of the Moors to the Island of Salsette; near these passages there are two castles seated on a rock over the water to defend this pass. The river then continues its progress to the west about three leagues, and forms the beautiful harbour of Bombay, which extends itself to the sea more than half a league in breadth, where all the ships from Portugal and other countries ride in, on account of its good soundings, having no sandbank nor any other impediments; and before it reaches the sea it extends one arm towards the south, which makes the Island of Caranja, and another towards the north which is the Island of Bandora. From this mouth of Bombay river it directs its course to the north coast about four leagues until it enters the harbour of Bassein, and leaves the Island of Salsette on the seaside, which is reckoned to be fifteen leagues in circumference and two in breadth."*

Francois Pyrard, a French traveller, who seems to have been in Bassein in the year 1607, writes about the trade of Bassein thus:— "From Bassein is exported the best timber for the building of houses and ships, the greater part of which latter are built here; it also yields a building stone that is fine and as hard as granite, and I never saw columns and pillars of entire stone so large as in this place. All the churches and sumptuous palaces of Goa are built of this stone."†

Dellon, another French traveller and a victim of the Inquisition, was in Bassein on January 2nd, 1674. He was landed as a prisoner from Damaun, and sent with other prisoners directly to the jail, which he

---

* *Decada* VII., bk. III., chap. x.

† *Viagem de Francisco Pyrard*, vol. ii., pp. 226-7.

describes thus:—"The jail of the city of Bassein is larger and cleaner than that of Damaun; there I met with a large number of companions in misfortune, whom the Rev. Commissary of the Inquisition of this city kept imprisoned for a long time, waiting the opportunity to send them over to Goa."* He embarked on the 7th on board a ship belonging to the fleet, along with his companions in chains, and set sail the next day for Goa.

Dr. Fryer, who visited Surat and Bombay in the year 1674, says that he was sent for by the captain of Bassein, by name John de Mendos, (Joaõ Mendes?) to treat his daughter. The captaincy, he says, was triennial, and was entailed on certain descendants of the conquerors, who succeeded to the office in rotation. The city is described as encircled with a "stone wall" with "a gate for each wind," where only the Christians lodge, the Banians repairing to the suburbs. There were in his time six churches, four convents, and two colleges, one belonging to the Franciscans and another to the Jesuits, who also possessed a fine library, consisting principally of commentaries and works on history and morals. Their college is said to have had fine square cloisters, with cells on two sides, a spacious refectory, and a goodly church. The Fidalgos, who tolerated no artisan among them or within the walls, had, according to this writer, stately dwellings two stories high, graced with covered balconies, and large windows with panes of oyster-shell or latticed.†

We have next the account by Dr. Gemelli Carcri, who visited Bassein in 1695, and describes it thus:—"The compass of Bazaim is three miles, and has eight bastions, not all finished," while "on the south side, towards the channel, there is only a single wall, that place being less exposed to the danger of enemies, and sufficiently defended by the ebb and flood. One third of the city, towards the north, is unpeopled,

* *Narraçaõ da Inquisiçaõ de Goa*, p. 48. The author of the *Historia das Inquisiçoens* adds to this quotation from Dellon the following:—"The city of Bassein is situated about twenty leagues to the south of Damaun; at the time it was under the Portuguese it was larger than Damaun, but wanting a good fortress, although possessing walls and a good garrison. It was built about a quarter of a league from the sea, on the margin of a river, where ships of any tonnage could enter and anchor any time in safety, for the harbour was well protected from winds. On this account it was the residence of a great number of merchants, and the emporium of a large trade; it had excellent houses, straight roads, large squares, rich and magnificent churches, the climate salubrious, and the soil fertile. The Portuguese had no city in India with so large a number of noblemen as Bassein, whence the proverb 'Fidalgo, ou Cavalheiro, de Baçaim'": p. 187.

† *A New Account of East India and Persia*, pp. 74, 75.

by reason of the plague which some years rages in it. The streets are wide and straight, and the great square or market has good buildings about it. There are two principal gates, one on the east and the other on the west, and a small one towards the channel or strait. The outskirts were then in a high state of cultivation, nothing appearing for fifteen miles but delightful gardens with several sorts of country fruit-trees, as palm, fig, mangas, and others, and abundance of sugar-canes. The soil is cultivated by Christian, Mahomedan, and Pagan peasants inhabiting the villages thereabouts. They keep the gardens always green and fruitful by watering them by certain engines, so that the gentry, allured by the cool and delightful walks, all have their pleasure-houses at *Cassabo* (Caçabé), to go thither in the hottest weather to take the air, and get away from the contagious and pestilential disease called *carazzo*,* that used to infect all the cities of the northern coast. It is exactly like a bubo, and so violent that it not only takes away all means of preparing for a good end, but in a few hours depopulates whole cities."†

Captain Hamilton, who visited Bassein about the same time, says :—"Its walls are pretty high and about two miles in circumference around the city, which has a little citadel in the middle of it. It contains three or four churches, and some convents and monasteries, with a college and hospital."‡

The Portuguese, though in full and uninjured possession of Bassein for about two hundred and ten years, were not unfrequently disturbed. The principal disturbing elements were the Mahomedans and the Marâṭhâs, whose opposition, it appears, was less provoked by the Portuguese government than by the religious intolerance of the Inquisition. Ovington writes that "the Mogul's army has made several inroads into this country, plundered some small towns, and threatened Bassein." He adduces several reasons for their pillaging incendiarism, one of which is that the Portuguese burnt formerly a Cogee (Kâzi), a person skilled in their law, at Goa. "Another reason is, because the Portuguese proselyte the children of all persons deceased among them, whether their parents are Moors or Pagans, and seize their estates into the

* *Carazzo* is not to be found in the lexicons of the Italian language; the symptoms, however, point to the plague.

† *A Voyage round the World*, by Dr. J. F. Gemelli Careri, Churchill's *Voyages*, vol. iv., p. 191. Also Burgess's *Notes of a Visit to Gujarât*, Bomb. 1870, pp. 6-7.

‡ Capt. A. Hamilton's *New Account of the East Indies*, vol. i., p. 180.

church, which raises a loud clamour against them, and grievous complaints to the Mogul."*

Orme mentions that Śivâji and his successors made raids into the Portuguese territory of Bassein, in revenge for the Inquisition burning the Marâṭhâ prisoners. In 1674 Moro Paṇḍit came down the Ghâṭs with 10,000 men, and, being quartered in the ruined town of Kalyâṇa, sent messengers to Bassein demanding the *chaut* or fourth part of the revenue of all the Portuguese territories in those parts. The cause of this demand was enmity borne towards the Portuguese, who, Orme adds, "had lately inflicted great severities on many families of the Morattoe religion within their districts, because they refused to become Christians; and this time of retaliation, by requiring them to become tributaries, seems to have been expressly chosen; the Portuguese having lately endured, with little resistance, a much greater insult from a much inferior force."†

Again, Goez, who was in India about the year 1603, says:—"When the Portuguese find an idol they burn or break it; they destroyed a tank at Bassein where the Hindus used to bathe for the remission of their sins; the persecution of the Portuguese had made many Hindûs, Mussulmans, and Parsees abandon their homes and live in the dominion of Shah Jehan, where they had liberty of conscience; and that between Bassein and Damaun there are few natives, the greater part of the village lands being uncultivated."‡

Modern Portuguese writers do not ignore the harm the Inquisition did to their Eastern empire. One of them§ says that very stringent decrees were issued throughout Portuguese India by the Provincial Council (a peripatetic institution auxiliary to the court of the Inquisitors at Goa) affecting populations of towns and parishes. The neophytes were strictly prohibited from living with the infidels under the penalty of paying one *pardao* (six annas) to the individual who should prefer the charge against them. It was also determined that no convert should keep friendship with a heathen, or even have him as a servant except as a groom, in which case the practice of his religion would not be allowed. In Bassein the Christians were not to employ

---

* *A Voyage to Surat in the year* 1689, by J. Ovington, Lond. 1696, pp. 206-207.

† Orme, *Hist. Frag.*, p. 45.

‡ *Calcutta Review*, vol. v., p. 271.

§ *Vasco da Gama*, No. 27, pp. 66-67.

the Parabûs,* neither lend them money, nor admit them into partnership, nor even give them shelter in their houses, under pain of transportation, subject to the approval of the Viceroy. No infidel was allowed to serve in a public office as a clerk, nayak, peon, mukâdama, receiver, *parpate*, interpreter, attorney, solicitor, broker, or shroff, nor were the Christians of Goa and Bassein permitted to rent their property to the pagans. It was, moreover, decreed that a roll or register of all infidels residing in each parish of the city of Goa, Bassein, &c., of a hundred persons each, should be kept, half of whom were compelled to attend every Sunday afternoon alternately a meeting where Christian doctrine or catechism was forcibly inculcated by a priest appointed for the purpose by a prelate of the diocese, and those who remained absent were mulcted one *tanga* (2½ annas) for the first occasion, two for the second, and three for the third, the amount to be paid to their accusers.

Another cause of the decadence of Bassein was more internal, and unfortunately more deeply rooted,—the laxity of morals. Soon after the middle of the sixteenth century,—or, more precisely, about the time Portugal was usurped by the Spanish crown,—the dissipation of habits was of public notoriety, and was not only animadverted upon both by foreign travellers and a few of the far-sighted among the Portuguese themselves, but were complained of to the King, Philip II. of Spain, who, apparently zealous both about the prosperity of his territory and the conduct of his delegates in the East, used to write to the Viceroy letters at each *monção* (*Arabicè* موسم),† advising him to be solicitous to punish those who should offend public morals by their demeanour.

The captains of Bassein were themselves engaged in trade, which the King being aware of, writes to the Viceroy that he is informed all the forts of the north are much injured for little or no care, or rather for positive negligence, on the part of the captains, who think more of their own trade and profits than of his service; that the captaincies of Bassein and Damaun are provided with timber for the building of ships of his armada from captains themselves, who charged far higher prices than their value in the market, which would not happen if they had no traffic of their own.‡

* The Portuguese used to call all the high-class Hindus of Bassein Parabûs.

† *Monçaõ* is the Portuguese term corresponding to 'monsoon,' or the season during which the ships from Lisbon used to sail for India.

‡ *Carta Regia*, dated the 13th March 1587—*Archivo Portuguez Oriental*, fasc. iii., p. 106.

Another proof of the royal solicitude about Bassein is to be found in the fact referred to in an excerpt of his letter to the Viceroy, Dom Duarte de Menezes, in the year 1587, of his having sent a miner (geologist?) named Agostinho de Souto-Maior to Bassein on being informed that there were signs of the existence of iron and also of copper and silver in that island; that he would be glad to learn whether anything of the sort had really been found.* Again, in January 1591 the King writes to the Viceroy, Mathias de Albuquerque, that he had been informed that a scandal had taken place in Bassein, and of which he had no knowledge until about two years had elapsed. The King then commands the Viceroy to prosecute the delinquents, as he had heard that for some years past it had been a very common practice in India to shoot people without the courts of justice putting a stop to it, which, the King regrets to say, is against both the service of God and his own.†

In spite of all these depressing causes, the prosperous condition of the court of Bassein was apparently as striking and as unshorn of its grandeur as in its former days; for we read that as late as 1720 the population of Bassein was 60,499, of whom 58,131 were Native Christians, the rest being Europeans. The revenue of Bassein in 1686 was 172,920 Xs., and the expenditure 91,588. In 1709 the revenue was 194,748, and the expenditure 100,161. From 1718 to 1719 the revenue was 310,779, and the expenditure 315,426. The last item we get is that of 1729, in which we are simply told of the revenue of 914,125. In the ecclesiastical department the sum of 14,357 Xs. was allotted to the priests as *congruas*, besides the emoluments they derived from their church ministrations. All this revenue was derived from the *seven* divisions to be described hereafter, which were subject to "the Court of Bassein," excluding of course Bombay, and the villages of *Mazagaõ, Parela, Warly*, &c., since its cession to the British crown according to the instrument of possession made by the public notary of Bassein on the 17th February 1665.

The Portuguese in India had, in the second half of the seventeenth century, received so many warnings of gradual decline of their power, that they became apprehensive that only a strong blow from a determined foe would be sufficient to wrest Bassein from their feeble grasp.

---

* *Archivo Portuguez Oriental*, fasc. iii., C. R. of the year 1587, p. 506.

† C. R. dated January 1591: *Archivo Port. Orient.*, fasc. iii., pp. 287, 288.

Corruption and depravity of manners* were making rapid strides among the citizens of every class; the original conquerors of India were not in existence; the mother-country, on the death of Dom Sebastian, was distracted by civil factions and overrun by the Spaniards; the flourishing colonies of Malabar snatched away by the Dutch; the spirit of religious intolerance and inquisitorial atrocities driving away from the Portuguese towns all native industry, riches, and talent; the trafficking of the captains; rapacity and unrestrained abuses in the management of the public money; the African slavery; and last, though not least, the absolute want of discipline, subordination, or love of glory, animating those squalid and drooping remnants of the Portuguese, would in themselves be enough to weaken beyond recovery any empire in the world, much less to cause Bassein to fall a prey to a powerful enemy, as it subsequently did.†

---

* The narrative entitled *Viaggio all' Indie Orientale* of the Carmelite Vincenzo Maria, one of the emissaries of Pope Alexander VII., explains better the culminations their depravity had attained. I forbear, however, quoting him. It is highly tinged with hatred, and the hatred of the priest knows no bounds. He is quite indignant with the ladies of Bassein for eating 'areca and betle' (*pân supâri*); but, though not so elegant, it is perhaps not worse than tobacco-smoking, at least physiologically.

† The organized system of plunder and despotism followed by the degenerate Portuguese of India was, according to the judicious remarks of Abbé Raynal, Teixeira Pinto, and latterly the distinguished American statesman and traveller William H. Seward, and several others, but the result of a small nation becoming of a sudden mistress of the richest and most extensive commerce of the globe. They lost the foundation of all their real power in the East through simply making themselves merchants, factors, sailors, and priests, to the utter neglect and even abandonment of agriculture, natural industry, and population; when their schemes of trade and projects of conquest, never being guided by the true spirit of international law, soon assumed the form of rapine. It was then evident that when a free and enlightened nation, actuated by a proper spirit of toleration, should appear on the stage, to contend with them for their empire in India, they would succumb; and so it proved. The travellers Linschoten, Tavernier, and others bear out the statements, and openly sympathize with the natives for forming confederacies to avenge affronts.

Amboyna was the first to avenge itself; other places followed, and at last from the very centre of their capital settlement of Goa rose that spirited confederacy of brave patriots known as '*sublevaçaô dos Pintos*,' which, though unsuccessful through the sheer stupidity of half a dozen priests who had assumed the *rôle* of leaders, was the harbinger of more peaceful and prosperous times, and of that true constitutional *régime* inaugurated under the auspicious reign of King Pedro IV. of Portugal, and first Emperor of Brazil, which, skipping over past resentments and old barriers of national antipathy, has concurred materially to reconcile the dependencies with the metropolis.

The patriotic Pintos, who, unlike modern Christians, sunk their time-honoured surnames to assume some commonplace Portuguese patronymic, and a couple of dozens of the old families in Goa, gave now their support to this new liberal government as consistently as they had formerly resisted the 'reign of terror and oppression.' Even yet it is mostly from their families, scattered over the three

Some element of valour and chivalry, however, inherited from "that nation of heroes" who, doubling the Cape of Good Hope, founded an empire extending from that promontory to the frontiers of China, still lingered in the breasts of the Portuguese of Bassein, and when, on the 19th May 1739, Captain Caetano de Souza Pereira capitulated, and handed over the noble court of Bassein, the seat of hundreds of feudal lords who spent their lifetime here, and whose bones are still there mouldering in vaults covered over by ugly heaps of brick and mortar,—nay, the very nests of venomous reptiles; the scene of many a romantic episode, of violence and martyrdom, of many a valiant soldier and not less heroic missionary; it was like the last groan of a lion that, enfeebled by decrepitude, still frightens his assailant. But "it is a melancholy view to contemplate the fall of nations," says Abbé Raynal. Let us hasten to the narrative of the siege.

The conduct of the Marâṭhâs towards the Portuguese was from the beginning marked by duplicity. They did not even dare to appear before the fort of Bassein until they had first taken possession of a small fort on the opposite side of the river, named Arnalla, and put the commandant and his whole garrison to the sword when their troops crossed.

The Portuguese governor of Salsette, Luis de Botelho, called immediately a council of war, at which it was decided that he should retire to Caranja, leaving Captain Pereira to defend the fort, and Captain Ferraz to command the garrison of Bandora.

A small attack followed, which was gallantly repulsed until the chief officers were severely wounded. Goa being itself distressed by the invasion of the Bhonslês, no aid could be procured thence, nor any assistance obtained from the English authorities at Bombay, notwithstanding constant representations made to them in pathetic terms by Joaõ de Souza Terras.*

All these circumstances concurred subsequently to encourage the Marâṭhâ general, Chimṇâji Appâ, the brother of Peshwâ Bâji Râo, to

---

old provinces of Goa, that have risen those distinguished men who have so honourably represented their native country in the Cortes of Lisbon and elsewhere. The University of Coimbra and the Polytechnic Institute of Lisbon have since those times numbered among their professors not a few of those who are either lineal or collateral descendants of these old patriots of Goa. These facts have their historical significance, and should not remain unknown to the student of Indian annals. For details of the above political blunder see *A Conjuração de 1787 em Goa*, by J. H. da Cunha Rivara, Nova-Goa, 1875.

* *Bombay Quarterly Review*, vol. iv., p. 80.

press the siege, scale its walls, and enter, sword in hand, overwhelming the Portuguese by numbers.

All these operations, however, occupied a considerable time.

When the Marâṭhâs laid siege to Ṭhânâ and Salsette, they took the precaution of occupying the islands of Varsova and Dhârâvi, and the creek between Bassein and the main, to prevent all assistance reaching the forts on the island; then advancing, on the 17th February 1739, and approaching the ramparts by sapping, they commenced the memorable siege of Bassein, which lasted for more than three months, and was conducted with such skill, courage, and perseverance as they have seldom, before or since, displayed. Notwithstanding all these qualities, the Marâṭhâs could not succeed until they had killed the brave commandant, Sylveira de Menezes, and, encouraged by their partial success and the tacit concurrence of the English, had sprung some twelve or thirteen mines, two of which exploded, making a large breach, which they promptly mounted, but a third blew up hundreds of the assailants in the air. The besieged kept up their defence by throwing hand-grenades among the crowds in the rear, and shells and huge stones from mortars* in their batteries and trenches, driving the besiegers away and plying with musketry those who had ascended, thus spreading terrible havoc and slaughter among the enemy. The Portuguese who had come from Europe exhibited prodigies of valour; it was with difficulty that Captain Pereira could restrain them from sacrificing their lives. Many of them would sally out in the dead of the night to attack the besiegers in their lines. The Marâṭhâs at length succeeded in effecting a breach in one of the curtains, but, as it was not large enough to be of use, other mines were fired, which made at last a very large breach under the tower of St. Sebastian, which, having been wholly brought to the ground, was resolutely mounted by the Marâṭhâs, who succeeded in gaining a position from which they could not be dislodged; and the garrison, worn out with famine and fatigue, and having lost the flower of their officers and men, and the sea-face being at the same time blockaded by the Angria, held out a white flag and offered to capitulate.

In this memorable siege the Marâṭhâs lost about 12,000 men in killed and wounded, while on the side of the Portuguese it is said the loss did not exceed 800, and when the treaty of surrender and capitulation was signed, on the 16th May 1739, it was stipulated

---

* Among the relics of the siege, some stone balls about six inches in diameter are still to be seen in a magazine in the fort

that "all the garrison, as well regulars as auxiliaries," should be allowed to march out of the town with all the honours of war, whilst eight days were allowed to those of the inhabitants who so wished, to leave it with all their moveable property.*

In conclusion, I cannot offer a more fitting remark on the subject of this remarkable siege and capitulation of Bassein than by quoting here the following words of an English writer:—"Thus fell a European city in India, as a stately tree, the growth of two centuries, which falls never to flourish again! Melancholy as was the issue, yet no contest had been so glorious for the Indo-Portuguese, in none had they earned such unsullied fame, since the days when Pacheco, with his four hundred countrymen, repelled the Zamorin's army, and Albuquerque twice conquered Goa." The writer then adds, "But no one who ever told the tale of Bassein's last days breathed an insinuation against the honour and courage of its Indo-Portuguese defenders, and this portion of Anglo-Indian annals would have had a brighter hue for us if the English had not been restrained by their calculations and mercantile propensity from rendering the unhappy city more prompt and valuable assistance, if for the sake of England's ancient ally the Government of Bombay had expended some of their increasing treasure, and responded to the moving appeals of the chivalrous Caetano de Souza."†

Bassein now, though in the hands of the Marâṭhâs, did not lose much of its lustre as a city, for it was soon made a *Sar Subhâ* and chief place in that section extending from the Bânkoṭ river to Damaun; but there being no Hindûs of high caste to take the place of those driven away by the Portuguese, Mâdhavarâo Peshwâ offered grants of land free to those who would like to settle in the city or its neighbourhood. He also instituted a tax in support of Brâhmaṇs to purify the native Christians, whom they regarded as polluted Hindûs, before receiving them into their former castes. Both these measures brought down a crowd of Hindûs from Mahârâshṭra and Gujârâshṭra, especially Parabûs, whose influence is still paramount in the country.

Bassein was again restored to the Marâṭhâs by the treaty of Salbai in 1782, and again resumed by the English on the overthrow and deposition of the last of the Peshwâs, in 1818, when it was incorporated into the Bombay Presidency.

To recapitulate, the Marâṭhâs did not long retain possession of

* This treaty is published in the *Bomb. Quart. Review*, vol. iv., pp. 84-85.

† *Bombay Quarterly Review*, vol. iv., pp. 71-87.

Bassein. In 1768 the East India Company began to covet the possession of Bassein and Salsette, and in 1773 Broach, Fort Victoria and Râjâpur were offered to the Marâṭhâ in exchange, but were not accepted. Next year, however, hearing that the Portuguese at Goa, with the aid of the army of 12,000 arrived from Brazil some time before, were preparing to seize Bassein and its dependencies, the Company hastened to take possession of them at once. By the treaty of Surat (1775) Râghobâ, then contending for power, readily ceded them, with other places, in return for the promise of the Company's aid. The Marâṭhâ ministry, however, did not accede to this in 1776, and it was with difficulty that Salsette was retained, while Bassein and other acquisitions were renounced.

Bassein was then taken from the Marâṭhâs by General Goddard's army in the year 1780, after a siege that lasted about twelve days.

The Marâṭhâs, when possessed of Bassein and the districts around, were strong enough to keep a firm hold of them, so much so that Niebuhr, writing in 1764, says : —"Depuis mon départ de ces contrées les Anglois ont tenté de se rendres maîtres de cette isle (Salsette), et, selon les nouvelles, ils doivent avoir fait en effet : mais je ne sais pas s'ils pourront bien défendre Salset contre les grandes forces de terre des Marattes."* A few years after, however, this hold grew loose.

The Portuguese in the meanwhile were, while waiting for a favourable opportunity, devising means to recover their lost province. They seem to have from the beginning nourished the hope of its restoration, the evidence of which is found in letters of the period exchanged between the Court of Portugal and the Viceroyalty of Goa with a political agent at the court of the Peshwâ.† At last, in 1774, the Portuguese sent a formidable armament from Europe for the avowed purpose of recovering their lost possessions, but this circumstance becoming known to the Government of Bombay, the then Governor, William Hornby, "determined to anticipate their enterprise, and seize upon the island for the English."‡ The Viceroy of Goa protested against such a proceeding, qualifying it as "breach of faith," "disregard to the right of nations," "infraction of peace," &c. The letter of the Governor and Captain-General, Dom Frederico Guilherme de Souza,

---

* *Voyage en Arabie*, &c., par C. Niebuhr, traduit de l'Allemand, Amsterdam, 1780, vol. ii., p. 2.

† *Chronista de Tissuary*, vol. ii., p. 158.

‡ Murray's *Handbook for India*, Lond. 1859, vol. ii., p. 305.

dated the 17th July 1780, is addressed thus:—"Honoraveis senhores Governador General e Conselheiros de S. Magestade Britannica na ilha de Bombaim."* This letter is the best index of the severe depression of spirits the Portuguese of India were labouring under at the time. It is but a *réchauffé* of frowns and smiles, of appeals and threats. Dom Frederico now appeals to the friendship of the English, and entreats them to spare the annexation of the Province of the North to their settlement of Bombay; then he says, "If the Government of Bombay insist on doing an act so injurious to good faith, and a breach of peace existing between two friendly and allied nations such as His Britannic Majesty and the Portuguese Crown, then he enters the most formal protest against it," and concludes thus:—"The gentlemen of the noble council ought to reflect that in that case (viz. of annexation) the English Bank runs the risk of losing all the millions that its steamers carry away from Portugal in order to maintain its public credit, and also that of losing all the trade in the parts of Lisbon and Algarve, if Her Most Faithful Majesty (D. Maria I.) ever think of recouping in Europe the damage done by the English to her dominions in Asia," &c.

Such is the half sentimental half diplomatic epistle of the Governor of Goa to the Government of Bombay. The threats are childish, but they indicate one thing, viz. the possession of what the French would call "la force du droit," but not "le droit de la force." Since this unfortunate time the Portuguese Government of India, still reeling under the hard blow struck by its great rival, the English, has not yet regained its former vigour. It continues most piteously to exhibit the same spasmodic and hysterically feminine demeanour in its relations with the foreign nations in India. Instance the Surat factory. It is a relief, however, to pass over from the letter of Dom Frederico to the manly though palpably sophistical reply of William Hornby and the Bombay Council to the Governor of Goa. It runs thus:—

"*To the Honourable Dom Frederick William De Souza, Governor and Captain-General of Her Most Faithful Majesty's Possessions in India at Goa.*

Honourable Sir,—We have now the honour to reply to your Excellency's letter dated the 17th of July, received here in the time of the monsoon.

When the reduction of Salsette was undertaken by the English troops in the year 1774, we received letters of protest from Signor José San-

* *Boletim do Governo, ut suprà*, 1874, No. 97.

ches de Britto, commander of His Most Faithful Majesty's fleet, and from your Honourable predecessor, Dom Pedro José de Camera. Our replies are, no doubt, deposited in the public Archives at Goa, and we conceived were very sufficient; but as your Excellency has now been pleased to revive the subject, and in like manner with your predecessor advanced arguments to prove that the right*........................ countries conquered by the Mharattas near forty-two years ago protested against this Government for an invasion of that right, and endeavoured to alarm us for the safety of the British interests derived from the national alliance with the Kingdom of Portugal, we are constrained to give a more minute reply, lest the public, unacquainted with the real circumstances of the case, should put a disavantageous construction upon our reserve.

We would have wished to confine ourselves to our former answers, because we confess we find a difficulty in treating seriously or with regular arguments a position so contrary to reason and received maxims as the existence of a right of sovereignty in your nation to territories dismembered from its dominions almost half a century, or that a regard on our part to such supposed right should prevent the English from carrying the war into such part of the Mharatta dominions as they may find most convenient or conducive to their success. The English in their proceedings have been governed by the plain dictates of reason, and of the laws of nature and of nations. They are engaged in a war with the Mharattas, and for their own safety and advantage they prosecute it with all possible vigour. They attack the Mharatta dominions wherever they judge an impression may be made with most advantage to themselves, or injury to the enemy, and when their armies come before the walls of a fortress where the Mharatta colours are flying, they are under no necessity to consult history before the batteries are opened to discover the ancient possessor, or to deliberate whether any of them may not possibly have an intention again to attempt the conquest at some future period.

The Portuguese acquired most of their territories in India by conquest and force of arms. In the same manner they were deprived of what they term the Province of the North, and their right consequently expired on the same principle that it originated,

We think it necessary to answer more seriously your charge of our having violated the public faith, and acted contrary to the Treaties

* These words are entirely obliterated.

subsisting between Great Britain and Portugal by the direction of our operations against the parts of the Mharatta dominions.

Your Excellency has endeavoured to support this charge by certain stipulations contained in the capitulations or Act of possession imposed upon the English at the time the Island of Bombay was delivered over to them by the Portuguese:

Were we to allow the fullest validity to those capitulations, or their utmost force to the words you have quoted, the obligation thereby laid upon the English would fall very short of fixing upon us a breach of national treaty: for take those words in their most extensive interpretation, they could only exclude us from making conquests or claims on the Province of the North so long as that Province continued in the possession of the Portuguese, or made a part of their dominions; but that bar has been long removed by its absolute and complete separation and dismemberment, and the consequent dissolution of the Portuguese sovereignty and jurisdiction therein.

As Your Excellency has been pleased to quote the Act of possession as an instrument of validity and a solemn convention between the two crowns, we are under the necessity to display the light in which that agreement was regarded by the King of Great Britain, by whom it was utterly disavowed, though it was far from our wish to revive the memory of disagreeable circumstances which happened so long ago.

His Majesty King Charles the Second, upon complaints of His subjects throughout the East Indies of unfriendly treatment from the Portuguese subsequent even to the Treaty of Marriage, and particularly of the delays and obstacles in the surrender of the Island of Bombay, and the unjust conditions exacted at its delivery, was pleased to send his Royal Letter to the Most Illustrious and Most Excellent Lord Lewis de Mendoza Furtado, then Viceroy at Goa, bearing date the 10th day of March 1675-76, wherein, after premising the bad treatment his subjects had experienced from the Portuguese, He declares his Royal intention in these words:—"Our intention is shortly to elucidate "and explain the eleventh article of the Treaty conjointly with our "aforesaid Brother the Most Serene Prince of Portugal, by whose "justice we doubt not our sovereign rights in the Port and Island of "Bombay and their dependencies will be vindicated from that *very* "*unjust capitulation* which Humphry Cook was forced to snbmit to "at the time when that place was first transferred to our possessions. "Which capitulation neither he, Humphry, was empowered to come "into, nor any one else to impose upon him a contravention to a "compact framed in so solemn and religious a manner. We there-"fore are determined to protest against the said Capitulation as pre-"judicial to our Royal Dignity, and derogatory to our right."

We have also very carefully considered the rights derived by the Portuguese from the Marriage Treaty in that particular point, which is the subject of Your Excellency's complaint.

We find it stipulated in the eleventh article that when the King of Great Britain shall send his fleet to take possession of the said port and island of Bombay, the English shall have instructions to treat the subjects of the King of Portugal throughout the East Indies in the most friendly manner, to help and assist them, and to protect them in their trade and navigation.

The extent and duration of the assistance and protection to be afforded by the English and received by the Portuguese is hereby very clearly limited and defined, and in the secret article the object of this stipulation is expressly declared to be against the States-General of the United Netherlands, with whom Portugal was then at variance; nor can we in any other part of this Treaty, which is the true basis of the relative rights of the two nations in India, and of their mutual claims upon each other, discover the smallest vestige of a title in your nation to the forbearance claimed by your predecessor with respect to the ancient possessions of the Portuguese in the Province of the North.

We have thus shown upon what slight grounds we have been impeached with breach of treaties and violation of public faith; but in what light will this charge be regarded by an impartial world, when, if we required any further justification for our proceedings, the Marriage Treaty itself gives us a most clear and expressed right to any territories formerly belonging to the Portuguese that we might at any time recover, for which the 14th Article makes effectual provision in the following words:—

"Article 14th—If however the King of Great Britain or his subjects "should *at any time hereafter* recover from the States-General of the "United Netherlands, *or from any others*, any towns, castles, or "territories, *that may have belonged heretofore* to the Crown of "Portugal, the King of Portugal with the assent and advice of his "council grants the supreme sovereignty, and the full, entire, and "absolute dominion of the same, and of every of them whatsoever, to

" the said King of Great Britain, his heirs, and successors for ever, " freely, entirely, and absolutely."

After this full explanation of the justice of the grounds upon which we have proceeded, we must, in our own vindication, reject and disclaim your protest as in no wise appertaining or applicable to this Government, and renounce every responsibility for any consequences that may result in Europe from any measures taken by the Crown of Portugal on your representation to the prejudice of the interests of Great Britain, though we have the firmest confidence that our Most August Sovereign His Britannic Majesty will afford those interests the most effectual protection and support from all injurious invasion. It cannot be unknown to you that the Honourable English East India Company, out of regard to the national alliance subsisting between Great Britain and Portugal, incurred a large expense by assistance afforded to the Portuguese in the defence of their possessions in the Province of the North, for which, notwithstanding repeated demands, they have not to this day been reimbursed; we must therefore hope that your Excellency will do justice to the Company, and discharge this debt of so many years' standing.

We are concerned to find that Mr. Henshaw has hitherto been able to obtain so little satisfaction relative to the capture of the English vessel at Mangalore, made by a vessel fitted out from the port of Goa, which will reduce us to a necessity of stating the affair to our superiors in Europe.

This will be presented to your Excellency by Mr. Henshaw, who will also have the honour of delivering to you a packet to your address from the Honourable the Governor General and Council.

We have the honour to be, with highest esteem, Honourable Sir, your most obedient humble servants,—William Hornby, J. Rapel, N. Stackboner.

Bombay Castle, 18th October 1820."*

From the moment this reply was received the Portuguese relinquished all hope of recovering their lost province of Bassein.

The English as early as December 1774 sent a force of 620 Europeans, 1,000 *sipâhis*, and 200 gun *laskars*, under General Robert Gordon, for the reduction of Ṭhâṇâ. The batteries opened on the 26th, and on the 27th an attempt to storm was repulsed with the

* *Boletim do Governo, ut supra*, 1874, No. 96.

loss of one hundred Europeans killed and wounded. Next evening a second assault was given, but with more success, resulting in the whole garrison being put to the sword. The third day of the siege was marked by the loss of Commodore J. Watson, who was killed by particles of sand, struck by a cannon shot close to him, penetrating his body. On the 6th of March, by the treaty of Bassein, the island of Salsette and the territory around was ceded to the English in perpetuity.

By the convention of Wargâm, concluded in January 1779, this latter acquisition, with others, was about to be restored to the Marâṭhâs, but Mr. Hornby disavowed the treaty, and determined at all hazards to resist the cessions to the Marâṭhâs on the one hand, and the entreaties of the Portuguese Government to try their chance of recovery on the other.

Very soon after, the Marâṭhâs cut off the supplies from Bombay and Salsette, which were usually brought to those places from the main, and this was a sufficient *casus belli* for the Government of Bombay to occupy the Konkaṇ opposite Ṭhâṇâ as far as the Ghâṭs, including Kalyâṇa.*

It appears that the representation made by the Governor of Goa to the Court of Portugal and then to the cabinet of St. James had the effect of the Directors of the E. I. Company in London and the Supreme Council at Calcutta denouncing the conquest and annexation of Bassein and Salsette by the Bombay Government as "unseasonable, impolitic, unjust, and unauthorized," and advising them to cancel the treaty. In those times communication with England was so slow that these orders were not received in Bombay until two years after the above events had taken place. Th Council of Bombay, however, protested against and disregarded the orders, being in the end successful in their negotiations. To the intelligent pertinacity of William Hornby and his Council, then, are the Bombay people indebted for the rise and prosperity of the city and its suburbs, which would not be what they are had they remained in other hands.

The town of Bassein is now called Bâjipura, or the city of Bâji Râo, while the whole district is divided into 161 villages, out of which four are *inâms*, and the principal divisions of which are Khani Vadem, where there is a small bandar; the mahâl of Mânikpura in the south-east, where there is a railway station four miles and a half distant from the fort; the mahâl of Aganâsi or Agâsî in the north; Sayavana, re-

* Grant Duff's *History of the Marâṭhâs*, vol. i., pp. 139-141; vol. ii., p. 414.

markable for its fort; the mountainous Tuṅgâr, known by its pagoda called Tuṅgâreśvara, already mentioned; Nirmala, above described; Suparâ, once a famous bandar, but now almost abandoned; and Pâparî, a village about a cannon-shot from Bâjipura, chiefly inhabited by Brâhmaṅs of Chitpâwan, Karâḍa, and Deshâstha divisions,* as well as Palshâs, Sonârs, and other inferior castes of the Hindûs. It yields an annual revenue of about 1,80,630 Rs.†

In 1840 the Court of Directors sanctioned the construction of an embankment across the Kalyâṇa creek to the island of Bassein, which has prevented the encroachment of the sea and reclaimed from it several hundred acres of culturable land, and lately an elegant and solid iron bridge has been built by the B. B. and C. I. Railway, which connects Bassein with Bombay.

The present condition of Bassein is that of a prosperous tâlukâ with its fertile soil, the island being generally low and flat, with the exception of two rugged hills of considerable elevation, laid out in plantain and sugarcane gardens, in which rice and *pân* (*Piper Chavica* or *Piper Betel*) are also cultivated.

In speaking now of the Antiquities of Bassein relative to the Portuguese period, I must begin with the enumeration of several districts that were under the jurisdiction of the "Capital of the North," each of which was as remarkable for the fortifications, churches, and convents it contained as the city of Bassein itself.

Here follows the list:—

Saibana de Baçaim.	A Ilha de Bellaflor de Sambayo.
O Caçabé de Tana.	A Pragana de Manora.
A Ilha de Salcete.	A Pragana de Asserim.
A Ilha de Caranja.	A Ilha de Bombaim.

Each of the above eight divisions consisted of a great number of villages, *tanadarias, mandovins, caçabés, hortâs, pacarias* and *sarretores*. Some of these terms are evidently of Eastern origin; for instance, *caçabé*, which is but the Persian كصب (kasaba), meaning a small town inhabited by decent people or families of rank. Again, *pragana* is the Marâṭhî परगणा (paragaṇâ), meaning a district, of which *caçabé* was the chief town. *Mandovim* is the मांडवी (mâṇḍavî), a custom-house. *Hortas* was the Portuguese term for *wâḍîs*, or groves, orchards, and cocoanut gardens, &c.

---

* Vaupell, *Trans. Bomb. Geog. Soc.*, vol. ii., pp. 138-9.

† ठाणें जिल्ह्या चें वर्णन, p. 26.

Some of the above words have now become quite obsolete; while others, which were either adopted from the natives or probably invented for the occasion, have even ceased to find a place in Portuguese lexicons. They are only found mentioned in official Portuguese documents of the 16th century, and I append them below in the order they are written.

Saibana de Baçaim.

The district thus named consisted of the whole island of Bassein, exclusive of the Fort, and of the land eastward, divided thus:—*Caçabé de Baçaim*, containing sixteen *pacarias* and eight *hortas; Caçabé de Agaçaim*, containing twenty *pacarias* and ten *hortas; Pragaña Salga*, eighteen villages and three *terras; Pragana Hera*, twenty villages; *Pragana Cama*, twenty-five villages and two *sarretores;* and *Pragana Anjor*, eighteen villages and seven *sarretores*.

The above divisions seem from the first to have comprised all the productive villages between Bassein and Tuñgâr. The *Caçabé de Baçaim*, as late as 1695, when visited by Gemelli Careri,* appears to have retained all its outward appearance of a rich and fertile district. It was taken possession of by the Portuguese on the 23rd December 1534, and as it was the custom of its former ruler to receive the revenue half-yearly from his subjects, the Portuguese got all the revenue due for that half-year, beginning, according to the native computation, with the 9th June. The revenue was paid in the Indian coin which the Portuguese chroniclers write *fedea*, equivalent to twelve reis. The amount for the year 1535 was 158,475 fedeas. This sum was derived from taxes and duties levied on the sale of cocoanut oil, opium, cotton, toddy, vegetables, fish, sugarcane, *pân* (*Piper Chavica* or betel), and on the professions of butchers, dyers, Koli fishermen, shepherds, &c.† This district was fortified by a stockade at *Saibana*, garrisoned by a captain, twenty-nine European soldiers, and 530 natives and slaves. The captain had the salary of 300 pardaos, the sum spent on the soldiers amounting to the total of 10,938 pardaos a year.‡

There were, besides, the fortifications of Agâsî, Suparâ, which the Portuguese chroniclers write Sopera, Nilla, and others of less note. That of Agâsî was well equipped with cannon and strongly garrisoned, and had a custom-house. The captain was paid 30,000 reis, and the clerk of

* Churchill's *Collection, ut supra*, vol. iv., p. 190.

† *Subsidios, ut supra*, pt. ii., pp. 140 *et seqq*.

‡ *Chronista de Tissuary*, vol. i., p. 31, and vol. iii., p. 246.

the custom-house 20,000 a year. The fortifications of Suparâ consisted of four wooden stockades, built by General Luis de Mello Pereira. All the above fortifications were last seen and described by Captain Dickinson in 1818, and were soon destroyed;* they have now almost entirely disappeared.

Close to Agâsî there is an island called Arnalla, and formerly *Ilha de vaccas*, or 'cows' island,' by the Portuguese, which commands the southern and main entrance into the Vaitaraṇî river. Its ruins are better preserved, and the buildings were probably repaired by the Marâṭhâs. It appears that before the arrival of the Portuguese this little islet was fortified by the Mahomedans, as evidenced by its domes, Saracenic arches and octagonal recesses, but the greater part of the fortifications were razed to the ground on its acquisition by the Portuguese. It was at last given over, for an insignificant quit-rent, to a Portuguese gentleman of Bassein, who built "an oblong square of about 700 feet with a circular tower," and had there posted a guard of five soldiers. The island is now inhabited, and has only two remarkable objects to notice, besides the fort itself, which is situated on an elevated spot, viz. an inscription in Marâṭhî stating that the fort was built during the reign of Bâjî Rao I. in the Śaka year 1659 (A.D. 1737) by an architect named Bâjî Tûlâjî, and a cave on the western side of the island, which is said to communicate with the sea. The island is divided into several villages, at one of which, by name Bhoegâum, the sea enters, runs through that of Vagholî, and debouches at that of Vatarî.

The whole district is dotted over with churches and convents, the former of which, having been renovated, are mostly in a good state of preservation, the latter in desolate ruins. As the population of Bassein increased, the rural districts became suburban, and mansions of fidalgos, with their private chapels and extramural parishes, arose. Agâsî was the first place of this district visited by Franciscan missionaries. Fr. Antonio do Porto as early as 1535 built there an orphanage for the education and maintenance of 40 boys, under the invocation of *Nossa Senhora da Luz*. This orphanage was destroyed by the Mahomedans in April 1540, when siege was laid to the island of Bassein under the command of the Mahomedan general Bramaluc, as he is called by the chroniclers. Profiting by the death of the Viceroy Garcia de Noronha, and the

* Captain Dickinson's *Report on the Forts of the Northern Konkan*, Govt. Selections, MSS.

absence of his successor Estevaõ da Gama, the Mahomedans fancied that the garrison of Bassein was in a state of disorganization, and invaded the island with an army of 5,000 foot and 3,000 horse. They were, however, most gallantly opposed by Captain Lourenço de Tavora with a mere handful of soldiers consisting of 500 Europeans and a body-guard of 50 chosen men. He surprised them in their own camp in the evening, while most of the men were, as usual with Mahomedans, bathing; and the hand-to-hand fight that ensued was one of the most fierce and terrific ever witnessed in Bassein; the Mahomedan general had at last to beat a retreat, and the king of Cambay, under whose auspices the invasion was planned, did not venture to attack that district again. On their march homewards, however, they plundered the orphanage of Agâsî, and it was here, Franciscan chronicles inform us, that the second batch of Christian martyrs was made, although it consisted entirely of native converts. The first batch of martyrs was made at Thâṇâ, but of this I shall have to speak when treating of that place.

The inmates of the orphanage of Agâsî, hearing of the approach of the enemy, fled precipitately away to take shelter within the walls of the fort of Bassein. Thus many pious orphan boys were saved, but five persons somehow stayed behind, either through illness or old age. The Mahomedans on taking possession of the almost deserted college with the five tenants, tried all means in their power, first of persuasion, and failing in this of cruel tortures, to force them to become converts to their own faith. The Christians resisted unflinchingly both the temptations of safety of life and of high prizes held out to them, preferring to suffer all torments rather than change their creed. The consequence was that they were all shut up in a room of the orphanage and the building set on fire. The poor Christians perished roasted in the lurid flames of the orphanage, and thus "gained," say the chronicles, "the glorious palm of martyrdom."

We hear no more of this orphanage after its burning down; but in 1634 there was a rich monastery of the Dominicans there, besides many handsome houses which were attacked by a Dakhaṇî king, plundered and destroyed.* There were many chapels and churches in the villages thickly populated by a Christian population, the principal being the chapel of *Sam Lazaro*, now in ruins; the parish church of *Sam Joaõ Baptista*, which was in the charge of the Franciscans; and that of *Nossa Senhora dos Remedios*, in that of the Dominicans,

* *Chronista de Tissuary*, vol. iii., p. 219.

both the latter being still in a fair state of preservation. The doors of this church once formed the lateral doors of the church of the Jesuits in the Fort. Diogo do Couto informs us that this church was built by the Dominicans, midway between the fort of Bassein and the village of Agâsî, close to a tank to the waters of which the natives ascribed peculiar virtue in healing the sick. The statement of Diogo do Couto, made about three centuries ago, is fully borne out by the feeling of veneration with which the Hindus of the day regard the waters of that tank. They venerate it now in fact with a vengeance, for during the Portuguese government the Inquisition had put a stop to all pilgrimage to the tank and to the use of its waters, under very severe penalties. Now they hold a *jatrâ* near the tank and a well-supplied fair.

Besides these, there were other churches, out of which the following are still standing, viz.:—*Nossa Senhora das Merces*—which was built by Dom Fr. Aleixo de Menezes, the Archbishop who fought the interesting sect of the Syro-Chaldæans of Southern India*—and that of *Monte Calvario*, both under the charge of the Franciscans. The Augustins had the parish church of *Nossa Senhora da Vida*, sometimes called in old documents *Nossa Senhora da Saude*, and the chapel of the *Annunciada*. All these were situated northward of the Fort. The churches to the eastward were the parish church of *Nossa Senhora da Graça*, of *Sam Thome*, of *Sam Thiago Maior*, and of *Espirito Santo*, which is the oldest among the rural churches, and the only one standing in its primitive state, *i.e.* whose restoration has not interfered with its former shape. All these were under the Jesuits. There is one more, of modern date, dedicated to Sam Miguel Archanjo, and is close to the railway station at *Purim* or Mânikpûra. The old one, on the same spot, belonged to the Jesuits.

Most of the above parishes throughout the island of Bassein are now in a more or less flourishing condition, containing a pretty large population of native Christians, which amounts to the total of 12,400, spread over the island and the adjacent country. They are distributed as follows:—

Pallî	800	Espirito Santo	2,000
Pâparî	1,200	N. S. das Merces	700
Monte Calvario	1,500	Mânikpûra	900
N. S. dos Remedios	3,000	Agâsî	900
Sam Thome	1,000		

* *Chronista de Tissuary*, vol. i., p. 63. Gemelli Careri says that this "small church was founded and served by an Augustinian, who did the office of curate": p. 192.

There are, besides, 400 native Christians at Târâpur, where there is a church of the invocation of *Nossa Senhora do Rozario,* which is included in the *varado de Baçaim, i.e.,* is under the jurisdiction of the Vicar-general of Bassein.

The native Christian population of Pallî had among them a parish church of the invocation of *A Madre de Deus,* but it appears that it has long been in a dilapidated condition.

There was another church, dedicated to the Holy Cross, built, as chroniclers tell us,* in 1560, on a piece of ground prepared from filling up a celebrated tank, the waters of which the Hindus believed were under the protection of a goddess, and purified both the body and the soul of those who used them. They were the Salette or Lourdes of the Hindus. The Jesuits, however, would not allow such an abomination to exist amidst them, especially where a yearly *jatrâ,* or pilgrimage in a semi-civilized fashion, was held, and a sacrifice of a shocking nature, as they inform us, was made. One of the fanatic pagans used to ascend a high tree close by and then cast himself headlong into the sacred pool below, the result being instantaneous death. While one day the *jatrâ* was being held, the Jesuits obtained from the Governor of Bassein a guard of soldiers, and went to the spot, where there was a large concourse of people, whom they put to flight; the pagoda was pulled down, the tank filled up, and on its site erected a temple to the Holy Cross. But the Hindus were not slow to console themselves in some way for the loss of their sacred pool. They soon got another, to which they transferred all the virtues ascribed to the one destroyed by the Portuguese. But even here the Portuguese would not leave them alone in the peaceful enjoyment of their holy waters. So they killed a cow and cast its entrails into the tank, that being considered by a Hindu profanation past all reparation. This tank is supposed to be the one above referred to, close to the church of *Nossa Senhora dos Remedios,* and to which Diogo do Couto refers thus:—"To some lakes particular virtue is ascribed, such as the one midway between Bassein and Agâsî, where the church of Nossa Senhora dos Remedios is built, in which the priests of the order of St. Dominic reside. This Lady has performed so many miracles that all the walls of the church are covered with pictures representing them. In front of the church is the tank,

---

* *Oriente Conquistado, ut supra,* and Juventius's *Epitome Historiæ,* &c., vol. ii., *ut supra.*

to which they attribute so great a virtue that they affirm that any person that gets into it will be healed of any complaint he may have, and the priests watch it with so great care that they never allow any Hindu to approach it, for fear of his performing any superstitious ceremony."* So it appears that the waters of the tank were, after all, either medicinal or mineral waters; or the curative virtues were accorded in consequence of the emotional nature of the individuals who resorted to them. For on what other ground can one account for the praiseworthy impartiality with which the sacred waters bestowed their favours on both the Christian believer and the infidel alike?

That was the way the Portuguese missionaries raised buildings throughout Bassein and the districts under its jurisdiction. It was, not unlike a well-known physiological law, a constant work of destruction and reconstruction, with this difference, that for every half-dozen Hindu temples destroyed they erected one Christian temple, assimilating all the property belonging to them; so they grew fat and became lazy. Philip Anderson says:—"The first people who had numerous congregations for whom they raised solid structures in Bombay and its neighbourhood were the Portuguese. Those zealous Roman Catholics induced a large number of natives to embrace their religion, and they built many Churches, a few of great magnificence. But the Portuguese attained their ends by unlawful means, and the carved stones of Bombay, Salsette, and Bassein, which they profusely raised to God's glory, are after all but records of fraud, rapine, and violence done to heathens' consciences."† This is partially true, and of this we shall meet more instances as we go on describing other districts of the old "Province of the North." But which nation is entirely free from this blame? The church of "Nossa Senhora dos Remedios," called by the natives Remedi, is, like that of Thâṇâ, the largest and most respectable parish church existing in the district, and appears to be renovated in almost the same style as when first built, although there is nothing very striking about its architecture. Gemelli Careri tells us: "Thursday the 3rd (February 1695), I went to visit the image of our lady *De los Remedios*, standing in a parish-church belonging to the Dominicans on the road to *Cassabo*. About five years since this church was burnt by *Kacaji*, a *Gentile*, subject to the *Great Mogul*, who, with a great multitude of

* *Decada* VII., bk. III., chap. x.

† *The English in Western India*, Bomb. 1854, p. 65.

outlaws and four thousand soldiers, went about like a rover, plundering and burning villages."*

The church of Agâsî was built after the destruction of the church and orphanage of the invocation of "Nossa Senhora da Luz." It is in point of time a comparatively recent building, as in that of architecture a very ordinary one. This church was visited in 1760, twenty-one years after the occupation of the island by the Marâṭhâs, by Anquetil du Perron on its feast day, although he was not treated there so hospitably as at the churches of Poinsar and Thânâ. He writes:—"J'arrivai dans cette Aldée (Agacim) le jour de la Fête de l'Église du lieu (16 Décembre 1760), par les plus beaux vergers du monde. Les chemins étoient remplis de Peuple qui se rendoit à l'Église, avec autant de liberté que dans un état Chrétien. Le Curé, occupé après la Messe à traiter les Prêtres Canarins qui l'avoient aidé dans les Cérémonies Ecclésiastiques, ne prit pas garde à moi, quoique mon Palanquin remplît la varangue de sa Maison, et sans une *Signare* qui voulut bien me faire chaufer de l'eau, j'aurois passé mon accès de fièvre sans rien prendre."†

This was on his way back to Surat, after visiting Bassein and the adjacent country, of which he speaks very accurately, and his remarks I shall have to quote from at their proper places. In the meanwhile his itinerary to Bassein from the north is so interesting, referring as it does to the ruins of forts and churches of Chikli, Târâpur, Mahim, 30 miles to the north of Bassein, now rapidly disappearing, that it may be advisable to give a *résumé* of it in the footnote below.‡

---

* Churchill's *Collection*, vol. iv., p. 192. This *Kacagi*, as Gemelli Careri calls him, was the king of Jawâr, called by the Portuguese chroniclers Koli King, who was in the habit of harassing the Portuguese of Bassein without the least warning or a *casus belli.* At last they made a treaty of friendship with him, but of this I shall have more to say hereafter.

† *Zend-Avesta*, &c., par M. Anquetil du Perron, Paris, 1771, vol. i., pp. ccccxxvii-viii. As this work is intended for scholars rather than the general reader the translation from Latin and French texts into English is deemed unnecessary.

‡ He speaks of the Fort of "le Kari de Tchikla" or Chikli thus:—

"Du côté de l'Aldée (Port. *aldea*=village), est un Fort quarré, consistant en quatre courtines flanquées de quatre bastions. Ce Fort commande le Kari; il venoit d'être réparé par les Marates, qui avoient bien la peine à protéger les habitans contre les courses des Pirates. Le bord de Kari est garni d'une espèce de parapet bas, long de cent toises." p. ccclxxix. Kari (*Khâḍi?*)=brackish part of the river. See also *Chronista*, vols. i.-iii.; *Instituto Vasco da Gama*, vol. ii., p. 28; and Vaupell, *Trans. Bomb. Geog. Soc.*, vol. vii., p. 142.

Reduced & Drawn by Ardesheer

MAHIM FORT.

Lieut. John McCluer's Surveys in the Library By. Geog. Soc.

VIEW OF THE LAND ABOUT MAHIM RIVER. Reduced & Drawn by Ardesheer.

Ibid.

VIEW OF THE LAND ABOUT MANORA. Reduced & Drawn by Ardeseer.

Ibid.

VIEW OF THE ENTRANCE OF THE MURVA RIVER. Reduced & Drawn by Ardesheer.

O Caçabe' de Tana'.

The *caçabé* or town of Thâṇâ was divided into eight *pacarias*. It was the seat of numerous rich *fidalgos* from Bassein, who had their

---

The Church of Cikli.

"J'allai descendre chez le Curé des Chrétiens de ce lieu. Il n'étoit pas alors dans l'Aldée. Son père, vieillard respectable, me donna l'hospitalité, et me régala d'une poule bouillie, qui me remit un peu."—p. ccclxxx.

On the way to Târâpur he says:—"On rencontre une petite Pagode quarrée, nouvellement bâtie."

Târâpur.

"La Forteresse Tarapour, réparée par les Marates dans le goût Européen, excepté les bastions du milieu, qui sont en partie ronds et en partie quarrés: en tout, quatre, canons sur les bastions. Le vieux côté de la Forteresse regarde Tchitchen, et le neuf la mer. A une heure vingt-cinq minutes, l'Aldée de Tarapour, dont l'Eglise dépend de celle de Dindou (Dhanu?).

"Je trouvai à Tarapour le Curé Dindou, qui me reçut dans la petite maison qu'il avoit dans l'Aldée, comme j'avais besoin de prendre langue avec lui, et qu'il étoit chargé de me faire avoir quelques Passeports Marates, je n'allai pas plus loin ce jour-là . . . . Ce bon Prêtre se donna encore la peine de me faire chercher deux Beras (coolies) pour compléter mon train . . . . Je quittai le Curé de Dindou, très satisfait de ses soins obligeans, et muni de Lettres pour le Curé da Ponjser, qui étoit l'Aldée de l'Isle de Salcette, la plus proche des Pagodes de Keneri."—pp. ccclxxx-ccclxxxi.

Mahim.

"Kari de Mahim . . . . l'Aldée de ce nom; petit Fort à l'Est de Mahim, formant un triangle flanqué de deux bastions pentagones, l'un au Nord, le second à l'Est: une embrasure à chaque bastion.

"Le Fort de Mahim est longue et baigné en partie par les eaux du Kari, qui est divisé en deux bras par une Langue de terre, dont la pointe répond au pied même du Fort . . . . Le second bras du Kari se passe au batteau. Ce qu'on voit de la Forteresse sur la route est une espèce de courtine basse, détruite, avec des bastions presque ruinés; et plus loin, une porte assez haute joignant la courtine au Sud. A droite du Fort de Mahim, sont des terres noyées."—p. ccclxxxii.

" . . . . Je rencontrai l'Aldée de Khelmi, avec un Fort commencé, dont les murs étoient déjà haut de cinq à six pieds. Près de-là sont trois tours abandonnées . . . . Plus loin, sur le *Kari*, est un bastion quarré, ruiné; ensuite une Eglise détruite."—*Ibid.* "On voit du bord du *Naddi* de Gantora (Dantura river) Bovamelangue, tombeau d'un Santon Musulman, élevé sur les Ghâtes, route le Ponin. Les dévôts y vont une fois l'an en pélerinage. Ce Monument est gardé par des Fakirs, et paroit de loin comme trois Forts."—p. ccclxxxii.

The *Itinerary* of Duperron, relating to Bassim:—"A six heures quarante minutes (du matin), Sipala (Suparâ?) . . . . A sept heures vingt-dix minutes, Vagoli, avec un *Kari* du même nom . . . . Eglise détruite. A sept heures cinquante minutes, Nermal (Nirmala), à deux *cosses* de Bacim; deux étangs; Pagode de Nana, dédiée à Maha Deo (au *Lingam*) . . . . A neuf heures dix minutes (après quelque repos), Gorkof (ou Vaserkot), Forteresse en terre, peu considérable, située sur une montagne, à l'Est. A neuf heures trente-cinq minutes, Guiridji. A neuf heures quarante minutes Vanssi. A dix heures Papri; ensuite Bacim de *Serra*, à l'Est, à une cosse. A dix heures quinze minutes Bacim, le Fort à l'Est."—pp. ccclxxxiii-iv.

villas there, surrounded by pleasant gardens, and whither they used to repair towards evening.

Thâṇâ was an ancient city, once the capital of the Northern Koṅkaṇ and a haven of importance, but long ago superseded, first by Bassein, and then by Bombay. It exists now almost as a thriving suburban town to the latter city, containing a population of about 12,000 inhabitants, since the G. I. P. Railway, which here crosses the strait separating Salsette from the continent, connected it with Bombay on the 16th April 1853, from which it is only twenty-four miles distant. Orme,* however, thinks that Kalyâṇa "existed early in the 14th century as the immediate metropolis of Salsette, Bombay, Bassien, and all the adjacent country, although under a higher power." And of Thâṇâ he writes:—"As no vestiges of magnificence have been discovered at Tannah, and no vessels of burthen can pass beyond it towards Callian, Tannah might be the port of deposit; to which merchants occasionally repaired to transact business with the ships, who, nevertheless, might consecrate the enjoyment of their fortunes to the more splendid residence of Callian." But others found at Thâṇâ "remains of an immense city;" although not so magnificent, perhaps, as those of Kalyâṇa, which were visited by Fryer in April 1675, and described as "the most glorious ruins," "the relics of stately fabrics," &c.† Two miles distant from Kalyâṇa is the village of Ambaranâtha, where a festival, Śivarâtra, is held in the month of Chaitra.

Those of the inscriptions of the Kânheri caves which refer to Kalyâṇa are the following:—

सिधं कलअणिकाय भोइभियाअ
पवइतिंकाय दामिलाय लेण
[पों] ढीच कणड सेले देय धम 卐

Translation.

"To the Perfect One. To Dâmila, inhabitant of Kalyâṇa, famed throughout the world, and purified, the religious assignation of a cave and cistern in the Kaṇha hill. Peace!"

Dâmila is a Buddhist saint of great renown. The inscription is said to be of an early date.

---

* *Historical Fragments*, Lond. 1805, pp. 216-217.

† *A New Account of East India*, *ut supra*, p. 124.

The other inscription runs thus :—

सेध कलय [णक] वसं [यकि सा]
यणसवमतस पुतसनेग
मस धम [नकस उपासाकनं] बुधकानं सहच सवेण परिवा
रेण पाव [नायठापिता] पिलेण पाणिय पोढी आसण पेढिका
योपाधे अ [थेमं] च कमोच देय धंम चातु दिसेभिखु सघह
ति टापित मातपितरो, उदिस सवत हित आवथ एथचे अखम निवीचदता

Translation.

"To the Perfect One. The religious assignation of a cave, a water-cistern, a seat, a cupboard, and a row of couches for the sick. These have been [bestowed] for the sancti[fication] of religious [devotees] and wise men, along with their attendants, by *Dharm*[*anaka*] skilled in sacred learning, son of Sayâna Sarvamata of Vas[ai] (Bassein), near Kaly[âṇa]. Come hither, all you monks from the four quarters [of heaven] to the house established from regard to the (donor's) father and mother. Come hither from every quarter, for here, too, is deposited an imperishable treasure!"

कलियण सुवणकरस समिदाभस सहसायण पनिक देयधम.

Translation.

"The religious assignation of a cistern, fitted to last a thousand seasons, by Samidâbha, a goldsmith of Kalyâṇa."*

The mention of Kalyâṇa in the Kânheri inscriptions, the most modern of which is supposed to be prior to the tenth century of our era, shows that place to have possessed, like Bassein and Suparâ, an ancient reputation.

Further testimony to the antiquity and splendour of Kalyâṇa is found in the *Ratnâmâlâ*, or 'Garland of Jewels,' in which the scene being laid at Kalyâṇa, where Râja Bhuvar the Solaṅkhî reigns in the year of Vikrama 752 (696 A.D.), the Brâhmaṇ Kṛishṇâjî celebrates the glories of the Solaṅkhî princess. The scene is described thus :—

---

* *Jour. Bom. Br. R. As. Soc.*, vol. v., pp. 15, 21, 29.

"The capital city, Kalyâṇa, is filled with spoils of conquered foes, with camels, horses, cars, elephants, jewellers, cloth-makers, chariot-builders; makers of ornamental vessels reside there, and the walls of the houses are covered with coloured pictures. Physicians and professors of the mechanical arts abound, as well as those of music, and schools are provided for public education. It is for the sole purpose of comparing the capital city of Ceylon with Kalyâṇa, that the sun remains half the year in the north, and half in the south."*

On the Mahomedans taking possession of Kalyâṇa, an attempt was made, according to their custom, to change the Hindu name, which means 'a fortunate city,' into Islamâbâd, or 'city of Islam,' but it met with, it appears, no popular acceptance.

The Portuguese had first taken possession of Kalyâṇa in 1535, but not having held it "with a constant garrison" it fell into the hands of the king of Ahmadnagar, then of Bijâpur in 1636, and at last into those of the Marâṭhâs in 1648, one of whom, by name Râmachandra Pant, Governor of Kalyâṇa, had a treaty of alliance drawn and signed with the Captain General of Bassein, dated the 10th January 1724.† Some of the Portuguese noblemen of Bassein had erected *quintas* or villas at Kalyâṇa.

No cave-inscriptions refer to Thâṇâ, but there are slabs and copper-plates, mostly of the Middle Ages, discovered in and about the old town, the *Śrî Sthânaka* and *Puri* of the Silhâra family, which distinctly allude to Thâṇâ. The mention of one of these copper-plates will be sufficient to give an idea of all the rest. This one was found in digging foundations for some new works in the fort of Thâṇâ in 1787, and purports to be a grant of land. It is dated Śaka 939 (1078 A.D.). A Hindu Râja, by name Arikesara Devarâja, sovereign of the city of Tagara, addresses "all who inhabit the city Śrî Sthânaka ('the mansion of Lakshmî,' or 'the prosperous city'), his own kinsman and others assembled there," &c.‡

Of the Arabian geographers and travellers of the Middle Ages who mention Thâṇâ as the capital of the Koṅkaṇ I have spoken more at length elsewhere.§ Marco Polo was at Thâṇâ about the end of the 13th century, and gives an account of it as follows:—

* A. K. Forbes's *Râs Mâlâ*, vol. i., p. 26.

† *Boletim do Governo do Estado da India*, 1874, p. 116. Tâlukâ Kalyâṇa contains 340 villages, of which 19 are inâms. It yields an annual revenue of about Rs. 1,79,024, of which Rs. 13,486 are given to inâmdârs.

‡ *As. Res.*, vol. ii., p. 357.

§ See *ante*, p. 14.

"Tanna is a great kingdom lying towards the west, a kingdom great both in size and worth. The people are idolaters, with a language of their own, and a king of their own, and tributary to nobody. No pepper grows there, nor other spices, but plenty of incense; not the white kind, however, but brown.

"There is much traffic here, and many ships and merchants frequent the place; for there is a great export of leather of various excellent kinds, and also of good buckram and cotton. The merchants in their ships also import various articles, such as gold, silver, copper, and other things in demand.

"With the king's connivance many corsairs launch from this port to plunder merchants. These corsairs have a covenant with the king that he shall get all the horses they capture, and all other plunder shall remain with them. The king does this because he has no horses of his own, whilst many are shipped from abroad towards India; for no ship ever goes thither without horses, in addition to other cargo. The practice is naught and unworthy of a king."*

Ibn Batûta (1334, Priaulx) also speaks of Thâṇâ as Kukin-Tâna, although he never visited it; but from its fame mentions it as one of the ports from which great ships used to go to Aden.† Some time before, Edrisi had described Thâṇâ as "a pretty town upon a great gulf where vessels anchor from whence they set sail;"‡ and although this looks rather exaggerated, Gildemeister§ has no doubt that "Thâṇâ was the only port known to the Arabs between Broach and Goa." Giovani Botero, although he speaks of Thâṇâ as containing "the remains of an immense city" and "a town that still contained 5,000 velvet-weavers," never saw it. He was charged by the Congregation *de propaganda fide* to collect and write notices of Christian missions. He was born in 1540, was in Spain in 1599, and died in 1617, without ever coming to India.

About twenty years before the conquest of Thâṇâ by the Portuguese the town is described by Duarte Barbosa under the name of Tana-mayambu thus:—"Twenty-five leagues further on the coast is the fortress of the before-mentioned king (king of Gujarât), called Tana-mayambu, and near it is a Moorish town, very pleasant, with many

* Yule's *Marco Polo*, vol. ii., p. 330.

† *Ibid.*, p. 302.

‡ Elliot, *ut supra*, vol. i., p. 89.

§ *De Rebus Indicis*, p. 46.

gardens, and very fertile—a town of very great Moorish mosques and temples of worship of the Gentiles. It is nearly at the extremity of the kingdom of Cambay or Guzarat, and it is likewise a seaport, but of little trade. And there are in this port small vessels of rovers like watch boats, which go out to sea, and if they meet with any small ship less strong than themselves they capture and plunder it, and sometimes kill their crews."* About a century before the arrival of the Portuguese, Thâṇâ was the scene of a fierce and long-continued struggle between the rival princes of the Dakhaṇ and Gujarât, until at last the Dakhaṇ monarch was entirely driven out of it in 1428. Exactly one century after—in 1528—Heitor da Silveira, after the defeat of the fleet of the Gujarât king in the Bombay waters, was extorting tribute of the panic-stricken Governor of Thâṇâ, Salsette, and Bombay, who appears to have owed fealty to the Gujarât prince, or had perhaps long been, as Elphinstone† believes, an independent little rajah, his small territory being a detached possession of the Gujarât kingdom.

Ferishta, as translated by Briggs, has the event thus recorded:—"In the same year (1428 A.D.) Kûtibkhan, the Governor of Mahim, dying, Sultân Ahmadshâh Bâhmanî thought this a favourable opportunity to obtain possession of that island, which he effected without loss."‡ He adds—"Tannah was taken at the same time. Among the articles captured on the island of Mahim were some beautiful gold and silver embroidered muslins, with which vessels were laden and sent to Ahmedabad."§

Elsewhere we are told that before the Mahomedans came to Thâṇâ, the town and the adjacent country were under the rule of the Bhaṅgolîs and Bhaṇḍârîs. The origin of this race is rather obscure. Mention is, however, made of it in the *Brahmottara Khaṇḍa* of the *Skanda Purâṇa* and in the *Kathâ Kalpataru*, wherein it is said that the progenitor of this race, by name Bharaguna, was created by Śiva for the purpose of bringing to him sweet toddy to allay his thirst after a severe fight with a demon. Bharaguna having thus acquired the esteem of Śiva was by him raised to the dignity of a treasurer, hence his name of Bhaṇḍârî, from भडार treasure. The Bhaṅgolîs are said to be a mere tribe of the Bhaṇḍârîs, so called from blowing their भोंगळी, a trumpet or cornet. It is

* *A Description of the Coasts*, &c., *ut supra*, pp. 68-69.

† *History of India*, Lond. 1854, p. 679.

‡ Briggs's *History of the Mahomedan Power in India*, Lond. 1832, vol. iv., p. 28.

§ *Ibid.*, p. 30.

supposed that on the overthrow of the Bhaṇḍârî rule the Mahomedans took possession of the country, and then gradually extended their power and mastered the neighbouring peoples. When the Portuguese arrived, it is stated that Bahâdur Khân, who was Governor of Bassein at the time, was allured by the former with the hope of gain, and consented to their establishing a factory there, which was to be seen, according to chroniclers, as early as 1526, and was eventually, as we have already learnt, changed into a fortress and the capital of all the northern settlements of the Portuguese in India. In the meanwhile the Bhaṇḍârîs and Bhaṅgolîs were all astir. Not being slow to profit by the advent of the new European comers, they sided with the latter for the expulsion of the Mahomedans, and thus perhaps retained, as at Chaul and elsewhere, those privileges of trumpeter chiefs, as they were called, to which there was no interruption since the dominion of the Portuguese.*

It appears that the Portuguese, subsequent to the conquest of Thâṇâ, harassed as they were with constant quarrels with the neighbouring princes, had little time or inclination to study the antiquities of the place, rich field though it be for study. But one day a Portuguese nobleman by name Dom Antonio de Souza, who was laying the foundation of his house at Thâṇâ, happened to discover in the excavations made among the ruins of a pagoda an engraving of a friar, which the chronicler believes was that of Friar Jordanus, of the order of Dominicans, who, after having buried his four fellow-missionaries, of the order of Franciscans, two of whom were presbyters and two lay brothers, was killed and buried there.†

The subject of the martyrdom of Jordanus being yet a *quæstio vexata*, let us first examine into its origin, and see who this Jordanus was.

Friar Jordanus was a Frenchman; he is said to have been a native of Séverac. But there being at least five places of the name of Séverac in France, it is difficult to determine to which of these should be accorded the honour of being his birthplace. It appears probable, however, that he was born in one of the three places in the district of Rouergue, in the department of the Aveyron, from a noble family, called from this province De Séverac, and which gave to France in the time of Charles VII. a Marshal by name Amaulry de Séverac. He is also called *Catalani*, which is supposed to be the genitive of his father's name.‡

* *Trans. Bomb. Geog. Soc.*, vol. i., p. 134.

† *Oriente Conquistado, ut supra*, tome I., conq. i., div. i.

‡ *Mirabilia Descripta*, translated by Col. Henry Yule, Lond. 1863, p. iv.

The dates of his birth and death are yet unknown, nor is there anything, in spite of papal bulls, to guide us as to the age at which Jordanus was appointed Bishop in India and first started for this country.

It is simply surmised that he was at first one of a party of twelve friars that, under the guidance of that venerable soldier of his order the well-known Thomas of Tolentino, journeyed to the East as early as 1302, proceeding first to Negropont and afterwards to Thebes.* That party was chiefly composed of Franciscans.

There are no other documents relating to Friar Jordanus than his two letters addressed to members of his own order (the Dominican), and to that of St. Francis, residing in Persia, found in a MS. in the National Library of Paris, and his own little work *Mirabilia Descripta*, the date of which is still undetermined. This work was first printed in France in 1839 by M. Coquebert Montbret, translated into English by Col. Yule, and published by the Hakluyt Society in 1863. Of the two other letters, the first is dated 12th October 1321 from Gogo, and the other 20th January 1324 from Thâṇâ. On the receipt of his second letter the Vice-Custos of the Dominicans in Persia, by name Nicolaus Romanus, is stated to have started for India. The only remaining document of any interest to the biography of Jordanus is a bull of Pope John XXII., the date of which is said to be equivalent to 5th April 1330, addressed to the Christians of Columbus or Columbum (modern Coulam or Quilon), and intended to be delivered to them by Jordanus himself, who was nominated Bishop of that place.† One of his letters appears to imply, however, that he had been to Columbum before his landing at Thâṇâ with the Franciscans, and that his *Mirabilia*, the heading of which sets forth his episcopal designation, was written in the interval between 1328, when he was appointed to that office, and 1330, when he is said to have left Europe.‡

The centre of the missionary operations was then Sultania in Persia, the seat of the Persian monarchy prior to its overthrow by Tamerlane. Here an Archbishop, by name John de Core, was appointed by the Pope. This metropolitan had three bishoprics—Tabriz, Semiscat or Samarkand, and Columbum—under him, and when Jordanus came to

* *Cathay, ut supra*, p. 184.

† *Mirabilia*, p. vii.

‡ *Cathay*, p. 184.

India he was deputed, together with the Bishop of Semiscat, Thomas of Mancasola, to carry the *pallium* to the archbishop.

But what is curious in the sequence of the narrative is that John de Marignolli, or John of Florence as he is called, who was a Minorite sent out to China as a legate from the Pope to the Great Khan, and was at Columbum only twenty years later, in December 1346 or 1347, probably the latter, although he mentions a church of St. George of the Latin communion there, is absolutely silent on the episcopate of Jordanus. And not only in the work of Marignolli, but in the works of several others who have written on the Syrian Christianity of Malabar, such as the Dominican Friar Navarrette in 1613, Father Vincenzo Maria in 1672, Michael Geddes in 1694, La Croze in 1723, down to Fra Paolino, Hough, and others in more recent times, except Whitehouse, who quotes from Yule's *Cathay* and *Mirabilia,* the name of Jordanus is simply conspicuous by its absence. It is known, moreover, that from the time of his alleged episcopate down to the arrival of the Portuguese, there was no Roman Catholic place of worship in the town of Quilon until Affonso Albuquerque imported a Dominican friar by name Roderic, who built a church there.*

But if there is so much doubt hanging over the fact whether Jordanus ever went to Columbum, there is little about one individual of that name having come to Thâṇâ. The question then arises, Was this the same that was going to Columbum? For the Portuguese claim him as a countryman of theirs, and the hagiologist Cardozo† declares that "Jordanus himself was eventually a martyr to the faith," but without particulars or evidence. These particulars are supplied by Pe. Francisco de Souza,‡ but they are unauthenticated. The only authority, then, that remains to be consulted on this obscure question, and which appears to throw some light on it, is the Franciscan friar Odoric of Friuli, commonly called *De Portenau,* a native of Pordenone, who came out as a missionary to Trebizonde, Ormuz, and Malabar, and after travelling sixteen years in the East returned in 1330 to Europe, and, having dictated his travels to G. de Solagna by order of his superior, died in the odour of sanctity on the 14th January 1331, which day is in the Roman Catholic calendar dedicated to his praise.§

* Rev. Thomas Whitehouse's *Lingerings of Light in a Dark Land,* Lond. 1873, p. 29.

† See *Kunstman* in Phillips and Görres, xxxvii., p. 152.

‡ *Oriente Conquistado, ut supra.*

§ *Acta Sanctorum,* January 14, tome i., p. 986.

He refers to the martyrdom of four Franciscan missionaries at Thâṇâ, but to Jordanus he does not even condescend to make the remotest allusion, which is, to say the least of it, extraordinarily strange. Can saints be jealous?

Regarding the martyrdom of the four Franciscans at Thâṇâ, if one collates the statements of Jordanus and Odoric he will find that the former, in his second letter, dated 20th January 1324, relates that having started from Tabriz to go to Cathay, he changed his mind and sailed towards Columbum with four Franciscan missionaries, but they were driven by a storm to Thâṇâ, in India, where they were received by Nestorians. There he left his companions, and, as he knew the Persian tongue well, he started for Broach, hoping to preach with success. He was detained, however, at Supera (Suparâ), and there he heard that his four brethren at Thâṇâ had been arrested. He returned to aid them, but found they had been put to death. He was, however, enabled to remove the bodies of the martyrs by the help of a young Genoese whom he found at Thâṇâ, and having transported them to Suparâ he buried them in a church there as honourably as he could. This, he says, took place two years and a half before the date of his letter, and he concludes by asking for more missionaries after the numerous conversions he had made at Broach and between Thâṇâ and Suparâ.*

There is, however, another work—a chronicle ending with the year 1320, which purports to have been written by one Jordanus, and has been traced with some plausibility to our author, although Muratori (*Antiq. Ital. Medii Ævi*, vol. iv., pp. 949 *et seqq.*) gives a number of extracts, and states "the author's apparent interests are to be Venetian and Franciscan." This chronicle gives minute details of the martyrdom, but being too long to enter here I give it in short.

Certain brethren of the orders of Minors and Preachers were sent on a mission to Ormus, but, finding that they could do no good there, they thought it well to go over to Columbum in India. On their arrival at Diu † the brethren of the order of Minors separated from the rest of the party, and set out by land to Thâṇâ, that they might there take ship for Columbum. Now there was at Thâṇâ a Saracen of Alexandria named Yusuf, who summoned them to the presence of the Malik, or gov-

---

* *Mirabilia, ut supra*, pp. vi.-vii., and *Cathay*, pp. 225 *et seqq.*

† Diu claims also the honour of having given birth to a saint, by name Theophilus, in the time of Constantine, whose foot is now being carried about in Goa, I am told, working miracles.

ernor of the land. He then demanded "what manner of men were they called." They answered that they were Franks, devoted to holy poverty and anxious to visit the shrine of St. Thomas. He questioned them on their faith, and they replied that they were Christians. The Malik then let them go; but Yusuf persuaded him to arrest and detain them. At length Malik, Kâzi, Pagans and Saracens questioned the brethren: "How can Christ, whom you call the Virgin's Son, be the son of God, seeing that God has not a mate?" They gave many instances of divine generation, and the infidels could not resist "the spirit that spoke in them."

Then at last the Saracens kindled a great fire and said to them, "You say that your law is better than the law of Mahomet; if it be so, go you into the fire and by miracle prove your words." The brethren replied that for the honour of Christ they would freely go. Brother Thomas then came forward to go in first, but the Saracens would not allow him to do so, he seeming older than the others. Then came the youngest of all, James of Padua, and incontinently went into the fire, and abode in it rejoicing and uttering praise, and without burning even his hair. Now those who stood by shouted with a great cry, "Verily these are good and holy men!" But the Kâzi, willing to deny so glorious a miracle, said: "I do not think so; his raiment is come from the land of Abraham." Then they stripped the innocent youth and all naked he was cast by four men into the fire; but he went forth from the fire unscathed. Then Malik set them free, but the Kâzi and Yusuf, bearing them malice for having been entertained in the house of a certain Christian, said to Malik, "If you let them go, all will believe in Christ, and the law of Mahomet will be utterly destroyed." Malik replied that he found no cause for capital punishment. But they said, "If one cannot go pilgrim to Mecca, let him slay a Christian, and he shall obtain a full remission of sins." Then the night following Malik sent officers who "despatched the three brethren, Thomas, James, and Demetrius, to the joys of heaven, bearing the palm of martyrdom." After a while brother Peter, who was in another place, presented himself, when after two days' sore afflictions, on the third they cut off his head and accomplished his martyrdom.*

Then Jordanus took away their bodies and buried them, as above stated, at Suparâ. Wadding† relates that soon after their death great

* *Mirabilia*, pp. x. *et seqq.*

† *Annales Minorum.*

miracles were wrought. One of these was that Friar Jordanus cured the young Genoese who had helped him to bury the bodies, of a bad dysentery, by means of a tooth of Thomas of Tolentino. Again, one Giovannino, son of Ugolino of Pisa, a merchant, having been lucky enough to appropriate the head * of one of these martyrs, saved his ship when attacked by pirates, by holding out this head as a buckler, whilst his two consorts were captured. And a part of the relics were deposited in the house of their order at Sultania, where they gave rise to further marvels, but nothing of this sort has come down to us from Jordanus himself.†

The account of Odoric is still longer. But it is in substance just about the same as that of Jordanus, with only a few discrepancies. He says that having embarked on board a vessel called *Jase* (جهاز), Persian *Jahaz*, a generic name for ship, after twenty-eight days he landed at Ṭhâṇâ, "where for the faith of Christ four of our Minor Friars had suffered a glorious martyrdom." He adds that whilst the friars were staying in the house of a Christian at Thâṇâ one day there arose a quarrel between the good man of the house and his wife, and in the evening he gave her a sound beating, In the morning the woman went and made a complaint of the beating to the *Cadi* قاضي, (Kâzi,) or Bishop and Magistrate, and the latter having asked if she had any proof of what she alleged, she answered that there were four "Frank Rabbans" or monks. They were sent for. Their names were Thomas of Tolentino, James of Padua, Demetrius, a Georgian lay brother "good at the tongues," Friar Peter of Senna being left at home to take care of their things. After some discussion on religion, the Kâzi asked Friar Thomas what he thought of Mahomed; the friar replied that "Mahomed was the son of perdition, and had his place in hell with the devil his father." When the Saracens heard this, they all began to shout with a loud voice together, "Let him die, let him die, for he hath blasphemed the Prophet." Then, after the friars were killed, "the Christians," Odoric continues, "who were in that place, seeing this, took the bodies, and caused them to be committed to the tomb," thus avoiding all mention of Jordanus and the martyrs' burial at Suparâ. At last Odoric says that he opened their tomb and humbly

* The alleged skull of Thomas was afterwards carried from India to Italy, and was in the 17th century, and may be still, preserved at his native place of Tolentino, where his feast used to be celebrated by his fellow-townsmen, who held a fair on that day (*Acta Sanctorum*, 1st April).

† *Cathay*, p. 73.

and devoutly took up their bones, and they wrought many miracles; and that the natives of the place "when caught by any disease, they go and take of the earth of the place where the friars were slain, and wash it in water and then drink the water, and so are immediately freed from all their ailments,"*—which sounds like a parody of the tomb of the apostle St. Thomas, and of some Buddhist Śrâmaṇas.

There is here one discrepancy in date which requires correction. We have seen that the letter of Jordanus Redivivus, as he is sometimes called, which mentions the martyrdom of the Franciscan friars, is dated 20th January 1324, whereas the chronicle attributed to him is dated 1320. But according to the *Acta Sanctorum* of the Bollandists the martyrdom took place on the 1st April 1322, or the Thursday of the week before Palm Sunday of that year; while the celebrated traveller Odoric of Friuli was at Thâṇâ in the same year, and sent home a letter describing the martyrdom as having occurred in the preceding year. Thus this error in date, and the martyrdom of Jordanus himself at Thâṇâ, after having buried the four Franciscan missionaries, remain yet to be corrected and confirmed. The martyrs appear as *Beati* in the *Acta Sanctorum*, and their feast is celebrated on the Wednesday of the Holy Week.

Of Thâṇâ Odoric writes:—"The city is excellent in position, and hath great store of bread and wine (one of his MSS. has 'abundance of victuals, but especially of butter, of *sesuan* [sesame?] and of rice'), and aboundeth in trees. This was a great place in days of old, for it was the city of king Porus, who waged so great a battle with king Alexander.† The people thereof are idolaters, for they worship fire, and serpents, and trees also. The land is under the dominion of the Saracens, who have taken it by force of arms, and they are now subject to the Empire of *Dili*."‡ The name of Dili has by some been

---

* *Cathay*, pp. 57-62 *et seqq.*

† Col. Yule says that Gasparo Balbi (1580) speaking of the cave of Elephanta, "at Cape Bombaim," says that it was formed by Alexander the Great to mark his furthest conquest. This may have been, he thinks, a current Mahomedan story, and might account for Porus being translated to Thânâ. I have noticed the same story in Portuguese writers of the sixteenth century and others, as well as that of the caves being built by the Chinese. But may not the word Porus have been first conjectured by some European writers at Thânâ, who thought they had found that name in the sound of Purî, applied to that city, to mean the name of the king? See *ante*, p. [illegible].

‡ *Cathay*, pp. 57-58.

rendered into Deli, and by others into Dodri. The Sultân of Delhi at this time must have been Gherass-uddin Toghlak, who ascended the throne in 1320. This Sultân ordered the Malik and his family to be put to death on account of his cruelty to the martyrs. The Kâzi on hearing this fled from the city and the emperor's dominions.

There is another point in this narrative which requires to be noticed. Jordanus tells us that he buried the Franciscan friars at *Supera.* Now this place, which is evidently the *Soupara* of Ptolemy and *Oopara* of the *Periplus*, was supposed by the French editor of Jordanus's *Mirabilia* to be the *Sefara el Hind* of the Arabs, which he places on the north of the first great river south of the Namadies (Narbadâ), *i.e.* Tapti, over against Surat, probably as the ancient representative of the fort of Suali.* It is the *Sufâlah* of Abulfeda, a contemporary of Jordanus, and of which place Gildemeister writes, *de cujus sitû omnis interiit memoria.* D'Anville places Supara at Siferdam.

Lassen thinks Suparâ to be a corruption of the Sanskṛit *Śurpâraka*, which means 'fine shore.' But this name is applied by Purâṇic writers to the Paraśurâmakshetra, from its winnow-shaped shore—from सूर्प (*sûrpa*), a winnow.† In the *Atlas Antiquus* of Sprunner-Menke I notice the word Śurpâraka placed about the Tapti, but there is no justification for such a location. Mas'ûdi says, "*Separa* is four days' journey from Cambay," while Albîrûnî writes:—"From Sindan to *Subarah* 6 parasangs; and from thence to Tanah is 5 parasangs" (Reinaud, *Frag. Arab. et Pers.*, p. 121), which is supposed by Mr. Burgess (see *Notes of a Visit to Gujarât*, Bomb. 1863, p. 13, and *Ind. Ant.*, vol. i., p. 321) to be identical with the Suparâ near Vasâi, an identification that has merited the approval of Col. Yule (see *Ind. Ant.*, vol. ii., p. 96), who says moreover that *Idrisi* refers to it thus:—"They fish for pearls here. It is in the vicinity of Bâra, a small island on which some cocoanut trees and the costus grow." We know nothing of pearl-fishery about Suparâ, but may not Bâra be another Mahomedan per-

* Vincent's *Periplus*, p. 385; *Mirabilia*, p. vi. See Reinaud's *Mém. sur la Géog.*, *ut supra.*

† शूर्पारकक्षेत्र (Surpârakshetra), a name applied to the western coast of the Paraśurâmakshetra, as newly acquired land extending from the river Vaitaranî to the Cape Kumâri (Comorin), and from the Sahyâdri Range to the Arabian Sea, is placed by Purâṇic geographers outside the then known world, which was divided into seven continents, thus:—Jâmbudvîpa, Gomeda, Shalmalî, Kusha, Krauncha, Shâka, and Pushkara.

version of Vasâi? Regarding the narratives of the missionary travellers I must not omit to mention that grave doubts have been raised on the genuineness of Jordanus's travels. Frequent extraordinary coincidences of statement and almost of expression have been noticed between this writer and Marco Polo, and what is not contained in Polo is supposed by Col. Yule to be pilfered from "the traditional yarns of the Arab sailors with whom they voyaged, some of which seem to have been handed down steadily from the time of Ptolemy—peradventure of Herodotus almost—to our day."* It may truly be said with the same writer:—"The more we learn, the further goes back the history of Eastern navigation:" p. 31.

Suparâ is also referred to in an inscription of the Kânheri caves thus:—

	Translation.
सापारगा नगम स समि कुपासक स पांदी दंयधम.	"The tank of Samyakupâsaka, skilled in sacred learning, of the town of Suparâ. A religious assignation."

The Rev. Dr. Stevenson thought† that Suparâ or Sopâr was the town of Sûpa or Sopa, thirty miles to the south-east of Puṇâ. Had that learned Orientalist known of the existence of the town of Suparâ in the proximity of the caves, he would certainly not have gone so far to identify it.

About the date of this and other inscriptions in the Kânheri caves I have already said enough elsewhere.

It is also doubted whether Odoric ever visited the East. But this is carrying one's scepticism rather too far. He may not have visited Cathay (China), Sumatra, &c., but of his visit to Thâṇâ there is, it appears, not the least doubt. Thus we have it that in Thâṇâ, now one of the suburbs of the city of Bombay, four Franciscan missionaries, comrades of Friar Jordanus, suffered martyrdom at the hands of the Mahomedan Governor in 1321, were buried at Suparâ near Bassein, and their bones removed to Europe by Friar Odoric only a year or two later.

It is apparent from the above statements that Thâṇâ when visited by Jordanus and Odoric was under a Musalmân Governor, subject to the Delhi sovereign, while only forty years before, at the time of Marco

* *Mirabilia*, p. xvii.

† *Jour. Bom. Br. R. As. Soc.*, vol. v., p. 19.

Polo, it was still under a Hindu prince, and it was during the interval that this change took place.

Abulfeda, who was, as above stated, a contemporary of Jordanus and Odoric, speaks of Thâṇâ as "a very celebrated city of trade for producing a kind of cloth which was called *Tanasi.*"* The cloth has still retained its former name, and is as well known among the Portuguese at Goa and elsewhere as *roupa de Thaña* as in Bombay, where it is almost daily hawked about the streets as "Thâṇâ cloth," although the importation of new fabrics from Europe and the establishment of mills in Bombay appears to have lessened the demand for it, and interfered with the reputation it once enjoyed.

Before drawing the subject of Jordanus and Odoric to a close, it is necessary to advert to another point which requires elucidation. Both the friars mention that there were at Thâṇâ in their time about fifteen Christian families of the Nestorian sect. In the seventh century Cosmas Indicopleustes also refers to a Persian Bishop at Kalyâṇa, and there must have consequently been a Christian congregation of the same denomination. Nevertheless, when the Portuguese came to Thâṇâ there was no Christian of any sect to be found there. In the interval between the martyrdom of the four Franciscans and the arrival of the Portuguese they seem to have disappeared, or, anyhow, abandoned the place. But what is really surprising is that Philip Anderson should tell us that "Sir Thomas Herbert found also Christians of St. Thomas at Thâṇâ amongst other places," and then add, "We are glad to ascertain how they appeared to an intelligent Englishman of the seventeenth century."† But the "intelligent Englishman of the seventeenth century" never said such a thing. What Sir Thomas Herbert refers to is Tanor, and *not* Thâṇâ.‡ Tanor, now Tanore or Tannûr, was a mediæval port of Malabar, and an ancient city with many Christian inhabitants, and the seat of an independent râjâ. It was well known to the early Portuguese writers.§ It is a pity that so excellent a work in other respects as *The English in Western India* is, should contain such a wrong interpretation and hasty conclusion. But this is not the only one of his blunders. Mr. J. H. da Cunha Rivara says:—

* Yule's *Marco Polo*, vol. ii., p. 331.

† *The English in Western India*, Bomb. 1854, p. 64.

‡ *Some Years' Travels into Divers Parts of Africa and Asia the Great*, Lond. 1665, p. 357.

§ See *Decadas*, Barros, tome i., pt. ii., p. 159; and Diogo do Couto, tome i., pt. i., p. 259.

" Philip Anderson...........has extracted from Pyrard these events (in Surat) relative to the English, but briefly and inexactly. Among other inaccuracies we shall point out one; speaking of these Englishmen ....Pyrard says, '*mais ils eurent temps de tirer leurs deux bateaux et de s'embarquer dedans environ quatre-vingt qu'ils estoient,*' &c., while Anderson writes, 'The crew, twenty-four in number, having contrived to reach the shore near Surate,' &c., thus making *quatre-vingt* 'twenty-four,' instead of eighty, with great discredit to his erudition, and serious disturbance of the order and sense of history, which nobody has the right to alter."*

The fortifications built by the Portuguese at Thâṇâ consisted of two towers and one small square fort with two bastions at opposite corners, well placed so as to command two creeks on both sides. It appears that the latter place is now called Kâmbê, about one mile north-west of Bhivaṇḍî, and of the two creeks Lakivlî and Bhivaṇḍî itself, which form the estuary of the Kâmwârî river. About two miles distant there is a hamlet called Firangpâḍâ, and this was once a Portuguese *quinta*, or villa residence, much resorted to by the Thânâdâr and Captain of Thâṇâ. Close to these forts are some wells which are also the work of the Portuguese.

The above fortifications were inspected and described by the two aforementioned Portuguese officers, in 1634 and 1728. The two round towers were called after the names of Sam Pedro and Sam Jeronimo, and the square fort with two bastions Reis Magos. They had first a small garrison of eight soldiers (reduced to four) under a captain, and were equipped with four guns. They were, until their capture by the Marâṭhâs, incomplete, and although urged by the above-mentioned inspectors to complete some, and build others, the Government seems to have turned a deaf ear to them, to repent of it at the last moment. Grant Duff says that the recommendation to build a new fort was at last acted upon, but with too little vigour, for the fatal year 1739 arrived before it was finished.† They had besides the above garrison one bombardier, one torchbearer, and a boat with two rowers. The disbursements on each of the fortifications made by the Factors of Bassein amounted to about 700 xerafins a year. The Governor of the town of Thâṇâ, who was called *Thânâdâr*, or more properly a collector, had the salary of 30,000 reis a year, and five peons under him. One *ouvidor* or judge

* *Viagem de Francisco Pyrard*, Nova Goa, 1862, vol. ii., p. 234.

† *History of the Marâṭhâs, ut suprà*, p. 237.

had 100,000 reis, and five peons; one *meirinho*, or police magistrate, 18,000, and eight peons; one jail-keeper 12,000, and two peons; and one clerk of the *mandovim*, or custom-house, 20,000. The yield of the customs dues of Thâṇâ was about the average of 16,000 pardaos a year.*

There was in 1634 one Cathedral at Thâṇâ, named 'A Igreja da Sé' under a vicar; one parish church of the invocation of Sam Joaõ; a convent of the Augustins with twenty monks; one of the Jesuits with eleven inmates; another of the Capuchins with twelve; and one of the Dominicans with two. Outside the town there were two chapels, one of the invocation of "Nossa Senhora do Rozario" under the Jesuits, and another of "Nossa Senhora da Graça" under the Augustin friars. Each of the above convents had 500 xerafins a year from the royal treasury, and each parish church or its vicar 42,000 reis.†

When visited by Fryer in 1675, Thâṇâ, which he writes *Tanaw*, had "seven churches and colleges, the chiefest of the Paulistines; the houses tiled, but low." "Here are made," he adds, "good stuffs of silk and cotton."‡ In 1634 Antonio Bocarro says:— "In this town there are many weavers' looms of cotton and silk, all very perfect; and also excellent writing-desks, counters and tables inlaid with black wood and ivory, much more durable than those of any other part in this country."§

Thâṇâ was visited about twenty years after Fryer, in 1695, by Gemelli Careri, who describes the town thus:—"There are also in *Salzete* the forts of *Bandora* and *Versava* with their villages; as also *Tana*, about which there are five (?) small forts garrisoned and furnished with cannon. The country, though open, is excellent good for *India*, and has three monasteries of Dominicans, Augustinians, and *Recolets* (a reformed section of Franciscans). It is famous for calicoes, no place in the Portuguese dominions exceeding it in this particular, even for table service. Eight years since one brother killed another at *Tana* about the possession of a village."‖

---

* For details of the revenue and disbursements on fortifications, their garrisons, &c., see *Subsidios, ut supra*, pp. 139 *et seqq.*; *Chronista de Tissuary*, vol. i., pp. 32 and 56, and vol. iii., pp. 246 *et seqq.*

† *Chronista*, vol. i., pp. 245 and 258.

‡ *A New Account*, &c., *ut supra*, p. 73.

§ *Chronista*, vol. iii., p. 258.

‖ Churchill's *Collection of Voyages*, &c., vol. iv., p. 198.

The Cathedral of Thâṇâ was built by that zealous Franciscan Antonio do Porto, besides a church and convent dedicated to St. Anthony. Although the religious chronicles of the time are silent on the point, it appears that the Cathedral was under the invocation of "Nossa Senhora da Conceiçaõ," as deduced from subsequent writers and travellers. One of the latter is the celebrated Anquetil du Perron, who has immortalized this church on account of his having sung there the *Credo* on the feast-day of the patron saint. His account is rather amusing, although sarcastic. Let us hear in his own language what he has to say on the church, the *padres*, and his singing in the Cathedral of Thâṇâ. He writes:—

"Descendu à Tanin, je me rendis chez le Curé des Chrétiens de cette Ville, à qui celui de Ponjser m'avoit annoncé. La réception qu'il me fit, fut très-polie. Il m'offrit sa table. Mais, comme ces Prêtres Canarins se mettent en général fort à leur aise, et que je m'étois apperçu que les manières Européennes les gênoient, je le remerciai, et allai m'in. ller dans une Chambre haute attenante à son Église, délâbrée, et dont le plancher n'étoit pas plus sûr que celui du Presbytère de Ponjser. Un cadre, une méchante table, et une chaise, furent les meubles dont on la garnit.

"Les Marates en s'emparant de Tanin, ont laissé aux Chrétiens une partie de leurs Églises, and la plus grande liberté d'exercer leur Religion; aussi les fêtes s'y célèbrent elles avec la même pompe qu'à Goa; les Processions se font sans danger, et même avec une sorte de respect de la part des Gentils.

"Le lendemain de mon arrivée, 8 Décembre, jour de la Conception de la Vierge, on célébroit la Fête de l'Église de Tanin. Les Chrétiens s'y rassembloient déjà de tous les endroits de l'Isle, et la plûpart des Curés des environs devoient s'y rendre pour augmenter le Clergé de la Paroisse. J'ignore d'où le Curé de Tanin avoit pu sçavoir que j'eusse de la voix. À peine commençois-je à prendre quelques momens de repos, après avoir arrangé ce qui regardoit mon petit domestique, que je le vis entrer dans mon galetas avec deux faces noires, armées de basses et de violons: c'étoit pour prier de chanter le *Credo* en faux-bourdon, le lendemain à la Grand' Messe. La proposition me parut singulière. Dans mes voyages, j'avois été pris plusieurs fois pour Médecin, et je m'étois tiré d'affaire, en n'attendant pas l'effet de mes avis: mais je ne sçavois pas qu'un François dût être Musicien. J'eus beau alléguer mon incapacité, le repos dont j'avois besoin; mes excuses furent prises pour un excès de modestie ; et il fallut être Chantre malgré moi. La soirée se passa a répéter avec les deux joints du Curé.

" Le spectacle du lendemain me dédommagea de la fatigue de la veille. J'allai sur les neuf heures à l'Église, que je trouvai remplie de plusieurs milliers de Chrétiens, tous noirs et repandant une odeur très-forte. La Nèf étoit ornée de branchages disposés en arcades accompagnées de colonnes et de balustrades faites avec du papier de couleur, en or et en argent. J'étois seul de blanc au milieu de cette foule de Noirs ; et je chantai le *Credo* en faux-bourdon, avec quatre instrumens, qui m'accompagnerent, ou que je suivis tant bien que mal.

" La vûe de ces Chrétiens étoit fixée sur moi ; on m'écouta dans le plus grand silence. Les cérémonies se firent avec beaucoup de décence. Je vis après la Messe, plusieurs Indiens païens amener leurs enfans, et leur faire dire des Évangiles sur la tête ; d'autres emporter de l'huile de la lampe qui brûloit devant la chapelle de la Vierge. Quand il fallut sortir, la tribune sur laquelle j'étois avec mes Musiciens, ebranlée en bas et en haut par l'affluence du Peuple, manqua effondrer. Nous en fûmes pour la peur ; et en effet, c'eût été dommage de périr, avant le splendide repas qui m'attendoit.

" C'étoit chez le Curé de Tanin, qui donnoit à dîner à ses Confrères, au nombre de quinze, aux Marguillers, aux Chantres et par conséquent à moi, sans parler de ma qualité d'Européen et de frère du Chef François de Surate, qui me valût les honneurs de la Table. Sa maison étoit en face d'un grand étang entouré d'arbres, et au milieu des paillottes des Chrétiens du lieu.

" Je trouvai en entrant la table dressée dans une longue salle, et entourée de bancs. Bientôt on la couvrit de deux Cochons de lait, de plusieurs plats de riz et de *Caris*, ceux que l'on appelle à Goa, fi da pout, et de pesch *Carvate*. Les Convives en soutanes noires, la tête rasée et nue, sans bas ni souliers, prirent séance, et l'on me plaça au haut de la table. Que l'on se réprésente ce qu'il peut y avoir de dégoutant dans les repas des Lapons et des Hotentots, et l'on aura une idée juste de ce banquet. Chacun y mangeoit avec ses doigts, un coude sur la table, la jambe nue et pliée sous la cuisse. La sauce qui ruisseloit de toute part, l'odeur forte de l'arak, la sueur des Officians, les rôts, les propos libres, la malpropreté du service, tout faisoit tableau ; je regrettois de n'avoir pas un second avec qui je pûsse philosopher sur une pareille assemblée.

" Le repas fini, chacun se rétira pour faire la siesté ou fumer la chiroute. Le Vicaire-Général de Carlin fut du nombre de ces derniers, et voulut me chercher querelle au milieu de cette peuplade qu'il croyoit à sa dévotion ; mais je le malmenai de manière qu'il partît le lendemain : le Curé de Tanin le pria d'être plus modéré ; et le Peuple, à qui j'avois chanté le plus beau *Credo* qu'il eût jamais entendu, ne me regardoit qu'avec une sorte de vénération."*

This took place in December 1760. The picture is rather overdrawn, but there is a great deal of truth in it.

Next to the Igreja da Sé of the invocation of Nossa Senhora da Conceiçaõ, where our traveller sang the *Credo* that gained him so much respect and sympathy from the Christians of Thâṇâ, were the Church and Convent of St. Anthony. These were built by the aforementioned Fr. Porto. He appears to have been all the while, from the day he landed at Bassein in 1534 with the invading army of his nation, on a building excursion. He began with Bassein, where he built a number of churches and convents, to which I shall have to refer hereafter ; then he went to Agâsî, where he built the Church and College of Nossa Senhora da Luz, which was, as above stated, burnt down with five Christians on the 30th April 1540 ; then went to Thâṇâ, and here, among other things, built the Church and Convent of St. Anthony. It is said that in order to build this church and convent he pulled down twelve pagodas which were round a great tank, which may be the one still observed in front of one of the churches there, and raised over the ruins of the Hindu temples his own. It was thought then, the chroniclers inform us, that this was the very place where the four Franciscan friars had been murdered two centuries before.† The martyrs were now avenged.

The next traveller who has left us a detailed description of Thâṇâ, after the *spiritueux* Du Perron, is the venerable Bishop Heber, who visited the place in 1825. He writes :—

" Tannah is chiefly inhabited by Roman Catholic Christians, either converted Hindoos or Portuguese, who have become as black as the natives, and assumed all their habits."‡ Then he states that in Thâṇâ

---

* *Zend Avesta, ut supra,* vol. i., pp. ccccxxiv. *et seqq.*

† *Gabinete Litterario das Fontainhas,* Nova Goa, 1846, vol. i., p. 38.

‡ This is quite true. Although most of the black Christians are Hindus of the low caste, there are not a few well-known half-castes, or *mestiços* as they are called, who are even blacker than the low-class Hindus. In habits a Pariah is far less disgusting than a Portuguese half-caste.

there is a considerable cantonment of British troops, a collector and magistrate, for whose use a very neat church was being built when the bishop visited it, and when completed was consecrated by him on the 10th July 1825. Then he mentions the small but regular fortress, from which Trimbakji escaped, all the news of the arrangements being conveyed to him by a groom's singing. He says at last that Thâṇâ is famous for its breed of hogs, and the manner in which its Portuguese inhabitants cure bacon.

The latest fact connected with the antiquarian history of Thâṇâ is the discovery, about a year ago, amidst the ruins of the old fort—which had for some time been used as a jail, and where foundations were being laid for a new one—of some gravestones of individuals of no particular interest to history, with short epitaphs engraven on them, and of some coins made of an alloy of tin and zinc called *rodas* by the Portuguese, which are very rare nowadays. They have St. Catherine's wheel on the obverse, she being the patron saint of Goa, which was conquered on the day of her feast, and where this coin was first struck by the Senate, and Dom Manuel's crown or cross on the reverse. There was also a Roman Catholic medal, with the head of Christ with the marginal legend of *Salvator Mundi* on one face and the year 1525, P. S. for Petri Sedis, and Rome on the other, dug up among archaic *débris*.* There is now very little of archæological interest at Thâṇâ. All the convents I have mentioned before have been almost entirely swept off the earth's surface, and what remains is about to be so, notably the Church of St. John, which, although rebuilt in 1609, is in a very dilapidated condition, the walls moss-grown, covered with jungle all around, without being repaired or whitewashed for a great many years, the whole surrounded by some old, venerable large trees, which appear to have been standing there for some three or four centuries, and the lofty chapel surmounted by a square tower and a dome threatening to tumble down. There is one of the largest bells the Portuguese ever brought to this place, suspended in its belfry, making a sonorous noise in that sequestered spot, where there are a few native Christians living, who seem to take great delight in listening to its deafening sound. There is every evidence of the building having been raised over the ruins of one or more pagodas destroyed by the pious zeal of the Portuguese missionaries.

Among the ruins now to be observed are those of the Church of the Jesuits, dedicated to the Blessed Virgin, "A Madre de Deus," and a

* See the *Indian Railway Service Gazette*, Jabalpur, vol. i., No. 34, p. 6.

residence for two Fathers. It was built by Father Melchior Gonsalves in 1552. After the building of the above temple and convent we are told by the before-mentioned Pe. Souza that he converted in a few months over 400 heathens, and collected a great number of pagan children who had been abandoned by their unnatural parents.

The Hindus of Thâṇâ were, it is said, in the habit of selling their children to the Musalmâns, who bought them with the object of making them their slaves. Father Melchior, moved with compassion at so inhumane a sight, appealed to the Christians of Thâṇâ, and received abundant contributions to build an orphanage in which these poor children could be fed and educated. Hundreds of children were thus saved and made Christians. But, unfortunately, the humane Jesuit was not destined to prosecute his work any further, for about the same year (1552) he is said to have been poisoned by a pagan, and died a holy death. It may, perhaps, be necessary to warn the reader against these ecclesiastical chroniclers being often apt to make of every one of their party a martyr, or a persecuted being, as well as to magnify the most ordinary affair of theirs into something of surpassing magnificence and grandeur; *magno conatu, magnas nugas*. There is indeed no absolute lack of vanity even in beings so little worldly as the religious chroniclers appear to be.

But to continue the narrative. The orphanage of Thâṇâ was in 1556 removed to another place. Finding that the town was growing in size, and that a large city, where there is always corruptness of morals, was unsuitable for the Indian youth, who they knew by sad experience is too susceptible to bad example, they resolved to break up this establishment and found a colony of orphans somewhere in the country, sufficiently distant from the city of Thâṇâ. They hit at once on the very fittest place that could be found in the island of Salsette, where there were already a church and a college of 130 boys erected by Father Silveira, who had obtained for that purpose, and for the propagation of the Catholic religion in the island, from the royal treasury, an annual allowance of 300 ducats. The place selected for the building of this orphanage was in the midst of a forest, where there was a famous temple of the Trimurtî, which Father Silveira—already known as a Provincial of their order at Goa, where he had seen that such a desecration of the poor Hindus' temples could well be done without much hurting their feelings (Jesuits even thought the Hindus had no feelings)—pulled down, and over its foundation raised the orphanage—which he dedicated, as if in ironical allusion to the three-headed Śiva, and in defiance of him, to the "Blessed Trinity," naming it "The Orphanage of the Blessed Trinity." The number of colonists soon rose to 300, and later on to a still higher number. The concord and harmony that reigned there had a salutary influence on the heathen, and served, we are told, to confirm many a wavering Catholic in his new faith. To the orphanage was soon added a farming establishment, where both the orphans and the children that were bought during a famine that raged there in those times were employed. From this farm were obtained all sorts of vegetables and grain for the support of, the orphanage. It is supposed that the ruins of this church and college are now at the bottom of the Vehar lake; while the ruins of the orphanage are still visible.

A Ilha de Salcete.

The island of Salsette was the third division of the "Province of the North" subject to the Capital of Bassein. It was divided into a Praganâ and ninety-five villages.

Its name is derived from Sanskrit षष्टी (Shâshṭî), Marâṭhî साष्टी (Sâsṭî), meaning sixty villages, in contradistinction to षट्षष्ठी (Shaṭshâshṭî), Marâṭhî सासष्टी (Sâsâshṭî), or sixty-six villages, the name of the district of Salsette to the south-east of Goa. The other distinction is that while the Salsette of Bombay, about ten miles to the north of the latter city, is an island, the Salsette of Goa, lying about twenty miles distant from the new city of Goa, is a peninsula. They were both indiscriminately written by the Portuguese Salcete or Salsette. Mr. K. Graul inferred from the sound of the word that it was derived from the Portuguese *sal* (salt), which was prepared during the occupation of the island by them, as it is now, not far from the causeway that unites Salsette to Bombay.* Another writer says:—"Thomas Stevens, of New College, Oxford, the first Englishman who visited the Western Coast of India, landed in Goa in 1579, and in 1608 was rector of a college in Salsette. He, too, wrote an account of his travels, but he is equally reticent about the neighbouring island of Bombay."† Stevens never came to Salsette near Bombay, and was all the while engaged in the rectorship of a Jesuit college at Margaõ first, and at Rachol afterwards, in the

* K. Graul's *Travels in* 1850, vol. iii., pp. 124 *et seqq.*

† *The Times of India Hand-book of Hindustân,* Bomb. 1875, p. 116. See also my Life of Father Thomas Stevens in the "Recordações da minha Viagem pelo Egypto, França, Inglaterra e Escossia," *Instituto Vasco da Gama,* vol. ii., pp. 245, 263, 283 *et seqq.*

Salsette of Goa. The mistake has evidently arisen from two different places being named alike. The first Englishman who even came close to Bombay was Ralph Fitch, in 1583. He was at Chaul and Kalyâṇa, but does not mention Bombay.

The island of Salsette is connected with the earliest period of Indian history. It was first a stronghold of Buddhism, and subsequently of Śaivism, as evidenced by the five groups of caves existing therein, viz. Kâṇheri, Kondevatî, Jogeśvara, Maṇḍapeśvara, and Magathan.

It is supposed that Salsette was visited by the Chinese pilgrim Hwen Thsang in the seventh century. General Cunningham writes:—"In this case I would read western frontier of the kingdom, and identify his cave-monastery with the well-known excavations of Kânheri in the island of Salsette. Indeed, if I am correct in the identification of Kalyâṇa as the capital of Mahârâshṭra in the seventh century, it is almost certain that the pilgrim must have visited the Buddhist establishments of Kânheri, which are not more than 25 miles distant from Kalyâṇa." Then about the date of the caves he adds:—"The numerous inscriptions at Kâṇheri show that some of its excavations must date as early as the first century before Christ, and the bulk of them during the first and second century after Christ."*

Next to the Buddhist and Śaivite monuments of Salsette are copperplates and inscriptions. It appears from them that Salsette was first subject to the Châlukya dynasty of Kalyâṇa, whose copperplates have been found in the island, and then to the Yâdavas, an inscription of which dynasty, besides several copperplates, is found in the abovementioned temple of Ambarnâtha, dated Ś. 782 (A.D. 860).

The remaining history of the Hindu period until the time of Râmadeva in 1295, and of the Mahomedan rule until the occupation of the island by the Portuguese, does not differ from the neighbouring town of Thâṇâ already described.

Passing on now to the Portuguese period, it was as early as 1535 that the Portuguese sent the above-mentioned Fr. Antonio do Porto on a missionary tour to the island, which resulted in the conversion of thousands of Hindus, in which respect Fr. Porto almost equalled the great St. Francis Xavier. He built numerous churches, convents, and orphanages in it, and in this respect he even excelled the Indian Apostle.

---

* *Ancient Geography of India, ut suprà*, p. 556.

The first stronghold of paganism his attacks were directed against were the Buddhist excavations of Kânheri. This fact is mentioned by Dr. Garcia d'Orta in the earliest work ever written by a European that refers to the Kânheri caves. He writes:—"There is an island called Salsette, where there are two underground pagodas, one of which, under a hill, is larger than the fortress of Diu, and may be compared to a city of Portugal containing about four hundred houses. There is a way leading to this great pagoda, hewn out of rock, where the monks of St. Francis have built a church of the invocation of St. Michael. There are other pagodas along the way, and at the top many houses with apartments, all made of stone. In one of these houses there is a tank or cistern of water, with conduits bringing to it rain water. There are altogether three hundred houses, with images of idols carved out of stone; notwithstanding all this they are sombre and frightful, as if made for the worship of the devil."*

Diogo do Couto refers to the caves more in detail. He describes numerous chambers and tunnels with windings, into one of which the indomitable Friar Porto went. Diogo do Couto writes:—"The priest, desirous of getting in to see this wonder, and the magnitude of this work, about which so much was said, took one of his companions, and collected twenty persons with arms and matchlocks to defend themselves against wild beasts; and some servants to carry the necessary provisions for the journey............................Thus prepared, they entered the caves by an entrance about four fathoms in breadth, where they placed a large stone, to which they fastened the end of the rope. They travelled through the caves for seven days without any interruption, through places some of them wide and others narrow, which were hollowed in the rock....................................The priest, seeing that they had expended seven days without being able to find any opening, and that the provisions and water had been almost consumed, thought it necessary to return, taking for his clue the rope, without knowing in these windings whether he was proceeding up or down, or what course they were steering, as they had no compass for their guidance."† Couto then mentions that the same missionary found the caves inhabited by *yogis*, one of whom was a hundred and fifty years old, who being made a Christian was named Paulo Rapozo; and another named Colete, who had a more saintly reputation than

* *Colloquios dos Simples e Drogas*, Lisbon, 1872, pp. 211-212.

† *Decadas, ut supra.*

his colleague Rapozo, was also converted and named Francisco da Santa Maria. To the former the King, John III., made a present of three villages of Pare, Arengal, and Mânikpûra, which on his death, following soon after, became by his will the property of the college of Mont-Pezier. The latter was instrumental in the conversion of several of his brother-*yogîs* and other heathens. He then informs us that there were more than 3,000 cells, each with a cistern supplied by one conduit, and that the above-mentioned caves led, according to some, to Cambay, and according to others to Agra, and that an inscription on the gate had led them to believe that this work was ordered to be built by King Bimelamenta.

All these marvellous statements are at last brought to a close with the assertion that the Kânheri Pagoda was ordered to be made by the father of the prince St. Josaphat, whom Barlao converted to the Christian faith, with the view of shutting him up there in consequence of his astrologers having foretold that the prince would profess the Christian religion.* This is altogether, with slight modifications, the legendary life of Gautama Buddha.

The passages in Diogo do Couto referring to these caves are found translated into English by the Rev. W. K. Fletcher in *Jour. Bo. Br. R. As. Soc.*, vol. i., pp. 34 *et seqq.*, and also in Dr. Wilson's lecture on *The Religious Excavations of Western India*, pp. 7 *et seqq.*

It appears that as late as the end of the seventeenth century the Kânheri caves were unknown to Europeans, except to those who could read the works of Garcia d'Orta and Diogo do Couto. Gemelli Careri, writing in 1695, says:—"What I most admire is, that it is almost unknown to Europeans; for, though I have made much inquiry, I do not find that any Italian, or other European traveller has written of it; and it is very strange to me that so ingenious a man as our Peter de la Valle should omit to see both this *Pagod* and the palace of Darius, with the antiquities of *Celmonar*, that were but a few leagues out of his way," &c. Then again, "I know not what judgment Portuguese authors make of it, because their books are scarce at Naples; but they, it is certain, are well acquainted with it, the viceroys themselves sometimes coming from Goa to see it; yet it is most likely they could never discover the truth."†

---

* *Decada* VII., bk. III., ch. x.

† Churchill's *Voyages*, *ut supra*, pp. 193 and 195.

These caves have been so often and so thoroughly described that they need no further mention here except in connection with one of its divisions which Fr. Porto consecrated and turned into a chapel of the invocation of St. Michael.

The other caves, which were almost entirely turned into a Roman Catholic chapel, were those of Maṇḍapeśvara, called Mont-Pezier or Monpacer by the Portuguese. On the side of these caves they erected another church and college, so that the caves became, as it were, a crypt to the church. This church was by the same Fr. Porto dedicated to N. S. da Conceiçaõ. The college was meant for the education of 100 orphans. All round the hill was a colony of two thousand native converts, the traces of whose dwellings are yet visible. Both Garcia d'Orta under the name of Maljaz, and Diogo do Couto under that of Monpacer, describe this place in the height of its prosperity in the works above referred to.

In its decline it was visited by Gemelli Careri, who writes:— "I went to the village of *Monopesser*, a mile distant, from the village of *Deins* belonging to the nuns of St. Monica of Goa, and six miles distant, from Bassein, to see a church underground, formerly a *Pagod* cut in the rock, on which stands the college and monastery of the Franciscans. It is a hundred spans long, and in breadth thirty. The side walls, as has been said, are of the natural rock, and only the front is made by art. Close by is another *Pagod* cut in the rock, formerly serving for their idolatrous worship." This was also converted into a church and dedicated to N. S. da Piedade, and appears to be the present church of Poinsar. Gemelli then adds:— "This church and monastery are like all the rest in India. Five religious men live there, to whom the king of Portugal allows 200 *Murais** of rice, all which they give to the poor except only as much as serves for their own sustenance. One of their fathers does the office of a curate in the village of *Cassi*, two miles distant, and has a good dwelling there. On the mountain near the said college is another hermitage, with a chapel."†

Anquetil du Perron saw these buildings in 1760 when abandoned, and describes their ruins circumstantially in reference to a plan which he has given by the side of his description. He refers to an open

* Elsewhere he writes:—"A *Murais* (mura) is twenty-five *paras*, and the *para* twenty-four pounds Spanish; measures the Portuguese use for provisions, as they do the *Covedo* (covado) for long measure."

† *Opus cit.*

space, where he says there must have been an inscription slab. It stood outside the caves to the left of a small cistern near a window, where the Portuguese had made a little cross in relief. In the church to the left of the caves Du Perron discovered a gravestone with a Portuguese epitaph with the date 1590. He says the Marâṭhâs after destroying this edifice carried the timber away to Thâṇâ. He then describes the cistern close by, whose waters, the natives informed him, blackened the skin of those who bathed in them. Our auther was about to try the experiment, but there being no water at the time (December 1760) he changed his mind.*

These caves were visited by Lord Valentia in November 1804. He writes:—"We went on to dinner to Mont-pesier, where our tents were pitched for us. Here are the ruins of a very handsome church and monastery, which, I understand, formerly belonged to the Jesuits: Monsieur Anquetil du Perron says, to the Franciscans; but I am inclined to consider my information as correct, from there being the remains of an observatory on a small hill in the neighbourhood, which was more probably the work of the intelligent followers of Ignatius Loyola than of the lazy monks of St. Francis. (Du Perron was right.) The church was originally lined with panel-work of wood, disposed in compartments, and richly ornamented with carving. In the centre was the head of a saint, tolerably executed, surrounded by wreaths of flowers, and other fanciful sculpture in a very excellent taste. The whole is in ruins, the roof having fallen in. The author, whom I have before mentioned, attributes this to the devastations of the Mahrattas, who, he says, carried away the woodwork to Tannah; but this appears improbable. Timber is not scarce; and if they had carried away the more solid work, they would hardly have left behind them the parts that were richly ornamented. Under the church a small pagoda has been formed out of the rock; it is square, and flat-roofed, with a few deities, and other figures, in basso-relievo. These the good priests had covered up with a smooth coat of plaister, and had converted the whole into a chapel. At present the original proprietors have been uncovered, and have again become objects of adoration to the ignorant native."†

Malte Brun writes:—"The Portuguese converted the place into a Christian church. They did not destroy the images, as in many other

* *Discours Préliminaire*, vol. i., pp. cccxc. *et seqq.*

† Viscount Valentia's *Voyages*, Lond. 1809, vol. ii., pp. 195 *et seqq.*

instances; but, not having coolness enough to allow them to stand as simple monuments of art and of antiquated opinions, they converted them into Christian emblems, painted them red, and, with pious zeal, cherished them as valuable proselytes; many others, of an ugliness incorrigibly heathen, they utterly effaced."*

Another fact in connection with the ruins of Monpaeer is of a melancholy nature, and is thus referred to by Vaupell, who paid a visit to it in May 1838:—"From the wall of this harmitary (hermitage?) a gentleman (Mr. J. Forbes) met his death some years ago. He, it seems, imprudently climbed the wall at a corner with his boots on, where the roots of a peepul tree served as a ladder: he got safely to the top, and after sitting for a while on the wall admiring the surrounding prospect, in the act of rising, it is supposed, part of the crumbling wall giving way under his feet, he slipped, and was precipitated into the court of the temple below, a height of between sixty and seventy feet. He never spoke afterwards, but was carried home to Bombay senseless, and died the same evening." The same writer describes the ruins thus:—"The ruins of Manpesir consist of a large church and tower, dedicated to N. S. de Conceiçaõ, and a quadrangular court adjoining, the stone arches of which are in a good state of preservation. The church contains one noble stone arch of fifty span near the entrance, a carved baptismal font sufficiently large for pedo-immersion, and a figure of the Virgin as large as life, standing on the altar: below there are a dead Christ, without arms, and the Virgin-mother supporting a dead Christ, all in wood. From the expression of the countenances of these figures, which excels anything of the kind I have ever seen, they would seem to be of European workmanship. Over the altar, the arched roof is inlaid with richly carved work, in square compartments. Adjoining the quadrangular building there are several others of various sizes, intended probably for Students' apartments and the residence of the venerable Jesuitical (Franciscan) professors: these are terminated at the north end by an hermite or chapel of ease. * * * (It was from the wall of this hermitage that Mr. Forbes was precipitated into the court of the temple below.) "The College is raised over an ancient Hindoo temple, carved out of the solid rock, which is still in pretty good preservation: it consists of one long room, supported upon pillars, and one room on each side, except the east, facing which is the entrance. The northernmost room is the largest, and in the best

* *Univ. Geog.*, Lond. 1822, vol. iii., p. 161.

order; it appears as if lately fitted up for some one's residence: on the south is the tank, or well of water, which is delicious, and refreshingly cool. I could not find out whether it proceeded from a spring, or was the collection of last rains. Over the door of the college is an inscription in Portuguese, with the arms of Portugal above it, purporting that the erection was made in 1623 (1643?) by order of the Infant Dom John III. of Portugal (King Dom Joaõ IV.?), as an appendage to the church N. S. de Conçeicaõ. On a hill adjoining to the south stands the tower, built of a circular form, with a dome about twenty feet high; the platform has a parapet wall running round, and the shaft below contains several chambers in its circumference, for soldiers: it appears to have been a watch-tower."*

Besides the two above-mentioned caves, which were turned to religious uses by Roman Catholic missionaries, they built a great number of churches in the island of Salsette, some of which are still in a fair state of preservation. To write the history of each of these buildings and the collegiate institutions in connection with them would carry me far beyond the limits assigned to this work. I must content myself with enumerating them thus:—

Church of Sam Boaventura at Yerangal, which was spelt by the Portuguese Arengal, and sometimes called Altomar. This church, with the parochial house attached to it, is now in ruins. It is about ten miles from Bandora, and is situated on a pretty little bay close to the sea. A mass is performed on its altar once a year, on the feast of the Epiphany, when a pilgrimage of the Roman Catholics of the adjacent villages takes place.

Church of N. S. da Piedade at Poinsar, before alluded to. It is within a mile's distance from the ruins of Mont Pezier.

Church of Sam Thome at Nave.

Church of N. S. d'Assumpçaõ at Haystana, sometimes called Candolim.

Church of Sam Jeronimo at Cassi.

Church of N. S. de Nazareth at Bainel.

Church of N. S. do Socorro at Manorim.

Church of Sam Braz at Ambolim.

Church of N. S. do Mar at Utana.

Church of N. S. da Saude at Varsava, the little island off the coast of Salsette.

---

* *Trans. Bo. Geog. Soc.*, vol. vii., pp. 145 *et seqq.*

Church of Santo Antonio at Malvane.

Church of Sam Sebastiaõ at Marole.

Church of Santo Antonio de Trumpa, or Perumpa, at Mane.

Church of Santos Reis Magos at Goray.

Church of Santo André at Bandora.

Chapel of N. S. do Monte at Bandora, a shrine also held in high veneration by the Hindûs, who call the Holy Virgin 'Matubâi.'*

The Church of St. Andrew is the oldest Church at Bandora. It was built by the Superior of the College of "the Holy Name" at Bassein in the year 1575, just three centuries ago,—Fr. F. Manuel Gomes, a Portuguese born in India, who, from the number of converts he made at Bandora and the neighbouring villages, is styled by chroniclers "the Apostle of Salsette." Bandora appears to have first resisted the efforts of the Jesuits to convert it to Christianity, and, being considered an unpromising field for missionary labour, was almost abandoned, until it was again taken up in the above-mentioned year by Fr. Gomes. When the latter entered Bandora he found no Christians there, but in 1588 he could boast of 4,000 converts, which by the year 1591, when the great missionary died, had increased to 6,000. He had founded for them, besides the parish of St. Andrew, two others, viz. the parish of Condit, now named Marole, above referred to, and that of Corlem or Curlâ. The town of Bandora had under its jurisdiction sixty-five villages, thirteen of which were entirely converted to the new faith.

The church of Bandora had a residence for two Jesuit missionaries attached to it; so had the churches of Marole and Curlâ. The latter is referred to by Du Perron thus:—"Depuis que les Marates s'en sont emparés, les Moines Portugais et les autres Prêtres blancs se sont retirés à Goa; les Curés Canarins occupent les débris des couvents et des Églises sous l'inspection d'un Vicaire-Général aussi Canarin, qui réside à Carlin, dans le Sud de l'Isle." Again: "Je trouvai à Carlin, dans un ancien couvent de Religieux un peu mieux conservé que celui de Ponjser, le Vicaire-Général de Salsette......................enflé de quelques *distinguo* scholastiques qu'il avait appris à Goa dans les écoles de théologie des Franciscans. L'abord de son Presbytère me plut; c'étoit une petite plaine entourée de cocotiers et de palmiers, qui avoit un air très-riant."† The parish church of St. Andrew was

* ठाणें जिल्ह्याचें वर्णन, p. 19.

† *Opus cit.*, pp. cclxxxv. and ccccxiv.

the only one in Bandora up to the end of the first quarter of the seventeenth century, when a college was built in 1620 under the invocation of St. Anne This was when founded a mere residence for two Fathers dependent on the College of Bassein at first, and on that of Thâṇâ afterwards. But when visited by Fryer, in 1675, it had acquired greater dimensions, for he says:—"It was not long before I was employed to wait on the Father Superior of the North, a learned man, and a Spaniard by nation, of the order of the Jesuits. The President (of the Bombay E. I. C. establishment) commanded his own baloon (a barge of state of two and twenty oars) to attend me and one of the Council, to compliment the Father on the island of Canorein (Couto calls it Canaria, another name for Salsette), parted from Bombaim by a stream half a mile broad. Near our landing place stood a College, not inferior to the building, nor much unlike those of our universities, belonging to the Jesuits here, more commonly called Paulistines (Paulistas)—whose Visitor was now my patient—who live here very sumptuously, the greatest part of the island being theirs. Our entertainment was truly noble, and becoming the gravity of the Society. After I had done my duty, the Fathers accompanied us to the barge; afore the College gate stood a large cross, thwacked full of young blacks singing vespers. The town is large, the houses tiled; it is called Bandora. At our department they gave us seven guns, which they have planted on the front of their College for their own defence, besides they are filled with good store of small arms: following therein the advice given by a statesman to the King of Spain, about the Netherlands; that 'if the Society of the Loyolists were multiplied, their convents might serve for castles.'

"In the middle of the river we had a pleasant prospect on both sides; on Bandora side, the College, the town, the Church of St. Andrew a mile beyond, and upon the hill that pointed to the sea, the Agoada, blockhouse, and a Church; on the other side the Church of Mahim, with other handsome buildings."

That was the first visit of Fryer. Then he paid a second one in company of a large party of friends, and a train of servants, horses and palankeens, which were ferried over before them. Our author then adds:—"We, coming soon after, were met by the Fraternity, and conducted to the Fathers, who detained us till afternoon by a stately banquet, showing us the civility of the Church and College; diverting us both with instrumental and local music, and very good wine.

"After which we were dismissed, and four miles off Bandora were stopped by the kindness of the Padre Superior, whose mandate wherever we came caused them to send his *recarders* (recados)—a term of congratulation, as we say 'our service'—with the presents of the best fruits and wines and whatever we wanted. Here, not adjoining to any town, in a sweet air, stood a magnificent rural church; in the way to which, and indeed all up and down this island, are pleasant *Aldeas*, or country seats of the gentry; where they live like petty monarchs, all that is born on the ground being theirs, holding them in a perfect state of villainage, they being lords paramount."*

When Bombay was made over to the English, the Bandora College of St. Anne claimed much land and various rights in the island, which not being acknowledged, the Fathers revenged the affront by receiving and assisting Humphry Cook, a dismissed English officer, in 1667, to attempt to raise a force for the capture of Bombay.† Again in 1720 and 1722 there were "disagreements and skirmishes" between the English of Bombay and the Portuguese of Bandora, led by the Jesuit Fathers.‡ Of the College now remains but the celebrated cross, which was removed in 1870 to the churchyard of St. Andrew's Church.

The Chapel of N. S. do Monte above alluded to seems to have been built about the same time that the Agoada bulwark, which commands the bay, was built, the date being possibly the one over the doorway leading to the Bandora Point, viz. 1640. It was probably in its origin a garrison chapel for the soldiers stationed at the Agoada fort. The fame of this shrine, however, appears to be from a recent date. Formerly the most celebrated images of the Virgin Mary, resorted to by both Roman Catholics and infidels for miraculous cures, were those of N. S. das Angustias at Dhânu, now completely ruined, of Madre de Deos at Chaul, and of N. S. dos Remedios in the island of Bassein, which was held in high veneration not only by the Roman Catholics and Hindûs, but even by the iconoclast Mahomedans, who are said to have spared that church, while they plundered and destroyed every other building during their repeated incursions in the country.

Both the above images seem now to be superseded by that of N. S. do Monte, which, in order to add a mystic lustre to her other triumphs,

* *A New Account*, &c., *ut supra*, pp. 70-71.

† Bruce's *Annals*, vol. ii., p. 213.

‡ Hamilton, in Pinkerton's *Collection*, vol. viii., p. 328.

is credited with the following legend :—Towards the end of the year 1738, when the Marâṭhâs conquered Salsette, they destroyed many of the Roman Catholic churches, convents, and sanctuaries, and among others the College of St. Anne, the Church of St. Andrew, and the Chapel of N. S. do Monte. The statue of N. S. do Monte was thrown into the sea, but it was picked up by a Kolî fisherman and concealed in the fissure of a rock near the Bandora Point for the period of six months, after which it was carried in solemn procession to the church of St. Andrew. There it remained until the year 1761, when a chapel was built on its former site, and the statue carried back to it.

Besides the above-mentioned churches of Salsette, there were three others at Thâṇâ, viz. N. S. da Graça, N. S. do Rozario, built by subscriptions for the Jesuits in 1605, and Madre de Deos.*

On the other side of the creek which separates the island of Salsette from the continent is the Church of N. S. do Egypto, near Kalyâṇa.

There was a church at Ghorbandar, situated in a delightful spot by the side of a monastery and fort, described by Fryer, Heber, and others, but now in ruins. The church was dedicated to St. John. It is now converted into a bungalow. Many of its features make it appear to have originally been a Mahomedan rather than a Christian building. Instead of the spire it has the round dome of Musalmân mosques. A tradition accounts for this anomalous feature by the assertion that there being a *pir* at the place where this church was built, the builders tried hard to make a spire, but through the virtue of the *pir* buried there, it *would* grow a dome.†

The Christian population of each of the above parishes varies between 500 and 2,000 souls. The resident priests, or vicars as they are called, lead a happy life. They have generally a small monthly salary from the Goa government, varying from 10 to 50 rupees, and 15 rupees from the British government. But their chief dependence is on the fees they receive from their parishioners for performing the offices of their religion. They also get in some cases allowances from the British government for the repair of the churches.

---

* Details on the above subjects will be found in the *Oriente Conquistado*, and in the excellent work in German by Mullbauer entitled *Geschichte der indischen Missionen*, principally drawn from Orlandini.

† *Oriental Christian Spectator*, vol. x., 1839, p. 338.

There were no forts of any importance in the island of Salsette except those of the islets of Dharavî, Varsava, and one small watch-tower at Bandora. Some of the monasteries were either themselves fortified, or built close to the forts and stockaded posts or round watch-towers to give notice of the approach of the enemy. The fort of Varsava was rebuilt by the Marâṭhâs (see Plate 13). That of Bandora, where there was a place called *Agoada* for the ships of the Portuguese fleets to take in water, is almost entirely destroyed. The Jesuits' College at Bandora, rendered famous by the visits of Humphry Cook and Fryer, had, as above stated, "seven guns mounted in front of it, and a good store of small arms."* The site occupied by this fortified college is now converted into a slaughter-house, the shed that is built on it bearing every appearance of the Roman Catholic cemeteries at Goa.

The defenceless condition of the island of Salsette was brought to the notice of the Goa government by the before-mentioned Factor of Bassein, André Ribeiro Coutinho, in 1728, who writes:—"To the island of Salsette it is necessary to pay all attention, not only because it is left uncared for, but because its villages minister to the sustenance of a great number of the population of the jurisdiction of Bassein and the capital of Goa. The whole of this island is unarmed, and exposed on the sea side to attacks of the enemy of the coast (Angria), and on the land side to those of the Sidî, English, and Marâṭhâ."†

It is quite true that the revenue derived from the island of Salsette was a great help to the Portuguese government, and to the innumerable idle fidalgos who had nothing else but empty titles to live upon. There was at Salsette a *tanadar* and some custom-house clerks, who undertook the collection of land revenues, excise dues, &c.

Most of the villages were given for an insignificant quit-rent, generally in perpetuity, to the Portuguese families resident in Bassein and Goa. The possessors of these villages were to all intents and purposes like the feudal lords of the mediæval times. Gemelli Careri says:—"If the peasants take the land to till in the place of their abode, they pay no other duty to king or landlord (though some exact some days of personal service); but those that hold in fee pay an imposition according to what they are worth, every four months, to the king's factors or treasurers,

---

* *New Account*, &c. *ut supra*, p. 70.

† *Chronista de Tissuary*, vol. i., p. 56.

Plate 13.

REDUCED & DRAWN BY ARDESHEER.

BASSEIN FORT, AS SEEN FROM THE RIVER.

LIEUT. JOHN McCLUER'S SURVEY IN THE LIBRARY BY. GEOG. SOC.

REDUCED & DRAWN BY ARDESHEER.

DARAVI POINT IN THE BASSEIN RIVER.

Ibid.

REDUCED & DRAWN BY ARDESHEER.

VIEW OF THE LAND ABOUT BASSEIN & DARAVI.

Ibid.

REDUCED & DRAWN BY ARDESHIR.

VIEW OF VARSAVA.

LIEUT. EDWARD HARVEY'S PLAN IN 1777, IN THE LIBRARY BY. GEOG. SOC.

residing in all the northern cities. These villages are given in fee to soldiers who have served long; or to other persons that have well deserved of the crown, for three lives, after which they generally endeavour to renew; but to the church they are given for ever."*

A Ilha de Caranja.

The island of Caranjâ was the fourth division of the territory subject to the jurisdiction of Bassein, consisting of one *Caçabé*, one *terra de Bendolac*, and three islands, viz. *Nevem*, *Seveon*, and *Elephante*.

The island of Caranjâ is one of the earliest known in Hindû history. It would appear to be the fate of its villages to have for centuries been the gifts of princes or rich devotees to monastic institutions, whether Buddhist or Christian. During the Buddhist period the monks living in the Kânheri caves were made, by the liberality of an opulent minister, the proprietors of a village in the island of Caranjâ, just as the village of Vihâr, now covered by the lake from which water is brought by an aqueduct to Bombay, was assigned for their support by another party. When the island came into the hands of the Portuguese, the Dominicans and Jesuits shared between themselves the greater portion of the island, the remainder being distributed among a few fidalgos and soldiers. These religious assignations or gifts by royal personages, ministers, or opulent devotees, who on entering the priesthood thus disposed of their property, were once very common among the Buddhists, and even now the granting of all the rents of a village for the support of religious establishments is not a rare thing at all among the Hindûs.

The archæological remains of the former sect in the island are cells of a very insignificant character, being now, like those of the Tungâr hill, mostly filled with water. "They are here noticed only," writes Dr. Wilson, "as vestiges of the Oriental asceticism in another of our Bombay islands, in all of which, capable of supporting a small population, there appear to have been hermitages, either Buddhist or Brâhmanical."†

The Roman Catholic churches and convents first built here by the same distinguished missionary, Fr. Antonio do Porto, who having accomplished his mission in Bassein and Salsette went to Caranjâ, and from this island to Chaul, date from 1535. Fr. Porto built the follow-

* Churchill's *Voyages*, *ut supra*, p. 198. For details see *Subsidios*, *ut supra*, pt. ii., pp. 139 *et seqq.*; and also *Chronista de Tissuary*, vol. iii., pp. 242 *et seqq.*

† *Jour. Bo. Br. R. As. Soc.*, vol. iii., pt. ii., p. 43.

ing churches :—Sam Francisco (to which was attached an orphanage for 40 boys), N. S. da Salvaçaõ, and N. S. da Penha. All these churches are now in ruins. It is written of the last church—N. S. da Penha—that when the above-mentioned Franciscan was laying its foundations he happened to unearth a blue stone with the image of the Blessed Virgin engraven on it. From the presence of this sculpture our pious friar inferred that the island must have been formerly inhabited by Christians, and from the circumstance of its having been found on a hill he named the engraving "N. S. da Penha," "Our Lady of the Hill;" and the hill itself "Serra da N. S. da Penha."* Bishop Osorio also informs us that when Caranjâ was first visited by the Portuguese they found there a majestic Christian temple.† But on the matter of finding remains of early Christianity in India the Portuguese writers are, to use the mildest expression, simply untrustworthy.

In order to know where these remains are now to be found, it is necessary to give a brief topographical description of the island, which consists of two hills, called Great Hill and Little Hill, and an intervening plain. Viewed from Bombay the island looks as if these two hills were placed side by side, and as if forming part of that range of hills that constitute the western boundary of the continent of India, but being in reality separated from the mainland on the south by a narrow arm of the sea, and on the east by another creek.

The island is four miles long and half as much broad. It is on the "Great Hill" that are to be found the ruins of the church of N. S. da Penha, as well as of other churches. A long and winding flight of steps leads to it. The only church existing at present in the island is of modern construction, and is of the invocation of N. S. da Purificaçaõ. This parish has about 200 souls, out of a population of 5,000.

There were two forts built by the Portuguese, one on the eastern side of the island, and the other on the top of the "Great Hill" before alluded to. The latter was the larger of the two, and built in the form of a square, three angles of which had a bastion each, all well equipped with cannon. Close to it were the barracks of the garrison, which consisted of one captain, six soldiers, one bombardier, and five peons, the sum of whose pay amounted to 480 pardaos a year, besides the 30,000 reis paid to the captain. But there were also, besides the above little gar-

* Paes's *Definiçoes Indicas*, Trat. 2, chap. i.

† *De Rebus Gestis Emmanuelis*, &c., bk. vi., p. 174.

rison, about 100 armed men, who were maintained by the owners of villages and others who had an interest in the defence of the island. In 1634 the Captain of the island for life was Fernaõ de Sampayo da Cunha, and the administration of the island was so well managed that after paying all the expenses it left a pretty good balance to be sent to the treasury of the state.* The expenses were, as above mentioned, incurred, besides the pay of the garrison, in the support of a great number of religious and missionary bodies both in and out of India. The vicar of Caranjâ, *i.e.* of the principal church, and of that of N. S. da Salvaçaõ had each of them 42,000 reis a year, besides some allowances for vestry expenses, the archbishop of Cranganore 5,000 pardaos a year, and the Jesuits at Japan 800 from the revenues of the island.

When inspected in 1728, the Factor of Bassein advised the government to have a little rock in the sea close to the island fortified, but it appears that it was then too late to do anything for the defence of a place that was rapidly gliding away from their grasp. Caranjâ was the southern extremity of the late province, subject to the jurisdiction of Bassein, and its fort was the fourteenth in order from Bassein downwards, including the watchtowers which studded the whole passage from Bassein through Thâṇâ to Bombay.†

Besides the above-mentioned churches, the Dominicans had a hermitage and a church of the invocation of N. S. do Rozario, built by Father-General Fr. Jeronimo da Paixaõ, and subject to the priory of Chaul, with a house wherein used to reside the *Pater Christianorum* of the island, a member of that order. The Christians of Caranjâ had once offered ground and money sufficient to build a convent for the Dominicans, but it appears that their offer, for some reason or other, was not accepted.

On the 13th April 1613 Caranjâ was the scene of one of the greatest riots ever witnessed in this part of the Portuguese settlements; but it was soon quelled by the brave Captain, Fernaõ de Sampayo da Cunha, whose display of energy and courage on that occasion is eulogized by the chroniclers.‡

Some years after the capture of the island by the Marâṭhâs it was visited by Forbes, who writes in 1774:—"I sailed from Salsette to

* *Chronista*, vol. iii., pp. 247 and 260.

† *Ibid.*, vol. i., pp. 32 and 57.

‡ *Anno Historico*, por Francisco de Santa Maria, Lisboa, 1714, day 13th April, pt. i.

Caranjah, and landed about two miles from the principal town, situated between two lofty mountains, on the west side : it was nothing more than a large Mahratta village, with low straggling houses, near a tank covered with wild ducks and water-fowl, hitherto unmolested by Europeans. On its banks a small fort, a Portuguese church, and a Hindoo temple embellished the view. The principal fort stands on the summit of a lofty mountain romantically diversified by woods and rock : the ascent is steep and difficult. This castle, small, badly constructed, and mounting only fourteen guns, was incapable of defence, but its situation rendered it almost inaccessible. It commands a western view of the town and harbour of Bombay, Salsette, and all the adjacent islands, and to the east the mountains of the continent, and nearer plains of Caranjah, abounding with rice-fields, cocoanut, palmyra, mango, and tamarind trees, filled with monkeys, parrots, owls, and singing birds of various kinds."*

The islands of Nevem and Seveon are now called Hog and Butcher's Islands. Hog Island was also called Deodevî by the Hindûs, and by the Portuguese *A ilha de patecas*, or 'water-melon island,' a name that Fryer corrupted into *putachos*, if he did not get it in that guise from some Portuguese *gamin* who wished to speculate with the credulity of the English doctor, as it is an exceedingly ill-sounding word to Portuguese ears. The names of Nevem and Seveon were used as such as late as 1760 by Du Perron.† Water-melons were formerly brought to the island for sale from Panvel. They are now brought straight to Bombay.

The island of Elephanta, with its rock-temples, has been so often and so thoroughly described by others that I need not refer to it here, especially as that part of the history of the island during the Portuguese sway, which is not generally known, the reader will find in my notes published in a supplementary form to William Erskine's description of the cave-temples in the new edition of the *Transactions of the Literary Society of Bombay*, vol. i., which is being edited by the Hon'ble Mr. V. N. Maṇḍlik.

I have, however, to enter a protest here against the carelessness with which accusations have been levelled by some writers against the Portuguese of having destroyed the rock-temples of Elephanta. Fryer in 1675 says :—They were "defaced by the Portugals, who have this

* James Forbes's *Oriental Memoirs*, Lond. 1813, vol. i., pp. 453-454.

† *Zend Avesta*, &c., vol. i., p. ccccxxiii

island also." Pyke in 1712 writes:—"The Portuguese now fodder all their cattle there in the rainy seasons, and to defend them from the violence of the monsoons: and lately one of their Fidalgos, to divert himself with the echo, which is here most admirable, fired a great gun into it with several shot, which has broken some of the pillars." Then follows Grose, who, materially exaggerating the latter circumstance, says: "In the blind fury of their bigotry, not suffering any idols but their own, they (the Portuguese) must have been at even some pains to maim and deface them (the figures), as they now remain, considering the hardness of the stone." Du Perron has jumbled his information, and makes the Marâṭhâs drag pieces of cannon into the temple to cause bas-reliefs, with the plaster used by the Portuguese to cover them, to fall off.*

Now these are all unfounded assertions. As for cattle, they were there in 1563, as the fact is noted with no little surprise and displeasure by Garcia d'Orta.† There is no evidence, therefore, to connect this sort of depredations with the Portuguese. The temples might have been desecrated and even injured long before by the Mahomedans, and who knows if some heterodox Hindus had not a share in it themselves! The Portuguese have already had too many sins to account for, and there is no need to add to the list others they never committed. The impartial authorities of Niebuhr and Lord Valentia bear out the above opinion. The former writes:—"Ces huit figures sont fort endommagées aux pieds, mais non point par le canon des Portugais, comme quelques voyageurs le prétendent, mais par l'eau de pluye qui ne fait que couler dans le temple depuis plusieurs années dans la saison pluvieuse, et y reste ordinairement fort long temps. Si les Portugais avoient effectivement eu le dessein de ruiner ces figures payennes, ils auroient agi d'une façon peu sensée, s'ils avoient voulu trainer pour cet effet des pièces d'artillerie sur une si haute montagne là, où cela pouvoit si faire à beaucoup moins de fraix au moyen d'un marteau, et peut-être s'en est on effectivement servi, à l'égard de plusieurs figures."‡

Viscount Valentia writes:—"There is no appearance of any great violence having been used to injure the figures. Had cannon been employed by the Portuguese for that purpose, the marks of the balls would have been visible, and the destruction would have been among

* Burgess's *Rock Temples of Elephanta*, Bomb. 1875, p. 55.

† *Colloquios*, *ut supra*, p. 212.

‡ *Voyage*, *ut supra*, p. 26.

the figures. As it is, the pillars are more rapidly decaying than any other part. The water is permitted during the rains to lodge in the cave, and the stone, being a soft one, moulders perceptibly away in the vicinity of the open air."*

It is true Diogo do Couto refers to the frolics of the Portuguese soldiers in the caves, but one does not know what these frolics amounted to; moreover Diogo do Couto is nothing if not hypercritical. The faults of the Portuguese altogether seem to have been in connection with the caves of Elephanta alone—for other caves known to them were converted to Christian use and worship—those of omission rather than of commission. They neglected to take care of the caves, situated as they were in an isolated island and too far from their seat of government.

A Ilha de Bellaflor de Sambayo; a Pragana de Manora; and a Pragana de Asserim.

These are the fifth, sixth, and seventh divisions subject to the "Capital of the North."

The first, also called *Sabayo,* and now Belâpur, had under it the Pragana Panechana with 30 villages, Pragana Cairanà with 17 villages, and Pragana Sabayo with 17 villages.

A Pragana de Manora had 42 villages and one sarretor.

A Pragana Asserim had 38 villages and 6 pacarias.

All these three districts were fortified, and had some churches and chapels built close to the forts; but they are now in ruins, and present no object of interest to the tourist or the antiquarian, except the fort of Asseri, which is described by Gemelli Careri thus:— "Besides its being seated on the top of the hill, where there is no other higher ground to command it, a crooked path cut out of the mountain, along which two men cannot go abreast, leads up to it, and is defended by several guards, who may withstand an army, only rolling down the stones placed there for that purpose."† Dickenson described it, after the Marâṭhâs had had it for eighty years, as accessible only at one point, and of such natural strength that, "with a handful of men to defend it, it may justly be considered impregnable. The latter part of the ascent up is an almost perpendicular staircase (with a precipice of several hundred feet immediately below it) hewn out of the solid rock forty feet higher, at the top of which is an iron door horizontally fixed, and from which the ascent is nearly as steep and of equal height

* *Voyages and Travels, ut supra,* vol. ii., p. 200.

† *Opus cit.,* p. 190.

to a second gateway." It was first taken by the Portuguese from an Abyssinian captain commanding the district, on the payment of Rs. 6,500, and was held by a garrison of sixty soldiers. Those who would like to know more about their past will find their description, the way their forts were garrisoned and equipped, the religious orders to which their churches belonged, the revenue derived from the *tanadarias, mandovins* or custom-houses, &c., and the sums the royal treasury devoted every year for their support, in the *Subsidios, ut supra*, pt. ii., pp. 139 *et seqq.*, pt. iii., pp. 17 and 18; *Chronista*, vol. i., pp. 31-56 *et seqq.*, and vol. iii., pp. 221 *et seqq.*

A Ilha de Bombaim.

The island of Bombay, as the eighth and last division of the "Province of the North," has a long and interesting history of its own, but as this forms the subject of a series of papers which I have contributed to the *Indian Antiquary*,* entitled *Words and Places in and about Bombay*, for the last three years, and which is to be continued, I need not write on it here.

Passing on now to describe the ruins of the city of Bassein, I must begin with its walls and ramparts, which are found to be in a fair state of preservation, except where they are breached at two opposite ends, due east and west, through which runs the modern high-road from the bandar, dividing the fort into two unequal parts. It is this road which prevents the old city from being utterly desolate. Besides the two artificial breaches, nature has made several along the sea-beach. At one place the sea has encroached upon the city to the extent of exposing some feet of the foundation of the wall, which must have been originally underground, the result being a breach. In its proximity a well eleven feet in diameter and twenty in depth has been left, like "a broken gigantic cask."† The general height of the works is from thirty to thirty-five feet, deriving its chief strength from nature, the river and swamps which surround it for the most part nearly to the foot of the ramparts on the north, south, and east sides, rendering it almost impracticable for the regular approach of the besieging army in any of the above directions. To this circumstance is to be attributed the very

---

* See vol. iii., pp. 247, 292, and vol. iv., p. 358.

† A coloured drawing of the above state of things by the late Dr. Buist will be found in the *Trans. Bo. Geog. Soc.* about the end of the volume for the year 1852.

scanty depth of the walls throughout the above portions of the works, the average thickness of which does not exceed five feet. Upon the western or land side the wall consists of a double front of the average thickness of forty-five feet, that being the only quarter which did not permit any natural obstacle to the approach of a besieging army, and was exposed to the repeated attacks of the armies of Gujarât, Jawâr, the Arabs of Muscat, and the Marâṭhâs. Its parapet, however, does not exceed five feet in thickness, being probably intended to resist the effects of musketry only. Capt. Dickinson declares this to be a grave defect in the fortifications, and adds :—"It is composed of irregular masonry, upon which time and neglect have produced the usual ravages; a very little battering, I conceive, would be sufficient to bring the whole of it down, while the chief accidents would arise from the scattered fragments of rock, which the work in question, in common with the rest of the extensive fort, is composed of."*

The Fort of Bassein was built in the form of an irregular decagon, the circumference of which is about a mile and a half, and the interior of the fort from east to west a little above two-thirds of a mile. Each of its angles has a four-sided bastion named Nossa Senhora dos Remedios, Reis Magos, Sam Thiago, Sam Gonçalo, Madre de Deos, Sam Joaõ, Elephante, Sam Pedro, Sam Paulo, and Sam Sebastian. There was another bastion, which is still partly standing, with an inscription on it, behind the citadel or circular fort about the middle of the city, and was named Cavalleiro. This is, unlike the others, round in shape.

Of the two mediæval gateways the one on the seaside, the "Porta do Mar," with its massive teak gates cased with iron bars and spikes, is in a state of perfect preservation. The other, on the land side—the "Porta da Terra," or "Porta do Campo" as some chroniclers name it —is imperfect, so far as those appendages are lying on the ground, almost blocking up the passage. Each of these gateways had, like those of Chaul, two gates, viz., interior and exterior. Out of these only the interior gate of the land gateway is ornamented with two detached sets of double columns, fluted and capitalled, with a window between, indicating that the space above the two gates was a floored one, possibly a room for the guard of the gate.

There was an ancient postern behind the cloisters of the Franciscans, which, from its undefended state perhaps, was eventually closed up by the building of the bastion Sam Sebastian, which bears an inscription.

* Capt. Dickinson's *Report on the Forts of the Konkan*, written in 1818, MSS.

Strange coincidence! The only bastion, with the exception of the bastion Cavalleiro, honoured with an inscription, evincing the great care of the Viceroys in its preservation, and in its strength by filling up the postern which might have been a source of weakness to it, was that by which the Marâṭhâs entered the fort in 1739! How fatal has the name of Sebastian been to the Portuguese!

The Fort of Bassein was in 1634, when visited by Antonio Bocarro, equipped with eighteen pieces of ordnance, and garrisoned by a certain number of companies, whose number varied according to the exigencies of war. There were, however, 400 Europeans and 200 native Christians within the Fort at this time, every one of whom was supposed to have under him three slaves. And this made in case of emergency an aggregate force of 2,400 men in a fair condition to resist the attacks of the native potentates, besides the handfuls of guards of soldiers which each fidalgo had in his village for its defence.* In 1728, when the Factor of Bassein made a detailed report on the defences of the North Konkaṇ, he drew particular attention to the insecure condition of the fort. Bassein had ninety pieces of artillery, ranging between three and twenty-four pounders, out of which twenty-seven were of bronze, and a garrison of eighty infantry and twelve artillerymen.† There were, besides, seventy mortars, seven of which were of bronze, and including those of all the forts of the districts subject to the jurisdiction of Bassein there were altogether one hundred and twenty-seven pieces of artillery, of which thirty-three were of bronze, and one hundred and eighteen mortars, of which only seven were of bronze. There were twenty-one armed boats in the Bassein port, each of which carried from sixteen to eighteen pieces of ordnance.‡

On the capture of Bassein by the Marâṭhâs all these warlike stores were taken possession of by them, but it does not appear that they made any effort to improve the fortifications. Du Perron, who visited the Fort only thirty years after its capture, writes:—

"Cette ville, autrefois soumise aux Portugais, est maintenant entre les mains des Marates.........Après Goa, je n'ai pas vu à cette côte de ville mieux située pour le commerce: elle est au commencement d'une Anse qui renferme plusieurs Isles, entr'autres celle de Salcette. La Forteresse a été bâtie par les Portugais, et seroit susceptible d'un belle défense

* *Chronista*, vol. iii., p. 243.

† *Ibid.*, vol. i., p. 30.

‡ *Diccionario Explicativo, ut supra*, p. 10.

entre les mains aguéries. C'est un exagone régulier. Les bastions sont à oreillons, et portent neuf canon de face : ceux du milieu ont les faces doubles. Le Milieu de plusieurs courtines est encore défendu par un bastion quarré ; et celle qui bat l'Anse est protégée par un pâté en maçonnerie construit sur le bord du bassin. Des deux portes, l'une qui est au Sud est ouverte ; les Marates ont condamné celle du Sud-ouest. Il peut y avoir maintenant, sur les bastions, quarante canon en batterie."*

Captain Dickinson in 1818, on the British taking possession of Bassein, found, "besides several pieces of ordnance and other stores scattered over the interior of the fort, upwards of one hundred gun-carriages upon the works, some of which were in good condition, or requiring little repair." The same writer advises the Bombay Government, in spite of "the great height of the works, which must of itself exclude much of the sea-breeze, the exhalations from the swamp jungle and old walls, impregnated as they are with putrid vegetation," to convert the fort into a big jail. He writes:—"It may become a question how far in its present state the fort of Bassein is not only available, but very useful, for purposes of police and the like. As a fine situation for a general as well as a provincial jail or place of security for prisoners in the event of any internal commotion or war with a European State, it unquestionably has its advantages, as well also in the numerous old buildings which might at any time and at a small expense be rendered habitable." He again reports on the advisability of repairing the fort of Bassein, for two other reasons, viz., "in the protection it would afford any boat or larger vessel, when in danger of being captured by an enemy, there being sufficient depth of water under cover of the guns for vessels of 200 tons' burthen, which considerably exceeds the general description of craft employed either in the carrying on or protection of the coast trade; and as a chief receptacle of timber from the forests of the interior," &c.†

Scarcely had seven years elapsed after the above Report was written when the ruins of Bassein had the honour of being visited by two eminent travellers, Bishop and Mrs. Heber. But they did not admire the ruins very much. The Bishop writes:—"About fifteen miles from Gorabunder, on the main land(?), is the city of Bassein, once a celebrated colony of the Portuguese, taken from them by the

* *Zend Avesta*, p. ccclxxxiv.

† Report, *ut supra*.

Maharattas, and lost by them to the English. It is of considerable size, and surrounded by a regular fortification of rampart and bastions, but without a glacis, which from the marshy nature of the surrounding country was, perhaps, thought needless. There is a small guard stationed in one of the gates, under an English conductor of ordnance, and the place is kept locked up, but is within perfectly uninhabited, and containing nothing but a single small pagoda in good repair and a melancholy display of ruined houses and churches. Of the latter there are no fewer than seven, some of considerable size, but all of mean architecture, though they are striking from the lofty proportions usual in Roman Catholic places of worship, and from the singularity of Christian and European ruins in India. * * * *

"The Portuguese churches in this place and Salsette are all in a paltry style enough, of Grecian mixed with Gothic. In Bassein they have tower-steeples without spires, in Salsette the small arched pediment to hang the bell which is usual in Wales. Their roofs, where they remain, are very steep and covered with tiles, and one of those in Bassein, which appears to have belonged to a house of Jesuits, has the remains of a handsome coved ceiling of teak carved and gilded. They are melancholy objects to look at, but they are monuments, nevertheless, of departed greatness, of a love of splendour far superior to the anxiety for amassing money by which other nations have been chiefly actuated, and of a zeal for God which, if not according to knowledge, was a zeal still, and a sincere one."

Mrs. Heber writes :—"I do not think the ruins themselves repaid us for the trouble we had taken to see them, as with the exception of a pagoda, with the sacred bull well carved at its entrance, they were all in the style of conventual architecture common in the early part of the seventeenth century ; but I was much struck, on entering the massive well-guarded gate, with the scene of utter desolation which presented itself ; it reminded me of some story of enchantment which I had read in my childhood, and I could almost have expected to see the shades of its original inhabitants flitting about among the jungle, which was grown in melancholy luxuriance in the courts and areas of churches, convents, and houses."* Mrs. Postans, however, had a more impressionable mind. She could see great architectural beauty in the buildings of Bassein, where others saw but everything mean and paltry,

* *Narrative of a Journey, ut supra*, vol. ii., pp. 185 and 188.

and often fell into raptures over them. She writes in 1838:—"The city of Bassein has been long forsaken; a few fishermen and shikarries alone occupy a spot once replete with luxury and power, and still containing magnificent evidences of taste, in the application of great and national wealth. * * * The city contains about eight churches, of considerable size and great architectural beauty," &c.* But the truth appears to lie between the two extreme stands made by the fair authoresses.

But to return to the ruins as they are now seen. Within the enclosure are still several buildings, but all more or less in a desolate and dilapidated condition. Standing near the portal of the ancient citadel, and viewing around the precincts of the once splendid city, the tourist beholds, with the exception of a few inscriptions, the Christian monogram I. H. S. carved on doors of churches, and which are still intact, nothing but crumbling walls everywhere; the antiquated moss-covered cross, that traditional symbol of Christianity, which the Portuguese loved to raise at every corner and cross-road; the broken masonry of gates, windows, and walls overgrown with sod and weeds, and overhung with creepers, the omnipresent *pipal*, the undying prickly-pear, and other tropical plants which thrive luxuriantly, sending their twisted tendrils into, and striking root down among, the chinks and crevices of massive walls, immense pillars with beautifully carved capitals, porches, pilasters, cornices, abutments, vaulted ceilings, and the remains of some elegant façades testifying to the opulence of olden times, now, alas! passed away for ever. Churches, convents, colleges, palaces and mansions are strewn about in fragments. Here a column, there a pedestal, yonder a long symmetrical mass pierced with a row of cells, some fallen and smothered in grass and briers, some still erect, bearing their wealth of foliage, trailing wreaths, waving tufts, and thick shrubbery, like hanging gardens high in the air. Silence and gloom reign supreme where once the air resounded with the clash of arms, the roar of cannon, and the tramp of gorgeous pomp and pageants; the traveller's step falls heavily on the ear, where once the chant of the religious, who kept high festivals and held gaudy and solemn processions within this recess, rang throughout its now deserted naves and aisles. A busy stage of missionary activity, with many a site consecrated by the footsteps of the celebrated St. Francis Xavier, Fr. Porto, and Fr. Manuel Gomes; a place that was

* *Western India*, Lond. 1839, vol. i., pp. 179-180.

signalized by sundry miracles, and whose walls were not seldom sprinkled over with the sacred gore of several martyrs.* But these sites are now obliterated, their edifices roofless, the whole a sublime chaos of huge steeples and towers, or mere shapeless mounds of ancient ruins, amidst which are found the tombs of their founders, some desecrated, dug up and plundered, and others without even a decent slab—a pregnant theme for the contemplation of the philosopher and the moralist, a Montesquieu or a Gibbon.

Now if one has the chance to stand on an elevated spot about the middle of the Fort and survey the whole area around, he will be struck with the peculiar marking off of it into two distinct sections, that towards the sea being covered with the ruins of numerous buildings, while the one fronting the land is found entirely unoccupied. What could be the reason of this strange arrangement? Three reasons have been brought forward:—one being that in the case of a siege the unoccupied area would be the quarter where the shot of the enemy would naturally fall thicker than on the other; the second, that in the event of the siege being prolonged, and the garrison starved for want of provisions, this space of ground would be utilized by easily converting it into a rice field, which whether in the rainy season or not, owing to the ample supply of water in its neighbourhood for irrigation purposes, would in less than six months yield rice enough for the support of the garrison. The third is that advanced by Gemelli Careri, who says that in consequence of a plague which towards the end of the seventeenth century is said to have devastated the island and the adjacent country, this space, which is about one-third of the city, became unpeopled, and the dwellings disappeared.

The exploration of the ruins must then begin on the sea side. And here the first thing the tourist will observe is an inscription on the wooden gate, in small characters partly covered by an iron bar. It runs thus:—

DO 20 DE NOV—DE 1720.

Part of this inscription being hidden under iron bars and spikes, its full wording would perhaps in an English guise amount to

"*This gate was made on the 20th November* 1720."

And it is no wonder that, massive teakwood as it is made of, the

* Besides the martyrs of Agâsî, Franciscans, Dominicans, and Jesuits were often murdered by Mahomedans within and outside the fort of Bassein. See *Oriente Conquistado.*

gate has withstood all ravages of time and neglect of man for more than a century and a half, and is even at present as strong, perhaps, as when first made.

Then crossing the gate and wending one's way along the main street—the lines of which, like those of several others in the same fort, can be easily traced—one sees first to the left a temple of mean architecture, dedicated to Hanuman. This appears to be a sarcastic intimation to the unwitting stranger, left as a memento of their rule by the myrmidons of Bâjî Rao *ad futuram rei memoriam*, that in the teeth of the Christian churches and saints at Bassein, the monkey-god has kept his ascendancy over all the ruins there. But the Hindu temples in the Fort of Bassein will be treated of further on.

Within a few yards from the sea gate and to the left of the street leading from it are the remains of the "Matriz," or Cathedral, of St. Joseph (see Plate 15), over the door of which is engraved the following inscription in stone:—

NO ANNO DE 1601, SENDO ARCEBISPO PRIMAZ O ILLMO. SR. DOM FREI ALEIXO DE MENEZES, E VIGARIO O PE. PEDRO GALVAO PEREIRA, SE REFORMOU ESTA MATRIZ.

Translation.

"In the year 1601, being Archbishop Primate the most illustrious Sr. Dom Frei Aleixo de Menezes, and Vicar the Rev. Pedro Galvaõ Pereira, this Matriz was rebuilt."*

This is a large building constructed after the same general architectural type which obtains elsewhere, viz. lofty belfries, vaulted sanctuaries, lancet windows, and arched doorways, with one towered frontispiece and a rectangular campanile besides. It is roofless, but the front and the side walls are in a fair state of preservation. A winding flight of stone steps leads to the top of the steeple. An attempt was made to explore it and obtain a view of the surrounding edifices from above, but scarcely was the ascent begun when two steps crumbled into dust. To persevere would have been not heroism, but folly. It is an inglorious death to die buried beneath the *débris* of a fallen edifice, a Westminster Abbey or a Pantheon though it be. The visitor should therefore be cautioned against going into these steeple-holes. Another word of warning, necessary to strangers, is not to be too eager to handle

* The above inscription, like several others, has been copied in a more legible form, abbreviations written in full, and clauses punctuated without any regard to the division of lines on the stones, all for the sake of better elucidation.

Plate 15.

COPIED & DRAWN BY ARDESHEER

BASSEIN.

THE "MATRIZ" OR CATHEDRAL OF ST. JOSEPH.

inscriptional stones. The writer had, whilst turning over a slab among the ruins of Chaul, a narrow escape from being bitten by a small snake; but, whether big or small, they are, after all, snakes. Besides, every one is not, like some persons, what the French would call *né coiffé*. Thus it is evident that even the chary work of an antiquarian has its perils.

In the chancel to the right of the main altar, which faces the east—in reference to the cardinal points the churches and chapels of Bassein seem to be quite indifferent—there is an oblong black tombstone with the following Latin epitaph:—

PETRI. GAL
VANI. TEM
PLUM. HOC QUI
REXIT. ET AU
XIT. HOC TRA
NSLATA. JACE
NT. FAMULI IN
DO× OSSA. SEP
ULCHRO.
OBIIT GOÆ
19 MARTII
ANNO 1618.

Translation:

"To this grave are transferred the bones of Pedro Galvaõ, servant of the Lord, who managed and enlarged this temple. Died at Goa on the 19th March of the year 1618."

This is the same man who was the Vicar of the "Matriz" at its rebuilding in 1601.

Would it not have been more fortunate for the mortal remains of poor Galvaõ to rest where they were first interred, than to be translated to Bassein? But then they could foresee the future just as much as we can.

It appears from some old documents that this Cathedral was built in or about the year 1546, during the Governorship of Dom Joaõ de Castro. In a long letter written by Dom Joaõ III., on the conversion of the natives of India, to the Governor, who was in the next year raised to the dignity of Viceroy, dated March 1546, the King among other things orders the Cathedral Church to be finished and endowed.* Simaõ Botelho, in his report on the Portuguese possessions

* The paragraph of the letter from the King Dom Joaõ III. to the Viceroy Dom Joaõ de Castro relating to the building of the Church of St. Joseph at Bassein runs thus:—"In the city of Bassein you shall build a church and dedicate it to St. Joseph, and provide for the subsistence of the vicar and his assistants; to accomplish which you may employ something out of our revenues, and the 3,000 pardaos formerly employed in the maintenance of the Mahomedan mosques and their service shall for the future be allotted for the subsistence of the priests, and such other persons as give a helping hand towards the conversion of the infidels."

in India, drawn up between the years 1546 and 1554—that of Bassein was written some time before 1550—gives a list of the disbursements relating to the Cathedral, thus ;—

Forty-eight canadas (a Portuguese measure of liquids) of wine a year	Two tangas per canada.
Twenty-four maunds of oil for lamps	One pardao a maund.
Thirty-four maunds of wax.........	15 tangas.
Flour for wafers, firewood, and laundry	12 pardaos.
Eight surplices, viz. for the vicar, four *beneficiados* or canons, one treasurer, and two choir-boys ...	12 tangas each.

In 1634 Antonio Bocarro writes :—

"The salary of the vicar of the "Sé Matriz," including the vestry expenses, and the salaries of two choir-boys, one treasurer, four *beneficiados*, four singers, and one player on musical instruments, amounts to	666 pardaos, and one larim a year.
Palm-leaves, flowers, &c., for ornamentation, and a kind of cloth called *canequim* for the altar ...	60 pardaos.
Twelve maunds of wax in candles to the confraternity of St. Sebastian, as patron of the city.	90 pardaos.

Gemelli Careri refers to this church briefly thus :—"Friday the 11th (February 1695) I heard mass in the parish church of Our Lady *da Sé*, where there are several altars and two chapels."*

Another tombstone, half-buried underground, has the name of Antonio de Almeida de Sampaio e Su...... It is about the western extremity of the nave.

Further on, at the end of the street to the left of the sea gate, are the ruins of the doorway of the castle, a circular citadel above alluded to, the entrance to which faces the sea. (See Plate 16.) This portal had until lately two sets of detached columns, two on each side, which

* Churchill's *Voyages*, p. 192.

BASSEIN.

THE RUINED GATEWAY OF THE CITADEL.

were removed, it is said, for the adorning of a rural church in the island, notwithstanding the mode they were separated being quite inartistic. The capitals, which are of Corinthian design, with the torus and plinth, are left behind, and only the fluted shafts carried away. The frieze is sculptured, the sculptural embellishments consisting of a Maltese cross, a coat of arms—probably of the Captain during whose time the portal was built—a sphere, and the date 1606, all in bas-relief. On each side of the frieze is now a vacant space, once occupied by inscriptional stones, which are lying about in utter neglect among the ruins, but with the characters entirely worn out. Above the frieze is a niche flanked by a pair of columns of the same order, proportionately diminutive in size, supporting a square slab on the top, on which are carved in alto-relievo the well-known letters I. H. S. The niche is said to have formerly contained a statue of the Blessed Virgin, which, like several other images in the fort, may have been taken care of by some vicar of one of the churches outside it.

Behind the portal the whole space of ground is strewn with the ruins of the castle. To its left, and opposite the ancient street which runs parallel to the newly made road that leads to the bandar, are the ruins of a bastion with the following inscription :—

HO PRIMEIRO CAPITAM QUE EDIFICOU ESTA FORTALEZA
FOI GARCIA DE SA POR MANDADO DO GOVERNADOR
NUNO DA CUNHA ERA DE 1536.

Translation.

"The first Captain who built this fortress was Garcia de Sa, by command of the Governor, Nuno da Cunha, in the year 1536."

This is the oldest inscription in Bassein, still standing, with a part of the wall in which it is let in. The way to it is choked up by ruins of the surrounding edifices, and by thick shrubbery with its dry foliage about two feet deep, the nests probably of snakes and other venomous reptiles. Bocarro refers to this bastion thus :—"This city of Bassein has in the inside, attached to the church of 'the Misericordia,' a house where the captain resides. It is surrounded by an old brick wall, and seems to have been the place of residence of the Moors, to whom it belonged. It has a round bastion which faces the pillory yard. This (the bastion) is a small thing, and being of little importance has been left unoccupied, and is now falling into ruin."*

* *Chronista*, vol. iii., p. 243. I am indebted for the discovery of the inscription on this bastion and for two others to Mr. J. H. Littlewood, a courteous old resident of Bassein.

The area in front of the portal was a market-place, which was daily thronged with people, being the busiest thoroughfare in the city. Gemelli Careri writes:—"The streets are wide and straight, and the great square or market has good buildings about it."* The area behind is covered with the ruins of the palaces of the General of the North and the Captain of Bassein; they consist but of mounds of rubbish, except a wall or two with doors and windows, which are a curiosity at the present time, as belonging to the Portuguese mediæval civic architecture, which is now fast disappearing. Fryer, who saw the above buildings when still in a fair state of preservation in 1675, or twenty years before Careri, describes them thus:—"The fort in the middle of the city is circular; towards the market appears a state house piatzed, where the Governor convocates the *fidalgos* every morning upon consultation, in which they all stand, a chair not being permitted the Governor, though gouty: towards evening they meet there to game."†

The captain of the fort and city of Bassein was the head of the settlement. He had a large establishment, not unlike that of Chaul, under him, paid by the royal treasury.

The following was the list of disbursements made by the royal treasury in defrayal of expenses entailed by the Captain of Bassein:—

Captain of the Fort	600,000	reis a year.
One naik, fifteen peons, besides two servants, their pay amounting to the total of	14,400	,,
Four torch-bearers.................	14,400	,,
Four *canadas* of oil for do.	43,200	,,
Three water and one umbrella carriers	14,400	,,

This was all in about 1550; but in 1634 the Captain of Bassein had under him eighteen peons, one naik, four torch-bearers, two water and one umbrella carrier, one doorkeeper, one *sobre-rolda* or chief of the night-watch department, and one Oriental translator, their pay amounting to 3,420 pardaos a year.

Having given in the preceding *Notes on the History and Antiquities of Chaul* the names of all the Captains that are found in the

* *Opus cit*, p. 196.

† *A New Account*, &c., p. 74.

Plate 24.

BASSEIN.

RUINS OF THE CHURCH OF THE AUGUSTINIANS.

chronicles, I append, in a foot-note below, those of the Captains of Bassein in chronological order.*

A little behind the portal of the circular citadel, and about the end of the street that leads from the sea-gate along the wall to the pillory-yard, are the ruins of a magnificent building, the uses of which have not yet been ascertained with precision. (See Plate 24.) While some assert that it was the house of the Captain, and others the Court of Justice, most people think it to have been the Church and Convent of the Augustinians. Its front, to which a stylobate of five deep steps, now partly covered with earth, forms an ascent, consists of an elegant portico supported by four pillars, dividing the entrance into three arches, leading into the vestibule. The background of the portico bears the Portuguese royal arms, and the remains of some other emblematic devices, now utterly undistinguishable. The entablature and the pediment used to bear until lately two inscriptions; both of them have now been removed. The lower one was carved on the architrave, the whole of which having fallen to the ground, the visitors often mistook it for an inscribed pillar. The upper inscription was placed in the tympanum, above the raking cornice of which was raised another piece of superstructure with a circular window crowning the frontispiece, which has now entirely disappeared. The whole of it made a graceful façade in the style of the mediæval ecclesiastical architecture of Southern Europe.

Of the two inscriptions given below—a copy of which, along with the photograph of the building, was taken while they were still together—the first was on the architrave, and the second on the tympanum.

---

* 1535 Garcia de Sá.
1536 { Rui Vaz Pereira.
Antonio da Silveira. }
1537 Manuel de Macedo.
1538 { Rui Lourenço de Tavora.
Garcia de Sá. }
1541 Dom Francisco de Menezes.
1545 Dom Jeronimo de Menezes (*o Bacalhao*).
1548 Jorge Cabral.
1549 Francisco Barreto.
1554 Francisco de Sá.
Then follows a long gap, which cannot be easily filled up.
1611 Nuno Vas de Castello Branco.
1620-23 Gaspar Pereira.
1630 Gaspar de Mello de Miranda.
1635 Rui Dias da Cunha.
1639 André Salema.
1650 Dom Alvaro d'Almeida.
1653 Manuel Corte Real Sampaio.
1661-64 Joaõ de Siqueira de Faria.
1667 Dom Antonio de Souto Maior.
1670 Manuel Teixeira Franco.
1671 Jeronimo Manuel Albuquerque.
1672 Henrique da Silva de Eça.
1675 André Pereira dos Reis.
1677-78 Fernando Antonio Souto Maior.
1693 Manoel Tavares da Gama.
1712-17 Dom Antonio Vasco de Mello.
1728 Francisco Pereira Pinto.
1738 { Joaõ Barbosa Barros.
Joaõ Xavier Pereira Pinto. }
1739 Caetano de Souza Pereira.

Both inscriptions are commemorative of St. Francis Xavier having been chosen patron of Bassein in the year 1631.* One runs thus:—

GOVERNANDO O ESTADO DA INDIA O VICE-REI DOM MIGUEL DE NORONHA, CONDE DE LINHARES, SE FEZ ESTE PORTAL, EM O QUAL SE POZ POR PADROEIRO D'ESTA CIDADE A SAM FRANCISCO XAVIER. A DES DE MAIO 1631.

Translation.

"Governing the State of India the Viceroy Dom Miguel de Noronha, Count of Linhares, this portal was built, on which was placed St. Francis Xavier as patron of this city. On the 10th May 1631."

The other is as follows:—

SENDO CAPITAO D'ESTA CIDADE GASPAR DE MELLO DE MIRANDA, E VEREADORES GONÇALO COELHO DA SILVA, PERO FERREIRA, E JOAO BOTO MACHADO COM OS MAIS OFFICIAES SE POZ N'ESTE (PORTAL?) A SAM XAVIER, QUE TOMARAO POR SEU PATRONO. ....NO ANNO DE 1631.

Translation.

"Being Captain of this city Gaspar de Mello de Miranda, and Aldermen Gonçalo Coelho da Silva, Pero Ferreira, and Joaõ Boto Machado, with other officers, (this inscription) of St. Xavier having been taken as its patron ......was placed on this (portal?) in the year 1631."

The first inscription was evidently commanded to be placed by the Viceroy, and the second by the Captain and members of the Senate, as it was called, or Municipality of Bassein.

The translations are literal, the only freedom taken being the addition of a word here and there in parentheses where the sense was ambiguous.

Next to the ruins of the Captain's Palace are those of the Factory. Close to the latter was a building of extraordinary size, called "Ambar," where rice belonging to the Factory was stored. The ruins of this building are now barely traceable.

* Yet only about a hundred years before, according to the testimony of Antonio Bocarro, the patron saint of Bassein at the time of its foundation was St. Sebastian. They appear, however, to have deposed him, and raised St. Francis Xavier to his place. There is as much of human nature in dealing with saints as with princes.

The Factor of Bassein was the second dignitary among the high officials of the city, with the pay of 200,000 reis a year. He had under him a staff consisting of the following:—

Two clerks, each of whom had	50,000 reis a year.
Two torch-bearers, whose pay with the price of two maunds of oil amounted to	28,800 ,,
Twenty peons, each of whom was paid ...	3 tangas a year.
Next to the Factor came the *Ouvidor* or judge, whose salary, like that of the *Ouvidor* of Thâṇâ, was............	100,000 reis a year.
He had under him five peons with the same pay as those of the Factor.	
Then followed the "Meirinho," a police officer, whose business was to apprehend criminals, his salary being also	100,000 ,,

He had for his service ten peons paid as above. Other officials were as follows:—

One "Alcaide do Mar," or sea bailiff, with the salary of	12,000 ,,
(To the above sum Jorge Cabral added one ducat a month).	
The "Almoxarife dos Almazens"	30,000 ,,
His clerk	12,000 ,,
King's solicitor................................	20,000 ,,
"Provedor de defunctos," or administrator of intestates	18,000 ,,
His clerk had the same pay.	
The chief of the night watch of the Fort	25,200 ,,
The master-builder	18,000 ,,

Bassein was once a place remarkable for shipbuilding. Also Thâṇâ was famous for its docks, as in 1588, when six small vessels were built and fitted out there. In 1636 two pinnaces were built for the Surat Factory at Bassein, which with two others built at Damaun formed the nucleus of what afterwards developed into the Bombay Marine.*

* Bruce's *Annals of the E. I. Company*, vol. i., p. 334.

The constable of the Fort had	38,920 reis a year.
The latter had under him twelve bombardiers, each of whom was paid......	3 tangas a month.
The architect and civil engineer	37,200 reis a year.
The gatekeeper of the Fort	3,700 ,,
The jailor	15,000 ,,
The *Tanadar-mór's* pay was	200,000 ,,

This *Tanadar* had besides, like those of Agâsi, Thânâ, Karanjâ, and Bandora, a house, *gratis*, belonging to the king. The house of the *Tanadar-mór* of Bassein was situated at what was called "Baçaim de cima," or Upper Bassein; while that of the *Tanadar* of Agâsi was a large mosque.

The Tanadar-mór had under him twenty peons, ten from Goa and ten from Bassein, each of whom was paid ..	5 tangas a month.
Four musketeers, each of whom had	7 ,, ,,
One Nâik..................................	2 pardaos a month.
One Nâfar	7 vintens ,,
One clerk	30,000 reis a year.
The latter had under him one Nâik and four Nâfars, whose aggregate pay amounted to	12,072 ,,
One Oriental Translator....................	14,400 ,,
One Parabu................................	10,800 ,,
One Tenoeyro (tanoeiro ?), a cooper	16,800 ,,
Each boatswain (comitre) of the ferry-boats in the Bassein river had	200 reis a month.*

There was also occasionally a high official placed at Bassein to superintend the work of others, named "Vedor," literally overseer. His name is not given in any of the three lists from which the above information is drawn, but he is referred to by chroniclers and travellers.

To crown the officialdom of Bassein was "the General of the North"—than whom, excepting the Viceroy and the high dignitaries of the Church, there was no greater officer in the whole of the Portuguese settlements—who always resided at Bassein.

Gemelli Careri says:—"The government is in a Captain, as they call him, or Governor, and the administration of justice in a *Vedor* and the *Desembargador*, who is a gown-man (probably a doctor of laws),

* *Subsidios, ut supra*, pt. ii., pp. 206 and 216; *Chronista*, vol. iii., pp. 245-246; *Instituto Vasca da Gama*, vol. i., p. 253.

and judge of appeals from all the *vedors* of the northern coast, along which in every city there are factors and treasurers for the revenue of the crown of Portugal. The Portuguese General resides at *Bazaim*, with sovereign authority over the Captain of that and all the other northern places, whence he is called General of the North."

Our traveller, a doctor of laws himself, was asked by the prior, Father Felicianus, to remain as advocate at Bassein for the various religious houses there, with a liberal annuity, because the native pleaders in the courts were extremely ignorant. But he says, "Having no inclination to live in those hot countries, I answered, that although he had offered me 100,000 pieces of eight portion, I should never be induced to quit Europe for ever."* Careri did well.

There being no *mandovim* or custom-house built at Bassein belonging to the king, a private house was rented for that purpose, paying 84 pardaos a year.

Little can be gleaned from chroniclers as to the social condition of the citizens of Bassein. Some of the travellers, however, refer to their customs and manners, the way the grand ceremonies of the Church were conducted, the etiquette observed at social gatherings, and the affluence and wealth that surrounded their dwellings, which throws a great deal of light on a subject that can never be elucidated by dry historical documents; although in some cases, perhaps, much subsidiary assistance can be derived even from them.

Among the travellers, Fryer and Gemelli Careri appear to have moved among the higher circle of society at Bassein, and the little glimpses we obtain from their writings are certainly worth recording. Fryer, after stating that the Captain of Bassein and those of other settlements held their appointments for three years, which were entailed on certain families of the conquerors, adds, "Every one in his course having his turn to rule in some place or other for three years, and upon these they can borrow or take up money as certain as upon their hereditary estates, the next incumbent being security for the payment: pursuant to this, a new Governor coming to *Choul*, his Honour the President sent to congratulate him; and the old Admiral of the *North* coming to *Baçein*, another was sent on the same message."

In regard to the villa residences of the citizens of Bassein in its suburbs and the adjacent country, I have already quoted from the

* Churchill's *Voyages*, p. 191.

above traveller a passage testifying to the opulence and good taste with which the Portuguese fidalgos of old lavished the surplus of their treasury on the embellishment of their houses.

Now turning to another phase of the social life of the Basseinese we find Gemelli Careri writing, "Thursday the 10th (February 1695), understanding there was a wedding of people of quality at the Church of our Lady *de la Vida*, I went to see the ceremony. I observed the bridegroom did not give his bride the right hand, and thinking it an extravagant custom, as being only used by crowned heads, I asked the reason of it of some Portuguese, who told me the same was practised in Portugal, and this that the gentleman might have his right hand at liberty, to put to his sword in defence of the lady. The bride was richly clad, after the French fashion; but some trumpets went along, sounding such a doleful tone, as little differed from that they use in conducting criminals to execution. I returned to the monastery in the *Andora* (palanquin); and here it is to be observed, that the manner of saluting those they meet, when they are carried in this sort of conveyance, in Italy would be taken for an affront and laughed at; for in token of respect they shut the little door of the *Andora* upon them. This in Naples would certainly produce a duel, and in India is done out of respect even to the Viceroy himself."

Again he writes:—"Sunday the 30th, Mass was sung at the Augustinians with music, which being in India was not disagreeable, and much gentry was there. The heat was greater than in *Damaun*... .... The people of fashion at that time wear silk and very thin muslins, having long breeches down to their heels, so that they need no stockings. Instead of shoes they wear sandals like the friars."* The Portuguese of those days appear to have understood hygiene better than we do nowadays.

The "people of quality" or Fidalgos here referred to were once numerous in the city of Bassein, as will be seen from a perusal of that excellent compilation *A Nobiliarchia Goana*, published by the late Mr. F. N. Xavier at New-Goa, 1862; but what is of interest to those who study the natural history of man living in different climes and countries, as in divers social media, is the fact that within three centuries out of a hundred families, to speak in round numbers, whose

* *Opus cit.*, pp. 191-192.

BASSEIN.

RUINS OF THE CHAPEL OF THE "MISERICORDIA."

names are recorded there, seventy-five at least have now become extinct. Of the remaining twenty-five, twenty have no lineal descendants, the collateral ones being an effete, degenerate race, morally and physically incapable of any exertion, dwelling in the meaner parts of the new city of Goa, and, although excessively proud of their pedigree and of their rights of conquerors, forming but the dregs of the Goanese society, whom the lowest pariah among the natives of the country despises and laughs at. It is in reference to this class of the Portuguese that the natives of Goa have given currency to the following proverb in Koṅkaṇî:—"Never say a snake is small, nor the Portuguese is yours." Whether the snake be small or the Portuguese friendly, they are both, notwithstanding, poisonous—utterly untrustworthy.

The remaining five per cent. are still prosperous, principally from their having reverted to the main trunk at home, in Portugal, where, in spite of their unnumbered reverses, and vices engendered by luxury and wealth drawn and accumulated from their former conquests, many a genuine man will yet be found.

There were no hotels at Bassein, but strangers who happened to visit the city were most hospitably treated by the monks. Thus Pietro della Valle was a guest of the Jesuits, and Gemelli Careri of the Augustinians. The latter traveller writes:—"There being no houses of entertainment in the city, we were received by Father *Felicianus* of the Nativity (Feliciano da Natividade ?), born at Macao, in the kingdom of China, and prior of the monastery of the Augustinians, who treated us all very courteously and like a true Portuguese."

But to return to the ruins. Next to those of the General of the North's palace, and separated from them by a large oblong area which was the garden of the palace, are the ruins of the "Misericordia" and of the Hospital attached to it. (See Plate 20.) This is a massive pile of considerable length, facing the wall on the river-side. It has a large and beautiful cloistered arcade adjoining it, built in the form of a square, enclosing a spacious courtyard completely shut in from the sight of the outer world. The Church of the "Misericordia" is, though not large, a handsome building. The frontispiece is constructed of finely hewn stone and delicately wrought pillars. Above the doorway is an escutcheon sculptured in stone, bearing a beautiful Maltese cross in the centre—most of the members of the "Misericordia" were in former days Knights of Malta—and on either side is the figure of a dragon holding in its teeth a roll, or what would appear to others a *fleur-de-lis*.

Within the body of the church are two tombstones, one large and the other small. The larger one bears the following epitaph :—

SEPULTURA DE Po. CÀBRAL
DE NAVAIS E DE SEU Fo. P.
HIERONIMO Po. CABRAL
E SEUS HERDEIROS.

Translation.

"The Grave of Po. Cabral de Navais, and of his son P. Hieronimo Po. Cabral, and his heirs."

The other runs thus :—

S^{A}
D^{A} L. H.
E$_{O}$ D$_{O}$ E.

This is a puzzle. Apparently a lady is buried here.

In reference to this church Gemelli Careri writes :—"Sunday the 6th I heard mass in the Church of the *Misericordia*, which is the parish of the city."

The "Misericordia" of Bassein, like that of Chaul, was a very old institution.* The Hospital adjacent to it had from the royal treasury 504,000 reis a year, or 140 pardaos a month. The "Misericordia" had, besides, 79,200 reis for the purchase of rice for the poor.

In a corner opposite the entrance of the church is a mound of stones and mortar, which seems to have once formed the pedestal of a cross, the latter having been removed. On one side of this pedestal is the Hindu temple dedicated to Mahâdeva (see Plate 19).

Running parallel to this is what appears to be the Church of N. S. da Vida. This is one of the oldest churches in Bassein. It was built close to the citadel. In fact, within a compass so narrow as the area between the citadel and the land gateway are found all the ecclesiastical edifices of Bassein. This is explained by the fact of there being various religious communities, about six in number, who, not finding room sufficient in the Fort, were obliged to build their churches and convents close to each other; and this not on a niggardly scale, for each of these buildings appears to be of dimensions large enough to accommodate all who resided within the Fort.

* See *ante*, p. 91.

BASSEIN.

THE TOWER OF THE CHURCH OF THE FRANCISCANS, AND THE HINDU TEMPLE.

In the nave of this church was some time ago established a sugar refinery, which imparted some life to the deserted city; but, not having in any way proved remunerative to the enterprising speculator, it was recently closed.

The space intervening between the "Misericordia" and the "Igreja de N. S. da Vida" is dug up into a tank in connection with the machinery in the latter church, just as another place close to the sea has been encircled by a wall with a flight of steps leading to the top, where sea-water used to be stored for the same purpose. While digging what would appear to be the garden of the General of the North's palace, they found there heaps of human bones. Were they buried there during the pestilence that raged in Bassein towards the end of the seventeenth century, or during the siege by the Marâṭhâs? In the Church of N. S. da Vida itself, while foundations were being laid for the factory within its nave, a grave came accidentally to be opened, where they found the bones of a man and horse together, with a rusty rapier amidst them. This is quite in keeping with the olden practice of burying a general along with his charger. Has this custom in the West any analogy with that of *Satî* in the East?

Gemelli Careri, besides the remarks already quoted anent a marriage ceremony which he witnessed there on the 10th February 1695, writes:—"Tuesday, the 8th, I heard mass in the parish of Our Lady *de la Vida*, where there are three very good altars well adorned."

Further on, to the right of the Church of N. S. da Vida, is another church, which was converted into a warehouse in connection with the sugar refinery. From its dimensions, and from being connected with what appears to be a conventual building in the vicinity, it would answer remarkably well for the Church and Monastery of the Hospitallers, which were also within the Fort.

The ruins of the monastery are now faintly discernible. The foundation of the order of the Hospitallers is of comparatively recent date. It was first instituted in Spain by a pious man named Joaõ de Deos, and all its members were laymen, doing the duties of nurses by attending on the sick and wounded in the hospitals. They came to Goa first in the 17th century, about the year 1681, and soon spread all over the other settlements. They were employed, after the Jesuits, in the Hospital of the "Misericordia" at Bassein, and the proximity of their monastery to the latter edifice would perhaps identify the pile of buildings close to the parish of N. S. da Vida, above alluded to, as the Monastery of the Fathers Hospitallers. Gemelli Careri refers to it thus:—"The Monastery of the Fathers Hospitallers, or *St. John de Dios*, where I was on Monday the 9th, is so poor, that it can maintain but three friars."

A little beyond, in front of the square, are the ruins of the Church and Monastery of the Jesuits, which must have formerly been a very handsome structure. The church presents the finest façade among the religious buildings of Bassein (see Plate 21). A noble arch, columns with fluted shafts and Corinthian capitals, the monogram I. H. S. surmounted with a cross sculptured in alto-relievo both on the lintel and above the pillars on either side of the entrance, with other architectural embellishments, combine to impart to the front of this church a very graceful and pleasing appearance. Attached to it are the ruins of the College, over the door of which is the date 1636, partly covered by rank vegetation. It probably refers to the time the College was rebuilt. Although more than three centuries old, the walls do not show the least sign of having settled, which is perhaps due to the Portuguese system of laying very deep foundations, as seen in Chaul, where the natives excavate several feet below the surface for stones. Within the nave of the church the walls bear the semblance of having settled, but this is entirely due to the *débris* of the fallen roof and arched ceiling having raised the pavement above its former level.

Several travellers refer to the Church and Convent of the Jesuits. Pietro della Valle, who was in the College on the night of the 29th March 1623, says that on his arrival in the port of Bassein from Damaun he sent word to Father Diogo Rodrigues, Rector of the college, to whom he had brought letters of introduction from the Rector of the Jesuit college at Damaun. The Rector despatched immediately Father Gaspar de Govea to invite him to pass the night in the monastery, as he had to embark the next day on board a vessel sailing with the "fleet of the north" to Goa. The invitation being accepted, Pietro della Valle took supper with the fathers, and, having been treated with great courtesy, thanked the Rector and the other fathers for their hospitality, and went to sleep on board the vessel. Of Bassein he writes:—"Della città di Bassaim non posso dir cosa alcuna, perchè di notte ci entrai, di notte ne uscii, e ci stetti dentro senza vederla: solo posso accennare, che è cinta tutta di mura forti, e se bene scorsi, mi parue più grande di Damàn; ma per un temporale terribile che patì gli anni addietro, aveva molti edificii rovinati; e

Plate 21.

BASSEIN.

JESUITS' CHURCH OF "HOLY NAME."

non rifatti. Trovai nel Collegio di Bassaim il Padre Paolo Giovio Italiano."*

As Pietro della Valle informs us, Bassein did in reality suffer from the effects of a terrible hurricane about the beginning of the seventeenth century. Ogilby also refers to this unfortunate occurrence thus:—"At the beginning of this age (century ?) many houses were swallowed up by an earthquake, in the room of which none have since been built."† An old MS. gives a rather exaggerated account of what happened, saying that it was an extraordinary deluge, and the force of the inundation had driven many a boat in the river up through the gate into the Fort. Although the accounts differ, some calling it a storm, and others an earthquake and inundation, there is no doubt that something unusual had taken place, although no notice of it is found in the chroniclers.

About fifteen years later (1639) Bassein was visited by Mandelslo; and although he did not land, being all the while in the harbour, his references to Bassein and the Jesuits are certainly worth reading. He writes:—

"Le 7e *Janvier* nous arrivâmes de grand matin devant la ville de *Baçaim*, située dans le Royaume de *Guzerate*, sur une rivière où les plus grands vaisseaux peuvent remonter depuis de Golfe de Cambaye; ce qui la rend marchande et riche; elle est aussi assez belle et assez bien fortifiée; il y a une fort bonne citadelle, et les *Portugais* en sont les maîtres depuis l'an 1534.

"Nous nous approchâmes de la ville, d'où le Gouverneur nous fit saluer de sept coups de canon, et nous répondîmes à sa civilité par trois coups de canon. Nous y attendîmes plus de quatre heures un *Jésuite Portugais*, que nous avions promis de conduire à *Goa;* mais voyant qu'il ne venoit point, nous remîmes à la voile et nous continuâmes nôtre route.

"Nous n'avions pas encore fait une lieue, que nous vîmes sortir du port une frégate *Portugaise;* ce qui nous fit croire qu'elle nous amenoit nôtre *Jésuite*, et nous obligea à baisser nos voiles pour l'attendre; mais

---

* "Of the city of Bassein I can say nothing; because I entered and left it during the night, and was inside without seeing it. I can only hint that it is surrounded by a strong wall, and, if well glanced at, it appeared to me larger than that of Damaun. But on account of a terrible storm, some years back, many of its edifices had been destroyed and not yet repaired. I met in the College of Bassein the Italian Father Paolo Giovio."—*Viaggi de Pietro della Valle il Pellegrino*, Venetia, 1667, pt. iii., pp. 131-132.

† *English Atlas*, vol. i., p. 214.

le capitaine qui aborda nos vaisseaux nous dit, qui le Gouverneur prioit le Président *Anglois* de souffrir que la frégate pût aller à *Goa* sous la protection du pavillon du Angletere, parce qu'il apprehendoit la rencontre de vaisseau *Hollandois*, qui courent incessamment cette côte. Il nous fit présent, de la part du Gouverneur, de trois bœufs, de quelques moutons, de pain, de plusieurs paniers de citrons et d'oranges, et de divers autres refraichissemens, avec lesquelles nous continuâmes gayement nôtre voyage."*

Next to Mandelslo comes Fryer, who writes on the Jesuit Church and College thus:—"Within the walls are six churches, four convents, two colleges, one of the Jesuits, another of the Franciscans. It bears the name of an Academy; the students are instructed in the Jesuits' college, but live in town: where is a library, with classes of historians, moralists, expositors, and no more. It is a college of polite structure, in the *Portuco* is a copy of *Angelos* representing the resurrection; above stairs, as well as below, are fine square cloisters, as all their collegiate churches have, on the sides whereof are their cells; they have a spacious refectory and a goodly church; three parts of the city are devoted to their use."† (See Plates 22 and 23.)

Gemelli Careri writes:—"Friday the 4th, I saw the church of the Jesuits, in India called *Paulistas*. It is richly gilt, not only the three chapels, but the walls and arch; but the workmen knew not how to make that rich metal show itself to the best advantage. The dormitory and cloister are the best in the city. In the garden, besides the Indian, there are some sorts of European fruit, and among the rest figs and grapes, which the father rector told me came to maturity twice a year, that is, in December and March."‡

The foundations of the church and monastery of the Jesuits at Bassein were laid in the year 1548. Previous to this the missions in and about Bassein were under the charge of the Franciscans and Dominicans, although the latter, being very few at that time, had not joined as yet in communities. The Franciscans had hitherto practically been since the days of Fr. Porto the sole ministers of the Christianity of Bassein and its neighbourhood. They had done excellent work up to that year, but having embraced too much at a time they could scarcely keep up what they had got, much less could they extend their field of operations.

* *Voyages du Sieur Jean Albert de Mandelslo*, Amsterdam, 1727, p. 233.

† *A New Account*, &c., p. 74.

‡ Churchill's *Voyages*, vol. iv., p. 192.

BASSEIN.

ONE OF THE SQUARES OF THE JESUITS' MONASTERY.

Add to this the dissensions that arose in that religious body at home, as well as in India, breaking up their order into two irreconcileable branches of the "Old Observance" and of the "Reform," when each of them having their own superiors, and making themselves almost independent of the mother-country, only a scanty supply of missionaries could be obtained. Thus arose a great relaxation in their duties, and the Christianity newly founded by them was languishing for want of ministers to carry on their evangelizing, and was about to revert to heathenism, when the opportune arrival of St. Francis Xavier and his companions saved the Roman Catholic missionaries from this ignominy. With the year 1542 dawns a new epoch in the missionary history of Portuguese India, the 6th of May being the memorable day on which the great Apostle St. Francis Xavier landed at Goa. Between this date and that of his death, the 2nd December 1552—ten years of a highly successful missionary life—St. Francis Xavier visited Bassein three times. First about the end of the year 1544, on his way to Diu to confer with the Governor Martim Affonço de Souza, who was then in that city, as to the best means of chastising "the tyrant of Jaffnapatam," as the king of that place was called, for his persecution of the new Christian converts.* He could not however, have stayed long in any of the cities he lighted upon on the coast, for we find him at Cochin about the middle of January 1545.

The second visit he paid to Bassein was in 1548, soon after his arrival at Goa from his second tour to the Fishery coast, on the 29th March, together with an envoy of the king of Kandy. He came to see the Viceroy, Dom Joaõ de Castro, and, having accomplished the object of his interview, returned immediately to Goa.

His third and last visit to this city was about the end of the same year, 1548. He was at Goa in June, attending on the Viceroy, Dom Joaõ de Castro, who was on his death-bed, and who died on the 6th of that month. Soon after the monsoon the great Apostle, whose name is still found recorded as written with the pen of steel on the slab of stone at several places in the ruined city, came to Bassein, and this time with the object of extending the missionary operations of his Society to this place. On his arrival in India in 1542 the Franciscan fathers of Bassein had requested him to take charge of the seminary which the King John III. had established for the conversion of the heathen; but the Apostle had been obliged to decline their offer, on account of his having but few

* See my *Memoir on the History of the Tooth-Relic of Ceylon*, &c., p. 42.

companions to help him in the work he had proposed himself to accomplish. But now, availing himself of the arrival of nine Jesuits from home, he laid the foundation of a splendid mission which his Society extended throughout the Northern Koṅkaṇ, and, leaving it in the hands of Melchior Gonsalves and another companion, sailed to Cochin, from which place he writes a long letter, dated 28th January 1549, to his Provincial in Portugal, Fr. Simaõ Rodrigues.*

Fr. Melchior Gonsalves, having taken charge of the new mission, began to build the Church and College, on the completion of which he was appointed Rector. It was called the "Church and College of the Holy Name of Jesus." St. Francis Xavier, although deeply absorbed in missionary labours of great moment elsewhere, never ceased to evince the interest he from the first took in the Jesuits' mission at Bassein. In one of his letters addressed to Fr. F. Gomes, Rector of the College at Goa, from Cangoxima, and dated the 5th November 1549, he writes :—"I want to hear from you about Melchior Gonsalves, about the College of Bassein, the Franciscans who before held it, whether any friars of that order have lately come from Portugal, whether the College which has once been given up to our Society is still governed by ours, and whether it is expected that it will be so perpetually."†

About this time the number of Jesuits in India was very limited, and even these few did not display, with the exception of St. Francis Xavier, in any marked degree abilities for their work. They were simply eminent in mediocrity. Cosme Annes, the "Vedor Geral da Fazenda" at Bassein, in a letter to the King written from that city and dated the 30th November 1547, after announcing the death of the Vicar-General, Miguel Vaz, says :—"All the fathers of the Order of Jesus who have come here, are, with the exception of 'Mestre Francisco' (St. Francis Xavier), incapable for this."‡

Fr. Melchior Gonsalves, however, worked successfully at the College of Bassein, and, notwithstanding the arduous duties of the Rectorate, found time to make occasional missionary excursions into the neighbouring villages, where he is said to have made a great many converts. Three years after, on his being succeeded by Fr. Melchior Nunes Barreto,

* This letter is given by Fr. Coleridge in his *Life and Letters of St. Francis Xavier*, vol. ii., chap. iii.

† Coleridge, *ut supra*.

‡ *Resumo Historico*, &c., p. 86.

BASSEIN.

ANOTHER OF THE SQUARES OF THE JESUITS' MONASTERY.

nominated by St. Francis Xavier on the 29th February 1552, shortly before his last voyage to China,* to this important post, Fr. Gonsalves went to Thânâ, where he remained until his useful career was put an end to by a violent death through poisoning, by one of the pagans of the town. The second Rector of Bassein, Melchior Barreto, was a brother of the Patriarch of Ethiopia, Francisco Joaõ Nunes Barreto, also a Jesuit, who being prevented from entering his diocese remained at Goa, living in the residence of his order at Choraõ like a simple Father. In the meanwhile the bishop of Goa, Dom Joaõ d'Albuquerque, having died, the Patriarch of Ethiopia was called upon to act as Administrator of the diocese of Goa. During the seven years that the episcopal See of Goa remained vacant it was governed by the chapter, all the episcopal functions and ordinations being performed by the Patriarch. The second Rector of Bassein was an esteemed comrade of St. Francis Xavier, whose three excellent letters addressed to him have been lately published, and show the affection the apostle had for him.

Fr. Barreto did not, however, remain long at Bassein. On the death of Gaspar Baerts, Rector of the "Santa Fé" College at Goa, and Provincial of the Jesuits in India, which took place on the 9th October 1553, he was appointed Provincial. His predecessor died quite suddenly, while preaching in the pulpit of the Cathedral from the text of the gospel of the day (27th Sunday after Pentecost), "The kingdom of heaven is like unto a king who would take account of his servants." Fr. Baerts had been ailing for some time from a cardiac affection, and was regretting, says their chronicler Pe. Souza, that he could not die on a cross in Japan. Next to St. Francis Xavier he was the greatest missionary that ever came to India, and the saint himself not unfrequently refers to him in his letters in terms of praise of his self-denial, zeal, and talents.

In the beginning of the year 1655 a goodly supply of missionaries of the Society of Jesus was despatched from Lisbon. Twelve of them started, their first destination being Abyssinia, but three of them—Fr. André Gonsalves, Fr. Pascoal de Chalons, and Brother Affonso Lopes—having had the misfortune to be shipwrecked and thrown on a desert island in the ocean, where they died starved, only nine arrived in safety at Goa, where some of them remained, and lent their help to both the colleges of Goa and Bassein.

* Other important dates relating to St. Francis Xavier are his canonization in 1612 and his election as a patron of India in 1631.

The next year brought another fine band of Jesuit missionaries. Fr. Gonçalo Silveira, whom their leader, St. Ignatius Loyola, had himself appointed Provincial, was at the head of this distinguished body; he died at Goa in 1562. It was in this year that the first printing-press in India was introduced by the Jesuits in the College of the "Holy Faith" at Goa, where numerous works and tracts on Christianity in Portuguese and vernaculars, romanized according to the phonetic system of the Portuguese, were published.

The year 1573 is a red-letter epoch in the annals of the Jesuit Church of Bassein. It was in this year that the largest number ever known of baptisms, amounting to 1,C00 heathen, was celebrated in their church. The number of converts by the Jesuits had hitherto been confined to mere hundreds, or never reached the thousand, but now they adopted a plan that as it had already been tried and found successful at Goa, promised to prove as fruitful here also. Their method consisted first in the conversion of a high-caste man, a Brâhmaṇ, who was sure to be imitated by a number of his and other classes. The next step was to solemnize his baptism with all possible pomp and splendour, to hold a grand procession in his honour with the assistance of the Governor, the nobility, gentry, and clergy of the town, and give a sumptuous banquet at the end of the ceremony to the new convert and his friends. Those were the halcyon days of Jesuitism. Their bait was alluring and irresistible, and the native convert was led by the nose.

These periodical public christenings went on increasing year by year in a progressive ratio, by means of agencies throughout the island of Bassein and the adjacent country, such as the one at Bandora, established in 1575, and others, until the year 1588, when in the church of Bassein alone 9,400 heathen were baptized. Owing to the large number of these converts new parishes arose in the island, three of which owe their origin to the Jesuits, viz. N. S. da Graça, Sam Thomè, and Sam Miguel Archanjo. There was an express order from Rome for the Jesuits in India, as if to stimulate their zeal, not to administer any parish church except those founded by themselves out of a pagan community by its conversion to the Christian faith.

The Jesuits of Bassein had also their local martyrs, the most conspicuous among them being the above-mentioned Fr. Melchior Gonsalves and Fr. Vicente Alvares, the latter a scholastic, who was murdered by Musalmân pirates on his way from Bassein to Goa.*

---

* *Oriente Conquistado, ut supra.*

As early as 1550 the King of Portugal, as before mentioned, used to contribute to the Franciscans of Bassein the annual sum of 2,070 pardaos, derived from a source which before the conquest was solely applicable to the lighting of the mosques in Bassein. On the establishment of the Jesuits this amount was equally divided between the Franciscans and Jesuits. It was disbursed under the heading "Conversaõ da Fé," or conversion to the faith. In 1634 the Jesuits of Bassein had this sum raised to 3,000 pardaos a year.*

There was also at Bassein a Commissary of the Inquisition. The transition from the history of the Jesuits to that of the Inquisition is but natural. It was through their influence that that dreaded tribunal was first established at Goa in 1560, resulting in the burning alive and other cruel tortures of about 1,250 persons in about ten or twelve *autos da fé*. The illustrious Marquis of Pombal suppressed it in 1774, but during the reign of D. Maria I., about the year 1779, when it was the fashion to revoke every measure of that great minister, it was re-established, until the year 1812, when it was, mainly through the representations made by the English Government, entirely extinguished.† Baldæus‡ refers to the origin of the institution of the Inquisition at Goa thus :—

"Certain blasphemous papers against our Saviour, with some severe reflections against the Jesuit Gonsalves (Gonçalo ?) Pereira, who afterwards suffered martyrdom at Monopatapa (Monomotapa ?), being found in a box set in the great church for the gathering of alms, and the same being supposed to be laid there by some European Jews, who now and then used to resort thither privately, this gave occasion to introduce the Inquisition into Goa."

Diogo do Couto§ gives more lengthy reasons for the establishment of this tribunal, and Pyrard|| tells us that only the rich, the confiscation of whose property profited the Inquisition, suffered, while the poor escaped.

When Dellon was brought to Bassein in 1583 on his way to Goa, to be tried by the inquisition there, he was detained in the port until the Commissary of the Inquisition at Bassein had added to the list of

---

* *Subsidios, ut supra*, pt. iii., p. 209; *Chronista*, vol. iii., p. 245.

† *Narraçao da Inquisiçao*, &c., by M. V. d'Abreu, Nova Goa, 1866, p. 5.

‡ *A Description of the East Indies, &c.*, p. 631.

§ *Decadas*, VII., cap. v., p. 335.

|| *Viagem, ut supra*, vol. ii., pp. 80 *et seqq.*

prisoners brought down from Damaun "a large number of companions in misfortune," who were all carried down to Goa fettered in irons.

Goa was the head-quarters of the Inquisition, but every one of their principal settlements, such as Bassein, Chaul, Damaun, Cochin, &c., sent yearly a large number of victims through their so-called Commissaries.

The prisoners at Bassein, until the arrival of "the fleet from the north," were kept in the Jail, which was somewhere near the Captain's Palace. There is no appreciable vestige of this building now in Bassein, except an inscriptional slab, partly worn out, to be seen near the travellers' bungalow outside the Fort.

The inscription runs thus :—

SENDO V. REI PERO DA SILVA E CAPITAM DESTA FORTALEZA RUI DIAS DA CUNHA A CIDADE DE BAÇAIM, D. LUIZ D'ATAIDE, FRANCISCO PEREIRA..............E ALVARO COELHO MANDOU FAZER ESTA PRISAM, A QUAL SE ACABOU SENDO CAPITAM ANDRÉ SALEMA, E VREADORES ANTONIO TELES, TRISTAM ....

Translation.

"Pero da Silva being Viceroy, and Rui Dias da Cunha Captain of this Fortress, the city of Bassein, Dom Luiz d'Athaide, Francisco Pereira...... and Alvaro Coelho caused this Jail to be built, which was completed while André Salema was Captain, and Antonio Teles, Tristam...... Aldermen."

The date is entirely worn out, but the mention of the name of the Viceroy Pero da Silva indicates it to be between 1635 and 1639, during which time he governed. But before this there must have been some other such place close to the Castle, about the middle of the Fort.

The Commissary of the Inquisition appears to have put up with the Jesuits, or perhaps had an apartment in their large pile of buildings fitted up especially for his use.

The greater part of these buildings—the college and cloisters—is now more or less dilapidated ; but their ruins are still interesting, not only as the most extensive in the Fort, but also as having belonged to a religious order that worked with great zeal and made numerous converts. Their style of architecture, in which there is no poverty of design, strikes one as essentially appropriate to the climate, skies, and the visible surroundings of the country, forming in this respect a singular contrast with the modern so-called Gothic buildings in the neighbouring city of Bombay, which are thoroughly out of place, or, rather, more fit to withstand the inclement weather of the dreary north than the sultry and oppressive heat of the tropical plains.

About the nave of the church, nearer the chancel, are two gravestones covering the mortal remains of two fair benefactresses of the Jesuits' Church and College; one runs thus:—

SEPULTURA DE ISABEL DE AGUIAR, DONNA VIUVA, INSIGNE BEMFEITORA DESTE COLLEGIO. FALLECEO A 24 DE JANEIRO ANNO DE 1591.

Translation.

"Grave of Isabel de Aguiar, widow and notable benefactress of this College. Died on the 24th January 1591."

The other is as follows:—

SEPULTURA DE DONA FILIPA DA FONSECA, DONA VIUVA, INSIGNE BEMFEITORA DESTA IGREJA, A QUEM EM SUA VIDA DEU TUDO QUANTO TINHA. FALECEO A VINTE DE JULHO DA ERA DE 1628.

Translation.

"Grave of Dona Filipa da Fonseca, widow, and famous benefactress of this Church, to which she gave during her lifetime all she possessed. Died on the 20th July 1628."

A little beyond, overtaken by similar misfortune, and belonging to the order of the Franciscans, is the Church of the invocation of "Santo Antonio." This is the oldest and one of the most extensive religious edifices of Bassein. Its foundation dates from the time of the venerable Fr. Antonio do Porto, who, after a very successful apostolic career through Bassein, Salsette, Caranjâ, Chaul, &c., where he is said to have "built 11 churches, converted 10,150 heathen, and destroyed 200 pagodas," * returned to Bassein to devote his mind entirely to it, where he worked with success for some years more, until an advanced age, and died there. It is a great pity that there is not only no record left of the

* *Gabinete Litterario*, vol. i, p. 37.

date of his death, nor even of the place where he was buried. The details of the life and labours of this truly great, holy, and zealous worker in the conversion of the heathen would be in interest second only to those of St. Francis Xavier.

The ruins of the Franciscan Church and Monastery are still visible, and its divisions fairly traceable.* This was the largest and most important monastic building after that of St. Francis at Goa, erected soon after the conquest of that city in 1510. There was a college in connection with it, and on it were dependent the filial churches of Espirito Santo, Monte Calvario, Madre de Deus at Pale, N. S. da Luz at Agâsî, and numerous others in the island of Salsette and elsewhere, mostly built by Fr. Antonio do Porto, each of which churches became at last a central station, where two or three friars usually resided, and had charge of all important churches or chapels in the neighbouring villages. But the churches they built, until the arrival of the Jesuits, when they considerably increased, being simply missionary stations, their congregations were very limited.

The principal chapel of this church has the arched ceiling with its elaborate mouldings in a tolerable state of preservation. The great arch near the chapel of the baptismal font is built in the style of the "flat arch" of the church of Belem near Lisbon, and is still well preserved (see Plate 25). The church has four lateral chapels, each of which, as well as the central nave and the chancel, contains a number of tombstones, some with and others without epitaphs.

The following are still legible. One runs thus :—

....E DO CONSELHO DE SUA MAGESTADE, FÁLECEU EM 24 DE AGOSTO DE 1558, E DE SUA MOLHER, DONA LUIZA DA SILVA E SEUS ERDEIROS."

Translation.

.................."His Majesty's Councillor, died on the 24th of August 1558, and of his wife, Dona Luiza da Silva and his heirs."

---

* An attempt was made by myself to prepare a plan of the ruins of the Church and Convent of the Jesuits, while that of the Church of the Franciscans was kindly drawn for me by my very esteemed friend Dr. Carlo de Marchesetti of Trieste, but being only two, and other buildings in ruins admitting of no such procedure, I regret that I am obliged to refrain from printing them here, in spite of my own wish and the request of others to do so.

BASSEIN.

RUINS OF THE CHURCH AND CONVENT OF THE FRANCISCANS.

In one of the side chapels to the left of the high altar may be read:—

AQUI JAZ DONA FRANCISCA DE MIRANDA, MOLHER DE MANOEL DE MELO PEREIRA, INSTITUIDORA D'ESTA CAPELLA, E SUA FILHA DONA INES DE MELO E SEU NETO LUIS DE MELO, A QUAL FALECEU A 10 DE NOVEMBRO DE 1606.

Translation.

"Here rests Dona Francisca de Miranda, wife of Manoel de Melo Pereira, founder of this chapel, and her daughter Dona Ines de Melo and her grandson Luis de Melo; she died on the 10th November 1606."

It is perhaps to this inscription, as far as the date is concerned, or to one similarly situated but now removed, that Bishop Heber refers thus:—"The largest of these churches, I was assured by a Maharatta of rank, a *protégé* of Mr. Elphinstone's, who accompanied us, was built by a man who had made a large fortune by selling slippers. It contains no inscription, that I could see, to confirm or invalidate this testimony, nor any date whatever, but one on a monument to a certain Donna Maria de Souza, of 1606."*

The assurance of this "Maharatta of rank" is, after all, a fiction. The church and convent were built with the money of the King of Portugal, and several chapels were built, as seen in this inscription, at private expense.

In another place, about the centre of the edifice, is the following:—

SRA. DE DONA GIOMAR D'AGUIAR, MOLHER QUE FOI D'ALVARO DE LEMOS, QUE DEOS AJA. FALESEO A 4 DE MARÇO DE 96 (1596?). HE SUA E DE SEU FILHO.

Translation.

"Grave of Dona Giomar d'Aguiar, widow of Alvaro de Lemos, may he be with God! Died on the 4th March of 96 (1596?). Is hers and her son's."

In the third chapel, to the right of the chancel, is legible:—

ESTA CAMPA POS DONA PRA DE BERREDO POR ESTAR SEPOLTADO NESTA SEPULTURA SEU MARIDO ANTO TELES DEMES, QUE FALECEO EM 26 DE OUTUBRO DE 1676. ESTA COVA FOI COMPRADA POR MANOEL DE CARVALHAR PERA E SEUS HERDEIROS.

PADRE NOSSO.

* *Narrative*, &c., vol. ii., p. 188.

Translation.

"This gravestone was placed by Dona 'Pra (Francisca ?) de Berredo for being buried in this grave her husband Antonio Teles de Menezes, who died on the 26th of October of 1676. This grave was purchased by Manoel de Carvalhar Pereira and his heirs. Our Father."

In the same is the following :—

ESTA SEPULTURA E DE BALTAZAR FREIRE DA CAMARA, FILHA DE DONA SIMOA FREIRE. FALECEO A PRº. DIA NV DE 1601.

Translation.

"This grave belongs to Baltazar Freire da Camara, daughter of Dona Simoa Freire. Died on the 1st of November of 1601."

Baltazar is generally the name of a man, but here it is given to a lady.

In the first chapel, to the left of the main altar, is one short epitaph which runs thus :—

SEPULTURA DE BENTO DA COSTA E DE SEUS ERDEIROS.

Translation.

"Grave of Bento da Costa and his heirs."

The corridor round the cells forming the cloisters placed on the four sides of a square courtyard, planted with trees, is still in a fair state of preservation. The arcade is supported by four complete and two half columns; whereas the corridor of the cloisters of the Jesuits has only four complete columns. The vestibule of the Church of the Franciscans is very elegant, its front consisting of three high arches, the portion above having fallen into ruin. Again, while most of the buildings of Bassein are built of irregular sharp fragments of basalt stone joined together by pretty hard mortar and clay, the building of the Church and Monastery of the Franciscans consists principally of cut stones of laterite for the walls, and of basalt for staircases, arches, windows, and door-posts. One staircase finely constructed of this stone is still found well preserved beside the vaulted sacristy.

The Franciscan Church and Convent were built at the sole expense of the king Dom Joaõ III., who endowed it with the annual stipend of 1,272 xerafins, to which was added by a pious gentleman the gift of 100 xerafins.* They had once, as stated above, 2,070 pardaos paid annually from the royal treasury, but this sum was eventually distributed between them and the Jesuits, under the heading of "conversion to the faith." The village of Mont-Pezier, yielding about 60 pardaos a year, was made over to them during the governorship of Jorge Cabral. This amount was to be applied to the use of the monks and neophytes dwelling in the residence attached to the Church of N. S. da Piedade.†

In 1634 the number of friars in the convent of the Franciscans was thirty; while that of the Jesuits was fifteen; of the Dominicans ten; and of the Augustins eight: all maintained by the State. The half of the gift of 2,070 pardaos paid to the Franciscans was about this time raised to 3,000.‡

It may not perhaps be generally known that the natives of Bassein and its neighbourhood have had the honour of one of their compatriots being enrolled among the Buddhist saints. This is the great Damila, whose name is recorded in some of the Kânheri inscriptions. This person was until lately the only celestial glory—if such a thing can be said of those who believe in nihilism—which the Basseinese could lay claim to. But now they have an undisputed right to flatter themselves with having one of their citizens' names inserted in the already long file of the *Flos Sanctorum*, and this not only surrounded with the ordinary halo of sanctity, but also with the crown of martyrdom. This holy man is no less a person than Brother Gonçalo Garcia, a native of Bassein, who, having had the happy thought of joining the Franciscan Convent as a lay brother, went to Japan with some friars belonging to his order, had the good fortune to be murdered by the Japanese, and is now worshipped by the Roman Catholics, and by none more so than the pious Basseinese and the Salsette devotees, as a saint. St. Gonçalo Garcia, who was murdered at Nagasaki in Japan, on the 5th February 1597, was declared first, along with his companions, by Pope Urban VIII., in a bull dated the 14th September 1627, to be a genuine martyr, and as such called "*beatus* Gonçalo Garcia," or blessed Gonçalo Garcia; but Pope Pius IX., on the 8th June 1862, before a large assembly of Cardinals, Patriarchs, Primates, Archbishops, and Bishops, amounting to about three hundred, raised the "*beatus*

* *Gabinete Litterario*, vol. i., p. 60.

† *Subsidios*, &c., pt. ii., p. 210.

‡ *Chronista*, vol. iii., p. 245.

Gonçalo Garcia" to the highest honour to which a living man can raise the dead. He was canonized, with other Japanese martyrs, and from that date he is styled St. Gonçalo Garcia, and is worshipped as such.*

The native Christians of Bassein and Salsette, who are mostly descendants of the once sturdy race of the Bhaṇḍârîs and the industrious Kolîs, have every reason to feel elated at such an event. Gifted with less than a mediocre proportion of intellectual faculties necessary to stand the struggle of life, they naturally comfort themselves with the hope that although placed by their fates at the lower end of the social scale, they may yet rise in the next world to the top, by following the example of their countryman St. Gonçalo Garcia, who managed so well to find his way to heaven. They are in their present circumstances, it is true, quite incapable of entering the portals of the temple of Minerva, being utterly devoid of even a moderate degree of mental power; but they have, in compensation, a great amount of piety, and under the guidance of the priesthood, whose conduct is extremely exemplary, there is every hope that St. Gonçalo will have many a follower among his countrymen, without the necessity of their ever going abroad to be crucified, as in Japan, in the cause of Christianity.

Having done for the present with the Buddhist and Christian saints of Bassein, let us turn our attention to the accounts of the travellers allusive to the church and monastery of the Franciscans. Gemelli Careri writes:—"Continuing to visit churches, I came on Monday the 7th to that of the Franciscans. Both church and monastery are built after the manner of Europe, the church having many chapels, contrary to the custom of India."†

Mrs. Postans refers to this and the Church of the Jesuits thus:—"The most perfect and handsome churches now remaining at Bassein are those of St. Paulo and St. Francis: both have square towers, with cloisters and priestly residences attached, but the most exquisite remnants of the past are to be found in the interiors of beautiful chapels, where through a vista of ruined arches the eye dwells on the richly wooded scene beyond, and Nature, in her sunniest dress, contrasts with the dark and mouldering stone, which she, like a laughing child decking its grey and aged sire with summer blossoms, hangs with bright lichens and many-coloured weeds. In one of

---

* *Anno Historico*, &c., "Dia 5 de Fevereiro."

† *Opus cit.*, p. 192.

these picturesque and beautiful buildings a lofty arch remains, supporting the roofless walls, worn in unequal turrets by the season's change." Elsewhere, in reference to the tombs in these churches, she writes:—" But thirty years have elapsed since the city of Bassein was inhabited; and still in one church the human sympathies of the observer may be excited, by the whitened remnants of mortality exposed in an open grave, doubtless desecrated, from the opinion, commonly received among natives, that individuals blessed with the goods of fortune often, with selfish anxiety, desire that their treasure should, rather than pass to other hands, be deposited with themselves, when corruption hastens into dust." Then again:—

"Tradition and romance have shed a charm of enchanting interest around the ancient history of that singular people, which is here touchingly recalled, as the traveller's eye traces many names which he at once must recognize as claiming ancestry with the noble blood of the first among those who fought for and established their country's power on the Indian soil. The names of Don Lorenço and of Alfonso Albuquerque, of many of the greatest and heroes whom the policy of Portugal selected to fix her empire in the East, cannot be read without emotion, the more so when surrounded by ruin and desolation, the relics of a power itself tottering in decay."* Very well; but our gifted authoress simply draws upon her imagination. Affonso d'Albuquerque was buried at Goa, and his bones were afterwards carried away to Portugal. It would not, certainly, speak well for the patriotism of the Portuguese if the bones of Affonso d'Albuquerque, whose memory is as much cherished by them as that of Clive by the English or of Koen by the Dutch, were to be seen by Mrs. Postans at Bassein in 1838. Dom Lourenço d'Almeida, to whom she evidently refers, died, as we have seen before, in the Chaul river.

The last fact recorded in the annals relating to the Church and Convent of the Franciscans of Bassein is that every time the great Apostle St. Francis Xavier visited Bassein it was here that he fixed his residence.

To the right of the ruins of the Church and Convent of the Franciscans, and almost intervening between them and the ruined Church and College of the Jesuits, are the ruins of the Dominican Church and Monastery. They were built in 1583, thirty-five years after the building of their mother-church and convent at Goa in 1548, under the

---

* *Western India in* 1838, vol. i., pp. 180 *et seqq.*

invocation of Sam Gonçalo. Here lies buried Fr. Jeronimo de Paixaõ, who was murdered near the walls of Bassein.

In 1634 there were ten monks in it, and it had 280 pardaos a year from the royal treasury, besides numerous donations from rich fidalgos. The Church of N. Sra. dos Remedios and several others in the neighbourhood were in their charge.

The vast Church of the Dominicans is now roofless, except a part close to the chancel, which is vaulted (see Plate 26). Like the English churches, its length is extraordinary in proportion to its breadth. Its walls, partially discoloured, are still standing. The *Capella-mór*, or principal chapel, with its beautiful arch, is in a very good condition. On the Gospel side of the altar is the tomb of the patron, in ruins, the epitaph being scarcely legible. The monastery is also in ruins, and an attempt made to trace its plan resulted in utter confusion. The corridors, halls and cells are now occupied by mounds of rubbish covered with rank vegetation. When visited by Gemelli Careri it had an excellent dormitory. He writes:—"Saturday the 5th, I visited the monastery of the Dominicans, with the famous dormitory. The church was large and had but three altars, as we said was used in India, opposite to the great gate, and all well adorned."*

Now strolling along silent walks and wide alleys between the high walls of the fort and of the monasteries of the Dominicans and Franciscans, stained with mould and fringed with delicate mosses, with branches of evergreen shrubbery interlocking, the tourist is confronted by the bastion Sam Sebastiam with a postern close by, which is thoroughly blocked up. A blank oblong space alone indicates the place which the inscription, now lying about in utter neglect near the land gateway, occupied. This inscription runs thus:—

REINANDO HO MUIO ALTO E MUITO PODEROSO REI D. JOAM DE PORTUGAL 3 DESTE NOME, E GOVERNANDO A INDIA O VICE-REI D. AFONSO DE NORONHA, FILHO DO MARQUEZ DE VILLA REAL, SENDO FRANCISCO DE SA CAPITAO DESTA FORTALEZA E CIDADE DE BAÇAI, FUNDOU ESTE BALUARTE, PER NOME SAM SEBASTIAM, AOS 22 DIAS DO MES DE FEVEREIRO ERA 1554 ANNOS.

* *Opus cit.*, p. 192.

BASSEIN.

RUINS OF THE CHURCH OF THE DOMINICANS.

Translation.

"During the reign of the most high and the most mighty King D. Joam of Portugal, the third of this name, and governing India the Viceroy D. Afonso de Noronha, son of the Marquis of Villa Real, Francisco de Sá being Captain of this Fort and City of Baçai, this bastion, named Sam Sebastiam, was built, on the 22nd of the month of February of the year 1554."

On the outer side of this wall, and leading from the postern, are the ruins of the once much-frequented pier, which juts out into the sea. Inside, almost opposite the ruins of the bastion, and a few yards distant from it, is a modern English tombstone, the epitaph being partially legible. It runs thus :—

"Here lies the body of...........Durham, wife of Andrew Durham, Surgeon, who departed this life in...........

Before dismissing the subject of the bastions and fortifications, it is necessary to advert to a curious intramural passage towards the river-side, which has existed there for a very long time, and baffled every attempt at explanation by putting out the lights carried in to illumine this dark recess. The air is evidently deleterious, but the cavernous passage appears to have had, like that of Chaul, some military purpose to serve.

The next object worth seeing is a very ancient street, which, running almost parallel to the new highroad, leads along the middle of the fort to the sea gateway. It is on both sides of this street that are to be found the architectural remains of the private mansions of fidalgos, which yet testify to the splendour and opulence of former times. When visited by Fryer in 1675, just two centuries ago, these buildings were "stately dwellings, graced with covered balconies, and large windows two stories high, with panes of oyster shell, which is their usual glazing among them in India, or else latticed." On the style of living of these fidalgos Fryer adds :—"They show their greatness by their number of *sumbreeroes* (sombreiros, *i.e.* umbrellas) and *Cofferies* (Caffrarias, *i.e.* African slaves), whereby it is dangerous to walk late, for fear of falling into the hands of those pilfering, abusive rascals. Only the Fidalgos had their stately dwellings, and none but Christians could lodge within the city, the Banians repairing to the suburbs upon tatoo."*

* *A New Account*, &c., p. 74.

It is a tradition that the ladies of Bassein would not walk in streets unless they were carpeted, and had private entrances to churches, to avoid defilement by contact with people destitute of blue blood. This little vanity may account, perhaps, for the existence of an arched passage over the way which connected the Cathedral with a private house to its right. If not ornamental, it may have served the purpose of conveying, unobserved by plebeian eyes, the ladies of the households of the fidalgos living in that quarter of the city direct over the street into the Cathedral.

An instance of the public spirit and opulence of the ladies of Bassein is found in the subscriptions which only a few of them, and those of the noblest blood, excluding every other of the lower grades of nobility, collected among themselves for the building of a monastery of the invocation of St. Clara of the Patriarchate of St. Francis d'Assisi for two hundred nuns at Goa. The subscription list amounted in a very short time to 200,000 xerafins, a pretty large sum in those days; but the Archbishop, D. Fr. Aleixo de Menezes, spent it in the erection of the College of S. Boaventura, built in 1602.*

Of the "stately" dwellings now remain but heaps of stones and mortar overgrown with dense forest, and they have thus lost the features by which they could be identified. This whole quarter is now like unto the ancient *campus ubi Troia fuit*.

There are, however, two objects worth hunting after, and these are an inscriptional slab let into a wall to the left of the street in the neighbourhood of the newly built cottages for the artizans who once worked at the sugar factory set up in the Church of N. S. da Saude, and an ornamental bath-room, which is still well preserved, owing to its being built entirely of hard cement studded with shells and pieces of porcelain.

The inscription is engraven in an extremely confused manner. Only a few words are intelligible, and its translation should rather be left as an enigma for the reader to solve. This is the last of the inscriptions of Bassein existing there, as none has escaped search. It runs thus:—

ESTAS CASAS S
EARA BATRADE
SAM EAFAOE
SAE ... NO ANO. DE
1617. POR MA

---

* *Resumo Historico, ut supra*, p. 374.

BASSEIN.

RUINS OF THE CAPTAIN GENERAL OF THE NORTH'S PALACE GARDEN.

DADO DO DOOM
E DO RCLAFL. O
O MAENCOICAE
DON OLÒI............A
....
....
....
20 ....
NIALFEIAC
AELACDELE.
SE ESUL OD ....
AEN ... SE SE SOMO
DIE CIO AGNEF
CAN PAMEINI
MAAPORMNATNDO
VPORESLPADIAO

This slab is about 5½ feet long by 2 feet broad.

It is matter for melancholy reflection that most of the families formerly living in this quarter, whose fathers reared these stately edifices, are now extinct.

In proximity to the above buildings, in a square which overlooks the road, are the ruins of the Chapel of N. S. da Annunciada, which was under the charge of the Augustins. The altar of this chapel, in defiance of the usages observed in similar temples, faces the north. The front presents two arches, the upper one being rather larger than the lower. The vaulted chancel, which has some painted mouldings on it, has considerably fallen in on the left side, but the walls, with four lateral windows, are still well preserved.

Thus far the ruins of Bassein. But architectural remains are not the only monuments of the Portuguese sway at Bassein. It was one of the centres from which radiated the influence of their polity, the effects of which are yet discernible in the religion and race they left behind ; and when all that is made up of stone and mortar is entirely swept off the earth's surface, or washed away by the action of the annual deluge that attends every monsoon, there will yet remain in Bassein and its vicinity vestiges of a kind far more lasting than the materials, that are liable to changes and permutations decreed by Nature.

One cannot venture to presume the estimation in which this sort of traces of their former rule in India is held by the thoughtful in

Portugal; one cannot be sure whether that country does feel at all proud of these monuments of "social amelioration and moral and religious regeneration," planted by her adventurous sons on both the western and eastern coasts of our peninsula. Of one thing, however, he may be certain, that the Christianity of Bassein and the neighbouring villages is but a mixture of Christian dogma and Hindu ritual, of Roman Catholic liturgy and Pagan ceremonial; it is in fact a *religio sui generis*. It has been undergoing so many phases of spasmodic progress and retrogression, that a treatise replete with interesting details might be written on the subject. It is not seldom that several of these so-called native Christians have renounced Christianity and reverted to the faith of their fathers, then forsworn the latter and embraced Christianity again. If one were to meet a specimen of these strange people and ask his name, he would incontinently reply that his name was Bairû, Janiâ, or other such Hindu name common enough among the Kolî tribes. Then if asked the name of his father or grandfather, it would surprise the inquirer to learn that he bore the designation of Joaõ Fernandes, Pascoal da Silva, &c.

The untutored state of their minds and their love of mimicry is displayed to the utmost in that religious festival of the Roman Catholic Church in India which is termed "Santos Passos." This grand melodrame, with some farcical episodes attached to it, is represented in every one of their churches, both in Bassein and other Catholic communities elsewhere, in all its serio-comic incidents and details. The passion of Christ—a subject otherwise too grave for such ridiculous exhibitions—is told with all vividness of imagination by an over-excited priest in ludicrous recitals, with the accompaniments of gestures more like those of a violent maniac than of a sober minister of the altar. Then follow images and other scenical decorations, which at a certain stroke or ringing of a little bell at the command of this tonsured actor are exposed to the gaze of the bystanders by the lifting of the screen, behind which all these theatrical paraphernalia are carefully concealed. The redundant and highly periphrastic narrative, with considerable spurious interpolations of his own, of what took place about nineteen centuries ago on the mount Calvary, with which the priest edifies his auditors, is then crowned by bearing the image of the Christ in procession, with which the play ends.

In some churches the tragedy is performed during the whole of Lent in multipartite acts, the last being that of the Crucifixion, which, as at Bandora, is represented with all its mournful effect. Usually a platform is erected within the chancel of the church, or, rarely, in *pandáls* raised in the yard with all the stage adjuncts. The comparative study of this play as acted in India and the famous Passion-play of Ober-Ammergau, in the Bavarian Alps, would result, it appears, in inferences of great value to sociology; for how truly applicable to this subject, as to others, are the words of Don Emilio Castelar, who in his *Old Rome and New Italy* says, "Those who look upon life from one side, upon time from one age, the doctrines of one religion only, humanity from one people, will never understand the human mind."

In some parishes in India, when there are no images to represent the several incidents of the play, there are not wanting magnanimous individuals to perform it all themselves, carefully avoiding, of course, the final crucifixion.

The history of the "Santos Passos" or Passion-play at Bassein is extremely curious. It originated with the Jesuits. The "Santos Passos" were first performed in the church connected with the Jesuits' College of "the Holy Faith" at Goa, as a sequence to an event of religious revival in 1551, when the Pope, in compliance with the request of St. Francis Xavier, granted a general jubilee for India, the first ever celebrated in this country. A Jesuit, by name Gaspar Berzeo, established then a society of the so-called "disciplinántes," whose business it was, while the preacher raised their religious emotions to the pitch of insanity, to chastise themselves with scourges, which in some instances had little iron blades attached to them, so as to make incisions into the skin deep enough to allow the blood to flow. Sometimes the theopathy of the faithful, as is usually the case, was of so catching a nature that whole congregations were found busy in the process of flogging themselves. In some instances the voice of the preacher, who had in the meanwhile worked himself up to a frenzy, was quite drowned in the whack and thwack of the lash and stripe. The hysteric penitents, of course, fainted; but then there were the Jesuit brothers always ready by their side to help them into another room, where consolations were liberally dispensed to them. The sermon of the Jesuit preacher was generally on the text "multa flagella peccatoris," and at the end of it a crucifix was held out to the contemplation of the entranced congregation, when the hardy "disciplinantes" began their work of self-torture. This enthusiasm, however, could not last long, and soon gave place to the so-called "Santos Passos," or Passion-play, performed in successive stages in weekly parts during the course of Lent, which, having begun in the Jesuits' church at Goa, spread, as if by infection, in a very short time to every Roman Catholic community in India. It was brought first to Bassein by the above-mentioned Jesuit Fr. Melchior Nunes Barreto.

The race of the native Christians of Bassein is well known to us. The title of *Portuguese*—for it is but a title—assumed by them is both ethnologically and politically incorrect. The physical and mental organization of this people cannot be described under one type, for they are pretty numerous clans of different types of the Koḷîs and Bhaṇḍârîs, though perfectly miscible, besides the hybrid product or bastard offspring of such heterogeneous elements as a European soldier and a low-class native woman,—for no high-class woman would marry him,—which altogether make up the community of the Roman Catholics of Bassein and the adjacent country. They are extremely ignorant, nor have they any talent worth developing for anything useful, except perhaps the lower walks of handicraft, such as carpentry, cotton-weaving, and the curing of bacon. From the day Nuno da Cunha conquered Bassein up to the present there has not been a single literary or scientific celebrity among them. The highest in the class are but clerks in English and Parsee offices, where they carry on the mechanical work of copying. Occasionally a pamphleteer or two put in their appearance, but their productions are written in excessively bad English and worse Portuguese. Of vernaculars, except perhaps a little colloquial corrupt dialect of the Marâṭhî, they know nothing, and appear to have renounced them from the day of their conversion to Christianity. They are as much despised by the dominant race as by the Hindus, and might, in fact, have got almost out of sight but for their occasional ebullitions of temper in doggrel pamphlets against their parish brothers, their minds never rising above the parochial lumber, although futile attempts are not unfrequently made to draw into it persons far above them and outside their community. As for the moral character of the hybrid race, it may be summed up in the following dictum, which has been found true elsewhere—they have inherited the vices of both their parents and the virtues of neither.*

* *Apropos* of the vices of one class of the population.

There is no descendant of any high-class native amongst them. This fact is best proved by their physiognomy, which is, in short and general outline, a receding forehead, small eyes, prominent cheek-bones, nose sunk at the root with wide nostrils, large mouth and thick lips. In the more depressed classes and those addicted to drink, the expression of the face is scowling and unsteady. Another proof of their low descent is the spite and hatred they bear, from the very bottom of their heart, against high-class natives, who, from their natural shrewdness and superior intellect, seem destined to domineer over them.

The architectural remains of the Marâṭhâ sway at Bassein are but two temples, before mentioned, the one close to the sea gate of the Fort, and the other near the ruins of the "Misericórdia." They have nothing striking about them, except, perhaps, the *Nandî* or sacred bull well carved at the entrance of the latter temple, and to which Mrs. Heber refers in her diary in terms of praise.

Of Bassein and its vicious administration, Captain Hamilton, who visited that city about 1695, writes :—"It is a place of small trade, because most of its riches lie dead and buried in their churches, or in the hands of indolent, lazy country gentlemen, who loiter away their days in ease, luxury, and pride, without having the least sense of the poverty and calamity of their country." Then our author adds that the governor was a Captain, and there resided also the *General of the North,* whose authority extended over Damaun, Diu, &c. ; "but," he says, "the Church superintends, which makes his government both uneasy and precarious."—Captain A. Hamilton's *New Account of the East Indies,* vol. i., p. 180.

APPENDIX.

CHAUL.

Tourists desirous of visiting the ruins of the forts and cities of Chaul and Bassein will require to learn for themselves, in the absolute want of guides, how the trips are to be undertaken, which the most convenient routes, what accommodation is procurable at those places, and all about the supply of provisions for the sail or journey, before starting.

The visitor to Chaul has not, unlike the one to Bassein, a choice between the land and sea routes. He has but the latter, and the trip is one of the most picturesque and enjoyable that can be imagined. There are steam ferries plying every alternate day, beginning with Monday, across the Bombay harbour, calling, according to circumstances, at more than one bandar on the way, but generally touching off Thull and Alibâg, and then going straight to Revadaṇḍâ or Chaul. The steam communication is only regular during the fair season, when the steam ferry starts from Carnac Bandar early in the morning (6-30), and after three hours' run reaches Chaul. The visitor then has almost the whole day before him to see the ruins, seek repose in the ruined city during the night, and return the following morning by the steamer, which leaves Dasgaum at daylight and touches off Revadaṇḍâ, arriving at Bombay the same afternoon.

There is no travellers' bungalow at Chaul; but the villagers will be found hospitable enough to afford shelter to the respectable excursionist in their hovels. Having examined the ruins of the Fort of Chaul, the visitor should then cross the river to see the more picturesque ruins of Kôrlô, or the "*Mórro.*" The most convenient ascent is on the land side from the foot of the hill where the Church of N. S. do Carmo is built. The church itself is worth looking into for its old altars and images of Our Lady of Carmel and St. Francis d'Assisi, transferred there from the old churches of Chaul. The ascent of the "Môrro" is rather steep, and the footpath narrow, but from a little beyond the remains of the pedestal of a cross a flight of about forty steps leads to the top of the hill, where the first gate of the Fort is situated. Having read the inscriptions, examined the gates, walls, bastions, and the ruins of the cistern and church with its vaulted chancel, high arch and beautiful mouldings, whose paintings are yet visible, the visitor will do well to go to the highest point on the ridge behind the church, from whence an excellent panoramic view of the sea, the city of Bombay and its suburbs, may be enjoyed. The descent by the slope towards the sea is made easy by a flight of steps, some of which are mouldering, while others are still in a fair state of preservation.

The first-class fare from Bombay to Chaul is Rs. 3-8-0. "Passengers are recommended to provide themselves with refreshments, nothing being obtainable on board."

Before closing the subject of Chaul, two additional facts, which have been overlooked, may be mentioned here. The excellent work entitled *A Historia das Inquisições* states that the Dutch tried more than once to invade Chaul, but without success. The chroniclers, however, are absolutely silent on this point. The other fact worth recording is that Isaac, the Armenian who accompanied the Jesuit Benedict Goes, a native of Azores, to China, on his return to India settled himself at Chaul.*

BASSEIN.

The tourist to Bassein may have his choice of a trip by water or land. The former is a pleasant route, especially on a moonlight night, the sail round by Thâṇâ to Bassein, winding in and out amongst numerous little islands, with a scenery which may be equalled but scarcely surpassed by any river or lake scene in the world, being one that is often resorted to by those who have time to spare; but two-thirds of tourists, being hard pushed for time, especially in these days of a high-pressure life, will always prefer the journey by railway.

The journey by land, then, from Bombay to Bassein, about twenty-nine miles, lies along the seaboard, and presents no very remarkable variety of scenery. The route for the first twenty-five miles leads through the low lands of the western sides of the islands of Bombay and Salsette, having nothing remarkable along the line, except the cave-temple of Jogeśvara, not far from Pahaḍî, or, as it is now called, Gorgaum Station, and those of Maṇḍapeśvara, or Mont-Pezier as it is vulgarly called, about ten miles further north. The ruins of Mont-Pezier have already been described. The cave-temple of Jogeś-

* *Cathay, ut supra*, p. 591.

vara, about 120 feet square, is considered to be the most modern of the Śivaite excavations of Western India, and of the same character of structure as the temple of Amaranâtha in the vicinity of Kalyâṇa. It is said to be built, unlike those of the *Ghârapuri* or Elephanta island and *Vira-Chola* or Elora, which belong to the Southern India type, after the Northern type of the Gujarât and Râjput districts, such as Kâṭhiâvâḍ, Paṭṭan, and Mount Âbu. The delicacy of workmanship displayed both in the architecture and sculpture of the Jogeśvara cave-temple, though in hard black basalt, shows it to have been already attained by artizans who had accustomed themselves to work in softer stone—the marble and calcareous sandstone of the north.

Beyond the island of Salsette the railway crosses the Bassein and Thâṇâ creek, with the intervening little island of Pânju, or Ju, as it is called by some, by a long substantial and elegant iron bridge, and the train then stops at the Mâṇikpûra or Bassein Road station. While traversing the bridge, the tourist will observe at a distance westward the scene of utter desolation among the brown moss-covered high walls of the Fort of Bassein, and the lofty spires of the ruined churches which it encloses. It has an imposing appearance as it is approached from the south, which cannot fail to be impressive. One is struck with the thought that when in the zenith of its splendour, it must have been one of the finest places on the western coast, or one of the most flourishing Christian cities in India, a thought that will be amply confirmed by a more close observation of the ruined fortifications and its interesting ecclesiology.

At the Bassein Road station the excursionist will have his choice of conveyances among bullock-carts, saddle-tattoos, and palanquins, which are all easily procurable and at a moderate charge, according to the tariff laid down by the Collector of Thâṇâ. There is close to the station a travellers' bungalow, with a resident messman. Of all vehicles the bullock-cart, or *ghâḍâ* as it is called, whose primitive use appears to have been that of a hay-wagon, is the most interesting. It is innocent of springs, and the jog-trot of the bullocks is enough to give one an unpleasant idea of what a break-bone fever is ; but considering the novel situation, the surrounding country so exquisitely beautiful, with rich rice-fields, salt-pans, and sweet-water ponds literally covered with the cordate leaves and lovely blossoms and flowers of the sacred lotus, and the belts of cocoanut palms that fringe the road the whole distance between the station and the land gate of the Fort—about four miles and a half,—and the fellow-travellers of a cheerful and resigned disposition, the jolting will but afford continual matter for merriment, and be felt as indispensable to the day's enjoyment. The down train leaves Bassein Road station about 4 P.M. Bombay time; but this is often altered.

The visitor to the Tuṅgâr hill will find his route lying along a bridle-road for the first two miles, and terminating at the foot of the hill. It crosses a bridge, a short distance from the Mâṇikpûra station, over the shallow channel which separates the island of Bassein from the continent, and is a frequent resort of anglers from Bombay.

The Tuṅgâr hill is situated between the two tâlukâs of Bassein and Bhivaṇḍî, the villages of both marching on to the top. It is a detached hill of the Koṅkaṇ, and, in common with Matheran and other mountainous regions of India, presents a variety of scenery. To the west and south there are numerous spurs, all thickly wooded; to the north and east the slopes, falling into terraces carpeted with perennial verdure, are steep. In two or three places the sides of the hill are not only steep, but bare and generally inaccessible.

There are six lines of ascent to the top of the hill, but the one in use in the present circumstances, when no route can be called excellent, is what lies along the metalled forest road, above referred to, leading for a distance of two miles to the foot of the hill between the villages of Anchola and Rajavalî to Gokîrva. About the latter place is a shrine of Mahâdevâ inside a *maṇḍap*, and close to the remains of a tank, where large carved flagstones are lying about. The tank may have been desecrated by the Portuguese, who had also a building there of their own, the ruins of which are in a state that does not permit of one's identifying them with a stockaded fort or a residence. The next part of the route to the base of the hill skirts the south end of Valiv and the north end of Satavlî village, where just on the crest of a hillock are the ruins of a Portuguese tower. The Portuguese, to whom all these villages belonged, had often serious contests with the Râja of Jawâr, called by the Portuguese annalists "*o Cole,*" or the king of Kolîs. The latter penetrated with his army quite up to the foot of the Tuṅgâr, and in 1583 ravaged almost all the villages to the eastward of the Bassein island, the Portuguese suffering considerable loss, from the wooded condition of the country and the agility of the Koli warriors, whom the annalists*

---

* Diogo do Couto, *Decadas*, vol. ix., p. 257.

describe as "monkeys jumping along from tree to tree." The eminent Darwin might have perhaps detected in these monkeys the "missing link" he and other biologists are in search of. But, "monkeys" though they are called by the chroniclers, the Captains of Bassein were not seldom compelled to sign treaties of alliance with them, who were thenceforward their steadfast friends. The treaties of the Portuguese with the king of Sarceta, Jaeda Rânâ, and with the Marâthâs, also refer to them.* The ancestor of this freebooting Kolî, named Jagappâ Nâyak Mukne, was the person who founded this little principality, early in the 14th century, and his son was in 1341 recognized by the court of Delhi under the title of Nem Shâh.†

From Satavlî the incline road passes through the Wârlî hamlet of Dhonvirâ to the temple of Śri Tuṅgâreśvara, the legendary history of which deity has been given elsewhere. The temple of Tuṅgareśvara consists of a group of small square buildings, four in number, which stand in a romantic little valley almost surrounded by hills, the slopes of which, with the land in the valley, are held in inâm for the temple. The inâm boundary lies on the top of the ascent to the hill, and the land included in the inâm is quite distinct and separate from the inâm hill itself, which is included in the forest lands of the different Government villages adjoining each other in this part of the Kaman and Śaivan mahâls of the Bassein and Bhivaṇḍî tâlukâs.‡

The little temples of Tuṅgâreśvara are of a very remote origin; but it appears that they were rebuilt more than a hundred years ago by Śaṅkarâjî Keshava, a celebrated Sar Subedâr of Bassein under the Marathâ government. This chieftain's handiwork is also seen in the fine temples of Vajrâbai at the hot springs of Gaṇeśpurî, in the valley of the river Tansa, the thermal waters of which, although not looked on with any religious veneration, are freely used by all classes for ablutions, especially by those suffering from skin diseases. Of the four temples of Tuṅgâreśvará, the largest is situated about the centre of this little plateau. It is about ten feet square, and is raised on a plinth about two feet high with a surrounding platform of six feet in extent. The roof has a *ghumata* or dome terminating in a small *śikhâra* or spire. It is closed on all sides except at the entrance, where there is a bell

---

* *Chronista*, vol. iv., pp. 22 *et seqq.*; and *Pazes e Tratados do Estado da India com os Reis e dominantes visinhos*, in the *Boletim*, *ut supra*, 1874, No. 21.

† S. Marriott's *Rough Notes on Jawâr*, Bombay, 1823.

‡ See *Proceedings of the Government of Bombay in the Revenue Department* between March 1866 and August 1870.

suspended from the lintel. Opposite the door, which is flanked on either side by a *gokhle* or niche holding the carved image of *Chaturbhujâkâr*, or four-armed Śiva on the right, and that of Gaṇapatî, with several *gaṇas* or "merry fellows" behind, all smeared over with red paint, are the principal deities—the beautifully carved figure of Pârvatî, without the usual exaggeration or monstrosity, communicating by a groove, the classic *yonî*, with the phallus, which is daily dressed by the *pujârî*, who lives in the adjacent village of Dhondirâ, with the three transversal white lines of the Smârta sect and a few flowers on the top, usually of the common *Dev Champa* (*Plumeria acuminata*). It need scarcely be added that the phallus or *liṅga*, the sexual symbol, although non-Vedic, and ever unmentioned in the epic poems of the *Râmâyaṇa* and *Mahâbhârata* or in the *Amarakosha*, having been in later times introduced into the Hindu pantheon from the aborigines of the south of India, although even this assertion has been lately disputed by some scholars, is now very popular. It is supposed that the original idea of the symbol was got from the Sun, and mythological analogy is in favour of this conjecture, the bull in Egypt and other countries having been sacred to it. Just in front of this shrine is a little square building with four arches supporting a *chattrî* or canopy, wherein is the figure of a Nandî and the pair of Śrî Datatrya's *pâdukâs* or footprints. Behind the principal shrine is another little room, about four feet square, with the image of Kâliyâmardhana, an incarnation of Kṛishṇa, holding a *nâga* or cobra in his hands.

Close to the Naṇḍî is a *van*, or square stone with a hole dug in the centre, for the preparation of the *gandha* or *tilaka*.

A few paces in front of this is another shrine containing the image of the monkey-god, Hanuman, by the side of which are the sacred trees the *pipal* (*Ficus religiosa*) and the *tulsi* (*Ocymum sanctum*), the latter planted in a little flower-vase poised on a pedestal, and a circular *dîpamalâ*, or pillar for holding lights.

About one of the corners of this quadrangular level plateau is the hut of the *Bâwâ*, or resident priest, the inventory of his chattels being made up of a plain grass mat, a piece of rag, and an earthen pot. The walls of the hut are of wattle and dab, the principal material being the common *Karvi* (*Strobelanthus asperrimus*), while the thatch consists of *Chirka* grass, interlaid with the leaves of the *Ság* (*Cedrella Toona*) and *Kumbia* (*Careya arborea*). There is a *kuṇda*, or well, and a spring of clear water behind the shrines, which is used by the above-mentioned

Báwá in common with the beasts of the neighbouring forest. There is also a grove of choice trees, such as the mango (*Mangifera indica*), *Aptâ* (*Bauhinia racemosa*), *Auli* (*Phyllanthus Emblica*), and *Dev Champa* (*Plumeria acuminata*). The leaves of the mango and Aptâ trees are held by the Hindus in such high esteem, as indicative of health and prosperity, that strings of them are used for ornamenting their doors on festive occasions, such as the Divâli, Shimgâ, &c. All these objects appear to contribute in imparting to the plateau of the Tuṅgâreśvara shrine a really enchanting and picturesque view all around.

This group of shrines is about five miles up the hill, and just as much from the summit. From the temple to the top of the hill the ascent is not only steep and much obstructed by jungle, but even, in some places, extremely dangerous. The mule track is from three to four feet wide, flanked either on one or both sides by deep ravines, to cross which at full gallop would simply amount to seeking an inglorious death. It is said, however, that an ascent on a more easy gradient is in contemplation, but its accomplishment is in the mean while transferred to the Greek kalends. Within a short distance from the hill summit there is a break of this zigzag ascent, and the last part of the hill rises abruptly.

The summit of the Tuṅgâr hill consists of the main plateau and the ridge, besides numerous knolls or points and two considerable separate hills on the line of ascent, which may perhaps be utilized if the area of the plateau and ridge happen to be occupied by buildings, dwelling-houses, and such public edifices,—as a church, bazar, hospital, &c.,—as contemplated, and for which sites have already been allotted and marked out, containing five acres each, at the rate of two rupees of ground-rent a year. The above area, both on the plateau and ridge, is about three miles long, and nearly one mile wide at its broadest part, the general width being from a quarter to half a mile. The height of the hill is 2,300 feet above the level of the sea, from which, as the crow flies, its summit is only ten miles distant, being open to the sea-breeze, there being no hill of size to intercept the wind. The neighbouring valleys to the eastward are notorious for being sources of malaria, from which the summit is free. The heat is never oppressive. The following were the readings during the month of May 1876:—at sunrise 74° Fahr., at 10 A.M. 78°, at 4 P.M. 82°, and at 10 P.M. 77°. The fall of rain is said to be only a few inches above the annual average fall of Bombay, which is 80 inches; but this is questionable. The hygrometric condition of the hill is very high; no reliable records appear, however, to have been made.

There is one tank at the Vaitaraṇî Point, and several springs on the summit and slopes of the hill. Reservoirs may also be formed by damming several hollows or fissures between spurs, whence rills are continuously issuing and running to waste, as well as by sinking wells in different places near thick groves of trees, all green and vigorous, and which, in the absence of springs, would be sufficient to provide a perennial supply. One spring, called "Gidpânî," from its being a drinking-place of vultures, is conspicuous by these birds having, by their long residence there, stained of a light colour the otherwise black surface of the trap rock.

The history of the Tuṅgâr hill as a sanitarium is of recent origin. It appears that it was in 1866 that Mr. Hope brought it to the notice of the Government. From the area, supply of water, and accessibility, it was thought that it would rival the Matheran hill as a sanitarium, and draw, besides the Bombay invalids, those of Gujarât, from their proximity to the hill. This was, however, long before the opening of the Suez Canal, since which event it has been practically demonstrated that the sanitaria of Matheran and Mahableshwar are more than sufficient for the local wants of those suffering from malaria and feebleness brought on by long residence in an enervating climate; nor can they have greater pretensions than these. All complex ailments, therefore, must avail themselves of the healing influences of the European climate, with its beneficial adjuncts of a far better society, and more wholesome food, through the rapid route of the Suez Canal. Thus Tuṅgâr hill, as a sanitarium, appears to be doomed to utter forgetfulness, as the most that can be made of it is an occasional resort for sportsmen from Bombay and Gujarât. There are only two bungalows on the hill, one belonging to Mr. Hope, and the other is a hotel containing four rooms, under Mr. C. de Souza, the resident messman at the travellers' bungalow at Bassein. The antiquities of the Tuṅgâr hill consist of a few cells —which, like those of the Caraṇjâ island, have been filled with water—and the sculpture of a Tîrthaṅkara or emancipated Jaina. The cells appear to be the work of Jainas, and probably date from the same period as the other Jaina excavations of Western India, being the most modern of all, viz. *Śaka* 1146, *i.e.* 1234 A.D., or thereabouts. But although about six centuries and a half old, their isolated position had precluded the possibility of their ever being meddled with by others, and they appear as if excavated but recently, all the fragments and splinters from the caves lying about in utter neglect, and untouched by any human hand, just as they were scattered about at the time the cells were excavated. These cells when filled with water are known by the name of Pâṇḍu springs. They consist now altogether of four reservoirs, some of them supported on pillars; and one was barely commenced when given up. They are all hewn out of the living rock, and the Jaina monks were probably assisted in the operation of excavation by the ancient residents of the hills, who had dug holes in stones all along the footpath to the cells from the southern extremity of the hill. These holes appear to have served the purpose of husking rice. The cells are all situated on a knoll on the northern side close to the tank, which might have been built at the same time. The largest of the cells is some twenty feet by eighteen.

The other object of antiquarian curiosity on the Tuṅgâr hill is the sculptured figure of a Tîrthaṅkara, the fragments of which were discovered near the site marked 21, formerly occupied by the hotel, now transferred to another spot. The stone, which is of trap, was about three feet square, and had, besides the figure of the Jaina saint in the centre, some worshipping figures around. The style of drapery and the head-dress appear to be of Râjputana origin. This sculpture was until lately entire, when the iconoclastic hotel-keeper, a Roman Catholic, feeling qualms of conscience at allowing such an idolatrous abomination to exist in his neighbourhood, broke it into pieces, with the decided applause of the priest, who had climbed up from Bassein to bless the hotel, which, in spite of all his blessings and the thoroughly Inquisitional smashing of the Hindu idol to fragments, has proved a complete failure. The hotel has now been opened for the last three years, its charges are six rupees a day and *extras*, but it scarcely receives a couple of visitors a year.

The geology, plants, and animals of the Tuṅgâr hill are just the same as those of Matheran.* There is so much similarity between the flora of the two hills that plants which are rare elsewhere, as for instance a certain species of the *Capparis* and others, are found only on the two sanitaria. Big game is also much the same in both places. The panther (*Felis pardus*), the *Bakrî* (*Cervellus aureus*), three varieties of monkeys and hares, besides numerous species of partridges, climbers, woodpeckers, barbets, and several other birds of beautiful metallic

* See *Matheran Hill*, by J. G. Smith, M.D., Edinburgh, 1871.

plumage, that warble, if they do not sing, appear to have their habitats equally on both hills. Tigers are, however, seen oftener on the Tungâr than on the Matheran hill; and the sambur. hog, bear, and civet cat, though still abundant on the former, seem to have disappeared from the latter. The hill tribes of the two hills differ considerably; while those of Matheran consist of Dhangars, Thâkurs, and Kâtharis, the only two races found on Tungâr at the present day are the hill Kolis and the Wârlîs.